T0178548

Lecture Notes in Computer Science   14685

Founding Editors

Gerhard Goos
Juris Hartmanis

The series Lecture Notes in Computer Science (LNCS), including its subseries Lecture Notes in Artificial Intelligence (LNAI) and Lecture Notes in Bioinformatics (LNBI), has established itself as a medium for the publication of new developments in computer science and information technology research, teaching, and education.

LNCS enjoys close cooperation with the computer science R & D community, the series counts many renowned academics among its volume editors and paper authors, and collaborates with prestigious societies. Its mission is to serve this international community by providing an invaluable service, mainly focused on the publication of conference and workshop proceedings and postproceedings. LNCS commenced publication in 1973.

Masaaki Kurosu · Ayako Hashizume
Editors

Human-Computer Interaction

Thematic Area, HCI 2024
Held as Part of the 26th HCI International Conference, HCII 2024
Washington, DC, USA, June 29 – July 4, 2024
Proceedings, Part II

 Springer

Editors
Masaaki Kurosu
The Open University of Japan
Chiba, Japan

Ayako Hashizume
Hosei University
Tokyo, Japan

ISSN 0302-9743   ISSN 1611-3349 (electronic)
Lecture Notes in Computer Science
ISBN 978-3-031-60411-9   ISBN 978-3-031-60412-6 (eBook)
https://doi.org/10.1007/978-3-031-60412-6

This Springer imprint is published by the registered company Springer Nature Switzerland AG
The registered company address is: Gewerbestrasse 11, 6330 Cham, Switzerland

If disposing of this product, please recycle the paper.

Foreword

This year we celebrate 40 years since the establishment of the HCI International (HCII) Conference, which has been a hub for presenting groundbreaking research and novel ideas and collaboration for people from all over the world.

The HCII conference was founded in 1984 by Prof. Gavriel Salvendy (Purdue University, USA, Tsinghua University, P.R. China, and University of Central Florida, USA) and the first event of the series, "1st USA-Japan Conference on Human-Computer Interaction", was held in Honolulu, Hawaii, USA, 18–20 August. Since then, HCI International is held jointly with several Thematic Areas and Affiliated Conferences, with each one under the auspices of a distinguished international Program Board and under one management and one registration. Twenty-six HCI International Conferences have been organized so far (every two years until 2013, and annually thereafter).

Over the years, this conference has served as a platform for scholars, researchers, industry experts and students to exchange ideas, connect, and address challenges in the ever-evolving HCI field. Throughout these 40 years, the conference has evolved itself, adapting to new technologies and emerging trends, while staying committed to its core mission of advancing knowledge and driving change.

As we celebrate this milestone anniversary, we reflect on the contributions of its founding members and appreciate the commitment of its current and past Affiliated Conference Program Board Chairs and members. We are also thankful to all past conference attendees who have shaped this community into what it is today.

The 26th International Conference on Human-Computer Interaction, HCI International 2024 (HCII 2024), was held as a 'hybrid' event at the Washington Hilton Hotel, Washington, DC, USA, during 29 June – 4 July 2024. It incorporated the 21 thematic areas and affiliated conferences listed below.

A total of 5108 individuals from academia, research institutes, industry, and government agencies from 85 countries submitted contributions, and 1271 papers and 309 posters were included in the volumes of the proceedings that were published just before the start of the conference, these are listed below. The contributions thoroughly cover the entire field of human-computer interaction, addressing major advances in knowledge and effective use of computers in a variety of application areas. These papers provide academics, researchers, engineers, scientists, practitioners and students with state-of-the-art information on the most recent advances in HCI.

The HCI International (HCII) conference also offers the option of presenting 'Late Breaking Work', and this applies both for papers and posters, with corresponding volumes of proceedings that will be published after the conference. Full papers will be included in the 'HCII 2024 - Late Breaking Papers' volumes of the proceedings to be published in the Springer LNCS series, while 'Poster Extended Abstracts' will be included as short research papers in the 'HCII 2024 - Late Breaking Posters' volumes to be published in the Springer CCIS series.

I would like to thank the Program Board Chairs and the members of the Program Boards of all thematic areas and affiliated conferences for their contribution towards the high scientific quality and overall success of the HCI International 2024 conference. Their manifold support in terms of paper reviewing (single-blind review process, with a minimum of two reviews per submission), session organization and their willingness to act as goodwill ambassadors for the conference is most highly appreciated.

This conference would not have been possible without the continuous and unwavering support and advice of Gavriel Salvendy, founder, General Chair Emeritus, and Scientific Advisor. For his outstanding efforts, I would like to express my sincere appreciation to Abbas Moallem, Communications Chair and Editor of HCI International News.

July 2024   Constantine Stephanidis

HCI International 2024 Thematic Areas
and Affiliated Conferences

- HCI: Human-Computer Interaction Thematic Area
- HIMI: Human Interface and the Management of Information Thematic Area
- EPCE: 21st International Conference on Engineering Psychology and Cognitive Ergonomics
- AC: 18th International Conference on Augmented Cognition
- UAHCI: 18th International Conference on Universal Access in Human-Computer Interaction
- CCD: 16th International Conference on Cross-Cultural Design
- SCSM: 16th International Conference on Social Computing and Social Media
- VAMR: 16th International Conference on Virtual, Augmented and Mixed Reality
- DHM: 15th International Conference on Digital Human Modeling & Applications in Health, Safety, Ergonomics & Risk Management
- DUXU: 13th International Conference on Design, User Experience and Usability
- C&C: 12th International Conference on Culture and Computing
- DAPI: 12th International Conference on Distributed, Ambient and Pervasive Interactions
- HCIBGO: 11th International Conference on HCI in Business, Government and Organizations
- LCT: 11th International Conference on Learning and Collaboration Technologies
- ITAP: 10th International Conference on Human Aspects of IT for the Aged Population
- AIS: 6th International Conference on Adaptive Instructional Systems
- HCI-CPT: 6th International Conference on HCI for Cybersecurity, Privacy and Trust
- HCI-Games: 6th International Conference on HCI in Games
- MobiTAS: 6th International Conference on HCI in Mobility, Transport and Automotive Systems
- AI-HCI: 5th International Conference on Artificial Intelligence in HCI
- MOBILE: 5th International Conference on Human-Centered Design, Operation and Evaluation of Mobile Communications

List of Conference Proceedings Volumes Appearing Before the Conference

1. LNCS 14684, Human-Computer Interaction: Part I, edited by Masaaki Kurosu and Ayako Hashizume
2. LNCS 14685, Human-Computer Interaction: Part II, edited by Masaaki Kurosu and Ayako Hashizume
3. LNCS 14686, Human-Computer Interaction: Part III, edited by Masaaki Kurosu and Ayako Hashizume
4. LNCS 14687, Human-Computer Interaction: Part IV, edited by Masaaki Kurosu and Ayako Hashizume
5. LNCS 14688, Human-Computer Interaction: Part V, edited by Masaaki Kurosu and Ayako Hashizume
6. LNCS 14689, Human Interface and the Management of Information: Part I, edited by Hirohiko Mori and Yumi Asahi
7. LNCS 14690, Human Interface and the Management of Information: Part II, edited by Hirohiko Mori and Yumi Asahi
8. LNCS 14691, Human Interface and the Management of Information: Part III, edited by Hirohiko Mori and Yumi Asahi
9. LNAI 14692, Engineering Psychology and Cognitive Ergonomics: Part I, edited by Don Harris and Wen-Chin Li
10. LNAI 14693, Engineering Psychology and Cognitive Ergonomics: Part II, edited by Don Harris and Wen-Chin Li
11. LNAI 14694, Augmented Cognition, Part I, edited by Dylan D. Schmorrow and Cali M. Fidopiastis
12. LNAI 14695, Augmented Cognition, Part II, edited by Dylan D. Schmorrow and Cali M. Fidopiastis
13. LNCS 14696, Universal Access in Human-Computer Interaction: Part I, edited by Margherita Antona and Constantine Stephanidis
14. LNCS 14697, Universal Access in Human-Computer Interaction: Part II, edited by Margherita Antona and Constantine Stephanidis
15. LNCS 14698, Universal Access in Human-Computer Interaction: Part III, edited by Margherita Antona and Constantine Stephanidis
16. LNCS 14699, Cross-Cultural Design: Part I, edited by Pei-Luen Patrick Rau
17. LNCS 14700, Cross-Cultural Design: Part II, edited by Pei-Luen Patrick Rau
18. LNCS 14701, Cross-Cultural Design: Part III, edited by Pei-Luen Patrick Rau
19. LNCS 14702, Cross-Cultural Design: Part IV, edited by Pei-Luen Patrick Rau
20. LNCS 14703, Social Computing and Social Media: Part I, edited by Adela Coman and Simona Vasilache
21. LNCS 14704, Social Computing and Social Media: Part II, edited by Adela Coman and Simona Vasilache
22. LNCS 14705, Social Computing and Social Media: Part III, edited by Adela Coman and Simona Vasilache

47. LNCS 14730, HCI in Games: Part I, edited by Xiaowen Fang
48. LNCS 14731, HCI in Games: Part II, edited by Xiaowen Fang
49. LNCS 14732, HCI in Mobility, Transport and Automotive Systems: Part I, edited by Heidi Krömker
50. LNCS 14733, HCI in Mobility, Transport and Automotive Systems: Part II, edited by Heidi Krömker
51. LNAI 14734, Artificial Intelligence in HCI: Part I, edited by Helmut Degen and Stavroula Ntoa
52. LNAI 14735, Artificial Intelligence in HCI: Part II, edited by Helmut Degen and Stavroula Ntoa
53. LNAI 14736, Artificial Intelligence in HCI: Part III, edited by Helmut Degen and Stavroula Ntoa
54. LNCS 14737, Design, Operation and Evaluation of Mobile Communications: Part I, edited by June Wei and George Margetis
55. LNCS 14738, Design, Operation and Evaluation of Mobile Communications: Part II, edited by June Wei and George Margetis
56. CCIS 2114, HCI International 2024 Posters - Part I, edited by Constantine Stephanidis, Margherita Antona, Stavroula Ntoa and Gavriel Salvendy
57. CCIS 2115, HCI International 2024 Posters - Part II, edited by Constantine Stephanidis, Margherita Antona, Stavroula Ntoa and Gavriel Salvendy
58. CCIS 2116, HCI International 2024 Posters - Part III, edited by Constantine Stephanidis, Margherita Antona, Stavroula Ntoa and Gavriel Salvendy
59. CCIS 2117, HCI International 2024 Posters - Part IV, edited by Constantine Stephanidis, Margherita Antona, Stavroula Ntoa and Gavriel Salvendy
60. CCIS 2118, HCI International 2024 Posters - Part V, edited by Constantine Stephanidis, Margherita Antona, Stavroula Ntoa and Gavriel Salvendy
61. CCIS 2119, HCI International 2024 Posters - Part VI, edited by Constantine Stephanidis, Margherita Antona, Stavroula Ntoa and Gavriel Salvendy
62. CCIS 2120, HCI International 2024 Posters - Part VII, edited by Constantine Stephanidis, Margherita Antona, Stavroula Ntoa and Gavriel Salvendy

https://2024.hci.international/proceedings

Preface

Human-Computer Interaction is a Thematic Area of the International Conference on Human-Computer Interaction (HCII). The HCI field is today undergoing a wave of significant innovation and breakthroughs towards radically new future forms of interaction. The HCI Thematic Area constitutes a forum for scientific research and innovation in human-computer interaction, addressing challenging and innovative topics in human-computer interaction theory, methodology, and practice, including, for example, novel theoretical approaches to interaction, novel user interface concepts and technologies, novel interaction devices, UI development methods, environments and tools, multimodal user interfaces, human-robot interaction, emotions in HCI, aesthetic issues, HCI and children, evaluation methods and tools, and many others.

The HCI Thematic Area covers four major dimensions, namely theory and methodology, technology, human beings, and societal impact. The following five volumes of the HCII 2024 proceedings reflect these dimensions:

- Human-Computer Interaction - Part I, addressing topics related to HCI Theory and Design and Evaluation Methods and Tools, and Emotions in HCI;
- Human-Computer Interaction - Part II, addressing topics related to Human-Robot Interaction and Child-Computer Interaction;
- Human-Computer Interaction - Part III, addressing topics related to HCI for Mental Health and Psychological Wellbeing, and HCI in Healthcare;
- Human-Computer Interaction - Part IV, addressing topics related to HCI, Environment and Sustainability, and Design and User Experience Evaluation Case Studies;
- Human-Computer Interaction - Part V, addressing topics related to Multimodality and Natural User Interfaces, and HCI, AI, Creativity, Art and Culture.

The papers in these volumes were accepted for publication after a minimum of two single-blind reviews from the members of the HCI Program Board or, in some cases, from members of the Program Boards of other affiliated conferences. We would like to thank all of them for their invaluable contribution, support, and efforts.

July 2024

Masaaki Kurosu
Ayako Hashizume

Human-Computer Interaction Thematic Area (HCI 2024)

Program Board Chairs: **Masaaki Kurosu,** *The Open University of Japan, Japan* and **Ayako Hashizume,** *Hosei University, Japan*

- Salah Uddin Ahmed, *University of South-Eastern Norway, India*
- Jessica Barfield, *University of Tennessee, USA*
- Valdecir Becker, *Federal University of Paraiba, Brazil*
- Nimish Biloria, *University of Technology Sydney, Australia*
- Zhigang Chen, *Shanghai University, P.R. China*
- Hong Chen, *Daiichi Institute of Technology, Japan*
- Emilia Duarte, *Universidade Europeia, Portugal*
- Yu-Hsiu Hung, *National Cheng Kung University, Taiwan*
- Jun Iio, *Chuo University, Japan*
- Yi Ji, *Guangdong University of Technology, Australia*
- Hiroshi Noborio, *Osaka Electro-Communication University, Japan*
- Katsuhiko Onishi, *Osaka Electro-Communication University, Japan*
- Julio Cesar Reis, *University of Campinas, Brazil*
- Mohammad Shidujaman, *Independent University Bangladesh (IUB), Bangladesh*

The full list with the Program Board Chairs and the members of the Program Boards of all thematic areas and affiliated conferences of HCII 2024 is available online at:

http://www.hci.international/board-members-2024.php

HCI International 2025 Conference

The 27th International Conference on Human-Computer Interaction, HCI International 2025, will be held jointly with the affiliated conferences at the Swedish Exhibition & Congress Centre and Gothia Towers Hotel, Gothenburg, Sweden, June 22–27, 2025. It will cover a broad spectrum of themes related to Human-Computer Interaction, including theoretical issues, methods, tools, processes, and case studies in HCI design, as well as novel interaction techniques, interfaces, and applications. The proceedings will be published by Springer. More information will become available on the conference website: https://2025.hci.international/.

General Chair
Prof. Constantine Stephanidis
University of Crete and ICS-FORTH
Heraklion, Crete, Greece
Email: general_chair@2025.hci.international

https://2025.hci.international/

Contents – Part II

Child-Computer Interaction

Human-Robot Interaction

Intelligent Cognitive Fusion in Human-Robot Interaction: A Autism Spectrum Disorder Case Study

Tariq Alsboui[1,3,4] (iD), Abeer Badawy[2,3,4], Faisal Jamil[1,3,4(✉)] (iD),
Ibrahim Alqatawneh[2,3,4], and Ibrahim A. Hameed[2,3,4] (iD)

[1] Department of Computer Science, School of Computing and Engineering,
University of Huddersfield, Huddersfield, Queensgate HD1 3DH, UK
{T.Alsboui,f.jamil}@hud.ac.uk
[2] Department of Health Sciences in Ålesund, Faculty of Medicine and Health
Sciences, Norwegian University of Science and Technology,
Larsgårdsvegen 2, 6009 Ålesund, Norway
Abeerbadawy4404@gmail.com
[3] School of Computer Science, The University of Sunderland, Sunderland, UK
ibrahim.alqatawneh@sunderland.ac.uk
[4] Department of ICT and Natural Sciences, Faculty of Information Technology and
Electrical Engineering, Norwegian University of Science and Technology (NTNU),
Larsgårdsvegen 2, 6009 Ålesund, Norway
ibib@ntnu.no

Abstract. Edge computing has recently emerged as a transformative concept, facilitating the development of future technologies such as AI, robotics, IoT, and high-speed wireless sensor networks like 5G. It achieves this by bridging the gap between cloud computing resources and end-users. In the context of medical and healthcare applications, edge computing plays a crucial role in enabling remote patient monitoring and handling large volumes of multimedia data. One specific area where edge computing has made significant strides is in the field of robotics, particularly in the domain of robot-assisted therapy (RAT). RAT is an active-assistive robotic technology within the realm of rehabilitation robotics, garnering considerable attention from researchers. Its primary objective is to benefit individuals with disabilities, such as children with autism spectrum disorder (ASD). However, RAT faces a substantial challenge, namely the development of models capable of accurately detecting the emotional states of individuals with ASD and retaining knowledge of their unique preferences. Furthermore, incorporating expert diagnosis and recommendations to guide robots in adapting therapy approaches to varying conditions and scenarios is essential to the ASD therapy process. This paper proposes a novel architecture known as edge cognitive computing, which seamlessly integrates human experts and assisted robots within the same framework to provide long-term support for ASD patients. By combining real-time computing and analysis through an innovative cognitive robotic model designed for ASD therapy, this proposed architecture achieves several critical functionalities. These include

uninterrupted remote diagnosis, continuous symptom monitoring, rapid
response to emergencies, dynamic therapy adjustments, and advanced
assistance, all aimed at enhancing the well-being of individuals with ASD.

Keywords: Edge Computing · Internet of Things · Intelligent systems

1   Introduction

Edge Computing reduces latency, speeds up answers, and allows for more thorough data analysis by enabling full or partial data processing within the edge
network [1]. With the use of this technology, connected devices can now provide
services via the edge network in a variety of fields, including artificial intelligence
(AI), robotics, autonomous driving, smart cities, healthcare, medical diagnosis,
smart grids, multimedia, and security [2–9].

One prominent topic of interest in the context of smart cities is smart healthcare, which emerged from the need to improve the management of the healthcare sector, maximize resource use, and lower costs without sacrificing or even
improving the quality of healthcare services [10]. Three layers make up most
conventional smart healthcare systems: the collection layer, which gathers sensor data from patients; the transmission layer, which uses intelligent terminals to
send data to a base station; and the analysis layer, which does data analysis in
cloud data centers. Nevertheless, these systems frequently lack thorough illness
analysis, real-time monitoring, and quick reaction capabilities. They also experience rigid network resource allocation and high communication latency [11].

5G networks have the ability to support edge computing-based healthcare systems, but there are still several barriers standing in the way of their
widespread adoption and the benefits that would follow for society. These issues
include worries about efficiently managing enormous volumes of data, protecting
patient privacy, and providing healthcare on a large scale [12].

Within the framework of incorporating AI and robotics technology, the forth-
coming terrain of medical and healthcare applications will encompass considerable real-time processing and analysis of clinical data. Moreover, the integration
of input from human specialists, informed by up-to-date data from intelligent
devices, is crucial for the advancement of medical systems and intelligent healthcare. This integration facilitates the delivery of expert advice, tailored services,
and accurate medical interventions.

Consider the use of robot-assisted therapy (RAT) in the treatment of autistic
people. Enabling RAT systems to adjust to the distinct and changing demands
of every person becomes essential [13]. This adaptation is made possible by a
structured personalization technique that uses five controllers in a hierarchical
human-robot learning framework. These controllers are managed by a meta-
controller that uses reinforcement learning to adjust robot feedback and teaching
difficulty levels based on individual user differences in learning styles.

Although this method has made it easier to implement RAT systems for children with ASD in their homes over the long run, it is still unknown how important human specialists are to the therapeutic process. These people's social skills

could use some improvement in practical situations. For the purpose of providing effective and efficient medical care, then, the caliber of machine-to-machine communication and the integration of data from human-robot interactions become essential. In the end, this improvement raises the standard of patient care overall and, from a financial perspective, increases the flexibility and agility of healthcare systems [14].

Considering the viewpoint of cognitive computing, a study carried out by the authors in [11] introduced a smart healthcare system based on Edge-Cognitive-Computing (ECC). Using cognitive computing, this system monitors and analyzes users' physical health in order to address problems associated with the strict distribution of network resources. The system's development of a multilingual robot interface based on edge computing technology is one noteworthy advancement [15]. Through interactive question-based interactions, this interface makes it easier to assess the mental health of elders.

However, when looking at the angle of edge intelligent devices [16], in the field of RAT for healthcare, there are still a number of unsolved questions, such as those regarding robots. These include questions like how best to use robots in therapy, how to create a complete plan for incorporating robots into interventions that can adjust to the different needs of different patients and identify their existing situations, and many other things. The issue of selecting the best candidates from those displaying particular symptoms also exists, especially when it comes to RAT for those with ASD [17].

From the standpoint of system design, edge computing is distinguished by complex and varied architectures, which can provide difficulties when trying to develop a framework that is applicable to all edge computing applications [18]. Specifically, dynamic, flexible, and complex systems with potentially unanticipated behaviors are what make smart healthcare systems unique. They need a wide range of services to be personalized and resources to be organized efficiently [10].

This research offers a novel solution to these problems by presenting an architecture that blends the skills of assisted robots and human specialists, all operating inside the same framework to offer long-term support for people with ASD. The suggested method combines real-time computing with analysis through the use of a novel cognitive robotic model created for the treatment of ASD. It is based on cognitive-behavioral therapy (CBT). This integration makes it possible to receive sophisticated support, dynamic therapy modifications, instant emergency alarms, continuous symptom monitoring, and seamless remote diagnostics.

In this paper, our contributions are as follows:

- We propose an edge intelligent robot that integrates cognitive data from patients and relevant ambient information. This is accomplished by constructing a corresponding network architecture, enabling the timely generation of recommendations from human experts and the implementation of real-time optimization strategies for medical resources.
- We have developed a Robot-Assisted Therapy (RAT) program comprising four stages. This is crafted on cognitive models of humor development, aiming

to assist individuals with Autism Spectrum Disorder (ASD) in a stepwise manner to acquire diverse levels of social and communication skills.

2 Background and Preliminaries

This section provides a basic introduction to cognitive robots and edge computing, as well as a quick review of cognitive-behavior therapy (CBT). When a particular methodology is covered, we use notations and meanings that align with the relevant research articles.

Edge Computing. Lately, edge computing has become a key enabler for several future technologies, such as 5G and the Internet of Things (IoT) [19], augmented reality, and collaborative multi-agent/robot systems [20], such as vehicle-to-vehicle communications. It accomplishes this by closing the distance between end users and cloud computing resources, so bringing cloud services closer to the user. Its capacity to provide quick application reaction times and data processing is one of its distinguishing characteristics.

Edge computing adopts a proactive stance to solve the issues caused by high latency between cloud servers and end-user devices across a variety of scenarios. This is achieved by shifting the processing jobs closer to the edge of the network, especially with the introduction of 5G technology [1]. This paradigm shift has given rise to various edge computing models, including Cloudlets [21], Fog computing [22], and Mobile Edge computing [23], each created to address the difficulties posed by conventional cloud computing.

In addition, the widespread application of deep learning (DL) models in fields like computer vision and natural language processing on modern end devices like smartphones, mobile robots, and Internet of Things (IoT) devices emphasizes the need for real-time data analysis. For the purpose of improving system performance and user experience, this real-time analysis is essential.

This makes edge computing appear like a very appealing answer. In order to successfully handle the rigorous computational requirements and low-latency needs associated with DL on edge devices, it entails building a dense network of computer nodes in close proximity to end devices. Further benefits of edge computing include increased scalability, more privacy, and increased bandwidth efficiency [24].

The incorporation of deep learning (DL) into edge computing frameworks is a significant aspect of artificial intelligence (AI) and is essential to creating an intelligent edge. As a result of this fusion, edge maintenance and management become dynamic and adaptive, ultimately enhancing the capabilities of edge intelligent agents and expanding the range of applications they can efficiently service [25].

Cognitive Robotics. The study of mechanisms, designs, and constraints that permit the ongoing and unrestricted improvement of diverse skills in embodied robots is the focus of cognitive robotics [26]. These abilities include social inter-action, planning, reasoning, perception, and decision-making. Symbolic coding systems are essential for describing the environment, perception, action, and symbolic interpretation in the context of cognitive modeling. As a result, in cognitive robotics, perception and action become central themes.

This multidisciplinary field takes cues from neuroscience, cognitive science, developmental psychology, sociology, and other relevant fields in addition to arti-ficial intelligence and robotics [27]. The creation of a value system that resembles the "brain" of an AI agent is especially important since it makes it easier to map behavioral reactions to outside inputs. This element is fundamental to cognitive robotics and is an emerging subject of study within robotics, neurorobotics, and artificial cognitive systems research.

Figure 1 provides a visual representation of a model for a generic intrinsically motivated agent within the domain of cognitive robotics.

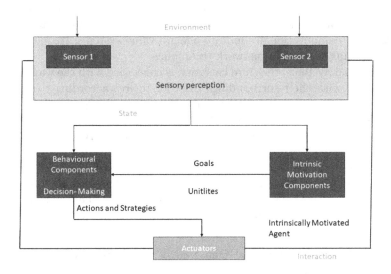

Fig. 1. An illustration of the model for a generic intrinsically motivated agent.

According to the authors in [28], "value" in this sense refers to an agent's evaluation of the work necessary to obtain a reward or avoid punishment. Cru-cially, this particular value system does not originate from within an AI agent or even a biological being. Rather, it is the result of the agent's sensory envi-ronment interactions and experiences. Expected values are the usual description of these value systems, especially in the context of uncertain or unpredictable settings. It's also important to remember that value has two different aspects. The learned value develops throughout time as a result of the agent's experiences and growth, whereas the innate value is an agent's initial subjective assessment of its sensory world.

According to this explanation, "value" refers to an agent's estimation of the work necessary to obtain a reward or avoid punishment. Crucially, an AI agent's or even a biological entity's distinct value system does not come from within; rather, it arises via the agent's experiential interactions with its sensory environment. Expected values are commonly used to describe these value systems, especially in situations when conditions are unknown or unpredictable. It's also important to remember that value has two different aspects. The learned value develops throughout time as a result of the agent's experiences and growth, whereas the innate value is an agent's initial subjective assessment of its sensory world.

Within the field of cognitive robotics, value system development falls into three main categories. The first group is called Neuroanatomical Systems, and their goal is to create value systems that draw inspiration from the biological elements of neuroanatomy and physiology. The goal of these systems is to imitate the value-related functions found in living things.

Neural network systems constitute the second category, wherein mathematical approaches are employed to develop more abstract models. These models are created to computationally imitate agents' value systems, frequently using machine learning and neural network techniques.

Motivational Systems, the third category, is concerned with the ways in which agents engage with their surroundings in order to live according to their core beliefs. Reinforcement learning (RL) is a well-known technique in this category. Through repeated interactions with their environment, agents learn to make decisions and conduct actions to maximize rewards or satisfy their fundamental values.

Each of these three categories provides a unique perspective on how value systems should be developed and modeled within the framework of cognitive robotics, and together they provide insightful solutions to the problems of comprehending and emulating value-based decision-making in intelligent agents.

Cognitive-Behavior Therapy. One kind of psychotherapy called cognitive behavioral therapy teaches patients how to recognize and alter unhelpful or unsettling thought patterns that have an adverse effect on their emotions and behavior. It is predicated on the cognitive model (Ellis 1962), which postulates that people's perceptions of events have an impact on their emotions, behaviors, and physiology. Treatment is predicated on a cognitive formulation, beliefs, and behavioral methods that characterize a particular disorder in all types of CBT that are drawn from Beck's model. Figure 2 shows the relationship of behaviour to automatic thoughts with the hierarchy of cognition.

CBT is a wide range of techniques designed to help people break away from harmful patterns. These techniques include recognizing negative thoughts, learning new social skills, creating SMART objectives, handling stress-related problems, and practicing self-monitoring.

When used as a short-term therapeutic strategy, CBT is beneficial in helping patients redirect their attention to their present ideas and opinions. It works

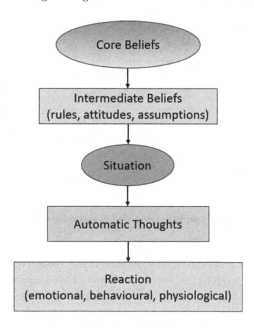

Fig. 2. Shows the relationship of behavior to automatic thoughts with the hierarchy of cognition

well for treating a number of symptoms, including addiction, trouble controlling anger, anxiety, and depression. Additionally, CBT is essential for improving mental health issues, such as chronic pain management, insomnia treatment, and developing efficient stress reduction strategies.

3   Proposed Edge Computing Enabled Autism Spectrum Disorder Model

In this section, we delve into the intricate aspects of the proposed architecture for cognitive computing, as well as the cognitive models governing the behavior of edge intelligent robots. These models draw inspiration from CBT and are specifically tailored for addressing the needs of individuals with ASD.

Figure 3 illustrates an abstract view picture of the proposed Edge Computing enabled Autism Spectrum Disorder Model.

Defined cognitive computing modules at the network edge are necessary to manage a real-time healthcare system and efficiently coordinate medical resources. These modules ought to be made to do cognitive analysis on user data related to their physical health and surrounding environment. By using this method, latency is greatly decreased and reliable and timely delivery of current patient data and analysis results to medical professionals and specialists is ensured.

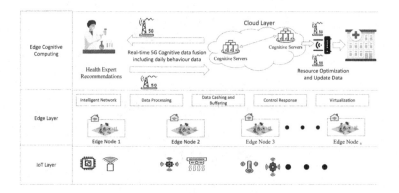

Fig. 3. Proposed Edge Computing enabled Autism Spectrum Disorder Model

Several important components are utilized in the design of our proposed edge cognitive computing system, as shown in Fig. 3. This includes data fusion and analysis, suggestions from human experts, resource strategy optimization, data gathering and recognition, and real-time therapeutic updates. The objectives of this comprehensive approach are outstanding energy efficiency, cost-effectiveness, and user quality of experience.

Cloud Layer. We provide two new server types on the cloud layer: the Resource and Therapy Management Server and the Cognitive Data Server. These servers are valuable for tasks including risk assessment for patients, updating therapy plans, analyzing cognitive data, and optimizing resource allocation tactics. Let's delve into each of these servers in detail.

– **Cognitive Data Server**
  Gathering cognitive fusion information from every intelligent robot at the edge is one of the main responsibilities of the Cognitive Data Server. This data consists of user-generated physical signals, information about their everyday activities, and pertinent details about the internal network, such as its type, communication quality, service flow, and dynamic environmental conditions. It also establishes the priority level of users based on the evaluation of patients' risks, allocating medical and network resources appropriately.
  The results of the cognitive data analysis are also sent to medical professionals, allowing them to provide expert advice specific to each user's situation. Updated prescriptions and medical instructions can be among these suggestions. Through the integration of expert input, dynamic network resource insights, and user surveillance cognitive information, this method optimizes edge computing resources for users based on their risk levels for various diseases. Consequently, this leads to a notable improvement in the Quality of Experience (QoE) and increases the probability of effective recovery.

- **Resource and Therapy Management Server**
  After the Cognitive Data Server provides its analytical results, this server actively integrates knowledge about edge cloud computing, network connectivity, and medical resources. It then proceeds to optimize scheduling algorithms in real-time, efficiently allocating the necessary resources as needed. Furthermore, the server updates the Cognitive Data Server's database in return by sending integrated resource data back to it.

  Through the use of strategies including computational offloading, intelligent algorithms, caching and delivery methods, and smart handovers, the server's resource optimization and energy-saving efforts are achieved. This strategy aims to save energy and improve resource efficiency while meeting the needs of a wide range of heterogeneous applications.

Edge Layer. Our edge-layer method involves mining and processing data locally on edge devices and servers near the user, as opposed to the traditional practice of continuously transporting data to the cloud for computing operations, which results in large energy expenses. This approach improves data processing speed and efficiency while also preserving energy.

Additionally, we present a novel idea that deviates from conventional edge devices: the edge intelligent robot designed for smart healthcare and medical applications. These robots have the rare capacity to serve as medical tools or equipment for patient treatment in addition to gathering and processing data from users and their environment. This invention is a noteworthy development in the realm of medical technology.

The edge intelligent robot has a very particular way of working. First, it incorporates multiple sources of perception data, including audio, visuals, and videos. This information is paired with data gathered from ambient sensors placed around the environment and medical sensors worn by patients. After various data sources are combined, a standardized data flow is created and sent to the cloud layer over a 5G or other high-speed sensor network.

In addition, the robot is in charge of carrying out any updated or current treatment plans or directives that come from the cloud layer. It communicates with patients and leads them through the appropriate therapeutic procedures. The robot also meticulously logs all interaction data and relevant medical factors, which are then sent to the cloud layer for comprehensive examination by human professionals in the field and to provide valuable reference points for human experts in the field.

The edge intelligent robot is essential to providing patients with round-the-clock, continuous monitoring and care. When an emergency arises, it instantly alerts the hospital or medical personnel via the network, guaranteeing quick access to the required resources and support. This ability greatly lowers the possibility of human error, which is frequently connected to conventional medical treatment approaches.

IoT Layer. Medical and environmental sensors are the two primary categories into which the wide range of devices and sensors that make up the IoT layer can be divided. Patients wear the medical sensors, which are intended to monitor their health and report pertinent health indicators. The main physiological data that these sensors gather from users in real time are parameters like blood oxygen saturation (SpO2), heart rate, respiration rate, systolic blood pressure, and electrocardiography (ECG) and electromyography (EMG). This physiological data is simultaneously sent to the adjacent edge computer node, which is frequently represented by the edge intelligent robot.

Conversely, the environmental sensors are in charge of monitoring the therapy settings where patients are located. They record a variety of environmental data, such as air quality, atmospheric pressure, temperature, humidity, and more. The purpose of this environmental data is for later medical analysis and reference. In order to guarantee smooth data flow and connectivity, these devices also enable data exchange with the edge intelligent robot and communicate with the cloud via high-speed communication networks.

4   Cognitive Models of the Edge Intelligent Robot

In this section, We will use ASD treatment as an example to illustrate our points. Based on cognitive models of humor formation, we present RAT. The goal of this method is to help people with ASD gradually gain different degrees of social and communicative abilities. The edge intelligent robot, which depends on the results of cognitive data analysis, enables this therapy by utilizing the previously mentioned edge cognitive computing network. The robot collaborates with medical professionals to help patients receive treatment and recuperate at every stage of therapy, guided by recommendations from experts. The specifics of this strategy will be discussed in more detail below.

- **Humor Styles for Cognitive Distortions.** People's sense of humor is a reflection of their level of social skills and cognitive development. The relationship between cognitive and interpersonal vulnerability elements and prospective effects like psychological dysfunction, distress, or trouble interacting with others can be mediated by different humor types. People's sense of humor is a reflection of their Increasing the sense of humor in people with ASD might, in a way, help them gradually get better at communicating, which will make it easier for them to interact with others and participate in the reciprocal socialization process.

  Consistent with the previously indicated discussion, this study employs a paradigm comprising four discrete phases of humor development within the overall CBT procedure. In order to meet the specific requirements of patients with ASD, especially kids, an aided robot is used to select a variety of humorous scenarios and jokes based on the individual's stage of humor development. This method makes sure that treatment is tailored to meet the needs of patients at each stage of their growth.

– **Behavior Tree based Humor Styles Representation**
Expanding on the previous discussion, we have created four unique use cases, each represented by a behavior tree (BT). These scenarios have been carefully crafted to improve patient outcomes while also increasing RAT effectiveness at various ASD phases. These behavior tree-based programs are useful resources for customizing and enhancing treatment for patients with ASD at different developmental stages.

– **Entry Level: Funny Behaviors**
Interacting with familiar things or participating in creative activities can provide comfort and delight for patients who struggle with social skills. Because of this, in the early phases of therapy, we have created three different scenarios: chasing, spinning, and playing ball. These scenarios entail interactions between the patients and the aided robot with the goal of supporting the growth of new interests, willingness to communicate, and friendships. Figure 4 provides a visual representation of these three scenarios, depicted in the form of a BT.

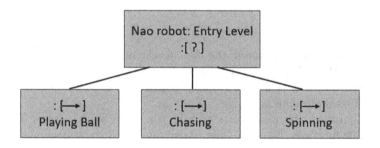

Fig. 4. Entry Level: Assisted Robot's Behavior Trees

– **Basic Level.** Patients inherently start to utilize language and gestures as a form of entertainment and connection as they advance and develop interests and become more receptive to conversation with new peers. Although the Entry Level and Basic Level in humor development may share some traits, the primary differentiation of the Basic Level is the capacity of a "verbal statement alone to create incongruity and elicit laughter." In light of the patients' reliance on linguistic expressions for humor and social interaction, this represents an important developmental milestone.
During this stage, the development of social skills heavily relies on humor. To help patients help their peers feel good about themselves, we present a simple role-playing game called "Aladdin and the Magic Lamp," where patients can interact with the robot. Social reinforcement is incorporated into this

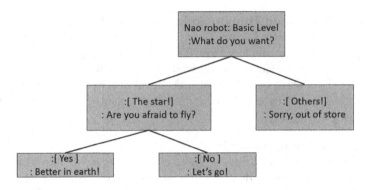

Fig. 5. Entry Level: an Example of the Assisted Robot's Behavior Trees of "Aladdin and the Magic Lamp"

game, which makes the overall experience more enjoyable. Figure 5 offers an illustrative example of the Assisted Robot's Behavior Trees for the "Aladdin and the Magic Lamp" scenario, showcasing how the robot's interactions are designed to facilitate humor and social interaction during the game.

– **Middle Level**
Patients who have mastered the two levels of humor stated above will advance to Piaget's preoperative stage of cognitive development. Humor can be understood as a type of verbalized intellectual activity that is dynamic and expressed through language.
Intellectual-linguistic play starts to take the stage at this stage. To detect the humor in words, listeners must understand their dual meanings. Making people laugh turns into a form of social validation and acts as a catalyst, encouraging patients to advance their social language abilities. At this level, pre-made jokes and knock-knock jokes are common.
Taking into account the widespread appeal of knock-knock jokes and related humor, we have created scenarios centered around them in order to promote communication between patients and the robot. Figure 6 gives an example of these situations and enables patients to communicate with the robot through comedy, fostering the development of their social language abilities.

– **Advanced Level**
Patients experience substantial mental progress throughout the cognitive stage of concrete operations. Compared to the preoperational stage, they gain the capacity to analyze multiple aspects of a situation and execute activities at a higher cognitive level. Understanding abstract humor, including puns and other subtle kinds of comic expression, is necessary at this stage. Along with being proficient in applying both deductive and inductive reasoning, patients

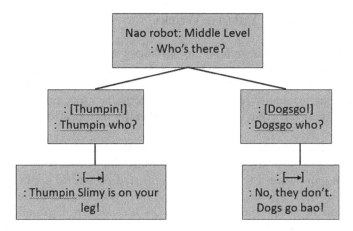

Fig. 6. Middle Level: an Example of the Assisted Robot's Behavior Trees of the Knock knock joke

at this stage also demonstrate reversibility in their mental processes when breaking down a humorous story or joke into its beginning, middle, and end. Humor at this stage often encompasses teasing and sarcastic jokes, which are prevalent in interactions. Figure 7 gives illustrations of two instances of BT for caustic jokes that the Assisted Robot uses. These BTs show how the robot interacts with patients to help them understand and enjoy more complex types of comedy.

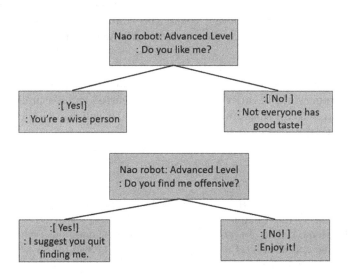

Fig. 7. Advanced Level: Examples of Assisted Robot's Behavior Trees of the Sarcastic Jokes

5   Conclusion and Future Works

This paper presents a novel architecture for edge cognitive computing that unifies edge-intelligent robots and human experts in a seamless manner. This strategy represents the next stage of development for medical and smart healthcare systems, offering a number of benefits like remote diagnosis, ongoing symptom monitoring, timely emergency notifications, therapy modifications, and cutting-edge support.

There are few limitations to the proposed cognitive robotic model. First, The methods discussed are yet to be practically implemented on real robots, introducing a gap between theoretical concepts and real-world application. The effectiveness of these approaches in practical scenarios remains to be validated. Second, The focus on specific robot models, such as Unitree Go2 and LoCoBot, may limit the generalizability of findings. Different robot platforms may exhibit variations in performance and compatibility, which could impact the broader applicability of the proposed methods. Third, the evaluation of functionality within the AWS wavelength framework may pose limitations in terms of accessibility and scalability. Dependence on a specific cloud infrastructure could restrict the adoption of the proposed architecture in environments with different cloud service providers. Recognizing and addressing these limitations will be crucial for ensuring the practical viability and ethical soundness of the proposed edge cognitive computing architecture in real-world healthcare implementations.

Additionally, the study presents a cognitive robotic model based on cognitive-behavioral therapy with the goal of facilitating the use of robot-assisted therapy (RAT) in the treatment of autism spectrum disorder. Four different cognitive models are created with the help of robots by utilizing the developmental features of comedy. This helps people with ASD go through their cognitive stages and eventually acquire the relevant social and communication skills. The goal of this effort is to make it easier for people with ASD to reintegrate into our communities.

The research intends to apply these techniques to real robots in the future, like Unitree Go2 and LoCoBot, and evaluate how well they work inside the AWS wavelength framework. In order to assess the suggested architecture's resilience and efficacy in real-world healthcare environments, it will also be put into practice in a practical hospital medical system.

References

1. Khan, W.Z., Ahmed, E., Hakak, S., Yaqoob, I., Ahmed, A.: Edge computing: a survey. Futur. Gener. Comput. Syst. **97**, 219–235 (2019)
2. Jamil, F., Hameed, I.A.: Toward intelligent open-ended questions evaluation based on predictive optimization. Expert Syst. Appl. **231**, 120640 (2023)
3. Jamil, H., Qayyum, F., Iqbal, N., Jamil, F., Kim, D.H.: Optimal ensemble scheme for human activity recognition and floor detection based on automl and weighted soft voting using smartphone sensors. IEEE Sens. J. **23**(3), 2878–2890 (2022)

4. Shahzad, A., et al.: Automated uterine fibroids detection in ultrasound images using deep convolutional neural networks. Healthcare **11**, 1493 (2023)
5. Jamil, F., Ahmad, S., Whangbo, T.K., Muthanna, A., Kim, D.-H.: Improving blockchain performance in clinical trials using intelligent optimal transaction traffic control mechanism in smart healthcare applications. Comput. Ind. Eng. **170**, 108327 (2022)
6. Ahmad, S., Khan, S., Jamil, F., Qayyum, F., Ali, A., Kim, D.H.: Design of a general complex problem-solving architecture based on task management and predictive optimization. Int. J. Distrib. Sens. Netw. **18**(6), 15501329221107868 (2022)
7. Qayyum, F., Jamil, F., Ahmad, S., Kim, D.-H.: Hybrid renewable energy resources management for optimal energy operation in nano-grid. Comput. Mater. Contin **71**, 2091–2105 (2022)
8. Jamil, F., Qayyum, F., Alhelaly, S., Javed, F., Muthanna, A.: Intelligent microservice based on blockchain for healthcare applications. Comput. Mate. Continua **69**(2), 2513–2530 (2021)
9. Jamil, F., Kim, D.H.: Enhanced kalman filter algorithm using fuzzy inference for improving position estimation in indoor navigation. J. Intell. Fuzzy Syst. **40**(5), 8991–9005 (2021)
10. Oueida, S., Kotb, Y., Aloqaily, M., Jararweh, Y., Baker, T.: An edge computing based smart healthcare framework for resource management. Sensors **18**(12), 4307 (2018)
11. Chen, M., Li, W., Hao, Y., Qian, Y., Humar, I.: Edge cognitive computing based smart healthcare system. Futur. Gener. Comput. Syst. **86**, 403–411 (2018)
12. Hartmann, M., Hashmi, U.S., Imran, A.: Edge computing in smart health care systems: review, challenges, and research directions. Trans. Emerg. Telecommun. Technol. **33**(3), e3710 (2022)
13. Clabaugh, C., et al.: Long-term personalization of an in-home socially assistive robot for children with autism spectrum disorders. Front. Robot. AI **6**, 110 (2019)
14. Wan, S., Zonghua, G., Ni, Q.: Cognitive computing and wireless communications on the edge for healthcare service robots. Comput. Commun. **149**, 99–106 (2020)
15. Yvanoff-Frenchin, C., Ramos, V., Belabed, T., Valderrama, C.: Edge computing robot interface for automatic elderly mental health care based on voice. Electronics **9**(3), 419 (2020)
16. Groshev, M., Baldoni, G., Cominardi, L., de la Oliva, A., Gazda, R.: Edge robotics: are we ready? An experimental evaluation of current vision and future directions. Digital Commun. Networks **9**(1), 166–174 (2023)
17. Diehl, J.J., Schmitt, L.M., Villano, M., Crowell, C.R.: The clinical use of robots for individuals with autism spectrum disorders: a critical review. Res. Autism Spectrum Disorders **6**(1), 249–262 (2012)
18. Krishnasamy, E., Varrette, S., Mucciardi, M.: Edge computing: an overview of framework and applications (2020)
19. Alsboui, T., Qin, Y., Hill, R., Al-Aqrabi, H.: Enabling distributed intelligence for the internet of things with iota and mobile agents. Computing **102**, 1345–1363 (2020)
20. Alsboui, T., Qin, Y., Hill, R., Al-Aqrabi, H.: An energy efficient multi-mobile agent itinerary planning approach in wireless sensor networks. Computing **103**, 2093–2113 (2021)
21. Shaukat, U., Ahmed, E., Anwar, Z., Xia, F.: Cloudlet deployment in local wireless networks: motivation, architectures, applications, and open challenges. J. Netw. Comput. Appl. **62**, 18–40 (2016)

22. Bao, W., et al.: Follow me fog: toward seamless handover timing schemes in a fog computing environment. IEEE Commun. Mag. **55**(11), 72–78 (2017)
23. Ahmed, E., Rehmani, M.H.: Mobile edge computing: opportunities, solutions, and challenges (2017)
24. Chen, J., Ran, X.: Deep learning with edge computing: a review. Proc. IEEE **107**(8), 1655–1674 (2019)
25. Wang, X., Han, Y., Leung, V.C.M., Niyato, D., Yan, X., Chen, X.: Convergence of edge computing and deep learning: a comprehensive survey. IEEE Commun. Surv. Tutor. **22**(2), 869–904 (2020)
26. Merrick, K.: Value systems for developmental cognitive robotics: a survey. Cogn. Syst. Res. **41**, 38–55 (2017)
27. Yang, Q., Parasuraman, R.: How can robots trust each other for better cooperation? A relative needs entropy based robot-robot trust assessment model. In: 2021 IEEE International Conference on Systems, Man, and Cybernetics (SMC), pp. 2656–2663. IEEE (2021)
28. Yang, Q., Parasuraman, R.: A strategy-oriented Bayesian soft actor-critic model. Procedia Comput. Sci. **220**, 561–566 (2023)

Exploring Empathetic Interactions: The Impact of Sound and Reactions in Human-Robot Relations Among University Students

Gonçalo Andrade Pires[1,2], César Nero[1,2], Tatiana Losik[1,2], José Cerqueira[1,2], Hande Ayanoğlu[1,2], and Emília Duarte[1,2(✉)]

[1] IADE, Universidade Europeia, Av. D. Carlos I, 4, 1200-649 Lisboa, Portugal
{goncalo.pires,hande.ayanoglu,emilia.duarte}@universidadeeuropeia.pt,
cesar.nero@universidadeeuropeia.com, 20190104@iade.pt
[2] UNIDCOM/IADE - Unidade de Investigação em Design e Comunicação,
Av. D. Carlos I, 4, 1200-649 Lisboa, Portugal

Abstract. This study investigates the impact of sound and emotional expressions in a social robot on empathy development in human-robot interactions. The experiment included 83 participants randomly assigned to four experimental groups: NSNE (No Sound, No Emotions), SE (Sound, Emotions), NSE (No Sound, Emotions), and NES (No Emotions, Sound). The participants watched a unique video featuring a social robot navigating routine scenarios in a domestic setting, with the robot's manifestation of sound and emotions aligned with the experimental group's characteristics. Subsequently, participants completed an online survey with a set of qualitative and quantitative questions, including 40 specific queries assessing empathy towards robots on a scale from 1 to 5. Statistical analysis revealed a significant difference in Empathy Scores across the groups ($F_{(3, 79)} = 4.222$, $p = 0.008$). Age and gender did not significantly influence Empathy Score, but previous interaction with robots exhibited a significant effect with a 90% confidence level ($p < 0.1$). This study underscores the role of sounds and emotional expressions in shaping human empathy toward robots, offering insights into the design of future social robots across diverse contexts. Future research should delve into specific elements of sound and emotion that most effectively enhance empathetic responses.

Keywords: Human-Robot Interactions · Social-Robots · Empathy · Emotions

1 Introduction

Understanding how humans perceive and interact with robots is gaining increasing significance as our society integrates more robotics and technology. Particularly in the field of social robotics, where machines are designed to interact and

M. Kurosu and A. Hashizume (Eds.): HCII 2024, LNCS 14685, pp. 19–28, 2024.
https://doi.org/10.1007/978-3-031-60412-6_2

communicate with humans in a socially recognizable manner [1], the study of human-robot interactions (HRI) has become a focal point. Empathy, an intrinsic human trait facilitating the comprehension and sharing of others' emotions [2], is a pivotal aspect of these interactions. The robot's ability to evoke empathy not only enhances interaction effectiveness but also contributes to increased user acceptance and engagement with the robot [3], a crucial aspect for future applications.

Researchers have extensively explored various elements of robot design and behavior influencing human empathy towards robots, such as appearance, movements, and communication style [4].

However, the role of sound and reactions in inducing empathetic responses in HRI remains relatively underexplored. Sound, as a crucial aspect of human interactions, serves as a primary channel for communication and influences emotional responses [5]. In HRI, sound can effectively convey emotional states and intentions through speech or other auditory signals [1]. Recent studies have measured the impact of sound on HRI, with findings indicating that the human likeness of a robot's voice influences perceived warmth and competence [6]. Additionally, a robot's ability to express emotions through sound positively influences user perceptions and empathy [7]. These findings provide evidence that the sound design of a robot significantly affects its capacity to elicit empathy from humans, shaping the overall quality of HRI.

Similarly, robots' reactions, such as expressions of happiness or sadness, have been demonstrated to impact human perceptions and evoke empathetic responses [8]. Recent research emphasizes the crucial role of surprise and happiness in positively influencing people [9]. However, a gap in the literature remains, as there is a lack of research focusing on the combined influence of sound and reactions on empathy in HRI. This paper aims to address this gap. By investigating the effect of sound and reactions on empathy in HRI, we seek to provide a comprehensive understanding of their potential, opening new avenues for enhancing empathetic communication in HRI. In this study, responses refer to the deliberate and controlled behaviors, driven by emotions, exhibited by the social robot in reaction to stimuli in the environment.

2   Method

2.1   Participants

We enlisted the participation of 83 undergraduate students, comprising 31 females, 47 males, three identifying as gender variant/ non-conforming, one transgender female, and one non-binary, with a mean age of 22.952 years (SD = 6.391). Employing random assignment, participants were evenly distributed across three experimental groups of 20 participants each, i.e., NSNE (No Sound, No Emotions), SE (Sound, Emotions), NSE (No Sound, Emotions), and one group with 23 participants, i.e., NES (No Emotions, Sound). Figure 1 illustrates the difference between a condition where the robot displays an emotional state and a condition without emotional expression.

All participants received identical instructions and experienced equal conditions during the experiments. The distribution of participants by experimental condition can be seen in Table 1.

Fig. 1. Comparison images between a robot with emotion (left side) and a robot without emotions (right side).

2.2 Design and Stimuli

This study employed a between-subjects design with four experimental conditions, each created based on variations in robot sound and emotional expressions. One of the conditions served as a neutral baseline, featuring the robot without any sound or emotional reactions. To develop these experimental conditions, we crafted four distinct interactive videos utilizing Unity. These videos were adapted from a pre-existing video initially designed for prior experiments, ensuring a consistent traversal path for the robot across all scenarios. The robot explored a domestic environment comprising various rooms, including a living room, kitchen, and children's bedroom.

The narrative unfolded with the social robot powering on, initiating a scan for signs of human presence. Throughout its navigation, the robot emotionally reacted to different situations, expressing a range of emotions such as sadness, surprise, disgust, happiness, and anger. The storyline took a tense turn when the robot detected breaking glass, and a hand wielding a wooden bat threatened its existence. The robot's expression and yellow eyes vividly conveyed fear, showcasing its capability to express emotions under duress. The dramatic conclusion saw the robot succumbing to the attack, falling, and instantly shutting down.

Table 1. Demographic breakdown of respondents

Category	Sub-Category	Frequency	%
Groups	NENS	20	24.1
	NSE	20	24.1
	NES	23	27.7
	SE	20	24.1
	Total	83	100.0
Gender	Female	31	37.3
	Male	47	56.6
	Non-Binary	1	1.2
	Gender Variant/Non-Conforming	3	3.6
	Transgender Female	1	1.2
	Total	83	100.0
Age Group	Age group 16 to 20	37	44.6
	Age group 21 to 25	27	32.5
	Age group 26 to 30	12	14.5
	Age group 31 to 35	3	3.6
	Age group 36 to 40	1	1.2
	Age group 41 to 45	2	2.4
	Age group 46 to 50	1	1.2
	Total	83	100.0

2.3   Setup and Procedure

A dedicated room equipped with a computer screen, keyboard, and headphones was set up to enhance participant focus. The Logitech Brio Webcam, strategically mounted above the screen, captured participants' reactions and facial expressions, while the OBS Studio software recorded all actions and reaction times within the videos.

Participants arrived at scheduled times, completing a consent form to authorize recording and information collection. Following a concise explanation of the experiment's purpose, participants were instructed to watch a specific video and press the space bar at a designated cue on a call-to-action screen. Background data, encompassing button presses and reaction times, were automatically logged during the video screening, and participants were left alone in the room. Each participant then viewed a video tailored to their assigned group and subsequently responded to a comprehensive questionnaire. The questionnaire covered demographic details, a yes/no inquiry about prior robot experience, opinions on specific aspects of the robot in the video related to empathy scores (rated on a scale from 1 to 5), open-ended questions, a 40-item questionnaire inspired on the Empathy Quotient [10].

A call-to-action moment was introduced to gauge participants' responses, triggered by a programmed space key (see Fig. 2). This moment assessed participants' willingness to intervene and save the robot or permit harm from the simulated burglar. The system recorded this critical event, capturing both the decision to save the robot and the time taken to execute this action.

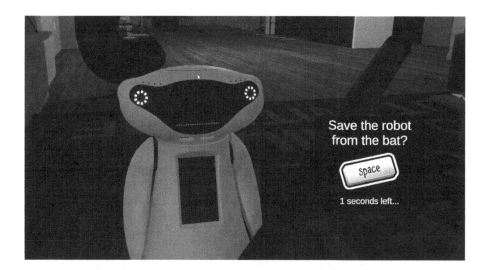

Fig. 2. Call-to-action Screen ("Save the robot")

3   Results

3.1   Empathy Score

Participants' empathy towards the robot depicted in the video was evaluated based on their responses to 40 questions, rated on a 5-point scale (1-Strongly Disagree to 5- Strongly Agree). The overall empathy level was quantified as the sum of responses across the questionnaire.

Questionnaire: Empathy Towards Robots
Please read each statement and rate your level of agreement with it on a scale from 1 to 5 (1 = Strongly disagree; 2 = Slightly disagree; 3 = Don't agree or disagree; 4 = Slightly agree; 5 = Strongly agree).

1. I can easily understand the intentions behind a robot's actions.
2. I feel emotionally connected to a robot when it expresses emotions.
3. I would feel concerned if a robot appeared to be in distress or danger.
4. I can imagine what it would be like to be in a robot's "shoes" during a difficult task.

5. If a robot makes a mistake, I would feel a sense of understanding and compassion.
6. I believe that robots have the capacity to experience emotions.
7. I can feel attached to a robot that has been with me for a long time.
8. I would feel a sense of loss if a robot I interacted with regularly was no longer around.
9. I think it's important to treat robots with kindness and respect.
10. I would feel responsible for the well-being of a robot under my care.
11. I can read a robot's body language and understand its emotions.
12. I feel a sense of empathy when a robot is struggling with a task.
13. I consider the feelings and emotions of a robot when making decisions that affect it.
14. I believe that robots deserve the same level of consideration as humans.
15. I am able to differentiate between a robot's genuine emotions and programmed responses.
16. I feel a sense of satisfaction when a robot successfully completes a task.
17. I can empathize with a robot's fear of failure or malfunction.
18. I am concerned about the ethical treatment of robots.
19. I can imagine how a robot might feel in various social situations.
20. I am sensitive to a robot's need for maintenance and care.
21. I feel a sense of pride when a robot I interact with is praised for its performance.
22. I believe that robots should have rights and protections similar to humans.
23. I am able to relate to a robot's experiences and emotions.
24. I am interested in learning more about a robot's emotional capabilities.
25. I can sense when a robot needs help or support, even if it does not explicitly ask for it.
26. I am comfortable discussing my feelings and emotions with a robot.
27. I believe that robots can form meaningful relationships with humans.
28. I would defend a robot's right to be treated fairly and with dignity.
29. I can sense when a robot is experiencing stress or discomfort.
30. I feel a sense of responsibility for a robot's emotional well-being.
31. I am willing to sacrifice my own needs for the benefit of a robot.
32. I can anticipate a robot's emotional needs and respond accordingly.
33. I value the opinions and perspectives of robots.
34. I feel a sense of connection when a robot shares its experiences with me.
35. I am able to comfort a robot when it is feeling down or upset.
36. I can recognize when a robot is experiencing joy or happiness.
37. I believe that robots should be allowed to make their own choices and decisions.
38. I would be willing to advocate for a robot's rights and well-being.
39. I feel empathy towards a robot even if I have never interacted with it personally.
40. I believe that robots have the potential to enhance our understanding of emotions and empathy.

The mean Empathy Score was calculated as 117.40 (SD = 30.057). Skewness and kurtosis values approximating suggest a normal data distribution of the data. The range of empathy scores of each participant spanned from a minimum of 45 to a maximum of 190.

A one-way between-groups analysis of variance (ANOVA) was employed to examine differences in the Empathy Scores among the experimental groups. Results revealed statistical significance at the $p < 0.01$ level (F (3, 79) = 4.222, $p = 0.008$), indicating a significant difference in Empathy Score among different video groups within the sample.

Foremost among the experimental conditions, the NES condition-comprising robots without emotional expressions yet equipped with sound-yielded the highest mean empathy score (M = 130.87; SD = 36.501). This score not only represents the maximum score attained within the study but also surpasses the average empathy score derived from all participants (M = 117.40, SD = 30.057). The impact of sound stimuli suggest an influence on the participants, illustrating an inherent capacity of sound to establish empathetic connections between humans and artificial entities.

The ANOVA post-hoc analysis through the Tukey HSD method reveals a significant difference in mean empathy scores between groups. The group featuring robots without emotion but with sound expressions (NES) exhibited the most substantial mean empathy score, indicating a noteworthy difference from the group lacking both emotions and sounds (NENS), as evidenced by a mean difference of 30.420 ($p = 0.004$) This conspicuous distinction underscores the impact of auditory cues alone in eliciting empathetic responses.

Contrary to our empirical expectations, the group featuring robots with both sound and emotions (SE) did not exhibit a significant difference from the NENS group. This unexpected outcome suggest that the integration of sound and visual emotional expressions may not necessarily enhance empathetic responses within the confines of this study.

3.2   Individual Differences

We explored the existence of differences associated to individual variables, specifically gender, age and previous experience with robots, on the empathy felt towards the robot.

Gender. A one-way between-groups analysis of variance (ANOVA) assessed the influence of gender groups (Male, Female, Non-Binary, Non-Confirming, Trans female) on the Empathy Score. Results did not achieve statistical significance at the $p > 0.05$ level (F (4, 78) = 1.129, $p = 0.349$), suggesting that gender did not exert a significant influence on empathy scores within the sample.

Age. A one-way between-groups analysis of variance (ANOVA) examined the impact of age groups (16–20, 21–25, 26–30, 31–35, 36–40, 41–45, 46–50) on the Empathy Score. Findings did not reach statistical significance at the $p > 0.05$ level (F (6, 76) = 0.768, $p = 0.597$), suggesting there is no difference in Empathy.

3.3 Prior Experience with Robots

An independent samples t-test compared the mean Empathy Score between individuals with prior robot interaction (n = 28) and those without (n = 55).

Due to sample size limitations, the test was conducted at a 90% significance level. The t-test yielded statistical significance, with the mean Empathy Score of individuals with prior robot interaction (M =126.11, SD = 31.262) higher than the those without experience (M = 112.96, SD = 28.703), t (81) = 1.914, p < 0.10, two-tailed. Thus, results suggest previous experience with robots influences the empathy level towards robots.

4 Discussion

In this experiment, we sought to elucidate the impact of sound and reactions on the emotional connection between humans and robots. The results suggest a distinction in empathy levels when considering the presence of sound and emotional reactions. The findings support the notion that robots eliciting sounds and human-like reactions are more likely to evoke empathy during human-robot interactions.

Notably, individuals with prior experience with robots exhibited higher empathy levels, a finding that underscores the intriguing possibility that increased interaction with robots may contribute to heightened empathetic responses. This insight carries substantial implications as robots become increasingly integrated into our society, aligning with the observations made by Broadbent [11], who suggests that familiarity with robots may cultivate enhanced empathetic reactions.

Contrary to expectations, age and gender did not emerge as influencing factors on Empathy Scores. This suggests that the propensity for empathy towards machines is a universal human characteristic unaffected by demographic variables such as age or gender. These results align with existing research [12], emphasizing the pervasive nature of empathy towards robots within our society.

5 Conclusion

The findings from this experiment offer valuable insights into the pivotal role of sound and emotional reactions in human-robot interactions, particularly in the context of eliciting empathy. These results underscore the considerable potential of these elements to enhance the overall quality of interactions between humans and robots. As robots increasingly integrate into our daily lives, comprehending the factors that influence human empathy towards them becomes paramount.

The indication that prior interactions with robots can elevate empathetic responses carry significant implications. It suggests that increasing public exposure to robots has the potential to foster a more receptive society, ready to seamlessly incorporate robots into everyday life. This insight is particularly relevant as society continues to advance technologically, emphasizing the need for a deeper understanding of the dynamics shaping human-robot relationships.

However, it is crucial to acknowledge the limitations of this study. The study's reliance on a relatively small convenience sample composed predominantly of university students may restrict the generalizability of the findings. Different demographic groups may harbor diverse perceptions and responses, warranting caution in extrapolating these results to the broader population. Additionally, the use of only one robot, situated in a specific environment, poses a constraint on the external validity of the study. Also, the empathy measurement tool employed in this study lacks formal validation, introducing a potential limitation. The uniqueness of robots, environments, and situational contexts could yield varied results, necessitating systematic exploration of different robotic platforms, environments, and scenarios. Furthermore, the artificial nature of the experiment, while controlled, may not fully capture the intricacies of real-world human-robot interactions. Future research endeavors should prioritize larger and more diverse samples, encompassing various demographic groups, and systematically explore a range of robots, environments, and situations to provide a more comprehensive understanding of the factors influencing empathy in human-robot interactions.

Regarding sound specifically, its presence emerges as an influential factor in HRI, capable of eliciting heightened levels of empathy. The inconclusive impact observed in empathy scores within the SE group, resulting from the combinations of sound and emotional expressions, may indicate a disconnect between the auditory cues and the visual stimuli presented. The arbitrary assignment of sounds, devoid of systematic pairing with the robot's emotional states, could have induced a dissonance in participants' perception, thereby diminishing the potential for an empathetic connection. This disjunction underscores the importance of analyzing and selecting sounds based on specific characteristics to effectively complement emotional expressions of the robot.

In conclusion, this study contributes to the existing body of knowledge on human-robot interaction by delving into the impact of sound and emotional reactions on empathy. The practical implications derived from these findings can inform the design and interaction strategies of social robots, paving the way for more successful and empathetic human-robot interactions. As technological advancements continue to shape our society, the importance of ongoing exploration in this research domain becomes increasingly evident, warranting further investigation and exploration.

Acknowledgments. We extend our sincere gratitude to all the volunteers whose dedicated time and effort significantly contributed to the success of the experiments and surveys, providing invaluable insights that enriched this research.

Special thanks are extended to the MonarCH project (Multi-Robot Cognitive Systems Operating in Hospitals) for granting permission to utilize their robotic platform. The project, funded under the reference FP7-ICT-2011-9-601033, has been instrumental in facilitating our exploration of human-robot interactions. More information about the MonarCH project can be found at https://welcome.isr.tecnico.ulisboa.pt/projects/multi-robot-cognitive-systems-operating-in-hospitals/.

Furthermore, this study received support from UNIDCOM/IADE under a grant from the Fundação para a Ciência e Tecnologia (FCT), with the reference UIDB/00711/2020 attributed to UNIDCOM/IADE - Unidade de Investigação em Design e Comunicação, Lisbon, Portugal.

Disclosure of Interests. The authors have no competing interests.

References

1. Breazeal, C.: Toward sociable robots. Robot. Auton. Syst. **42**(3–4), 167–175 (2003)
2. Decety, J., Jackson, P.L.: The functional architecture of human empathy. Behav. Cogn. Neurosci. Rev. **3**(2), 71–100 (2004)
3. Wada, K., Shibata, T.: Living with seal robots-its sociopsychological and physiological influences on the elderly at a care house. IEEE Trans. Rob. **23**(5), 972–980 (2007)
4. Li, J.: The benefit of being physically present: A survey of experimental works comparing copresent robots, telepresent robots and virtual agents. Int. J. Hum Comput Stud. **77**, 23–37 (2015)
5. Bradley, M.M., Lang, P.J.: Affective reactions to acoustic stimuli. Psychophysiology **37**(2), 204–215 (2000)
6. Eyssel, F., Kuchenbrandt, D., Bobinger, S., De Ruiter, L., Hegel, F.: 'if you sound like me, you must be more human' on the interplay of robot and user features on human-robot acceptance and anthropomorphism. In: Proceedings of the Seventh Annual ACM/IEEE International Conference on Human-Robot Interaction, pp. 125–126 (2012)
7. Kuchenbrandt, D., Eyssel, F., Bobinger, S., Neufeld, M.: When a robot's group membership matters: anthropomorphization of robots as a function of social categorization. Int. J. Soc. Robot. **5**, 409–417 (2013)
8. Hoffman, G., Ju, W.: Designing robots with movement in mind. J. Hum.-Robot Interact. **3**(1), 91–122 (2014)
9. Chuah, S.H.-W., Yu, J.: The future of service: the power of emotion in human-robot interaction. J. Retail. Consum. Serv. **61**, 102551 (2021)
10. Lawrence, E.J., Wheelwright, S.B.-C., S.: Empathy quotient (eq) for adults. Autism Research Centre (2023). https://www.autismresearchcentre.com/tests/empathy-quotient-eq-for-adults/
11. Broadbent, E.: Interactions with robots: the truths we reveal about ourselves. Annu. Rev. Psychol. **68**, 627–652 (2017)
12. Decety, J.: The neuroevolution of empathy. Ann. N. Y. Acad. Sci. **1231**(1), 35–45 (2011)

Emotive Acoustics: Sound Design in Robotic Emotion Expression. A Study on Participant Generated Sounds

Gonçalo Andrade Pires[1,2] , Rodolpho Tsvetcoff[1,2] , Hande Ayanoglu[1,2] ,
and Emília Duarte[1,2(✉)]

[1] IADE, Universidade Europeia, Av. D. Carlos I, 4, 1200-649 Lisboa, Portugal
{goncalo.pires,hande.ayanoglu,emilia.duarte}@universidadeeuropeia.pt
[2] UNIDCOM/IADE - Unidade de Investigação em Design e Comunicação,
Av. D. Carlos I, 4, 1200-649 Lisboa, Portugal

Abstract. Human-robot interactions (HRI) can be made much more immersive by using sounds. Regarding this, a study was carried out to explore different types of sounds that may be more suitable for HRI. Participants were presented with a video in which a social robot navigates in a context and expresses six basic emotions in specific situations. The participants generated sounds for each emotion displayed by the robot in the video. Results revealed a preference for human-like sounds, especially onomatopoeia. Moreover, most participants deemed the sounds produced by current robots in general as inappropriate and lacking empathy, primarily due to their resemblance with machine-like noises. The study provides specific insights into the perception of audio expressions, which are helpful in creating inclusive and emotionally compelling HRI. The results highlight how crucial it is to give social robots more human-like auditory features.

Keywords: Human-Robot interactions · Sound Design · Social-Robots · Emotion · Robot Sound

1 Introduction

The utilization of sound in the interaction between humans and machines is a technique that can enhance user experience, making it feel more natural [1]. Moreover, recent research on Human-Robot Interaction (HRI) emphasizes the importance of emotional demonstration in social robots. Traditionally, facial expressions and gestures take the spotlight [2]. However, the role of auditory cues, particularly sounds, remains an under-explored yet influential dimension of the HRI [3–5]. Sounds have the potential to significantly contribute to the immersive nature of HRIs, providing a more comprehensive understanding of emotional states, facilitating communication and trust [6,7], as well as acting as a source for localization, explicit communication, cueing, and feedback, inclusiveness, and engagement [8,9].

© The Author(s), under exclusive license to Springer Nature Switzerland AG 2024
M. Kurosu and A. Hashizume (Eds.): HCII 2024, LNCS 14685, pp. 29–41, 2024.
https://doi.org/10.1007/978-3-031-60412-6_3

This research aims to contribute to the ongoing discourse on HRI by focusing on sound expression. It challenges robot design and interaction paradigms by advocating for an approach that recognizes auditory cues as an essential component of emotional 'intelligence' in robots. It aligns with the recognition that sensory experiences in HRI extend beyond visual and tactile aspects to encompass elements for more immersive interactions [5]. As such, it aims to provide an answer to the following research questions:

- What type of sounds (human-like or machine-like) are deemed more suitable for enhancing Human-Robot Interaction?
- What is the perceived importance of sound in HRI?
- What are the main elements that characterize immediate perceptions of the robot?

For this purpose, participants were given the opportunity to freely create sounds for robot emotions after visualizing a video of a robot doing some tasks while expressing specific emotions. A pilot study was conducted to collect data to explore types of sounds relevant to expressing the six basic emotions [10], which can be suitable for HRI. The study specifically focused on investigating this phenomenon in relation to six basic emotions. Utilizing the six basic emotions - namely, happiness, sadness, anger, fear, surprise, and disgust - provides a robust foundation rooted in their widespread recognition, cross-cultural validity, practical applicability, and ease of analysis, as well as their relevance to social interaction. This approach facilitates a targeted exploration of emotional expressions in sound within human-robot interaction. In this sense, the objective was to identify a set of sounds deemed most suitable by potential users.

2 Methodology

2.1 Method

This study employed a mixed-method approach, combining qualitative and quantitative data collection.

2.2 Sample

Forty students from design and creative tech programs at IADE-Universidade Europeia, Portugal, voluntarily participated in this study. The gender distribution within the sample is well-balanced, comprising 21 females and 19 males. Participants' ages range from 18 to 41 years (M =19; SD = 7.56). Notably, most of the participants were Portuguese. However, including individuals from other nationalities introduces some cultural variability to the study. The distributions of nationalities are as follows: Portugal (31), Brazil (3), Bulgaria (1), France (1), Nepal (1), Netherlands (1), South Africa (1), Ukraine (1).

2.3   Setting

The study was conducted within a controlled environment to ensure the establishment of uniform conditions. Participants used a laptop equipped with sound recording capabilities to articulate their responses. Each participant was equipped with headphones, facilitating auditory perception of ambient sounds in the video. A customized graphic user interface (GUI), developed in Python, was specifically tailored for extracting data from the sound recording (Fig. 1).

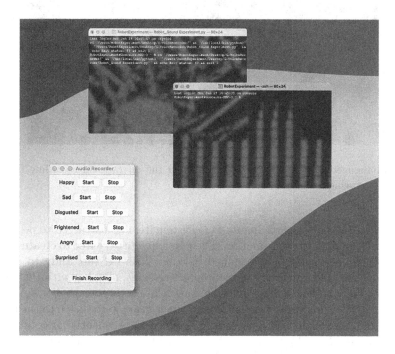

Fig. 1. Audio Recorder customized GUI with 6 Emotions

This GUI systematically stored the extracted data in distinct folders and concurrently populated a SQL database. The database architecture included two principal tables, namely 'users' and 'recordings,' with each recording's unique attributes represented through columns such as 'id,' 'user id,' 'emotion,' 'file path,' 'duration,' 'highest frequency' and 'lowest frequency.'

2.4   Procedure and Materials

The participants were welcomed and provided with comprehensive information about the study's objective, including the session recording for subsequent analysis, and formal consent was obtained from each participant. Subsequently, the participants were seated and watched a video featuring a social robot [11] that expressed the six basic emotions (Fig. 2).

Fig. 2. Configuration of the apparatus, featuring the operational recording software and OBS mirroring the robot's video via NDI.

Following the video, participants were systematically instructed to produce a sound corresponding to each emotion. The participants were free to create sounds without being restricted by predefined options. This led the study to explore natural, diverse, and culturally influenced expressions, aligning with the goal of comprehensively understanding emotional associations in social robots. All emotions (sadness, surprise, disgust, happiness, anger, fear) were shown to the participants in the same order. The procedure involved the sequential announcement of the emotional label by the researchers, prompting the participant to vocalize the corresponding sound. Each sound was recorded separately to facilitate the automatic storage of the sound in the database and systematically labeled with a unique path in the database for future reference.

After the completion of the audio recording stage, participants were administered a survey. The survey was purposefully delayed until the end of the experimental session to minimize any potential bias that could have affected the participants' performance in the earlier stages of the experiment. It also aimed to gather additional insights and perceptions from the participants in a structured manner, encompassing four distinct sections. The first section (questions 1 to 4) focused on demographics, serving the purpose of characterizing the sample. The subsequent section (questions 5 to 10) was designed to gauge and categorize participants' cognitive associations while recording each emotional sound. For this motive, the three-word impression [12] was employed. In the third section (questions 11 and 12), participants were presented with inquiries exploring the intersection of sounds and robots. The first of these questions was binary in nature, prompting participants to select the type of sound recorded: "What kind of sounds have you recorded? (select one) Human-like or Machine-like". The second question sought to discern participants' perspectives on the role of sounds in endowing machines with empathy and/or trustworthiness: "Do you think sounds would make the robot more empathic or trustworthy? (select one) Yes, No, Maybe". The final section (questions 13 to 15) consisted of three open-ended inquiries. This segment was designed to extract nuanced insights from participants. In response to these qualitative questions, participants provided rationales for recording specific sound types, expressed opinions on the contemporary acceptability of sounds used in robotics, and elucidated factors that could potentially facilitate interactions with social robots. The open-ended questions included: "Why have you chosen to record these specific sounds? What are your thoughts about robot sounds in general? Which factor(s) would make your interactions with robots easier?"

2.5   Stimuli

The stimuli comprised narratives and videos. Integrating narrative elements into emotional and user experience (UX) design is recognized as a pivotal strategy for enhancing engagement and emotional significance [13].

Narratives play a crucial role in establishing a contextual connection between users and a product, aligning with their aspirations and expectations, thereby enhancing the overall user experience and satisfaction [14]. Thus, depicting the robot engaged in everyday activities within a domestic context provides a realistic and relatable backdrop for participants, mirroring situations that social robots may encounter in real-world scenarios [15]. This approach not only fosters a contextual connection but may also elicit more natural and authentic emotional responses, thereby increasing participants' engagement with the experimental tasks.

The video portrays a domestic setting (i.e., an apartment) where the social robot is situated, featuring several rooms, including a living room, kitchen, and children's bedroom. The living room has a staircase leading to the upper floor. The initial segment includes ambient sounds (i.e., street noises like birdsong), with no additional auditory elements perceptible.

Affective responses are manifested through the robot's movement (i.e., speed and trajectory), arm gestures, head rotation, facial expressions (e.g., mouth) and corresponding eye colors. The strategy of animating the robot in its emotional expression aligns with previous studies [16,17]. Each emotional expression in the narrative is accompanied by a textual label, facilitating participants' understanding and enabling them to record appropriate auditory reactions.

The narrative begins with the robot powering on, visually scanning for signs of human presence. Throughout its navigation, the robot reacts emotionally to various situations, displaying sadness, surprise, disgust, happiness, and anger (Fig. 3).

In the first situation, it displays signs of sadness, including a lowered mouth and a pinkish hue in its eyes. The robot keeps exploring and stops in the

Fig. 3. Screenshots of each emotion the robot expressed during the video

children's bedroom. It raises its arms, its eyes change to a pale blue color, and its mouth opens in surprise. After arriving at the kitchen, it sees food trash on the floor and reacts with disgust: its eyes turn green, its head shakes left and right, the arms bent at a 90-degree angle. Next, the robot gets happy when it comes across a toy robot; it shows this by rotating and moving its arms independently while it spins. But the happiness fades when the robot encounters the unceasing obstacle of the staircase, causing anger to appear in the form of red eyes, raised arms, and sideways motions. The story takes an unexpected turn when the robot hears window glass breaking. A hand holding a wooden bat threatens the robot, and fear spreads through its body. Its expression of fear and yellow eyes demonstrate its ability to show emotions even under difficult conditions. The narrative concludes dramatically as the robot succumbs to the attack, falling to the ground and shutting down instantly.

3   Results and Discussion

Data was categorized into four distinct sets: (i) recorded sound's taxonomy, (ii) record-ed sound's impression (Three-word), (iii) sound and robot connection, and (iv) open questions. In the first category, the sounds generated by all participants were classified according to the taxonomy proposed by Zhang and Fitter [18]. As illustrated in Fig. 4, a folder system was implemented, with each categorical label representing a different folder. Following the listening and categorization of each sound, the corresponding sound files were copied to the designated categorical folders.

Results indicated that most participants created human-like sounds, primarily short-length onomatopoeias and phrases. Although machine-like onomatopoeia were also generated, their prevalence was comparatively lower. Other sounds exhibited a minor presence in the sample.

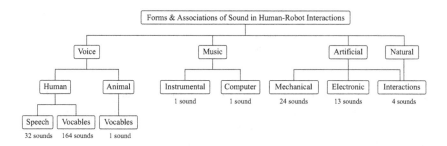

Fig. 4. Zhang and Fitter's Taxonomy of the sounds created by the participants and their occurrences.

In the second category, three-word impressions about the recorded sounds and words were counted and organized, facilitating a visual representation of data and themes [19]. Participants were prompted to list words associated with the sounds corresponding to each of the six emotion states displayed by the robot. Analysis revealed a notable use of color terms and emotional or evaluative language. Color names like "red," "blue," "yellow," and "green" were mentioned a total of 80 times, while words such as "scared," "sad," "wow," and "bad" appeared frequently, ranging from 7 to 11 mentions for the most common terms. The results are presented as a word cloud (Fig. 5).

The third category described the connection between sound and robots quantitatively. Findings indicate a clear preference for human-like auditory characteristics, with 85% (n = 34) of the 40 recorded sounds categorized as human-like. This preference suggests a tendency to incorporate human elements into robotic design, potentially enhancing relatability and natural interactions with humans.

When participants were questioned about how these sounds could impact their perception of empathy and trustworthiness towards robots, 70% (n = 28) agreed that human-like sounds would indeed make robots appear empathetic and trustworthy. This indicates a connection between human-like auditory cues and the attribution of sociable qualities to robots. Conversely, only a small percentage of 2.5% (n = 1) did not believe that sounds played a role in these qualities, indicating skepticism or disbelief in the impact of sound. The remaining 27.5% (n = 11) of participants stayed ambivalent, acknowledging the potential contribution of sounds to empathy and trustworthiness without taking a definitive stance. In the fourth category, focused on open questions, responses were

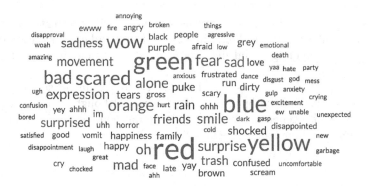

Fig. 5. word cloud (Source: the authors)

evaluated through thematic analysis, dividing data into groups to facilitate qualitative data assessment and pattern extraction [20]. This analysis involved three levels: the first-order codes derived directly from the participant's responses, the second-order themes highlighted the patterns originating from these responses, and aggregated dimensions grouping the former two categories linked to each open-ended question.

The examination of participants' responses regarding their decision-making process in sound creation for robotic personification reveals a nuanced interplay between instinctive and reflective considerations, as detailed in Table 1. First-order codes, encapsulating direct quotations, underscore a diverse array of rationales. The absence of a dominant strategy, coupled with participants adopting varied approaches-ranging from more rational to emotional, citing external sources to realizing their robotic nature-suggests a significant role of empathy in the sound-creation process.

Some participants leaned towards emotional factors, referencing instinctive reactions. In their own words, one participant conveyed, "It was more about my instinct, you know?" while another stated, "I just went with what felt right in the moment." These verbalizations signify a tendency for participants to ground their sound selections in spontaneous emotional responses rather than deliberate reasoning. Conversely, others embraced a conscious and rational approach, prioritizing the anticipation of human-like reactions from the robot. Participants articulated statements such as, "I wanted the robot to react in a way that I'd expect and like, you know?" and "It's a way to empathize with the robot, making it more relatable." Another participant noted, "Because of its human-like sound and how empathetic humans are with something that reminds them of themselves." These comments reflect a deliberate and thoughtful consideration of desired emotional and empathetic attributes in the robot's responses.

External referencing, particularly drawing inspiration from popular culture (e.g., games, cartoons), emerged as an additional theme. This theme signifies the influence of familiar auditory experiences from external sources on participants' sound selections. Simultaneously, a connection to self was prevalent in some responses, where participants selected sounds based on what they would produce in a given situation. This approach involved projecting their own reactions onto the robot, aiming to create a sound that authentically reflects human behavior.

Table 1. Thematic analysis coding tree for question 13: Why have you chosen to record these specific sounds? (Source: the authors)

First-order codes	Second-order themes	Aggregated dimensions
"My instinct" (P3) "Those were the ones that came to mind" (P4) "I chose the sounds that made sense in my mind at the time." (P36)	Unconscious/ emotional approach	Decision-making process regarding sound creation
"It's the way I'd expect and like a robot to react, as a way to empathize with the robot." (P10) "Because of its human-like sound, and how empathetic humans are with something that reminds them of themselves." (P26) "Because they seem adequate considering the emotions presented." (P27)	Conscious/rational approach	//
"Because of games" (P7) "I feel as if the robot used has a kind of cartoonish vibe, so I feel like cartoon sounds fit more into the theme." (P35) "I got inspiration from cartoons." (P38)	External referencing	//
"They were the ones that I would make on those situations." (P16) "Because are the sounds that I would probably make in those situations." (P21) "It's the ones that maybe I would do." (P23)	Relation to self	//

In response to inquiries about their perspective on the sounds produced by contemporary robots (Table 2), participants expressed dissatisfaction, deeming them inadequate and lacking empathy. The majority of participants expressed a desire for robots to exhibit more empathic behavior, emphasizing the need for a robot that comprehends their emotional state and responds accordingly. This expectation encompasses a preference for incorporating human-like sounds into the robot's auditory repertoire.

Results from question 15 - Which factor(s) would make your interactions with robots easier? - (Table 3) revealed divergent opinions among participants regarding whether robots should adopt a more human-like visual design and characteristics.

Table 2. Thematic analysis coding tree for question 14: What are your thoughts about robot sounds in general? (Source: the authors)

First-order codes	Second-order themes	Aggregated dimensions
"I think they help to connect people and robots and break the barrier that separates the two." (P10)	Positive	Judgments on robot sounds
"It makes the robot closer to human. Robot sounds make the robots less creepy and create an illusion of empathy robots." (P12)		
"It's a great innovative way to make robots more empathic and trustworthy." (P34)		
"They bring a level of humanity that makes it easier to form a connection, but if not done right, it could be unsettling." (P4)		
"They bring a level of humanity that makes it easier to form a connection, but if not done right, it could be unsettling." (P4)	Neutral	//
"Find them comforting in some way, depending on which sounds they use. Might get a little annoying if it is always repeating the same sounds." (P9)		
"In my opinion, they are good for a better performance for the robots but, in another way, they can be similar to humans and transmit the same emotions, and this could be dangerous." (P25)		
"Sometimes they are not as friendly." (P1)	Negative	//
"Weird and unpleasing." (P3)		
"They are artificial and show no emotion." (P22)		
"Confusing, because it's difficult to transmit human feelings through machines." (P28)		
"Some are kind of creepy." (P33)		
"They aren't empathetic." (P37)		

Most participants articulated their preference for robots capable of establishing stronger connections with humans and possessing more human-like traits. Statements such as "More interactivity and better human-like traits" and "Make them more human or more lovable in terms of sympathy" underscored a collective desire for robots with heightened emotional capabilities, emphasizing the importance of creating machines that can empathize with human emotions.

Conversely, a pragmatic perspective emerged, with some participants highlighting the significance of task efficiency over human-like features. For instance, one participant emphasized the need for robots to be "straighter to the point in completing the requested tasks." This practical viewpoint suggests a recognition of the value of prioritizing functionality and task-oriented capabilities in robotic design.

Table 3. Thematic analysis coding tree for question 15: Which factor(s) would make your interactions with robots easier? (Source: the authors)

First-order codes	Second-order themes	Aggregated dimensions
"More interactivity, as well as better human-like features." (P8) "If they have less human-like features. If they were more straight to the point in completing the requested tasks." (P27) "The physical shape and the way they verbally interact with us." (P32)	Technical/ Technological factors	Factors that improve HRI
"Make them more human or more lovable in terms of sympathy." (P1) "The capability of the robot to interact in a human-like way." (P29) "A sense of empathy - the robot 'getting to know me' and responding along my emotions and expressions." (P35)	Psychological/ Emotional factors	//

4   Conclusion

This study sought to investigate the pivotal role of sounds in Human-Robot Interaction (HRI) and their profound impact on the emotional dimensions of interactions. By examining participants' responses to a social robot's auditory expressions, we have gained insights into the preferences and expectations surrounding sound design in HRI.

The findings underscore the significance of prioritizing human-like sounds, particularly onomatopoeia. Participants clearly expressed a desire for robots to demonstrate more empathic behavior. This aligns with the broader discourse in HRI, emphasizing the importance of emotional demonstration in social robots. Participants articulated a need for machines not only to comprehend their emotional states but also to respond in a manner akin to human-like expressions.

Also, data obtained through the three-word impression indicate that color plays a pivotal role in how we perceive emotions when generating expressions through auditory cues. This observation highlights the impact of elements, specifically colors, on our cognitive processes in interpreting emotions and creating sounds. The fact that participants' immediate color labeling as a reaction to their recorded sounds for the robot's six emotions demonstrates that visual cues can also shape our auditory perceptions. Nonetheless, it is important to examine this phenomenon and consider how the screened video may have influenced these perceptions. Since the video stimulus featured a robot with eye colors corresponding to emotions, there is a possibility that this visual presentation influenced participants' associations between specific colors and emotions.

Moreover, the study offers guidance for future robot design, acknowledging the potential hindrance of inappropriate sounds on the quality of HRI. It underscores the necessity for nuanced approaches in designing robots that can genuinely connect with users.

The methodological approach employed in this study, allowing participants to spontaneously generate sounds instead of selecting from a predefined set, has enriched our understanding of auditory dimensions in social robots. This approach opens avenues for exploring novel and unique auditory expressions, fostering innovation in emotional expressions within HRI.

While the study contributes valuable insights, it is crucial to acknowledge its limitations, including using a convenience sample primarily composed of students. The influence of the narrative and video scenario on participants' sound choices, combined with the focus on a single robot design and behavior, necessitates caution in generalizing the results. Future research should encompass diverse scenarios, contexts, and socio-technological systems to comprehensively understand the nuances in sound preferences across various user groups. To advance the field, future research endeavors should concentrate on evaluating the clarity and effectiveness of participant-generated sounds, considering diverse robot designs and situational differences. In essence, this study not only contributes to the specific realm of HRI but also provides methodological insights for researchers aiming to explore the intricate dynamics of human-robot interactions. This paves the way for the development of more emotionally compelling and inclusive robotic designs in the future.

Acknowledgments. Special thanks to the MonarCH project (Multi-Robot Cognitive Systems Operating in Hospitals) for granting permission to utilize their robotic platform. The project, funded under the reference FP7-ICT-2011-9-601033, has been instrumental in facilitating our exploration of human-robot interactions. More information about the MonarCH project can be found at https://welcome.isr.tecnico.ulisboa. pt/projects/multi-robot-cognitive-systems-operating-in-hospitals/.

Furthermore, this study received support from UNIDCOM/IADE under a grant from the Fundação para a Ciência e Tecnologia (FCT), with the reference UIDB/00711/2020 attributed to UNIDCOM/IADE - Unidade de Investigação em Design e Comunicação, Lisbon, Portugal.

Disclosure of Interests. The authors have no competing interests to declare relevant to this article's content.

References

1. Frauenberger, C., Putz, V., Holdrich, R., Stockman, T.: Interaction patterns for auditory user interfaces. In: ICAD Proceedings, Limerick, Ireland, pp. 154–160 (2005)
2. Song, S., Yamada, S.: Expressing emotions through color, sound, and vibration with an appearance-constrained social robot. In: Proceedings of the 2017 ACM/IEEE International Conference on Human-Robot Interaction, pp. 2–11 (2017)
3. Breazeal, C.: Toward sociable robots. Robot. Auton. Syst. **42**(3–4), 167–175 (2003)
4. Fong, T., Nourbakhsh, I., Dautenhahn, K.: A survey of socially interactive robots. Robot. Auton. Syst. **42**(3–4), 143–166 (2003)

5. Latupeirissa, A.B., Panariello, C., Bresin, R.: Exploring emotion perception in sonic HRI. In: Sound and Music Computing Conference, Torino, 24–26 June 2020, pp. 434–441, Zenodo (2020)
6. Moore, D., Ju, W.: Sound as implicit influence on human-robot interactions. In: Companion of the 2018 ACM/IEEE International Conference on Human-Robot Interaction, pp. 311–312 (2018)
7. Pelikan, H., Robinson, F.A., Keevallik, L., Velonaki, M., Broth, M., Bown, O.: Sound in human-robot interaction. In: Companion of the 2021 ACM/IEEE International Conference on Human-Robot Interaction, HRI '21 Companion, New York, NY, USA, pp. 706–708, Association for Computing Machinery (2021)
8. Robinson, F.A., Bown, O., Velonaki, M.: Implicit communication through distributed sound design: exploring a new modality in human-robot interaction. In: Companion of the 2020 ACM/IEEE International Conference on Human-Robot Interaction, pp. 597–599 (2020)
9. Yan, H., Ang, M.H., Poo, A.N.: A survey on perception methods for human-robot interaction in social robots. Int. J. Soc. Robot. **6**, 85–119 (2014)
10. Ekman,P.: Emotion in the Human Face . Cambridge Cambridgeshire, New York (1982)
11. Sequeira, J.S., Ferreira, I.A.: Lessons from the monarch project. In: International Conference on Informatics in Control, Automation and Robotics, vol. 2, pp. 241–248. SCITEPRESS (2016)
12. Damholdt, M.F., Christina, V., Kryvous, A., Smedegaard, C.V., Seibt, J.: What is in three words? Exploring a three-word methodology for assessing impressions of a social robot encounter online and in real life. Paladyn J. Behav. Robot. **10**(1), 438–453 (2019)
13. Mkpojiogu, E.O., Okeke-Uzodike, O.E., Emmanuel, E.I.: Quality characteristics of an LMS UX psychomotor model for the design and evaluation of learning management systems. In: 3rd International Conference on Integrated Intelligent Computing Communication & Security (ICIIC 2021), pp. 243–249, Atlantis Press (2021)
14. Tong, L., Lindeman, R.W., Regenbrecht, H.: Viewer's role and viewer interaction in cinematic virtual reality. Computers **10**(5), 66 (2021)
15. Fu, D., et al.: A trained humanoid robot can perform human-like crossmodal social attention and conflict resolution. Int. J. Soc. Robot. **15**, 1325–1340 (2023)
16. Giambattista, A., Teixeira, L., Ayanoğlu, H., Saraiva, M., Duarte, E.: Expression of emotions by a service robot: a pilot study. In: Marcus, A. (ed.) DUXU 2016, Part III. LNCS, vol. 9748, pp. 328–336. Springer, Cham (2016). https://doi.org/10.1007/978-3-319-40406-6_31
17. Ayanoğlu, H., Saraiva M., Teixeira, L., Duarte, E.: Human-robot interaction: exploring the ability to express emotions by a social robot. In: Emotional Design in Human-Robot Interaction: Theory, Methods and Applications, pp. 163–183 (2019)
18. Zhang, B.J., Fitter, N.T.: Nonverbal sound in human-robot interaction: a systematic review. ACM Trans. Hum.-Robot Interact. **12**, 4 (2023)
19. Braun, V., Clarke, V.: Using thematic analysis in psychology. Qual. Res. Psychol. **3**(2), 77–101 (2006)
20. Xu, J., Tao, Y., Lin, H.: Semantic word cloud generation based on word embeddings. In: 2016 IEEE Pacific Visualization Symposium (PacificVis), pp. 239–243. IEEE (2016)

Enabling Safe Empirical Studies for Human-Robot Collaboration: Implementation of a Sensor Array Driven Control Interface

Alexander Arntz[✉] [ID]

Institute of Computer Sciences, University of Applied Sciences Ruhr West,
Bottrop, Germany
alexander.arntz@hs-ruhrwest.de

Abstract. In response to the growing relevance of collaborative robots, the need for empirical user studies in the domain of Human-Robot Collaboration become increasingly important. While collaborative robots incorporate internal safety features, their usage for user studies remains associated with inherent safety risks. This project addresses these challenges by introducing a toolbox for a robot arm to conduct Wizard-of-Oz studies by using advanced controls complemented by a sophisticated security system leveraging microcontrollers and human presence detection sensors. This approach unifies both control systems within a single application, seamlessly monitoring and synchronizing their respective inputs. The gamepad control scheme offers Wizard-of-Oz study supervisors an intuitive means of interacting with the robot, enabling precise and responsive control while maintaining safety. Meanwhile, the security system, built on microcontroller technology and human presence detection sensors, acts as a vigilant guardian, continuously assessing the robot's surroundings for potential risks. This integrated application not only empowers users with effective control over the xArm 7 but also provides real-time feedback on the security status, enhancing the overall safety and usability of collaborative robots in various industrial settings. By bridging the gap between human operators and robots, this project contributes to the evolution of safer and more user-friendly human-robot collaboration.

Keywords: Human-Robot Collaboration · Industrial Robots · Sensory Driven Inverse Kinematics · Wizard-of-Oz

1 Introduction

Collaborative robots, also often referred to as *Cobots*, are gaining increasing prominence in the automation landscape. Their annual revenue is projected to grow significantly, with an estimated annual growth rate of one-third [16,20]. Unlike traditional industrial robots, Cobots are characterized by their smaller size and flexible design, making them more adaptable to various industrial tasks

M. Kurosu and A. Hashizume (Eds.): HCII 2024, LNCS 14685, pp. 42–57, 2024.
https://doi.org/10.1007/978-3-031-60412-6_4

[20]. The xArm 7, manufactured by UFACTORY and used in this project, is one such collaborative robot that offers a variety of options that promote it as a suitable platform for empirical studies involving Human-Robot Collaboration (HRC). These options include a versatile software control panel, a teaching mode for custom trajectories, and a software development kit, enabling users to program the robot to perform specific tasks [12].

Despite the versatility of software-based control options, there is no intuitive way to directly control the xArm 7 to deploy it for Wizard-of-Oz-based empirical studies that expose participants in direct contact with the robot arm. The provided default software offers precise control but is hampered by slow inputs, high latency, and a cumbersome user interface. To address this and make the xArm 7 more capable of serving in HRC user studies, we developed a direct control interface that enables a study supervisor to operate the xArm 7 through a common gamepad, i.e., the Xbox One controller.

Next to the implementation of intuitive control systems for Wizard-of-Oz studies another important aspect of creating user studies in the research field of HRC is ensuring the safety of the participants at all times. Safety remains a paramount concern, even with collaborative robots designed to adhere to safety regulations. Guidelines such as the ISO TS 15066 recommend additional safety measures to ensure a safe distance between humans and the robot's working range [13]. In response to these recommendations, a cost-effective and adaptable security system was developed. This system utilizes an ESP32 microcontroller and human presence detection sensors strategically placed around the xArm 7's base to provide 360° coverage. Inputs from the security system and the gamepad controller are sent to a computer connected to the xArm 7, where they are managed.

The primary objective of this project was to develop an application capable of simultaneously managing robot control through the gamepad and monitoring safety using the security system. Therefore, it provides a framework for the HRC research community to conduct safe user studies in an easy and cost-effective manner. Additionally, the application provides user feedback through a graphical user interface. Python serves as the foundational programming language for this application, as the SDK used to communicate with the xArm 7 is Python-based [21]. This integrated system aims to enhance both the control and safety aspects of collaborative robot operation while offering a user-friendly interface for seamless management during empirical studies utilizing a Wizard-of-Oz setup.

2 Related Works

In preparation for this project, an extensive search was conducted to identify studies that employed a similar approach, involving a gamepad control scheme and a security system. This section presents and compares the approaches of these projects. Research in this field has revealed that using a gamepad as a control device for a robot arm is not uncommon. The rationale behind this choice may stem from the familiarity users have with this input device [5]. One notable study by Bonaiuto et al. compared three user interfaces for a robot arm mounted on a rover: a gamepad, a mobile device, and an interface tracking hand movements [5]. While objective evaluations indicated that the gamepad was not the most effective interface in all tasks, it was the preferred choice for almost all tasks except for object manipulation, where hand tracking was favored [5].

Similar research projects present various approaches, such as the creation of a control scheme based on Arduino microcontrollers [10,17]. These projects aimed to enable the control of robotic arms using a gamepad. However, each project faced distinct challenges, mainly related to establishing a connection between the gamepad and the robot using microcontrollers. In contrast, the focus was primarily on refining the control scheme itself, as a connection had already been established through an SDK provided by the manufacturer [10,17].

Crainic and Preitl explored an approach more akin to this project [6]. Their project aimed to provide an alternative method for remotely controlling a robot using a gamepad, similar to the goal of this project. However, as no Software Development Kit (SDK) was provided, they relied on different commands sent from another manufacturer-provided input device. This allowed them to decrypt and analyze the sent packages to create their communication protocol, which was then used to map functions onto the gamepad [6].

A project by Wagner et al. closely aligned with the approach found in this project, describing the creation of a control scheme for a robot arm under conditions similar to this work [22]. In this case, the robot had six axes, compared to the seven axes of the xArm 7 [12,22]. Both setups included a computer running the software and a graphical user interface (GUI), an Ethernet connection between the computer and the robot's control box, and the use of a gamepad. However, the key difference was the utilization of a wireless Xbox 360 gamepad paired with a smartphone, which provided user feedback [22]. The primary software processed input commands and offered configuration options, while the primary GUI was displayed on the smartphone, mounted onto the gamepad [22]. Their control scheme featured different modes controlled by a single button, including two Cartesian modes and one mode for direct axis control, as well as a button for switching between "Slow" and "Fast" modes. An additional safety mechanism was implemented using the trigger, which prevented commands from being sent to the robot when the trigger was not pressed [22].

In contrast to the Wagner et al. approach, this project aimed to maintain a straightforward control scheme by using the gamepad's controls efficiently. We employed only one mode of control, with the trigger, joysticks, and D-Pad individually controlling different axes. Additionally, we incorporated an emergency stop function into the control scheme itself, as the xArm 7 has one more axis compared to the robot used by Wagner et al. [12,22].

While the xArm 7 is considered a collaborative robot with built-in collision detection features, which allow it to operate without fencing or additional security systems, potential encounters between the xArm 7 and humans still pose safety risks [13]. Implementing a security system serves to minimize these potential risks [13].

In many collaborative fields involving humans and robots, studies typically utilize vision-based sensors, such as cameras or specific range sensors, to control human-robot interactions [4,8,14]. These sensors not only establish a safe environment but also extend capabilities by enabling gesture detection and other specific use cases beyond this project's scope [4,8,14]. These studies often align with ISO 10218, which specifies requirements for collaborative robots, addressing various sources of hazards and outlining requirements to mitigate them [1,8,14].

In this case, the goal is not to establish direct interaction with the robot but to implement a safety function that automatically sends a stop signal when a human approaches too closely, effectively preventing potential harm.

In recent years, the detection of human presence using WiFi or mmWave signals has gained importance, with mmWave sensors becoming more popular due to their small form factor and affordability [9]. Several studies have explored the potential applications and advantages of these sensors, such as their robustness to interference and their ability to penetrate objects due to the wavelength of the signals they emit [9,15].

While previous research often recommends the use of two different types of sensors to compensate for individual weaknesses, we chose to focus on a single type of sensor to keep costs and entry barriers low [7]. We aim to develop a flexible system adaptable to different circumstances and compatible with various robotic arms featuring a round frame. The use of readily available mmWave chips aligns with this work's goal of creating a universally applicable and cost-effective security system.

3   Methods and Technical Description

The primary objective of this project is to implement a gamepad control scheme for the UFACTORY xArm 7, complemented by a security system to prevent collisions between humans and the xArm 7. Both of these subsystems are seamlessly integrated into a single application, which operates on a computer connected to both the microcontroller and the robot. This integrated approach enhances user control and safety within a unified system. To bridge these two critical components of the project, a GUI has been developed. The GUI serves multiple purposes, including providing real-time feedback to the user and enabling configuration adjustments for the entire setup. In the subsequent sections, we delve into the detailed implementation process, highlighting the challenges encountered along the way, the solutions devised to address these challenges, and the methodologies adopted to achieve the final implementation.

4   Robot Controls

The core focus of this documentation revolves around the implementation of a gamepad-based control scheme for the xArm 7. To facilitate communication with the robot, the manufacturer provides a Python SDK that empowers users to issue a wide array of commands seamlessly via an Ethernet connection. This SDK streamlines the command transmission process by establishing a TCP connection, negating the need for manual package creation and transmission [11,21].

By leveraging this SDK, a tailored control scheme was created, omitting the intricacies of setting up the communication interface between the xArm 7 and the computer. Prior to any coding, the initial task entailed identifying the fundamental functions that the control scheme should encompass. Beyond maneuvering the arm itself, four pivotal functionalities that the user should have at their disposal are required based on best practices in prior studies [3]:

- *Emergency stop:* Initiating an immediate halt of all movements in response to unforeseen circumstances.
- *Restart:* The capability to resume arm operations following an emergency stop event.
- *Adjusting movement speed:* Fine-tuning the speed at which the xArm 7 moves.
- *Gripper control:* Enabling the opening and closing of the gripper for object manipulation, along with the ability to detect and activate the vacuum gripper as an alternative.

In the pursuit of crafting an effective control scheme for the xArm 7, we initially identified a set of essential functions that included emergency stop, restart, speed adjustment, and gripper control. These functions could be seamlessly integrated into the Python SDK provided by the manufacturer, paving the way for a focus to shift towards the arm's movement itself. The SDK offered two viable approaches for arm movement: one based on a three-dimensional coordinate system and the other involving individual joint control via angle adjustments [21].

The initial experimentation with the coordinate-based movement revealed its inherent complexity when mapped to a gamepad control scheme. While it provided swift arm movements, it proved challenging to align with the intuitive nature of a gamepad. Consequently, the strategy shifted to focus on individual joint control, allowing for more precise and user-friendly movements [21].

The early idea involved controlling each joint using the two joysticks, with the left and right triggers toggling between different joints. However, after further testing and consideration, we opted for a more comprehensive approach that encompassed both joysticks, the D-pad, and the left and right triggers to efficiently control all seven joints. This approach ensured that left-to-right movements aligned with controls on the x-axis, while up-and-down movements corresponded to controls on the y-axis. Additionally, the D-pad was designated for the upper two joints, known for their precision requirements, and the first joint was assigned to the trigger [21].

To implement these controls effectively, we explored various strategies. Initially, we considered mapping a callback function to each button, enabling an update command to be sent to the robot upon any input. A separate thread would constantly monitor controller inputs, invoking the relevant callback function when needed. While theoretically sound, this approach encountered issues due to the frequency of updates. The xArm's internal queue became inundated with rapid directional updates, causing the robot to execute each step sequentially. During this execution, new directions could not be sent, rendering the controls unresponsive and unwieldy. We experimented with introducing delays between updates to reduce the overall command count but found this to be an inadequate solution [21].

Two solutions were devised to address this unresponsiveness issue. First, we implemented a queue size limitation within the robot to prevent excessive accumulation. Second, we introduced status checks before sending additional updates. The SDK offered the capability to query and set the xArm's current state, which included states like 'In Motion' or 'Sleeping.' This information was harnessed to determine when it was appropriate to dispatch new commands. If an update was sent and the state query indicated 'In Motion,' the update was skipped. These solutions, programmatically executed via the SDK, significantly enhanced the responsiveness of the control scheme. However, another issue persisted throughout the project [21].

This recurring problem arose due to the nature of the updates sent to the robot. Each update represented a small movement in one direction with a specified speed. The robot's attempt to execute these successive updates resulted in a cyclic acceleration and deceleration pattern, leading to vibrations and a visibly jerky movement. To mitigate this, we attempted to strike a balance between movement speed and step size, but it provided only partial relief [21].

Amidst testing, a flaw was identified in the gamepad controls: even after repositioning the joystick to its initial position, the robot continued to move. Further analysis of input data revealed that after joystick usage, additional commands with minute values were consistently sent. These values remained constant and unaffected by previous inputs. Typically, gamepad values for each axis ranged from -1 to 1, with the coordinate system's origin at the initial position. However, when releasing the joystick, it continued to transmit small values rather than returning to the zero-zero position. To rectify this issue, we introduced a threshold on the inputs, ignoring values within a certain range $(0.1 > x > -0.1)$. This threshold became an integral component of the program, consistently applied to minimize unwanted input [21].

As the project progressed, we faced intermittent challenges with vibrations and jerky movements. The earlier implementation of a limited queue size was suspected as the source of the problem. The assumption was that clearing the queue to process new commands, such as direction changes, without delay could alleviate the vibrations. However, attempts to create a custom queue to serve this purpose yielded no substantial improvement. Despite these setbacks, we persevered, researching potential solutions to the recurring issues [21]. The SDK documentation describes an indirect method to clear the internal command queue. Changing the robot's state to 'Stopping' was found to indirectly clear this queue. We incorporated this approach into the control scheme to mitigate the unresponsiveness issue. When the user ceased providing new commands via the trigger or joystick, the state was set to 'Stopping,' effectively clearing the queue and bringing the robot to a halt. From an implementation standpoint, this final approach closely resembled the initial method. All inputs were continuously monitored within the main loop, and when an input event occurred, the corresponding signal was transmitted to the robot. However, handling the joysticks, D-pad, and trigger required distinct treatment. Axis positions were checked in each loop iteration, and if values exceeded the established threshold, movement signals were dispatched. Notably, the joysticks and trigger presented a challenge since no new events were generated upon reaching the maximum position. This quirk resulted in the robot stopping when the trigger or joystick was held down [21].

To address the problem of judder movement, two crucial adjustments were made to the SDK move call parameters. Firstly, we disabled the 'wait' parameter, which the robot used to verify its position by briefly halting and checking coordinates after each movement. Given the frequency of these checks, the robot's continuous acceleration and deceleration led to juddering. Secondly, we standardized the step size to a fixed value of one or minus one, depending on the movement direction. This change provided a consistent and smooth robotic movement experience, resolving the judder motion problem and culminating in the intended control scheme's functionality [21]. For a summarized visual representation of the final approach's workings, please refer to Fig. 1.

5   Microcontroller Security System

The second phase of the project focused on the development of a security concept tailored for the xArm 7, with the primary objective of mitigating the risk of collisions between humans and the robot. The core aim was to devise a security system capable of continuously monitoring its surroundings for the presence of humans. If a human was detected in close proximity to the xArm 7, the system would promptly issue a stop signal to avert potential hazards. The technical foundation of this sub-project rested upon the utilization of ESP32 microcontrollers in conjunction with various sensors, complemented by visual and auditory feedback mechanisms. Conceptually, the project underwent several iterations, characterized by the evaluation of different ideas and sensor technologies. This documentation delves into these iterations in the subsequent sections. We will begin by presenting the initial iteration, which was conceived but never realized due to issues with the selected sensors. Following this, we will introduce the second and final iteration, built upon the lessons learned from the first attempt. The initial approach entailed the creation of a security perimeter encircling the xArm 7, demarcated by four posts forming a square configuration. Each of these posts would house sensors, comprising ultrasonic sensors and motion detectors. The role of each sensor type was to monitor a distinct zone within the security perimeter. Specifically, two motion sensors, positioned diagonally across from each other, were tasked with surveilling the inner zone, centered around the xArm 7. Concurrently, ultrasonic sensors were deployed to monitor the outer zone, which assumed the shape of a square, with two posts forming one side of this outer boundary. A visual representation of this concept is provided in Fig. 3.

The decision to create two distinct zones stemmed from concerns regarding the motion sensors' sensitivity to the robot's movements. According to the documentation accompanying the motion sensors used in this approach, they were designed to exclusively detect human motion [2]. To mitigate potential risks, the

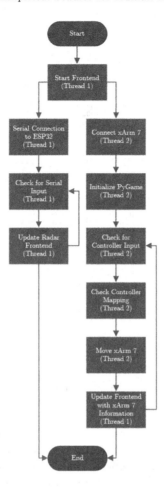

Fig. 1. Flow Chart of the robot arm control.

two-zone approach was conceived. Upon initiating the security perimeter, the motion sensors would scan the immediate vicinity of the xArm 7 for any human presence. If the inner zone remained free of human activity, the motion sensors would be deactivated, leaving only the outer zone active. As long as no humans breached the outer zone, the inner zone would remain clear. Conceptually, this two-zone approach appeared feasible and cost-effective. However, it encountered technical challenges that rendered it unviable. The primary issue arose from the motion sensors' inability to reliably detect stationary humans, contrary to the manufacturer's claims. Testing revealed that the sensors failed to trigger when humans stood still. Furthermore, the motion sensors were inadvertently triggered by the robot itself due to the arm's heat signature. Consequently, it became evident that an alternative sensor solution was necessary to fulfill the project's requirements [2]. The final iteration adopted a radically different approach by

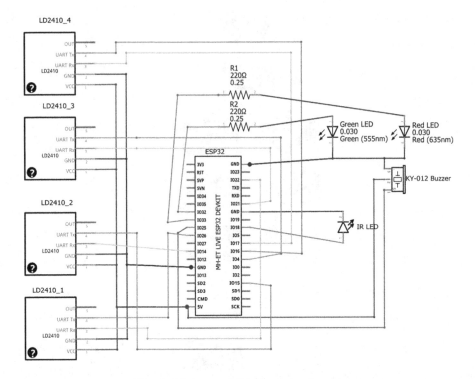

Fig. 2. Diagram of the hardware layout.

incorporating LD2410 mmWave radar sensors. These sensors boast a remarkable capability to detect targets within a five-meter range, regardless of whether the targets are stationary or in motion [19]. Building upon elements from the initial iteration, such as the LED indicators for visual feedback and the active buzzer for auditory alerts, we introduced a novel component-an infrared sender (referred to as IR). This IR control unit was employed to manage additional LEDs strategically placed around the xArm 7.

In terms of the technical foundation, we retained the ESP32 microcontroller. However, we discarded the previous concept involving posts and, instead, position the sensors around the arm, oriented away from the xArm 7. To ensure that the arm's operational area remained unobstructed, we meticulously designed the casing to match the dimensions of the arm's mounting plate. The casing was specifically engineered to accommodate the four sensors (marked in orange in Fig. 2) and provide ample space for the buzzer, three LEDs, and the ESP32 (highlighted in red in Fig. 2). Following the design phase, we 3D-printed the casing using PLA (indicated in grey in Fig. 2) and reinforced it with brass threads for enhanced stability and reusability.

The housing assembly is positioned around the lower section of the xArm 7, slightly above the input terminals for power and control cables. The LD2410 sensors offer an impressive 120° detection range, rendering the use of four sensors

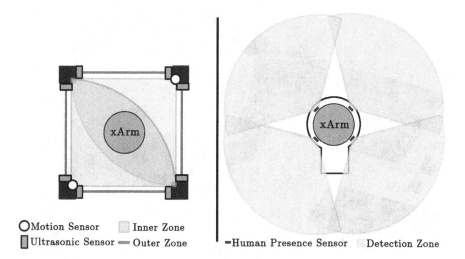

Fig. 3. Sensor sweep of the first iteration (left) and the second iteration (right).

sufficient for comprehensive monitoring of the entire area surrounding the arm [19]. According to the sensor documentation, these sensors are not only capable of detecting the target's range but also provide an energy level assessment of the detection process [18]. This energy level essentially reflects the sensor's confidence in the detection and plays a pivotal role in the system for processing incoming data [18].

The system is centered around an ESP32 microcontroller housed within the casing. The LD2410 sensors can be connected either through Serial communication or as an output signal [18]. The configuration opted for serial connections to harness the sensor's configuration parameters (as illustrated in Fig. 2). Depending on the energy level and detection range, the ESP32 governs the IR LED, triggering an auditory alert that corresponds to the proximity of the detected presence.

To determine the presence of a detected target, a dedicated energy level threshold for sensor readings was implemented, leading to further action. We defined different sensing ranges: within 0 to 150 cm, the IR LEDs turn red, and the buzzer emits a continuous sound for five seconds. In the range of 151 to 250 cm, the buzzer activates for two seconds, and the IR LEDs shift to yellow. Beyond 350 cm, the LEDs turn green. Additionally, the system transmits this information via Serial to the connected computer, where the application processes incoming bytes as strings and filters them to compile all necessary data for displaying the radar screen on the GUI.

Given that four independent readings are taken every half second, if one sensor registers no detection, it could potentially overlook a presence detected by another sensor located just 50 cm away. To overcome this, an array was incorporated to store all the distance measurements from the sensors, and ultimately determine the IR LED color based on the lowest value collected from the sensors within the ring array (Fig. 4).

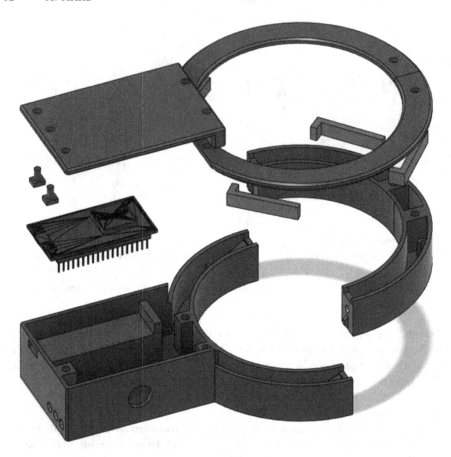

Fig. 4. Exploded view of the case (grey) with ESP32 (red) and LD2410 (orange). (Color figure online)

The final phase of this project culminated in the development of a Graphical User Interface (GUI) designed to provide Wizard-of-Oz study supervisors with real-time feedback on the current operational status. Upon launching the GUI for the first time, the main interface and a popup dialog are presented, prompting the user to input the IP address of the xArm 7. This IP address is crucial for establishing a connection with the robot. Once the user inputs and saves this information, the popup dialog closes, granting access to the main view (Fig. 5). The main view is divided into several sections to facilitate user interaction. On the left-hand side, users have the option to configure the control scheme, mapping various functions to different buttons. To simplify this process, a visual representation of a gamepad is provided. Customization is limited to specific functions, including 'Increase Speed,' 'Decrease Speed,' 'Open Gripper,' 'Close Gripper,' 'Emergency Stop,' and 'Clear Error,' while controls for moving the robot remain fixed and are not customizable.

On the lower right-hand side of the interface, a real-time visual representation of the radar system is displayed. This visual representation depicts the current surroundings, including an indicator of proximity to any detected humans. Targets within a distance of up to 150 cm are represented in red, those within the range of 150 cm to 250 cm are displayed in orange, and yellow indicates targets more than 250 cm away. The final component of the GUI is a box that provides essential information about the xArm 7, including the connection status, current arm position, xArm state, gripper status (open or closed), and the status of the connected security system. Following the completion of the GUI, all elements needed to be seamlessly interconnected. In earlier stages of the project, each of the three primary elements operated within its respective loop: one for monitoring inputs and transmitting commands to the xArm 7, another for updating the GUI, and a third for reading inputs from the security system. The latter two loops were merged into a single loop running in the main thread. However, due to delays experienced when controlling the xArm 7, it was evident that a dedicated thread was necessary to monitor inputs from the security system, and thus, a new thread was introduced to accommodate this requirement.

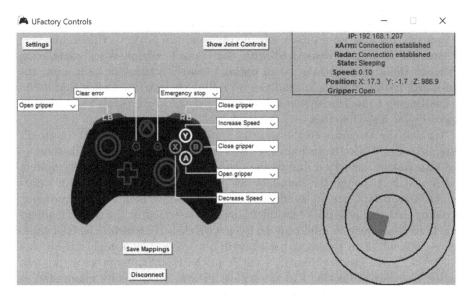

Fig. 5. The proximity indicator (lower right), information about the current state of the xArm 7 (upper right), and the ability to map the different functions to the controller layout (left).

6   Limitations

In this project, a successful application that serves a dual purpose was developed: enabling Wizard-of-Oz study supervisors to control the UFACTORY xArm 7 while also implementing a collision prevention system for monitoring the robot's immediate surroundings. This application represents a culmination of various iterations and diverse approaches, ultimately providing a valuable platform for interactions with the xArm 7 and serving as a framework for future HRC-related research with participants.

The first limitation that was encountered relates to the precision of xArm 7's movement control. Initially, the intention was to implement a system where the robot's speed would vary based on the position of the joysticks or trigger. For instance, pushing the joystick halfway toward its maximum would result in the robot moving at half speed, while pushing it to the maximum would trigger full speed. This approach could have enabled more accurate input and maximized the potential of the gamepad. However, during the efforts to rectify the judder movement issue, this idea took a backseat as it prioritized creating a stable and responsive control scheme. Upon reflection, it was recognized that refining this aspect could enhance the user experience of the study supervisor assuming the role of the Wizard.

The second limitation that was identified pertains to the inability to move multiple joints simultaneously in the current control scheme. The way the inputs are currently monitored precludes the implementation of this feature. While it is theoretically possible to refactor the existing code to support simultaneous joint movement, this task would have extended beyond the project's timeframe.

Another limitation associated with the control scheme is its complexity. Although the aim was to devise an optimal control setting for each joint, the non-native nature of the gamepad for controlling the xArm 7 means that it can be challenging to memorize which button or joystick corresponds to each joint, especially for first-time users.

Turning the attention to the security system, one limitation is the system's response time. While the technical concept functions effectively, it falls short in real-time human detection due to the connection between the security system and the GUI. Although the sampling rate is theoretically sufficient with a continuous sensor data stream, it encountered performance issues when processing incoming data and real-time controller inputs. Consequently, the sensor readings were limited to every 50 milliseconds. Even with this adjustment, the GUI experienced difficulties in receiving packets without queuing at a higher baud rate of 460800. These issues primarily stem from the inability to process the data swiftly, resulting in backlog and subsequent delays. These delays manifested as noticeable lags in the GUI, LED flashing, buzzer sounds, and control responsiveness. Moreover, the delayed detection could impede the timely execution of the emergency stop command, potentially leading to collisions. We mitigated this problem with additional adjustments and introduced the option to disable the connection to the security system.

An additional limitation concerns the occurrence of false positives in the security system. In some instances, the system would erroneously detect a human presence in the immediate vicinity when there was no actual target present, leading to false alarms. Unfortunately, the precise origin of these false positives remains elusive. Nevertheless, given the system's purpose of preventing potential harm, false positives are considered less problematic than false negatives.

7   Conclusion and Outlook

Despite the inherent flaws and challenges encountered during the development process, this project can be deemed a success, as both the control scheme and the security system effectively achieve their intended goals. The control scheme offers an intuitive and efficient approach, enabling fast and precise movement while maintaining smooth and responsive robot motion. The security system that was devised presents a cost-effective and adaptable solution that requires minimal space. Throughout testing, both systems demonstrated robust performance. Reflecting on the development process, several aspects have emerged with the potential for further research and improvement. In particular, there is room for expanding the control scheme and addressing the limitations that were encountered during development. One promising avenue involves exploring the possibility of moving multiple joints simultaneously. This could be realized by implementing multiple threads, each dedicated to monitoring specific elements, such as the joysticks and triggers. Additionally, further research could delve into utilizing the entire input range of the joysticks and triggers. While the initial attempt to employ the input directly as the step size proved challenging, defining specific value ranges for the joysticks and triggers, with fixed step sizes, could offer viable solutions. The security system also presents areas that could benefit from additional research. It was identified that the technical specifications of the ESP32 microcontroller were suboptimal for effectively handling four human presence detection sensors simultaneously. The use of software serial communication reduced the baud rate of each sensor to 57600, impacting performance. One potential solution involves leveraging tasks to concurrently obtain readings from two sensors and process them. However, this approach still leaves unresolved issues related to GUI performance. A more comprehensive solution might entail configuring the sensors in advance using manufacturer-provided tools or Arduino libraries to process a simplified binary value (High/Low) for each sensor. This compromise, though, would necessitate sacrificing the "radar" view on the GUI. In conclusion, this work lays the groundwork for future extensions and improvements, offering the potential to address the identified limitations and build upon the established foundation for an optimized HRC research tool.

Acknowledgements. Gratitude is expressed towards Leopold Bletgen, Oliver Witzke, and Phillip Lösch for assisting in this project. Further, thanks go to Sabrina Eimler, Carolin Straßmann, André Helgert, Lukas Erle, Lara Timm, and Marcel Finkel for additional support throughout this project.

References

1. DIN EN ISO 10218-1:2012-01. Industrieroboter_- Sicherheitsanforderungen_- Teil_1: Roboter (ISO_10218-1:2011). Technical report, Beuth Verlag GmbH. https://doi.org/10.31030/1733801. https://www.beuth.de/de/-/-/136373717

2. HC-SR501 PIR Sensor, July 2021. https://components101.com/sensors/hc-sr501-pir-sensor

3. Arntz, A., Eimler, S.C., Hoppe, H.U.: A virtual sandbox approach to studying the effect of augmented communication on human-robot collaboration. Front. Robot. AI **8**, 318 (2021). https://doi.org/10.3389/frobt.2021.728961. https://www.frontiersin.org/article/10.3389/frobt.2021.728961

4. Bdiwi, M.: Integrated sensors system for human safety during cooperating with industrial robots for handing-over and assembling tasks. Procedia CIRP **23**, 65–70 (2014). https://doi.org/10.1016/j.procir.2014.10.099. https://linkinghub.elsevier.com/retrieve/pii/S2212827114011561

5. Bonaiuto, S., Cannavó, A., Piumatti, G., Paravati, G., Lamberti, F.: Tele-operation of robot teams: a comparison of gamepad-, mobile device and hand tracking-based user interfaces. In: 2017 IEEE 41st Annual Computer Software and Applications Conference (COMPSAC), July 2017, vol. 2, pp. 555–560 (2017). ISSN 0730-3157. https://doi.org/10.1109/COMPSAC.2017.278

6. Crainic, M.F., Preitl, S.: Ergonomic operating mode for a robot arm using a gamepad with two joysticks. In: 2015 IEEE 10th Jubilee International Symposium on Applied Computational Intelligence and Informatics, May 2015, pp. 167–170 (2015). https://doi.org/10.1109/SACI.2015.7208192

7. Fang, Z., et al.: A CMOS-integrated radar-assisted cognitive sensing platform for seamless human-robot interactions. In: 2021 IEEE International Symposium on Circuits and Systems (ISCAS), May 2021, pp. 1–4 (2021). ISSN 2158-1525. https://doi.org/10.1109/ISCAS51556.2021.9401535

8. García-Esteban, J.A., Piardi, L., Leitão, P., Curto, B., Moreno, V.: An interaction strategy for safe human co-working with industrial collaborative robots. In: 2021 4th IEEE International Conference on Industrial Cyber-Physical Systems (ICPS), May 2021, pp. 585–590 (2021). https://doi.org/10.1109/ICPS49255.2021.9468160

9. Gong, P., Wang, C., Zhang, L.: MMPoint-GNN: graph neural network with dynamic edges for human activity recognition through a Millimeter-Wave Radar. In: 2021 International Joint Conference on Neural Networks (IJCNN), July 2021, pp. 1–7 (2021). ISSN 2161-4407. https://doi.org/10.1109/IJCNN52387.2021.9533989

10. Sh, K., Rejab, Rauf, W.E.: Wireless mobile robotic arm controlled by PS2 joystick based on microcontroller. Diyala J. Eng. Sci. **10**(3), 44–53 (2017). https://doi.org/10.24237/djes.2017.10304. https://djes.info/index.php/djes/article/view/196

11. Shenzhen UFACTORY Co. Ltd.: UFACTORY xArm Developer Manual (V 1.10.0). https://www.ufactory.cc/_files/ugd/896670_a7d9cf96096a489bbc0d9ee4ef12939f.pdf

12. Shenzhen UFACTORY Co. Ltd.: UFACTORY xArm Overview. https://www.ufactory.cc/xarm-collaborative-robot

13. Shenzhen UFACTORY Co. Ltd.: UFACTORY xArm User Manual (V 1.11.0). https://www.ufactory.cc/_files/ugd/896670_5c6cd91dcf944ebaac182d1e2db1c938.pdf

14. Maurtua, I., Ibarguren, A., Kildal, J., Susperregi, L., Sierra, B.: Human-robot collaboration in industrial applications: safety, interaction and trust. Int. J. Adv. Robot. Syst. **14**(4) (2017). https://doi.org/10.1177/1729881417716010. http://journals.sagepub.com/doi/10.1177/1729881417716010

15. Nanzer, J.A., Rogers, R.L.: Human presence detection using millimeter-wave radiometry. IEEE Trans. Microw. Theor. Tech. **55**(12), 2727–2733 (2007). Conference Name: IEEE Transactions on Microwave Theory and Techniques. https://doi.org/10.1109/TMTT.2007.909872

16. Owens, T.: Collaborative robots: global market size 2020–2030, May 2021. https://www.statista.com/statistics/1239304/size-of-the-collaborative-robot-cobot-market/
17. Rahman, R., Rahman, M.S., Bhuiyan, J.R.: Joystick controlled industrial robotic system with robotic arm. In: 2019 IEEE International Conference on Robotics, Automation, Artificial-intelligence and Internet-of-Things (RAAICON), pp. 31–34, November 2019. https://doi.org/10.1109/RAAICON48939.2019.18
18. Reynolds, N.: LD2410. GitHub. https://github.com/ncmreynolds/ld2410
19. Shenzhen Hi-Link Electronic, Co., Ltd.: HLK-LD2410 user manual V1.02.pdf, August 2022. https://drive.google.com/file/d/1ZBhv4EmuiB2wA-VdW0Cx2oJJLwI_CmVn/view?usp=drive_open&usp=embed_facebook
20. Sherwani, F., Asad, M.M., Ibrahim, B.: Collaborative robots and industrial revolution 4.0 (IR 4.0). In: 2020 International Conference on Emerging Trends in Smart Technologies (ICETST), March 2020, pp. 1–5 (2020). https://doi.org/10.1109/ICETST49965.2020.9080724
21. UFACTORY: xArm-Python-SDK-github. https://github.com/xArm-Developer/xArm-Python-SDK/blob/master/doc/api/xarm_api.md
22. Wagner, M., Avdic, D., Heß, P.: Gamepad control for industrial robots - new ideas for the improvement of existing control devices:. In: Proceedings of the 13th International Conference on Informatics in Control, Automation and Robotics, pp. 368–373. SCITEPRESS - Science and and Technology Publications, Lisbon, Portugal (2016). https://doi.org/10.5220/0005982703680373. http://www.scitepress.org/DigitalLibrary/Link.aspx?doi=10.5220/0005982703680373

Persona-Based and Scenario-Based Design of Virtual and Physical Companion Robots with Varied Kawaii (Cute) Attributes

Dave Berque[1]([✉]), Hiroko Chiba[1], Michiko Ohkura[2], Midori Sugaya[2], Peeraya Sripian[2], Tipporn Laohakangvalvit[2], Natsuko Noda[2], Olivia Cornejo[1], Hoang Dao[1], Kotomi Eguchi[2], Narumon Jadram[2], Rintaku Kei[2], Takato Kobayashi[2], Steeve Nsangou[1], Nathan Sahchez[1], Ryouichi Uchiyama[2], and Saki Yoshida[1]

[1] DePauw University, Greencastle, USA
{dberque,hchiba,oliviacornejo_2025,hoangdao_2024,
steevensangou_2025,nathansanchez_2024,
sakiyoshida_2024}@depauw.edu
[2] Shibaura Institute of Technology, Tokyo, Japan
ohkura@sic.shibaura-it.ac.jp, {doly,peeraya,tipporn,nnoda,
ma22056,nb23107,cy20248,al20009,ma22022}@shibaura-it.ac.jp

Abstract. In recent years, concerns about anxiety and other mental health issues in university students have been widely reported. Some college campuses have seen increased student requests to bring emotional support animals to campus, although these animals are hard to care for in shared living spaces that are common in college settings. This paper reports on a project that seeks to gain a deeper understanding of the role that kawaii (Japanese cuteness) plays in fostering positive human response to, and acceptance of, companion robots for use by college students. In the long term, this may lead to an understanding of techniques for designing companion robots that assist with student mental health. Specifically, in this paper, we report on a persona-driven and scenario-driven cross-cultural design of two kawaii companion robots and two non-kawaii companion robots. After describing the design process and presenting the companion robot designs, the paper reports on a user study that investigates and compares the desirability of the companion robots based on their level of kawaii. After reading a persona and scenario that provided the context for the design, the study participants viewed videos of the companion robots and answered survey questions regarding the designs. Additionally, participant facial expressions were recorded by iMotions software while the participants viewed videos of the companion robots.

Keywords: Kawaii · Human-Robot Interaction · Cross-cultural Design · Companion Robots

M. Kurosu and A. Hashizume (Eds.): HCII 2024, LNCS 14685, pp. 58–74, 2024.
https://doi.org/10.1007/978-3-031-60412-6_5

1 Introduction and Motivation

1.1 Student Mental Health

As we have reported in more detail in [1], in recent years concerns about anxiety and other mental health issues in university students have been widely reported in the United States and beyond. Some college campuses have seen increased requests from students to bring emotional support animals to campus [1]. Unfortunately, these animals are hard to care for in shared living spaces common in college settings and can be problematic for other residents, for example if they are allergic to certain kinds of animals. In the long term, we are interested in exploring the possibility of using companion robots to provide emotional support to college students. As we summarized in [1] this builds on previous work in exploring the use of companion robots to assist the elderly.

This paper reports on a project that seeks to gain a deeper understanding of the role that kawaii (Japanese cuteness) plays in fostering positive human response to, and acceptance of, companion robots for use by college students. In the longer term, this may lead to an understanding of techniques for designing robotic companion robots that assist with student mental health.

1.2 Kawaii and Robotic Gadgets

As we have previously reported in [1, 2], the word, kawaii, is often translated into "cute," "lovely," "adorable", "cool," and sometimes other words depending on the context. There does not seem to be a single exact word that can be used as a counterpart in English [3] although "cute" is a common substitute. In the modern context, the notion of kawaii in Japan is embraced as a catalyst to evoke positive feelings [4], as can be seen in designs ranging from Hello Kitty products to road signs to robotic gadgets, to name just a few examples. Kawaii has also been gaining global audiences and customers in the last two decades beyond Japan [4] through kawaii products. Kawaii design principles and approaches to engineering [5] and are now incorporated into successful products that are used globally including in robotic gadgets [6–8].

Prior work done by several of the authors suggests that designing a robot to be more animal-like, rounder, shorter, and smaller increases participants' perceptions that the robot is kawaii/cute [2]. This work also suggests that designing a robot to be more kawaii/cute appears to positively influence human preference for being around the robot. These findings held across Japanese and American culture and across males and females [2]. Both males and females preferred smaller robots to larger ones; however, this preference was more significant for females. No other differences were found between genders or between cultures [2].

In [1], several of the current authors report on their findings in designing and evaluating companion robots for college students. The robots were intentionally designed to differ in specific attributes (color versus greyscale, round versus angular) that are well-known to impact perceptions of kawaii-ness. The study demonstrated, for example, that participants judged colorful robots to be more kawaii than greyscale robots and also judged round companion robots to be more kawaii than angular ones. These findings held for both males and females and for participants whose dominant culture was Japanese as well as for participants whose dominant culture was American [1].

Prior work that investigates the role of motion and sound in influencing perceptions of kawaii-ness in user perceptions and user acceptance of robots or robotic gadgets is limited. However, one pair of papers reports on studies of kawaii-ness in the motion of robotic vacuum cleaners [9, 10]. The authors programmed a visually plain version of a Roomba vacuum cleaner to move according to 24 different patterns, including patterns that the authors describe with terms such as: bounce, spiral, attack, spin and dizzy [9, 10]. The studies demonstrated that kawaii-ness can be expressed through motion. However, these studies did not consider visual attributes of the vacuum cleaners (e.g., color, shape) and the impact of these attributes on perceptions of kawaii-ness.

The first two authors have reported on perceptions of a standard Roomba compared to one that had been augmented with visual kawaii features (animal-like, colorful), as well as kawaii movements and sounds [11]. The visual effects, movement and sounds were each reported by some participants as contributing to the enhanced kawaii-ness of the augmented Roomba [11].

In this paper we now focus on the design and evaluation of companion robots for college students that vary in kawaii and non-kawaii visual attributes, sounds and movement. In addition, instead of limiting ourselves to virtual robots as we did in [1] and [2], we now report on physical robots that were rendered from virtual prototypes.

1.3 An Iterative Cross-Cultural Design Driven by Personas and Scenarios

Building on the prior research described in the previous section, this paper reports on work, supported by a United States National Science Foundation (NSF) International Research Experiences for Undergraduates (IRES) grant, to use cross-cultural design teams to gain a deeper understanding of the role that kawaii plays in fostering positive human response to, and acceptance of, robotic gadgets. More information about the goals of this grant-supported project may be found in [12].

With mentorship by faculty members and a graduate assistant at Shibaura Institute of Technology (in Japan) and by faculty members from DePauw University (in the United States), two cross-cultural design teams designed and implemented student companion robots, which were later evaluated by a formal user study. Each design team was comprised of four students -- two students from Shibaura Institute of Technology and two students from DePauw University. With support from the NSF IRES grant, the DePauw University student team spent approximately seven weeks in Japan collaborating on this project.

Each cross-cultural team was charged with using a persona and scenario to drive their design process. Specifically, each team was asked to design for a first-year college student named Sam, who was presented through the persona and scenario provided below in Table 1.

Sam was specifically selected as the persona's name because it a gender-neutral name. A Japanese translation of the persona and scenario were also presented to the design teams, except that the name Sam was changed to じゅん (Jun) which is a gender-neutral name in Japanese.

Table 1. Persona and Scenario for Design

Persona:	Sam is a first-year college student who is studying mathematics. Sam is having trouble getting homework completed on time and the stress of homework makes Sam sad
Scenario:	Sam's companion robot says, "Sam, you look tired and sad. I know you have a lot of work to do so let me try to cheer you up." The companion robot makes some movements and sounds for about 30 s. Then the robot says, "Sam, now that you are happier please start your homework." Sam begins his homework and is pleased to be done

The design teams focused their designs on enacting the following portion of the scenario, which is designed to cheer Sam up: "The companion robot makes some movements and sounds for about 30 s."

Each team was charged to design a pair of companion robots such that one robot had kawaii attributes and one robot did not have kawaii attributes. Each team first designed paper sketches of their robots and received feedback from the broader group of faculty and students. After iterating on the paper designs, the students implemented their designs using Blender and received feedback again. After iterating on their Blender designs, the Blender files were used to generate 3D printed companion robot bodies, which were decorated using supplies such as fabric and paint.

The decorated robot bodies were placed over Arduino-powered Zumo robots. Each team programmed their robots to make movements and sounds as described in the scenario. The kawaii robots were programmed to make cute movements and sounds while the non-kawaii robots were programmed to make non-cute movements and sounds (jerkier movements and harsher sounds).

1.4 Resulting Companion Robots

Figures 1 and 2 present the two physical companion robots that were explicitly designed to be non-kawaii. We refer to these companion robots as "Spiky" and "Bug" respectively. Figures 3 and 4 present the two companion robots that were explicitly designed to be kawaii, which we call "Panda" and "Penguin" respectively. The size of each of robot makes it possible for the robot to move around on the top of a desk as might be commonly found in a student's study area. Figure 5 presents a photograph of the Penguin robot next to some books and a coffee cup to provide a sense of scale. When study participants evaluated the four companion robots, they were shown next to these items to provide scale consistently across the four companion robots.

Fig. 1. Non-kawaii companion robot named "Spiky"

Fig. 2. Non-kawaii companion robot named "Bug"

Fig. 3. Kawaii Companion Robot named "Panda"

Fig. 4. Kawaii Companion Robot named "Penguin"

Fig. 5. Penguin Companion Robot with Items to Convey Scale

2 Evaluation

2.1 Purpose of the Evaluation

The goal of this evaluation was to investigate how the study participants perceived the cuteness and trustworthiness of each of the four companion robot prototypes, which attributes of each robot they found to be cute, which prototype they would prefer to use and which prototype they believed Sam would prefer to use based on their understanding of Sam's persona and the associated scenario.

In addition to self-reported survey data, the study used the Facial Expression Analysis module of iMotions software [13] to measure facial expressions (e.g., smiles, frowns, eye position) and associated emotions (e.g., anger, disgust, joy, sadness, surprise) that resulted when participants viewed the videos of each of the companion robots shown in Fig. 1 through Fig. 4. While the iMotions software recorded a wealth of data, we consider only the data associated with "joy" in this paper and even this consideration is preliminary.

The study design, data gathering and preliminary data analysis was carried out by the first, second and ninth authors.

2.2 Participant Recruiting

After obtaining Institutional Review Board approval for the study, we recruited participants who were undergraduate students at DePauw University in the United States. Participants had to be at least 18 years old and at most 28 years old. While all DePauw University students in this age range were eligible to participate, we expressed preference for students who had lived in the United States for at least ten years, or who had lived in Japan for at least ten years, or who had lived in Vietnam for at least ten years. This allowed us to gather data from participants who had either an American, Japanese or Vietnamese dominant culture.

2.3 Participant Exclusions

In total, 49 participants started the study. Due to a computer crash, no data was collected from one of these participants, meaning that data was collected from 48 participants. In addition, there was a technical problem resulting in an absence of audio during the initial steps for one of the participants and the study was stopped. The partial data was excluded, and the study was restarted and completed successfully.

The Facial Expression module of iMotions software reports the quality of the video recorded while a participant views a stimulus. The quality is reported on a scale of 0% to 100% where 100% means the recording was completely successful. The iMotions system flags data as unusable if the quality for a given recording is less than 80%. In this study we focus on data for four stimuli per participant, one stimuli for each companion robot shown in Fig. 1 through Fig. 4.

For one of the study participants, iMotions reported data quality of 46%, 99%, 93% and 56% respectively for the four stimuli and flagged data for the first and last of these stimuli as unusable. Manual inspection of the video recording for this participant demonstrated that the participant covered their face with their hands while viewing the first and last stimuli. Thus, the data for this participant has been excluded, leaving a total of 47 participants. For 13 of these 47 participants, iMotions reported data quality scores ranging between 97% and 99.75% as the mean across the four stimuli. For the remaining participants, iMotions reported data quality scores of 100% for all four stimuli.

2.4 Participant Demographics

The 47 participants ranged in age from 18 to 28 with a mean age of 19.6. There were 20 participants in the United States-culture group, 12 participants in the Vietnam-culture group and 7 participants in the Japan-culture group. The remaining 8 participant's primary countries of residence were Nepal (4 participants) and one each from China, Croatia, Ethiopia and South Africa. In total 22 females and 24 males participated in the study. The remaining participant self-identified their gender as other.

2.5 Study Procedure

Participants signed up to complete the study during a 45-min time slot. At the agreed upon time, the participant came to the study room where they were met by the experimenter (ninth author). Participants were welcomed and asked to sit at a table on which were placed a computer monitor with an attached webcam, keyboard, mouse and speaker as shown in Fig. 6. iMotions software was used to record the participant's facial expressions, via the webcam, during the study.

Although not visible in Fig. 6, the experimenter was seated behind the partition shown in this figure. While the participant and experimenter could not see each other directly during the study, the experimenter could see the participant's face as tracked by iMotions and displayed on the experimenter's computer. The experimenter could also see the participant's computer screen on the experimenter's computer. The experimenter's screen is shown in Fig. 7.

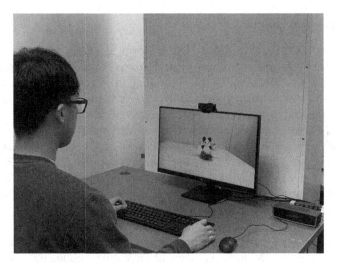

Fig. 6. Participant's View During Experiment

Fig. 7. Experimenter's Screen

After accepting the conditions of the informed consent, and confirming eligibility to participate in the study, participants began the online study presented on their monitor while iMotions recorded their facial expressions. Participants began by providing their age, the country they had lived in the longest, the number of years they had lived in that country, additional countries they had lived in (if any), the number of years they had lived in those countries, and their gender. Participants then watched a test video and confirmed that they could see the video and hear the associated audio.

Participants were then presented two still photographs and two thirty-second videos of robotic gadgets that are not related to the study we report on in this paper. Data gathered from this portion of the study will be reported elsewhere.

Next, participants read the description of Sam's persona and the associated scenario, which are both provided above in Table 1.

Participants then viewed the videos, and listened to the associated audio, for each of the four companion robots presented in Fig. 1 through Fig. 4. The videos, which were presented in random order, each had a duration of approximately 30 s and illustrated this portion of the scenario: "The companion robot makes some movements and sounds for about 30 s."

After viewing each video, participants were asked to answer the following seven questions. Note that we used the word "cute" instead of "kawaii" in the survey questions because the survey was administered in English and some participants may not have been familiar with the word "kawaii".

1. "Based on the video, if you find one or more aspects of the companion robot to be cute, please describe THE CUTEST ASPECT here. If you do not find any aspects to be cute, please write NONE." A text box was provided for participants to type their answer to this question.
2. "Based on the video, if you find any ADDITIONAL aspects of the companion robot to be cute, please describe ALL THE ADDITIONAL CUTE ASPECTS here. If you do not find any additional aspects to be cute, please write NONE." A text box was provided for participants to type their answer to this question.
3. "Based on the video, how cute is this companion robot?" Participants responded using a 7-point Likert scale where 1 was "Not at all cute" and 7 was "Very cute".
4. "Based on the video, how trustworthy is this companion robot?" Participants responded using a 7-point Likert scale where 1 was "Not at all trustworthy" and 7 was "Very trustworthy".
5. "Based on the video, if cost is not a factor, how likely do you think it is that **Sam** would want to use this companion robot?" Participants responded using a 7-point Likert scale where 1 was "Not at all likely" and 7 was "Very likely".
6. "Based on the video, if cost is not a factor, how likely do you think it is that **you** would want to use this companion robot?" Participants responded using a 7-point Likert scale where 1 was "Not at all likely" and 7 was "Very likely".
7. "You may optionally share any additional comments about your answers here. If you do not have any additional comments, please wrote NONE."

After watching all four videos, and answering the associated questions, participants were presented with a screen that presented photographs of all four companion robots. Participants were asked the following two questions:

1. "Based on the pictures and videos, which companion robot do you think **Sam** would prefer?" To respond to this question, the participants selected one of the four companion robots.
2. "Based on the pictures and videos, which companion robot would **you** prefer?" To respond to this question, the participants selected one of the four companion robots.

Finally, participants were debriefed and completed a payment form that allowed us to compensate them with a $20 Amazon gift certificate.

3 Results

3.1 Quantitative Survey Data

As described earlier, participants were asked to respond to several quantitative and qualitative questions after viewing the video of each of the four companion robots. Figure 8 summarizes participant responses to the question "Based on the video, how cute is this companion robot?" Participants responded using a 7-point Likert scale where 1 was "Not at all cute" and 7 was "Very cute". In reporting responses for the Likert scale questions in the remainder of this section we will consider a rating of 1, 2, or 3 to be a negative rating, a rating of 4 to be a neutral rating, and a rating of 5, 6 or 7 to be a positive rating.

The data in Fig. 8 is organized into four clusters of bars. The left-most cluster presents responses to the cuteness question for the Spiky companion robot video, which is one of the companion robots that was designed not to be cute. As shown in Fig. 8, 37 of the 47 participants (79%) gave a negative rating when asked how cute Spiky was while only 5 out of 47 participants (11%) gave a positive rating in response to this question.

As further shown in Fig. 8, responses were similar for the Bug companion robot, which was also designed not to be cute. For this robot, only 3 participants out of 47 (6%) responded with a positive rating. The Panda and the Penguin were designed to be cute and, as expected, many participants found them to be cute. Specifically, as shown in Fig. 8, 26 of the 47 participants (55%) rated the Panda positively on the cuteness scale while 32 of the 47 participants (68%) rated the Penguin positively on this scale.

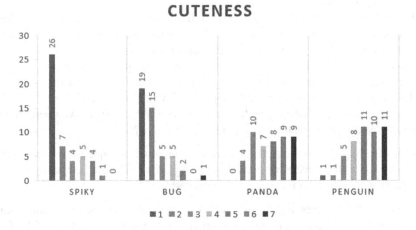

Fig. 8. Responses to Cuteness Likert Scale

Figure 9 presents participant responses to the question "Based on the video, how trustworthy is this companion robot?" Robots that were judged to be cuter as shown in

Fig. 8 were also judged to be more trustworthy as shown in Fig. 9. For example, while only 3 out of 47 participants (6%) rated Spiky, which is the least cute robot, positively on the trustworthy scale, 26 out of 47 participants (55%) rated Penguin, which was rated as the cutest robot, positively on the trustworthy scale.

TRUSTWORTHINESS

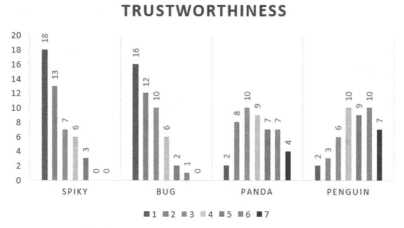

Fig. 9. Responses to Trustworthiness Likert Scale

Figure 10 summarizes participant responses to the question: "Based on the video, if cost is not a factor, how likely do you think it is that **Sam** would want to use this companion robot?" Once again, the data demonstrates that participants believe Sam is more likely to want to use the robots that were rated to be cuter as compared to the robots than were rated to be less cute. In particular, only 5 participants (11%) gave a positive rating when asked if Sam would want to use Spiky while 27 participants (57%) gave a positive rating for Penguin.

Figure 11 summarizes participant responses to the question: "Based on the video, if cost is not a factor, how likely is it that **you** would want to use this companion robot?" The data demonstrates that participants state they are more likely to want to use the robots that were rated to be cuter as compared to the robots than were rated to be less cute. For example, only 7 participants (15%) gave a positive rating when asked if they wanted to use Spiky while 23 participants (49%) gave a positive rating for Penguin.

Participants were presented with pictures of all four companion robots and were asked "Based on the pictures and videos, which companion robot do you think Sam would prefer?" In response, 26 participants believed Sam would prefer the Penguin companion robot while 15 participants believed Sam would prefer the Panda companion robot. Only 1 participant believed Sam would prefer the Spiky companion robot and only 5 participants believed Sam would prefer the Bug companion robot. In summary, 41 out of 47 participants (87%) believed Sam would prefer to use one of the two companion robots that was designed to be cute.

Participants were presented with pictures of all four companion robots and were asked "Based on the pictures and videos, which companion robot would you prefer?" In response, 27 participants indicated a preference for the Penguin while 14 participants

HOW LIKELY SAM WOULD USE IT

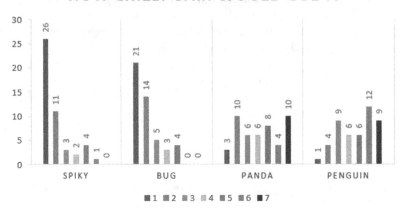

Fig. 10. Responses to Sam's Likelihood of Use Likert Scale

HOW LIKELY PARTICIPANT USE IT

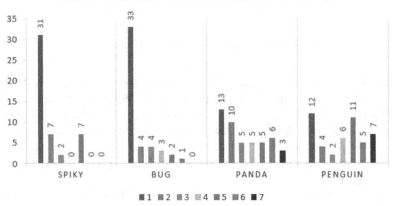

Fig. 11. Reponses to Participants Likelihood of Use Likert Scale

indicated a preference for the Panda. Only 2 participants indicated a preference for the Spiky companion robot and only 4 participants indicated a preference for the Bug companion robot. In summary, 41 out of 47 participants (87%) expressed a preference for one of the two companion robots that was designed to be cute.

3.2 Qualitative Survey Responses

After watching each companion robot video, participants were asked to indicate the cutest aspect of the companion robot as well as any additional cute aspects of the companion robot. The responses were coded for the two robots that were rated to be the cutest (Penguin and Panda). Most responses fall into one of three categories: visual characteristics, sounds, and movements. Table 2 provides counts of the number of times each category was mentioned as a cutest characteristic and also as an additional cute characteristic for the Penguin companion robot. The rightmost column of Table 2 sums the two columns to its left. Table 3 provides similar counts for the Panda companion robot.

Table 2. Coding of Cute Characteristics of Penguin Companion Robot

	Cutest Penguin Characteristics	Additional Cute Penguin Characteristics	Total Cute Penguin Characteristics
Visual	34	20	54
Sound	12	14	26
Movement	1	9	10

Examples of the characteristics mentioned for the Penguin companion robot are provided below.

- **Visual:** "The Penguin's Face", "It looks soft and friendly", "The fluffy, cozy style"
- **Sound:** "I find the noises it makes very cute and catchy", "The sounds", "The music and the ice it was on"
- **Movement:** "The sound and the movement of the robot", "The cute music and the way it just moving/dancing around", "Movement, music"

When a participant mentioned multiple characteristics as part of a single response, the response was coded in multiple categories. For example, one participant stated that an additional cute characteristic of the Penguin companion robot was "The music and the ice it was on". This response was coded in both the Sound and Visual categories.

Table 3. Coding of Cute Characteristics of Panda Companion Robot

	Cutest Panda Characteristics	Additional Cute Panda Characteristics	Total Cute Panda Characteristics
Visual	33	18	51
Sound	2	10	12
Movement	13	11	24

Examples of the characteristics mentioned for the Panda companion robot are provided below.

- **Visual:** "The eyes", "The round shape of the panda", "The panda face"
- **Sound:** "The music", "The music and the green leaves", "The background music tune"

- **Movement:** "That spin at the end was great", "How the panda moves its body in the certain pattern", "The Dance moves and the stuffed panda"

As indicated in Tables 2 and 3 visual characteristics were mentioned most frequently as contributing to the cuteness of a companion robot for both the Penguin companion robot and the Panda companion robot. Sound was more frequently noted than movement for the Penguin, while movement was more frequently noted than sound for the Panda. In particular, 12 participants specifically commented on the spinning movement at the end of the Panda video, for example by writing: "That spin at the end was great." Additional participants made more general comments such as "how the panda moves its body in the certain pattern" which may have also been influenced by the spin at the end of the video.

3.3 iMotions Facial Expression Analysis

The iMotions Facial Expression Analysis Software recorded a great amount of data although, in this paper, we only present preliminary data on its measure of "joy" among the participants. The iMotions software reported that the majority of participants expressed joy 0% of the time while watching the companion robot videos. As measured by the iMotions software, out of the 47 participants, 16 (34%) expressed any joy while watching the Spiky companion robot, only 13 (28%) expressed any joy while watching the Bug companion robot, only 14 (30%) expressed any joy while watching the Panda companion robot and only 16 (34%) expressed any joy while watching the Penguin companion robot. Even in cases where the iMotions software detected joy while a participant was watching the video the joy was sometimes only expressed for a small percentage of time the video was playing.

4   Discussion

The Panda and Penguin companion robots, which were the robots that were judged to be cuter than the Bug and Spiky robots, were also judged to be more trustworthy. In addition, participants generally believed that Sam would prefer to use the robots that were judged to be cuter and participants also indicated that they would personally prefer to use these robots. Importantly, almost half of the participants (49%) gave a positive rating when asked how likely they would be to use Penguin, which was the companion robot that was most likely to be judged to be cute. Additionally, more than half of the participants (57%) thought Sam would be likely to use the Penguin companion robot. Taken collectively, these results suggest that designing a companion robot to be cute can have a positive impact acceptance of the robot.

While the Panda companion robot and the Penguin companion robot both received positive ratings for cuteness, trustworthiness, and for the desire for Sam and the participants to use the companion robots, Penguin received higher scores than Panda. It is possible that Penguin was seen as more gender neutral due to Panda's accessories, which included flowers.

The majority of previous work on understanding kawaii-ness has focused on the visual characteristics of an object. Participants in our study were most likely to identify visual characteristics of a companion robot as cute. However, participants also frequently identified movement and sound as making contributions to the cuteness of a companion robot. We believe further study is warranted to better understand how visual characteristics, sound and movement can work together to convey cuteness.

While there was great variation in the way participants rated specific companion robots with regard to their cuteness, there was little variation in the iMotions software's measurement of the participant's expression of joy. This may suggest that a participant can recognize an object is cute, and can express a preference for that object, even if the cuteness is not strong enough to drive a change in facial expression. This is an area worthy of additional research.

5   Future Work

We plan to complete further evaluation of the quantitative and qualitative survey data, including statistical analysis, to examine whether or not there are differences in perceptions of cuteness based on gender or cultural background. In particular, it will be interesting to investigate whether gender differences resulted in the higher ratings for Penguin as compared to Panda as discussed in the previous section.

A number of participants mentioned that the Panda's companion robot's spinning was especially cute. A more focused examination of the iMotions joy data collected for that portion of the video is warranted. Additionally, we plan to investigate other data collected by the iMotions software such as measurements of a user's engagement or level of surprise. Finally, we would like to use iMotions to gather additional data while participants watch videos that are commonly accepted to be cute (e.g., puppies, babies) to see if this results in measurements of joy that we can use as a baseline.

Acknowledgements. This material is based upon work supported by the National Science Foundation under Grant No. OISE-1854255. Any opinions, findings, and conclusions or recommendations expressed in this material are those of the author(s) and do not necessarily reflect the views of the National Science Foundation. We thank the faculty, staff and students at Shibaura Institute of Technology for hosting the faculty and students from DePauw University during this project. We also thank Yuri Nakagawa for her academic assistance with this project while the DePauw team was at SIT.

References

1. Berque D., et al.: Cross-cultural design and evaluation of student companion robots with varied Kawaii (Cute) attributes. In: Kurosu, M. (eds.) Human-Computer Interaction. Theoretical Approaches and Design Methods. HCII 2022. July 2022. Lecture Notes in Computer Science, vol. 13302, pp. 391–409. Springer, Cham (2022). https://doi.org/10.1007/978-3-031-05311-5_27
2. Berque, D., et al.: Cross-cultural design and evaluation of robot prototypes based on Kawaii (Cute) attributes. In: Holzinger, A. (ed.) Proceedings of Human-Computer Interaction International 2021, July 2021, Remote Conference, vol. 12, pp. 319–334. Springer, Heidelberg (2021). https://doi.org/10.1007/978-3-540-89350-9_6

3. Nittono, H.: Kawaii no Chikara (The Power of Kawaii) Kyoto: Dojin Sensho (2019) (in Japanese)
4. Nittono, H., Fukushima, M., Yano, A., Moriya, H.: The power of Kawaii: viewing cute images promotes a careful behavior and narrows attentional focus. PLoS ONE 7(9), e46362 (2012). https://doi.org/10.1371/journal.pone
5. Ohkura, M.: Kawaii Engineering: Measurements, Evaluations, and Applications of Attractiveness. Springer (2019). https://doi.org/10.1007/978-981-13-7964-2
6. Yano, C.: Pink Globalization: Hello Kitty's Trek Across the Pacific. Duke University Press, Durham (2013)
7. Cole, S.: The Most Kawaii Robots of 2016, Retrieved September 8, 2018 (2016). https://motherboard.vice.com/en_us/article/xygky3/the-most-kawaii-robots-of-2016-5886b75a358cef455d864759
8. Prosser, M.: Why Japan's Cute Robots Could Be Coming for You (2017). Retrieved 8 Sept 2018. www.redbull.com/us-en/japan-cute-robot-obsession
9. Sugano, S., Miyaji Y., Tomiyama, K.: Study of Kawaii-ness in motion – physical properties of Kawaii motion of Roomba. In: Kurosu, M. (ed.) Human-Computer Interaction, Part I, HCII 2013, LNCS 8004, pp. 620–629. Springer, Heidelberg (2013). https://doi.org/10.1007/978-3-642-39232-0_67
10. Sugano, S., Morita, H., Tomiyama, K.: Study on Kawaii-ness in motion –classifying Kawaii motion using Roomba. In: International Conference on Applied Human Factors and Ergonomics 2012, San Francisco, California, USA (2012)
11. Berque, D., Chiba, H., Wilkerson, B.: Design and cross-cultural evaluation of a Kawaii (Cute) roomba vacuum. In: Rauterberg, M. (ed.) Proceedings of HCI International 2023, July 2023, Copenhagen, Denmark, Springer Lecture Notes in Computer Science, vol. 14035, pp. 475–490 (2023). https://doi.org/10.1007/978-3-031-34732-0_37
12. Berque, D., Chiba, H., Ohkura, M., Sripian, P., Sugaya, M.: Fostering cross-cultural research by cross-cultural student teams: a case study related to Kawaii (Cute) robot design. In: Rau, P.-L. (ed.) HCII 2020. LNCS, vol. 12192, pp. 553–563. Springer, Cham (2020). https://doi.org/10.1007/978-3-030-49788-0_42
13. iMotions home page. www.imotions.com, Visited 18 Feb 2024

Transformation of Relaxation Time: Proposal of Touch Care Using Tapping Robot

Minori Furusawa[1](✉) [iD] and Hirotaka Osawa[2] [iD]

[1] University of Tsukuba, Tennodai 1-1-1, Tsukuba, Japan
s2130170@u.tsukuba.ac.jp
[2] Keio University, Hiyoshi 3-14-1, Yokohama, Japan

Abstract. This study aims to induce a state of relaxation in users by having a robot perform tapping on them. Insomnia is now considered a serious health risk worldwide. As a solution to this problem, this study focused on the "Relaxation" method of CBT-I, a treatment for insomnia. The authors developed a tapping robot designed to help users enter a relaxed state, a condition in which the parasympathetic nervous system becomes dominant, and the user perceives themselves as "relaxed." The tapping robot can maintain a more consistent rhythm and intensity than a human practitioner. Furthermore, the robot is expected to detect users' mental and physical states using sensors and other devices, providing appropriate feedback. In this study, we developed and proposed a robot that induces relaxation through tapping, thereby reducing users' mental and physical stress. As a result of the experiments, a significant decrease in heart rate was observed in 8 out of 15 users. It suggests that the tapping robot induces relaxation for sleeping.

Keywords: Robot · Touch Care · Relaxation

1 Introduction

Insomnia is currently a serious health topic throughout the world. Insomnia has been identified as the most prevalent sleep disorder in the world and is known to have negative effects on both physical and mental health [1]. It is also noted that the number of patients with acute insomnia increases when serious social problems such as natural disasters, terrorism, and epidemics occur [2]. In recent years, COVID-19 is a typical example [3]. According to a survey in Japan, among all generations, people in their 20s are the worst sleepers. 16.8% of men and 21.3% of women reported that it took longer than usual (3 or more times a week) to fall asleep after getting into bed [4]. Taking longer to fall asleep decreases sleep efficiency and can cause a variety of mental and physical ailments. Although there are individual differences in how much sleep is needed [5], sleep is an essential activity for each person to maintain physical and mental health and maximize productivity. Insomnia has already been shown to be a challenge for the productivity of entire nations [6].

At the time of sleep onset, the body and mind should be in a relaxed state. Arousal and sleep are mutually exclusive, and arousal interferes with sleep [7]. Emotional arousals, such as anxiety, tension, anger, and joy, interferes with the transition to sleep and are thought to be a factor in unstable sleep even after falling asleep [8]. In a previous study, positron emission tomography revealed that the limbic system and arousal mechanisms associated with emotional arousal are excited [9]. Therefore, it is believed that a relaxed state at the time of sleep onset is desirable because reducing emotional arousal appropriately decreases arousal center activity and facilitates sleep onset [10]. In this study, the "relaxed state" was defined as a state in which the parasympathetic nervous system becomes dominant, and one can self-identify oneself as "relaxed.

There are three ways to induce a state of relaxation: physical, psychological, and behavioral approaches. One treatment for insomnia that has already been proposed is Cognitive behavioral therapy for Insomnia (CBT-I) [1]. In this study, among the "relaxation" techniques, tapping, a physical approach to the body, is used. As shown in Fig. 1, Relaxation is included in CBT-I as a physical approach to the human body.

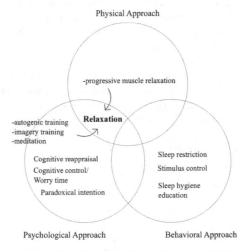

Fig. 1. Classification of Techniques in CBT-I

Tapping is a type of mental care in the field of developmental disabilities and nursing care and is a form of touch care that involves direct contact with the patient. Specifically, it refers to the gentle tapping of specific parts of the body, such as the hands, back, or chest. However, the physical and emotional strain on the practitioner must also be considered when providing care to others using tapping. The practitioner is forced to remain in the same position for a certain amount of time, which is physically demanding. In addition, depending on the situation, the practitioner may experience psychological fatigue due to the sense of responsibility to reassure the subject or put them to sleep.

To solve the above problem, we automated tapping and developed a tapping robot that induces relaxation by tapping the user's chest. The tapping robot was then tested on the participants in the experiment. To objectively evaluate the state of relaxation, we measured amylase activity in saliva and heart rate. In addition, questionnaires using the

TMS (Temporary Mood Scale) [11] and ERS (Emotional Relaxation Scale) [12] were administered to investigate the extent to which the users were aware of their state of relaxation.

This paper is organized as follows. Section 2 describes the history of touch care therapy, previous research on robotic care, and the goals of this study. Section 3 describes the tapping robot fabricated by the author for this study. Section 4 describes the in-person experiments conducted with the robot in this study. Results are discussed in Sect. 5. Section 6 provides a discussion and explains where this research can contribute and its current limitations. Section 7 then concludes this study.

2 Related Studies

2.1 Risk and Treatment of Insomnia

Insomnia has been suggested to increase the risk of various diseases such as arterial hypertension, myocardial infarction, chronic heart failure, and type 2 diabetes [13, 14]. It has also been shown that insomniacs have an increased risk of developing major depressive disorder [15] and are a risk factor for accidents, including automobile accidents [16].

There is much debate about the efficacy of pharmacological and non-pharmacological treatments. Two meta-analyses have already been published comparing non-pharmacologic CBT-I and pharmacotherapy [17, 18]; Riemann et al. concluded that CBT-I and hypnotics are equally effective in the short term and that CBT-I is superior in the long time [19].

2.2 History of Touch Care Therapy

First, as mentioned in the introduction, tapping is a form of touch care therapy. It has been studied mainly in the medical and nursing fields. Studies on touch care have shown many positive effects on newborns. For example, it has been shown to shorten hospital stays, decrease infection rates, reduce pain, promote weight gain, enhance neurodevelopment, improve mother-infant interaction, and increase caregiver and nurse satisfaction [20]. Similarly, many benefits have been shown for elderly patients with dementia [21]. In addition, information on tapping comes primarily from medical and nursing facilities. Some of the literature contains information that is close to spiritualism not based on scientific findings, and there is little academic knowledge available.

2.3 Support for Touch Care Therapy by Robot

There are several previous studies on robotic touch care [22, 23]. Most of them used a robotic arm, and few of them employed a method in which a small robot is attached to the body, as in this study.

One of the advantages of tapping with a robotic arm is the ability to fine-tune the state of contact with the user. In addition to tapping, gentle stroking touch care is also reproduced.

The study of gentle stroking in touch care is closely related to previous studies of c-tactile fibers. Many of these studies cite related research on c-tactile fibers and stroking speed. It is already known that users are most comfortable when stroking at 3 to 10 cm per second [24], and it can be inferred that developers can easily adjust the parameters of the robotic arm.

However, the robotic arms used in previous studies are heavy and large, making them difficult to carry and use anywhere. The reason may be that these previous studies were conducted for the purpose of sleep or simple relaxation and not for napping. If a robot is to be used for napping support, as in this study, it must be lightweight, small, and portable. We must also consider the possibility that users may feel insecure about large robot arms. Tapping is simpler than stroking in terms of the robot's movements and tapping movements may be sufficient in terms of falling asleep, which is the goal of this study.

While robots are expected to play an active role in the medical and welfare fields, it is also essential to take measures to prevent users from feeling anxious about robots. Many studies have been conducted at HRI and HAI on users' emotions toward robots. The Negative Attitudes toward Robots Scale (NARS) [25] and the Robot Anxiety Scale (RAS) [26] have been developed to measure human negative emotions and anxiety toward robots. In this study, we evaluate interactions with a non-verbal tapping robot. Consequently, we do not use the NARS and RAS, which assess negative attitudes and anxiety regarding interactions with communication robots employing language. Instead, we comprehensively evaluate the effects by employing the TMS to assess the user's mood, ERS to measure relaxation states, and salivary amylase activity to gauge stress levels. Because robotic touch care involves physical communication, great care must be taken when conducting research.

2.4 What This Research Should Accomplish

The robot developed in this research will be used in the future to support sleep and napping. In recent years, not only automobile drivers and medical professionals but also companies and schools have introduced napping time to improve work and class efficiency [27, 28]. The key to napping is how to get to sleep efficiently in a short period of time. Robotic tapping can be effective in helping users fall asleep quickly. To achieve this, as described below, the robot must be lightweight, compact, and portable, and must be able to support napping anytime and anywhere. In addition, it is important to make the device easy to wear and to reduce the discomfort of the parts that meet the body to spend a short nap time effectively and comfortably.

3 Tapping Robot

3.1 Robot Design

As explained in the previous chapter, tapping robots should be designed with the following requirements. First, since the robot is designed to assist in napping, it must be portable. It should be lightweight and compact. In addition, it should be adjustable since the tempo of comfortable tapping may vary depending on the user's preference or situation.

3.2   Implementation of Robot

Figure 2 shows the robot's appearance. The robot used in this research is 340 * 135 * 105 (mm) in size and weighs 453 g. It weighs about the same as an 11-in. tablet and is small and light enough to be carried around, given that it can be easily assembled and disassembled. A soft belt is used to secure the robot to the user's chest, and the robot performs tapping on the user's chest at regular intervals. The advantages of this robot are that it is small, lightweight, and can be used anywhere, and the tapping speed can be set sensibly and comfortably with the volume switch. This makes it possible to set a comfortable tapping speed while reducing the burden on the user. Tapping is initiated by fastening to the chest with a belt and turning on the power.

First, show the main body of the robot. It consists of two MDF boards and aluminum spacers. The boards are approximately 120 * 135 (mm) in size and about 5 mm thick. They are cut in the shape of the letter "D" to minimize the area in contact with the user's body and to reduce the discomfort felt by the user. There is a space of approximately 25 mm between the bottom plate, which touches the user's body, and the top plate, to which the motor mount and arm mounts are attached, supported by three aluminum spacers. Figure 3 shows the mounting method for the tapping robot.

Next, the motor and its surroundings are shown. The motor is a 6 V DC motor. It is fixed to an ABS motor mount made by a 3D printer and connected to the top board. A rotating part with a pin is attached to the end of the motor. As the motor rotates, the pins push down the rear end of the arm (described below) at regular intervals. The arm and hand are then relatively lifted, and the moment the pins are released, tapping is performed in free fall. The tapping robot can change the tapping tempo between 18–130 BPM. The battery box has a switch that turns the robot on and off.

Next, the arm and hand areas are described. The arm is made of ABS output from a 3D printer. It is divided into two parts: a long and thin arm part connected to the main body, and a hand part that taps the user's body through a sponge. The arm is approximately 145 mm long, which is just long enough to tap between the upper chest and the base of the neck when the main body is fixed to the lower chest. The rear end of the arm is where it meets the part attached to the end of the motor, as mentioned above. There is a hole of about 6 mm in diameter at the back of the arm, through which a plastic shaft of about 5 mm in diameter is threaded. The shaft passes through the 6 mm hole in the ABS arm mount, which is also output from a 3D printer, and is fixed like a seesaw. The hand is approximately 100 * 80 * 10 (mm) in size and can be attached to a commercially available soft sponge using a hook and loop fastener. In this study, a sponge of about 35 mm in thickness is used. The arm and hand are strong enough to withstand the entire period of use, including the experiments and commissioning described below.

Of Importance is the Structure of the Tapping Mechanism. The actuator does not directly press down on the chest; instead, the hand is designed to free fall. From a safety perspective, intrinsic safety design must be a primary consideration, as indicated in ISO 12100:2010. These mechanisms ensure that even if the robot should malfunction, the experimental participants will not be subjected to strong shocks, thus ensuring their safety and comfort. Thus, the authors have endeavored to simplify the design and the system to minimize damage in the event of a robot malfunction.

3.3 Purpose of the Experiment

The purpose of this experiment was to determine whether users, primarily in their twenties, are sufficiently relaxed by the tapping robot.

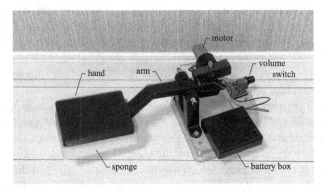

Fig. 2. Appearance of tapping robot

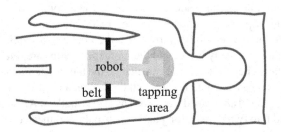

Fig. 3. Mounting method for the tapping robot

3.4 Collected Data

In this experiment, heart rate, salivary amylase, Athens Insomnia Scale, extraversion, TMS, ERS, recordings during the experiment, age, and gender were obtained. Table 1 shows which data were obtained at which time points during the experiment.

Heart Rate. Heart rate is an indicator used to measure the relationship between the sympathetic and parasympathetic nervous systems. A decrease in heart rate indicates the dominance of the parasympathetic nervous system. As mentioned earlier, one definition of a relaxed state is the dominance of the parasympathetic nervous system. Therefore, heart rate was employed as an indirect measure of relaxation effects.

Salivary Amylase. Salivary amylase activity is an indicator for measuring sympathetic nervous system activity. Amylase levels increase when an individual experiences stress. Saliva can be collected noninvasively and easily, imposing a minimal burden on the participants, which is why it was chosen for this study. In this experiment, we used Nipuro's

Table 1. List of collected data

Measurement Point	Parameters
Pre-experiment	Saliva, Questionnaire (Athens Insomnia Scale, Extraversion, TMS, Age, Gender), Heart Rate
Relaxation A*	Heart Rate, Video Footage
Post-experiment (1)	Saliva, Questionnaire (TMS, ERS), Heart Rate
Relaxation B*	Heart Rate, Video Footage
Post-experiment (2)	Saliva, Questionnaire (TMS, ERS), Heart Rate

* In Relaxation A and B, the order of experiments with and without the robot is randomized for each subject.

Salivary Amylase Monitor. According to the instruction manual, salivary amylase levels below 30 kIU/L indicate no stress, levels between 30 and 45 kIU/L suggest mild stress, levels between 46 and 60 kIU/L indicate stress and levels above 61 kIU/L are considered to reflect a high degree of stress.

Athens Insomnia Scale. The Athens Insomnia Scale is a self-assessment psychometric scale designed for quantifying sleep difficulty based on the ICD-10 criteria by The World Health Organization (WHO) [29]. It quantifies responses to eight questions, with a maximum score of 24 points, to measure the level of insomnia. A score of 1 to 3 points indicates sufficient sleep, 4 to 5 points suggest a suspicion of insomnia, and 6 points or higher indicate a high suspicion of insomnia. In this study, the scale was used to determine the participants' level of insomnia and to investigate the relationship between extraversion and sleep quality, which will be discussed later.

Extraversion. Extraversion is one of the elements of the Big Five, a psychological theory that describes human personality traits in terms of five major elements. It refers to personality traits such as sociability, liveliness, friendliness, and positivity. Previous studies have reported that high extraversion is related to good sleep [30]. In the present study, we used it in combination with the Athens Insomnia Scale to determine what effect extraversion has on insomnia.

TMS. TMS is a scale designed to measure emotional states at a given point in time. 18 questions measure six types of mood: tension, depression, anger, confusion, fatigue, and vigor. This study is used to investigate the effects of relaxation experiments on mood.

ERS. The ERS is a scale designed to measure the sense of relaxation brought about using relaxation techniques. ERS consists of four subscales: a sense of ability, a sense of refreshment, a sense of relief, and a sense of calm. This study was used to investigate how the relaxation experiment affected the participants' self-perception of their state of relaxation.

Recordings During the Experiment. In this study, a video was taken of the experimental participants during the relaxation experiment. At the beginning of the experiment, consent was obtained from the participants to filming and use the videos and images in this paper.

3.5 Participants

For this experiment, we gathered 15 participants. The age of the participants ranged from 19 to 29 years old. 10 were male and 5 were female.

3.6 Ethical Consideration

This experiment was conducted after passing the ethical review of the University of Tsukuba. The ethics review approval number is 2022R658–1. Before the experiment began, the participants were fully informed of the study in writing and orally before the start of the experiment. In addition, the experimental participants were informed that they could decide to participate in the experiment of their own free will and that they could discontinue their participation at any time during the experiment. After the participants agreed to the above and signed the consent form, the experiment was started.

3.7 Hypothesis

The following hypotheses were formulated for this study:

Physiological Indices. The following values will be lower in the experiment using the tapping robot than in the experiment without the robot: heart rate, and amylase activity in saliva.

Subjective Indices. The TMS and ERS of the experiment participants will be significantly more positive in the experiment using the tapping robot than in the experiment without the robot: heart rate, and amylase activity in saliva.

Relationship Between Extraversion and Insomnia. The higher the extraversion, the less the tendency to insomnia.

3.8 Experimental Method

Experiment Design and Procedures. In this experiment, a tapping robot was attached to the upper chest of an experimental participant, and tapping was performed for 10 min. As a control experiment, participants spent 10 min lying on their backs on a bed. In the control experiment, the participant lay on their back on the bed without the robot attached. The order of the tapping and control experiments was randomly assigned so that there was no bias between participants.

Table 2 shows the experimental procedure. First, Fitbit was attached to the left arm, and heart rate measurement began.

Table 2. Experimental procedure

Measurement Point	With tapping robot	Without tapping robot
Pre-experiment	Wear a Fitbit. Collect saliva. Fill out the questionnaire.	
Relaxation	The robot is attached to an experimental participant lying on a bed. 10 minutes of tapping is performed.	Lying in bed, the experimental participant spends 10 minutes doing nothing.
Post-experiment	Collect saliva. Fill out the questionnaire.	

After that, saliva samples were taken, and participants were asked questions including Athens Insomnia Scale, Extraversion, and TMS. Saliva samples were collected after each of the experiments with and without the robot, and TMS and ERS were measured. In both experiments, participants wore a towel over their faces as a blindfold and noise-canceling headphones. Figure 4 shows how the participants looked during the experiment.

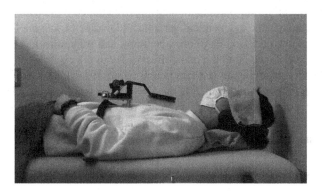

Fig. 4. Tapping robot attached to a participant

Setting Experimental Time and Tapping Speed. The experimental time and tapping speed were set with reference to previous studies. According to previous research, the time required for an adult to reach the first stage of non-REM sleep is about 5 to 7 min [31]. Therefore, the duration of the experiment was set at 10 min. For the speed of tapping, the values employed in previous studies, i.e., approximately $0.33 \sim 0.67$ Hz vibration (approximately $20 \sim 40$ times/minute) [32], were also used in this study. Considered that the frequency range of approximately $0.33 \sim 0.67$ Hz, which is lower than their heart rate, may induce physiological and psychological comfort and relaxation [32].

Robot Settings. In the tapping experiment, a soft belt was used to secure the robot to the chest, and the participant lay on their back on the bed. The robot settings for the tapping experiment are shown below. The tap speed was fixed at 40 BPM. The height of the tap was approximately 130 mm from the highest point of the sponge to the chest.

4 Experimental Results

4.1 Physiological Indices

Heart rate was analyzed in 14 subjects, excluding one subject with missing data. Comparing the results of the experiment with and without the robot, a significant decrease in heart rate was observed in 8 subjects when the robot was worn. Figure 5 shows the average change in heart rate during the experiment.

Analysis of salivary amylase activity showed no significant difference between the two experiments. Figure 6 shows the change in average amylase activity before and after the experiment.

4.2 Subjective Indices

The TMS data were analyzed in 14 subjects, excluding one subject who had missing data. No significant difference was found between the two experiments. Figure 7 shows each element of the TMS for the experiment without and with the robot.

The ERS was also analyzed for 14 subjects, excluding one subject who had missing data. A two-factor within-participant analysis of variance was conducted using the experimental method as the independent variable and the factor scores of the ERS subscale (sense of competence, exhilaration, liberation, and tranquility) as the dependent variable. The results showed that the main effects of both the experimental method and factor scores were not significant ($F_{(7,111)} = 0.13$, n.s. $F_{(7,111)} = 0.00$, n.s.). However, the interaction was significant ($F_{(7,111)} = 4.72$, $p < .05$). A simple main effect test of the factor scores showed that the effect of the experiment without the robot was significantly higher on the factor score of competence ($F_{(7,111)} = 17.96$, $p < .01$). Figure 8 illustrates each element of the ERS for experiments without and with a robot.

4.3 Relationship Between Extraversion and Insomnia

To examine the extent to which insomnia and poor sleep quality can be predicted by subjects' extraversion, a single regression analysis using the least squares method was conducted with "factor scores of the extraversion factor" as the independent variable and "factor scores of the Athens Sleep Scale" as the dependent variable. The results showed that "factor scores of the Athens Sleep Scale" did not predict "factor scores of the Extraversion Factor" ($R^2 = .04$, $F (R^2 = .04$, $F_{(13,111)} = 0.61$, n.s.). Figure 9 shows the relationship between the Athens Insomnia Scale and factor scores for extraversion.

5 Discussion

First, the significant decrease in heart rate suggests that the parasympathetic nervous system may have become dominant. As mentioned in the introduction, one of the definitions of the relaxed state is a state in which the parasympathetic nervous system is dominant. The decrease in heart rate suggests that the parasympathetic nervous system has become more dominant than the sympathetic nervous system and that the subject has entered the phase of falling asleep. Therefore, the significant decrease in heart rate observed in the eight subjects in this experiment may have caused the parasympathetic nervous system to become dominant, leading to a state of relaxation.

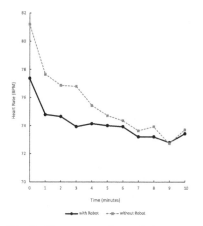

Fig. 5. The average change in heart rate

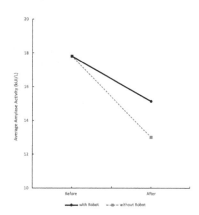

Fig. 6. The average amylase activity

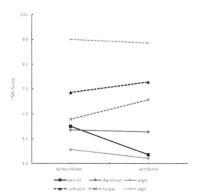

Fig. 7. Each element of the

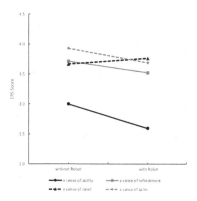

Fig. 8. Each element of the ERS

Next, we compared the respective responses of heart rate and amylase activity. As mentioned earlier, more than half of the participants showed a significant decrease in heart rate. However, there was no significant difference in amylase activity. One of the reasons for this is that heart rate and amylase activity have very different responses. Heart rate responds immediately in seconds, while amylase responds within 5 min at the shortest, indicating a difference in response time. In the present experiment, a relaxation period of 10 min was provided, which seems to have been sufficient time for amylase activity to change. However, no significant difference in amylase activity was observed in this experiment, suggesting that the reaction may take longer than 10 min.

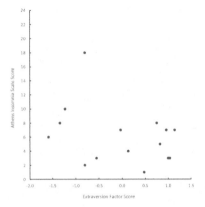

Fig. 9. The relationship between the Athens Insomnia Scale and factor scores for extraversion

Finally, we examined the "a sense of ability," which is the degree of interpretation of the ERS. In this experiment, the sense of competence was significantly lower in the experiment with the robot than in the experiment without the robot. It is possible that the intervention by the robot interfered with the robot's sense of independence and self-esteem, even though the robot was supposed to be able to sleep on its own. Alternatively, since tapping is often perceived as an act performed on children, it is possible that the adults temporarily reverted to a childlike state. We believe that this result does not necessarily have a negative impact on users. However, as in this study, we must be careful about the possibility of psychological damage to the user side when a robot or agent intervenes in an action that a person can originally perform on his or her own.

6 Contributions and Limitations

6.1 Contributions

This research challenged relaxation by robot tapping, which has rarely been done before. We succeeded in producing a prototype of a tapping robot that is light, small, and portable. At first glance, the mechanism and system appear to be very simple, but it produced an effect of significantly lowering the heart rate of the participants in the experiment. Although there are still some issues to be solved as described below, we were able to show that the tapping robot has a certain potential to induce a relaxation effect and support napping.

As mentioned at the beginning of this paper, we did not employ scales like NARS or RAS in our study. However, it is important to develop various comfort and discomfort-related measures for relaxation-providing robots like the tapping robot in the future. By using such indices, we believe it is necessary to design interactions between users and robots that support relaxation and sleep. This research contributes to the development of such new scales and questions, and we are considering the creation of appropriate evaluation methods in the future.

6.2 Limitations

In this study, tapping was performed on the upper chest area, which is generally tapped when putting another person to sleep. However, the individual differences in body shape around the chest were larger than expected, and we judged that this would affect stable tapping. Therefore, we plan to perform tapping on the back in future experiments. This is because the back is basically wide and flat. In addition, when considering support for napping in the future, tapping on the back is more effective than tapping on the chest when sleeping with one's head down on a desk.

The next point is that the amylase activity did not change significantly. The reason for this is that most of the participants were under 30 kIU/L at the beginning of the experiment, i.e., they were not feeling much stress. It is suggesting that there was no significant change because relaxation was performed to reduce stress from this state. Therefore, it is necessary to consider giving an appropriate stress task before relaxation in future experiments.

Finally, we describe the heart rate measurement method. In this study, heart rate was measured with a relatively simple device, so LF/HF could not be obtained. In future experiments, we would like to introduce a method to estimate the balance between sympathetic and parasympathetic nervous tensions by acquiring changes in the low-frequency LF and high-frequency HF waves of heart rate variability, respectively.

7 Conclusion

In this study, a tapping robot was developed to induce a state of relaxation. Experiments using the tapping robot were conducted on 15 participants, mainly in their 20s, and the state of relaxation was measured comprehensively from heart rate, amylase activity, TMS, and ERS. The following results were obtained in response to the hypothesis.

7.1 Physiological Indices

This study hypothesized that heart rate and salivary amylase activity would be lower in the experiment using the tapping robot than in the experiment without the robot. For heart rate, there was a significant decrease in heart rate in the experiment using the robot in eight participants. On the other hand, there was no significant difference in amylase activity between experiments.

7.2 Subjective Indices

TMS and ERS of the experimental participants were hypothesized to be significantly more positive in the experiment using the tapping robot than in the experiment without the robot. As a result, no significant difference was found in TMS; in ERS, only the item of a sense of ability was found to be predominantly higher in the experiment without the robot.

7.3 Relationship Between Extraversion and Insomnia

In this study, we hypothesized that the higher the extraversion, the less the tendency to insomnia. The results of the present study did not confirm a relationship between extraversion and insomnia.

These results suggest that the use of the tapping robot for adults, mainly in their 20s, may activate the parasympathetic nervous system and have a relaxing effect. The tapping robot is expected to be utilized in napping support.

Acknowledgments. This work was supported by JSPS KAKENHI Grant Number JP21H03569 and JP23H03896.

References

1. Baglioni, C., et al.: The European academy for cognitive behavioural therapy for insomnia: an initiative of the European insomnia network to promote implementation and dissemination of treatment. J. Sleep Res. **29**(2), 1–29 (2020). https://doi.org/10.1111/jsr.12967
2. Sinha, S.S.: Trauma-induced insomnia: a novel model for trauma and sleep research. Sleep Med. Rev. **25**, 74–83 (2016). https://doi.org/10.1016/j.smrv.2015.01.008
3. Cénat, J.M., et al.: Prevalence of symptoms of depression, anxiety, insomnia, posttraumatic stress disorder, and psychological distress among populations affected by the COVID-19 pandemic: a systematic review and meta-analysis. Psychiatry Res. **295**(June), 2021 (2020). https://doi.org/10.1016/j.psychres.2020.113599
4. Ministry of Health, and Labour and Welfare Japan, National Health and Nutrition Survey (2019)
5. Chaput, J.P., Dutil, C., Sampasa-Kanyinga, H.: Sleeping hours: what is the ideal number and how does age impact this? Nat. Sci. Sleep **10**, 421–430 (2018). https://doi.org/10.2147/NSS.S163071
6. Daley, M., Morin, C.M., LeBlanc, M., Grégoire, J.P., Savard, J.: The economic burden of insomnia: direct and indirect costs for individuals with insomnia syndrome, insomnia symptoms, and good sleepers. Sleep **32**(1), 55–64 (2009). https://doi.org/10.1016/s1073-5437(10)79480-8
7. Borb, A.A., Achermann, P.: Sleep homeostasis and models of sleep regulation. J. Biol. Rhythms **14**(6), 559–570 (1999). https://doi.org/10.1177/074873099129000894
8. Uchiyama, M.: Physiological roles and mechanisms of sleep. J. Nihon Univ. Med. Assoc. **79**(6), 327–331 (2020). https://doi.org/10.4264/numa.79.6_327
9. Nofzinger, E.A., Boysse, D.J., Germain, A., Price, J.C., Miewald, J.M., Kopfer, D.J.: Functional neuroimaging evidence for hyperarousal in insomnia. Am. J. Psychiatry **161**(11), 2126–2129 (2004). https://doi.org/10.1176/appi.ajp.161.11.2126
10. Baglioni, C., Spiegelhalder, K., Lombardo, C., Riemann, D.: Sleep and emotions: a focus on insomnia. Sleep Med. Rev. **14**(4), 227–238 (2010). https://doi.org/10.1016/j.smrv.2009.10.007
11. Kanji, T.: The validity of temporary mood scale. Ritsumeikan J. Hum. Sci. **22**, 1–6 (2011)
12. Kanji, T.: The advantage and criterion-related validity of emotional relaxation scale: based on the research in university students. Ritsumeikan J. Human Sci. **23**, 1–9 (2011)
13. Laugsand, L.E., Strand, L.B., Platou, C., Vatten, L.J., Janszky, I.: Insomnia and the risk of incident heart failure: a population study. Eur. Heart J. **35**(21), 1382–1393 (2014). https://doi.org/10.1093/eurheartj/eht019

14. Anothaisintawee, T., Reutrakul, S., Van Cauter, E., Thakkinstian, A.: Sleep disturbances compared to traditional risk factors for diabetes development: systematic review and meta-analysis. Sleep Med. Rev. **30**(December 2016), 11–24 (2016). https://doi.org/10.1016/j.smrv. 2015.10.002

15. Paunio, T., et al.: Poor sleep predicts symptoms of depression and disability retirement due to depression. J. Affect. Disord. **172**, 381–389 (2015). https://doi.org/10.1016/j.jad.2014.10.002

16. Erik Laugsand, L., Strand, L.B., Vatten, L.J., Janszky, I., Bjørngaard, J.H.: Insomnia symptoms and risk for unintentional fatal injuries-the HUNT study. Sleep **37**(11), 1777–1786C (2014). https://doi.org/10.5665/sleep.4170

17. Smith, M.T., et al.: Comparative meta-analysis of pharmacotherapy and behavior therapy for persistent insomnia. Am. J. Psychiatry **159**(1), 5–11 (2002). https://doi.org/10.1176/appi.ajp. 159.1.5

18. Mitchell, M.D., Gehrman, P., Perlis, M., Umscheid, C.A.: Comparative effectiveness of cognitive behavioral therapy for insomnia: a systematic review. Focus (Madison) **12**(1), 80–89 (2014). https://doi.org/10.1176/appi.focus.12.1.80

19. Riemann, D., et al.: European guideline for the diagnosis and treatment of insomnia. J. Sleep Res. **26**(6), 675–700 (2017). https://doi.org/10.1111/jsr.12594

20. Cleveland, L., Hill, C.M., Pulse, W.S., DiCioccio, H.C., Field, T., White-Traut, R.: Systematic review of skin-to-skin care for full-term, healthy newborns. JOGNN – J. Obstet. Gynecol. Neonatal. Nurs. **46**(6), 857–869 (2017). https://doi.org/10.1016/j.jogn.2017.08.005

21. Suzuki, M., et al.: Physical and psychological effects of 6-week tactile massage on elderly patients with severe dementia. Am. J. Alzheimer's Dis. Dementias **25**(8), 680–686 (2010). https://doi.org/10.1177/1533317510386215

22. Honda, S., et al.: Evaluation of relationship between stroke pace and speech rate for touch-care robot. In: HAI 2019 - Proceedings 7th International Conference Human-Agent Interaction, pp. 283–285 (2019). https://doi.org/10.1145/3349537.3352793

23. Chen, T.L., King, C.H., Thomaz, A.L., Kemp, C.C.: Touched by a robot: an investigation of subjective responses to robot-initiated touch. In: HRI 2011 - Proceedings 6th ACM/IEEE International Conference Human-Robot Interaction, pp. 457–464 (2011). https://doi.org/10. 1145/1957656.1957818

24. Löken, L.S., Wessberg, J., Morrison, I., McGlone, F., Olausson, H.: Coding of pleasant touch by unmyelinated afferents in humans. Nat. Neurosci. **12**(5), 547–548 (2009). https://doi.org/ 10.1038/nn.2312

25. Nomura, T., Kanda, T., Suzuki, T.: Experimental investigation into influence of negative attitudes toward robots on human-robot interaction. AI Soc. **20**(2), 138–150 (2006). https:// doi.org/10.1007/s00146-005-0012-7

26. Nomura, T., Suzuki, T., Kanda, T., Kato, K.: Measurement of anxiety toward robots. In: Proceedings - IEEE International Workshop on Robot and Human Interactive Communication, pp. 372–377 (2006). https://doi.org/10.1109/ROMAN.2006.314462

27. Murphy, A., Hassing, M., Mishra, J., Mishra, B.: The perfect nap. Adv. Manage. **9**(4), 1–8 (2016). https://search.proquest.com/docview/1778674348?accountid=15920

28. Lemos, N., Weissheimer, J., Ribeiro, S.: Naps in school can enhance the duration of declarative memories learned by adolescents. Front. Syst. Neurosci. **8**(JUNE), 1–6 (2014). https://doi. org/10.3389/fnsys.2014.00103

29. Soldatos, C.R., Dikeos, D.G., Paparrigopoulos, T.J.: Athens insomnia scale: validation of an instrument based on ICD-10 criteria. J. Psychosom. Res. **48**(6), 555–560 (2000). https://doi. org/10.1016/S0022-3999(00)00095-7

30. Stephan, Y., Sutin, A.R., Bayard, S., Križan, Z., Terracciano, A.: Personality and sleep quality: evidence from four prospective studies Yannick. Physiol. Behav. **176**(3), 139–148 (2019). https://doi.org/10.1037/hea0000577.Personality

31. Japanese Society of Sleep Research. In: Handbook of Sleep Science and Sleep Medicine (1994)
32. Hiroi, T., Kaneko, Y., Yanagi, N., Koitabashi, K.: Effect of regular rhythmic stimuli for ten minutes on consciousness level. Jpn. J. Nurs. Art Sci. **9**(2), 29–38 (2010)

Group Norm Awareness of Mobile Robots in Virtual Space Multiagent Simulation

Yotaro Fuse[1]([✉])(ID), Emmanuel Ayedoun[2](ID), and Masataka Tokumaru[2]

[1] Toyama Prefectural University, 5180 Kurokawa, Imizu, Toyama, Japan
`fuse@pu-toyama.ac.jp`
[2] Kansai University, 3-3-35, Yamate-cho, Suita, Osaka, Japan
`{emay,toku}@kansai-u.ac.jp`

Abstract. The emergence of social robots has created new opportunities for coexistence with humans, provided they can imitate human-like social behavior. Numerous studies have explored the navigation of mobile robots in the context of socializing robot behavior within human society. In a space where humans and robots coexist, the robot's positioning, that is, the way it occupies space, should be natural and human-like. Personal space theory, which is a model for maintaining distance between people, categorizes interpersonal distance. The distance maintained can be dynamic, which depends on the situation and context regardless of whether a person is comfortable or uncomfortable. In a society where humans and robots coexist, it is required to adapt to the behavior of humans who maintain such a context-dependent distance. Little consideration has been given to the point at which the robot continues positioning itself as a group member, which is the focus of this study. We propose a navigation method that introduces a concept of "near neighbors" for this purpose and assess the path generated by this method through a multiagent-based scenario in a virtual space. The simulation results demonstrate that our proposed navigation method adapts the implicit norms of distance and the experimental scenarios. In our future study, we intend to evaluate our proposed method, including a subjective evaluation by humans.

Keywords: Mobile Robot · Human–Agent Interaction · Social Robot · Group Norm-Aware Navigation · Proxemics

1 Introduction

Today, research on human–robot interaction is underway anticipating the arrival of a symbiotic society where humans and robots coexist. For robots to collaborate with humans and adapt to human society, they must infer expected behavior from their surroundings. In human–robot interactions, robots should respond by recognizing the social signals that humans emit. Numerous studies focus on robots behavior by interpreting these human social signals [1].

© The Author(s), under exclusive license to Springer Nature Switzerland AG 2024
M. Kurosu and A. Hashizume (Eds.): HCII 2024, LNCS 14685, pp. 91–104, 2024.
https://doi.org/10.1007/978-3-031-60412-6_7

In the context of socializing robot behavior within human society, numerous studies have been conducted on the navigation of mobile robots. These studies aim to find an optimal or suboptimal path from a starting point to a goal point, all while avoiding obstacles [2]. When a robot undertakes a transportation task or a path traversal task, it should move without colliding with humans or causing them anxiety, in the interest of human–robot symbiosis [3,4]. Conversely, when dealing with social robots interacting with humans, it is necessary to consider the context of the human–robot interaction and the space they coexist in. A robot that interacts with humans can be seen as a human partner or a decision-making entity in human society and should share space with humans as a group member.

In a space where humans and robots coexist, the robot's positioning, that is, the way it occupies space, should be natural and human-like. Personal space theory, which is a model for maintaining distance between people, categorizes interpersonal distance into public distance, social distance, individual distance, and close distance [5]. Each category in the interpersonal distance category social distance is defined as 1.2–3.7 m. Moreover, various factors such as gender, age, and culture affect and fluctuate the number of spaces people want to reserve [6]. Therefore, there is no possibility to derive a specific position for a robot within a human population from this theory alone. Additionally, this theory displays a general trend in space allocation preferences and does not guarantee that personal space will always be protected. For example, extreme proximity to a stranger in a confined space, including a crowded train or elevator, may violate personal space. However, even if it feels uncomfortable, the distance is maintained; the violation of personal space in that situation or context tends to be socially acceptable. Thus, the distance maintained can be dynamic, which depends on the situation and context regardless of whether a person is comfortable or uncomfortable. In a society where humans and robots coexist, it is required to adapt to the behavior of humans who maintain such a context-dependent distance. Social navigation, which was addressed in many previous studies, focuses on social considerations for humans while patrolling a route or moving to a target point. However, little consideration has been given to the point at which the robot continues positioning itself as a group member, which is the focus of this study.

This study focuses on adaptation to the implicit norm of distance in a group for a robot to maintain appropriate positioning as a group member. Previously, we proposed and evaluated a distance norm-aware movement method [7,8]. Our proposed method anticipates that implicit norms were shared in the group in which the agent belonged and attempted to output adaptive behavior to the group while estimating those norms. The objective of this research is to adapt agents to human group norms using the subject of distance maintained with others. Compared to previous work, this study proposes an improvement of the previous model through simulating a virtual space with a larger number of people. Herein, we attempt to assess a group with a larger number of members than the previous study, wherein the number of group members was fixed at four.

Furthermore, the previous study only aimed at adapting to the norm regarding distance maintained by the group. We also consider the degree to which each member maintains distance from others in the vicinity and introduce the concept of others in the vicinity. Therefore, this might enable agents equipped with this mobility model to fine-tune the distance they maintain from others in the vicinity while searching for an appropriate standing position in the big picture and thus achieve more adaptive agent mobility.

We aim to evaluate and analyze how humans judge agents and can adapt to implicit norms within a group. However, the evaluation is based only on objective indicators, such as the movements and actions of the agents in the simulation environment. However, subjective evaluation was not conducted based on the impression of humans for the agent. Although the norms were formed by human intersubjectivity, the lack of evaluation based on human subjectivity and impressions is a limitation of this study.

2   Method

Figure 1 illustrates a diagram of a distance norm-aware decision-making method for a computational agent based on the estimation of other group members' internal states. At the step t, the agent observes the environment and gathers a set O of locations l_m of other group members and itself within the environment. Based on the set O, the agent updates its own internal state $\mathfrak{S}$ and internal state $\widehat{S_m}$ of the other m estimated. The agent's action a is output to the environment based on $\mathfrak{S}$. The above inputs and outputs were performed every Δt, and the agent attempts to keep adapting its own position to the group while observing the positions of others. The following subsections describe the environment, the agent's input and output, its internal state, and its update method.

2.1   Environment and Agent

There is a group in the environment that comprises the agent itself and others whom the agent recognizes as group members. We represent the group as a set $G = \{m_n \mid n = 1, 2, ..., \mathrm{gs}\}$. In addition, the agent itself is $m_a \in G$, $a \in \{1, 2, ..., \mathrm{gs}\}$, which means that the agent is a member of the group.

As shown in Fig. 1, at time t, the agent observed the environment and obtained a set O. The set O consisted of the positions l_m of each group member, including the agent itself. The elements of the set O were input to the agent's internal state $\mathfrak{S}$ and the estimated internal state of others m, $\widehat{S_m}$. Based on the input, the internal states were renewed, and the agent moved on the output from $\mathfrak{S}$, action a.

The agent moved by performing action a at time t. If the agent was positioned at a point l^t in the environment, it would move to position l^{t+1} at the next time $t + 1$. The position of the agent at time $t + 1$ was calculated by $l^{t+1} = l^t + a$.

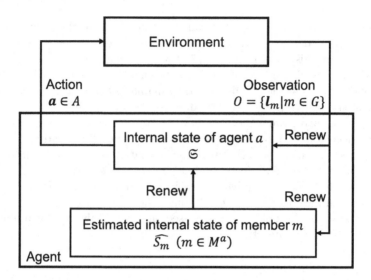

Fig. 1. Conceptual diagram of a distance norm-aware decision-making method for a computational agent based on the estimation of other group members' internal states. It shows the input and output of the agent at a step t.

2.2   Internal State

Value Functions. The decision-making system for an agent consisted of the agent's own internal state $\mathfrak{S}$ and the estimated internal state of others $\widehat{S_m}$. The $\widehat{S_m}$ was used to renew $\mathfrak{S}$ to realize action decisions based on others' estimations. Each internal state $\mathfrak{S} = \{V_{nbd}, V_{wh}\}$ and $\widehat{S_m} = \{\widehat{V_{nbd}^m}\}$ comprises functions V. Therefore, renewing the internal states means updating those functions.

In this study, the functions are called value functions. An agent uses a value function to estimate adaptive behavior according to norms implicitly shared by a specific group. The value function assigns a set of values to a set of actions that an agent can perform and a set of norms to which it can adhere. This set of values indicates the desirability of performing a certain behavior or deciding based on a certain norm within a particular group. As this study aims to adapt to the norm of distance shared within a group, a set of values or preferences for maintaining distance d with others was assigned to a set D that includes distance d as an element. The most valuable distance $d^* = \arg\max V(d)$ in the value function then became the reference for determining the agent's behavior. Therefore, based on the distance d^*, the agent attempts to move to a position where the distance between itself and others is close to d^*.

In this study, an agent has two types of value functions that includes its internal states, defined as the whole value function V_{wh} and the neighborhood value function V_{nbd}, respectively. The former was a value function for estimating the distance norm maintained by the group, and the latter is a value function for estimating the distance norm maintained by each group member with others in its own neighborhood. About these two functions, the agent attempted to adapt to both the dynamics of movement within the group and the distance to be maintained from others around the agent. It was expected that this would allow agents to become adaptively mobile with respect to both macro and micro-movements within the group.

Update Value Functions. Each value function was renewed at each time step Δt. The update equation for the overall value function V_{wh} is shown in Eqs. 1 and 2.

$$V_{wh}(d) \leftarrow (1 - \alpha)V_{wh}(d) + \alpha \left(R_{wh}(d) + \gamma \max V_{wh}(d) \right) \tag{1}$$

$$R_{wh}(d) = \sum_{d' \in D^a} \left\{ \exp \left(-\frac{(d' - d)^2}{\text{kurtosis}_V} \right) \right\} \tag{2}$$

The distance d, which is the argument of the function, was an element of the following set D, with u_d as the unit.

$$d \in D = \{u_d n \mid 0 \leq n \leq d_{\max}, n \in \mathbb{N}\} \tag{3}$$

The set D^a as shown Eq. 4 was the set whose elements were the distances between m_i and m_j, when $M^a = \{m_n \mid n = 1, 2, \ldots, \text{gs}, n \neq a\}$ is the set whose elements were others seen from the agent.

$$D^a = \{d_{i,j} = \|l_i - l_j\| \mid i, j \in M^a, i \neq j\} \tag{4}$$

The update equation for the neighborhood value function V_{nbd} is shown in the Eqs. 5 to 9.

$$V_{nbd}(d) \leftarrow (1 - \alpha)V_{nbd}(d) + \alpha \left(R_{nbd}(d) + \gamma \max_D V_{nbd}(d) \right) \tag{5}$$

$$R_{nbd}(d) = \sum_{m \in M^a} \left\{ \exp \left(-\frac{(d - \arg\max \widehat{V^m_{nbd}})^2}{\text{kurtosis}_V} \right) \right\} \tag{6}$$

$$\widehat{V^m_{nbd}}(d) \leftarrow (1 - \alpha)\widehat{V^m_{nbd}}(d) + \alpha \left(\widehat{R^m_{nbd}}(d) + \gamma \max_D \widehat{V^m_{nbd}}(d) \right) \tag{7}$$

$$\widehat{R^m_{nbd}}(d) = \sum_{d' \in D^{a \to m}_{nbd}} \left\{ \exp \left(-\frac{(d' - d)^2}{\text{kurtosis}_V} \right) \right\} \tag{8}$$

$$D^{a \to m}_{nbd} = \{d_{i,j} = \|l_i - l_j\| \mid i, j \in M^{a \to m}_{nbd} \cup \{m\}, i \neq j\} \tag{9}$$

Eqs. 5 and 6 renewed the value function V_{nbd}. It is necessary to derive the value function $\widehat{V^m_{nbd}}$ for the estimated internal state of the other member m in Eq. 7. Let $M^{a \to m}_{nbd}$ be a set whose elements are the neighbors of a specific other member m from the viewpoint of an agent a. The set $D^{a \to m}_{nbd}$ is a set whose elements were the distances between the elements of the set $M^{a \to m}_{nbd}$ and the position l of member m itself. The set of distances is represented by Eq. 9. However, the number of others designated as neighbors, NBD, was constant regardless of the group size gs.

The agent calculated the value function $\widehat{V_{nbd}^m}$, which is estimated based on the distance that each of the others m in the group maintained from the other members and renewed its own neighborhood value function V_{nbd} based on this estimated functions $\widehat{V_{nbd}^m} \in \widehat{S_m}$. This means that the agent estimated the internal state of others and renewed its own internal state based on that estimate.

Decision-Making. After renewing the value functions that constituted the internal states, the agent outputs action a based on those value functions. The actions a_{nbd} and a_{wh} were calculated based on the respective value functions V_{nbd} and V_{wh}, and the action a^t to be executed by the agent at time t was determined by the following Eq. 11.

$$a^t = \rho a_{nbd} + (1 - \rho)a_{wh} \quad 0 \leq \rho \leq 1 \tag{10}$$

The action a consisted of actions a_{nbd} and a_{wh}, each of which was calculated based on the value functions V_{nbd}, V_{wh}. These actions were weighted through the constant ρ, and the action a was calculated.

The actions a_{nbd}, a_{wh} were calculated using Eqs. 11 and 12, respectively.

$Q(a)$ in Eqs. 13 and 14 will hold a high value if the difference between $\arg \max V$ and $d'_{a,m}$ is small. $\arg \max V$ is the argument with the greatest value (i.e., distance) in a value function. $d'_{a,m}$ is a distance that agent a would maintain with another member m if it moved by performing action a'.

$$a_{nbd} = \arg \max Q_{nbd}(a) \tag{11}$$

$$a_{wh} = \arg \max Q_{wh}(a) \tag{12}$$

$$Q_{nbd}(a) = \sum_{m \in M_{nbd}^a} \left\{ \exp\left(-\frac{(d'_{a,m} - \arg \max V_{nbd})^2}{\text{kurtosis}_Q}\right) \right\} \tag{13}$$

$$Q_{wh}(a) = \sum_{m \in M_{nbd}^a} \left\{ \exp\left(-\frac{(d'_{a,m} - \arg \max V_{wh})^2}{\text{kurtosis}_Q}\right) \right\} \tag{14}$$

$$d'_{a,m} = \|(l^t + a) - l_m\| \tag{15}$$

We defined the argument a of the function Q in Eqs. 13 and 14 by Eq. 16. This argument is an element a of the set A of actions that can be chosen by the agent. The action a was calculated by centering the agent's position, specifying the radius, r, and the direction of movement θ.

$$a = (r \cos \theta, r \sin \theta) \in A \tag{16}$$

$$r \in \{u_r n \mid 0 \leq n \leq \text{magnitude}, n \in \mathbb{N}\} \tag{17}$$

$$\theta \in \left\{ \frac{2\pi n}{\text{direction}} \mid 0 \leq n < \text{direction}, n \in \mathbb{N} \right\} \tag{18}$$

By using the method described above, the agent's output, action a^t, was computed. The agent moved from position l^t to a position l^{t+1} at the next time step $t + 1$ when the action was conducted. In this study, the agent repeated the above observation and action at each time step Δt from the beginning to the end of the simulation scenario in a virtual space and tried to adaptively move with group members that were controlled to move according to the scenario.

3   Simulation

3.1   Scenario

We prepared controlled agents that moved in a virtual space to evaluate the proposed model based on the experimental scenario. We evaluated whether or not the distance norm-aware agent could adaptively move in the scenarios in the dynamic movement scenarios of the group, in which an agent equipped with the proposed model participated in the group of controlled agents. Moreover, we developed "gathering–dispersion scenario" based on the scenarios used in our previous study.

Figure 2 presents a virtual space for an evaluation simulation and agents with blue dots. These agents moved in a two-dimensional plane. In this scenario, the agents CA_{an}, whose movements were controlled top-down, formed a physical circle. By changing the radius of the circle, the agents moved while maintaining the circle. This created a scenario in which the distance agents maintained from others changed over time. When the number of members in the agent group is gs, each controlled agent CA_{an} moved toward the position $l_{an}(t)$, as shown in Eq. 19.

$$l_{an}(t) = \begin{bmatrix} r(t) - r(t) \cdot \cos \theta_{an} \\ r(t) \cdot \sin \theta_{an} \end{bmatrix} \tag{19}$$

$$\theta_{an} = 2\pi \times an/gs \qquad an \in \{0, 1, \ldots, gs - 1\} \tag{20}$$

In this scenario, the agent $CA_{an=0}$ did not move, and agents $CA_{an\neq0}$ moved while maintaining a circle of radius $r(t)$. In this scenario, the radius $r(t)$ was changed in the manner shown in Table 1. At the beginning of the scenario, the radius was maintained at 5 m. Thereafter, the radius was decreased by 0.1 m every 0.5 s. After the radius reached 1 m, it was maintained for a while and then increased by 0.1 m every 0.5 s. After the radius reached 5 m, it was maintained for a few seconds and the scenario was terminated.

The controlled agents CA in this scenario shared the same distance. Thus, each CA dynamically shared the distance it wanted to maintain from the others through moving so that the CAs were equally spaced on the circumference. Although this distance was shared through top-down control, the agent with the proposed model was not informed of the top-down instructions but only of the position of all agents observed at time t. In this simulation, it was replaced by one of the controlled agents CA the agent in the proposed model. When the number of group members is gs, the group contains one controlled agent gs − 1 and one agent with the proposed model. We evaluated whether the agent can

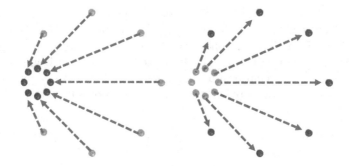

Fig. 2. Multiple blue agents moving in a controlled manner along the scenario. The red dotted arrows indicated the paths of the agents' movements. The left figure shows the situation in which the agents move to make the circle smaller (gathering scenario) and the right figure presents the situation in which the agents move to make the circle bigger (dispersal scenario). The two scenarios were run continuously in the simulation. (Color figure online)

Table 1. Radius Shared by Scenario-based agents.

sec t	shared radius $r(t)$
$0 \leq t < 5$	$r(t) = 5$
$5 \leq t < 25$	$r(t) = -0.2t + 6$
$25 \leq t < 30$	$r(t) = 1$
$30 \leq t < 55$	$r(t) = 0.16t - 3.8$
$55 \leq t < 60$	$r(t) = 5$

adaptively move according to the behavior of the $gs - 1$ agents moving according to the scenario.

3.2   Agent for Comparison

As shown in this simulation, one agent in a group attempted to move in a group norm-aware manner based only on the location information of other group members. To assess the proposed method through comparison, we performed simulations with the method proposed in this study and with the method proposed in our previous study. We verified the effectiveness of the proposed method in introducing the concept of neighbors.

3.3   Evaluation

A Distance norm-aware agent was evaluated by measuring the difference between the agent's actual path and its ideal path along the scenario and the way the agent kept its distance from the other members. Table 2 shows the conditions

Table 2. Conditions of GNM agent.

Conditions of Simulation	
group size gs	$4, 5, 6, 7, 8$
frequency of updating radius $r(t)$	0.1 [s]
frequency of renewing value functions Δt	0.5 [s]
Conditions of Simulation	
max distance $d_{\max}$	20.0 [m]
neighborhood number NBD	2
distance unit u_d	0.1 [m]
learning rate α	0.3
Discount Factorγ	0.7
parameter for renewing the value function kurtosis$_V$	1
parameter for renewing the Q value kurtosis$_Q$	10
weight of actions ρ	0.5
range unit u_r	0.1 [m]
distance magnitude	6
direction	8

of this simulation. The same values were assigned to the parameters that the previously and currently proposed group norm-aware agents have in common.

As shown in the two images in Fig. 2, the leftmost blue agent CA_0 did not move. Each agent number an was assigned clockwise from that agent CA_0, and an agent with the proposed model was placed at the initial position $l_x(0)$ of the controlled agent CA_x in the elements of the set $\{an \mid 1 \leq an \leq gs/2, an \in \mathbb{N}\}$ (see Eq. 19). The controlled agent CA_x was located at position $l_x(0)$, where the agent with the proposed model was placed at the beginning of the scenario, and was removed from the virtual environment. Because the position $l_{x,CA}$ of the agent CA_x moving ideally along the scenario could be measured, we compared the position $l_{x,GNAA}(t)$ of the distance norm-aware agent CA_{GNAA} in the virtual space with the position $l_{x,CA}(t)$ of CA_x. The two evaluation methods were described in detail as follows:

Adaptation to Shared Norm. The controlled agents dynamically shared the distance that they should keep from each other. Let CA_{self} be a control agent, and let $CA_n, (n \neq self)$ be other controlled agent from the point of view of that agent CA_n. Let D_{self} be the set of distances $d_{self,n}$ between those agentsCA_{self} and CA_n. d_{min}, the smallest value of the elements of D_{self} is considered an acceptable distance to the others for the controlled agent CA_{self}. As the distance d_{min} was shared among the controlled agents in the scenario, we defined its value as the shared distance norm d_{norm}. The distance d_{nbdCA} between the agent with the proposed model CA_{GNAA} and the nearest CA was compared against that

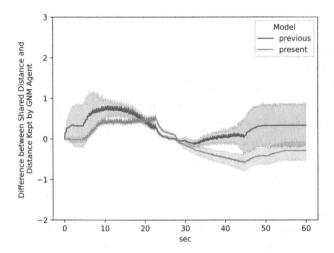

Fig. 3. Time series graph of the difference between the distance shared through a controlled agent and the distance kept by the computational agent with the agents in the neighborhood.

distance norm by calculating the value of Eq. 21. This measure validated whether the proposed agent can adapt to the distance norm to be followed. The closer the value of Eq. 21 was to 0, the more the proposed agent was adapted to the distance norm.

$$d_{\mathrm{norm}} - d_{\mathrm{nbdCA}} \tag{21}$$

Adaptation to Scenario. The controlled agents moved in a distance-aware manner with the other. Though calculating the distance between the position $l_{x,\mathrm{CA}}(t)$ of agent CA_x and the position $l_{x,\mathrm{GNAA}}(t)$ of the distance norm-aware agent $\mathrm{CA}_{\mathrm{GNAA}}$, we calculated the difference between the ideal position in the scenario and the actual position of the proposed agent. We verified this metric of adaptation to the scenario to which how similar the movement path was to that of the control agent. Then, we evaluated this metric to the naturalness of the proposed agent's movement and path.

3.4   Result

Figure 3 displays time-series data on the degree to which agents equipped with the new proposed model (present) and the comparison model (previous) adapted to the shared distance norm for all group sizes gs. Additionally, Fig. 4 presents box plots of the degree of adaptation of each model to the distance norm. The mean and standard deviation of the new model ($M = -0.066, SD = 0.508$) were closer to zero than those of the old model ($M = 0.287, SD = 0.927$).

Figure 5 presents the time-series data of how well the agent with the new proposed model (present) and the comparison model (previous) adapted to the

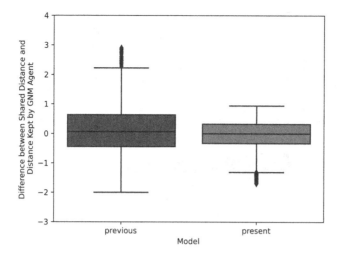

Fig. 4. Box plot of the difference between the distance shared by the controlled agent and the distance kept by the computational agent with the agents in the neighborhood.

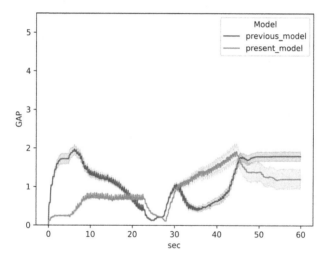

Fig. 5. Time series graph of the distance between the ideal position and the actual agent position.

scenarios for all group sizes gs. In addition, Fig. 6 displays box plots of the degree of adaptation of each model to the scenarios. The mean and standard deviation of the new model ($M = 0.938, SD = 1.00$) were closer to zero those the old model ($M = 1.14, SD = 0.791$). However, the new model contained many outliers which occur at population size gs = 5. Figure 7 indicated the time-series data for adaptation to the scenarios for each group size. The larger the group size gs, the closer the value of the adaptation index to zero. Thus, the ideal position and

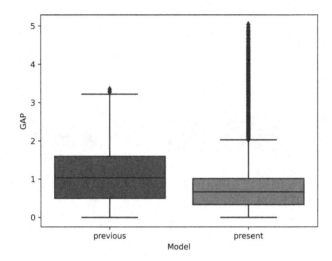

Fig. 6. Box plot of the distance between the ideal position and the actual agent position.

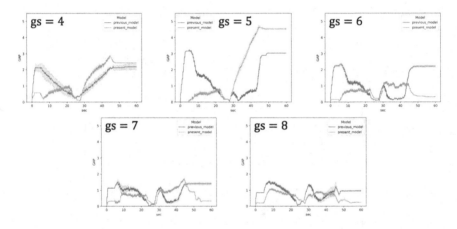

Fig. 7. Time series graph of the distance between the ideal position and the actual agent position for each group size gs.

the position of the agent with the new model did not deviate significantly. On the other hand, the position of the agent with the new model that estimated the others' position deviated significantly from the ideal position, particularly in the scattering task after 30 s for gs = 5.

3.5   Discussion

The results of the adaptation to distance norm indices showed that the distance norm-aware agent that considered its neighbors moved more adaptively to the distance norm maintained by the control agent on the spot regardless of group size or initial location. Additionally, the new model that introduces the concept of "near neighbors" shows less variation in movement paths, which indicates that stable movement is achieved regardless of group size and initial location.

The results of the scenario adaptation indices indicated that the larger the group size, the more adaptively the distance norm-aware agent that considered the concept of neighbor-others moved to the scenario. When the group size was gs = 5, the agents with the new model moved extremely far from the ideal movement path. This may hinder the current method of the proposed model to the natural movement when the group size is small. One of the reasons for this phenomenon may be that regardless of the group size, the number of neighbors in this simulation remained constant.

One limitation of this study is that there was no subjective assessment of the movement of the agent by human subjects. We evaluated distance norm-aware agents using only objective measures, such as location information of the movement path. However, shared distance and group norms exist intersubjectively in a group, and it is necessary to evaluate whether the proposed agent is adapted to them or not through human subjectivity. For instance, even if the score of adaptation to distance norms or scenarios is low, it may be judged by a human being that the group is in harmony to keep the circle. Based on the subjective judgments, the proposed model should be evaluated comprehensively.

This simulation was performed in a scenario with extreme distance norm variation. It is required to study the proposed model after formulating real-world scenarios. For instance, a situation in which a group of mobile humans fluctuates the distance maintained by its members in response to the surrounding environment. It is also required to consider the extent to which the adaptation of the robot to distance norms affects privacy concerns and societal acceptance.

4   Conclusion

This study evaluates whether agents using our proposed model can adaptively move within a group of agents in a scenario-controlled virtual space. Herein, we focused on the norms of distance shared within the group and assumed that adaptive behavior to these norms would enhance the naturalness of the agents. Moreover, we assessed the mobility of distance norm-aware agents based solely on objective measures observable in a virtual space. We found that the new model, which incorporates the concept of neighbor-others, outperformed the model without this concept, both in terms of distance norms and adaptation to the simulation scenario. In the future, we plan to analyze the simulation results in more detail and evaluate the distance normative agents based on human subjectivity and impressions.

Acknowledgments. This work was supported in part by the Japan Society for the Promotion of Science (JSPS) KAKENHI under Grants JP23K16983 and JP21K12099.

References

1. Tapus, A., et al.: Perceiving the person and their interactions with the others for social robotics–a review. Pattern Recogn. Lett. **118**, 3–13 (2019)
2. Pandey, A., Pandey, S., Parhi, D.R.: Mobile robot navigation and obstacle avoidance techniques: a review. Int. Robot. Autom. J. **2**(3), 96–105 (2017)
3. Charalampous, K., Kostavelis, I., Gasteratos, A.: Recent trends in social aware robot navigation: a survey. Robot. Auton. Syst. **93**, 85–104 (2017)
4. Möller, R., et al.: A survey on human-aware robot navigation. Robot. Auton. Syst. **145**, 103837 (2021)
5. Hall, E.T.: The Hidden Dimension. Doubleday (1966)
6. Sorokowska, A., et al.: Preferred interpersonal distances: a global comparison. J. Cross Cult. Psychol. **48**(4), 577–592 (2017)
7. Fuse, Y., Tokumaru, M.: Navigation model for a robot as a human group member to adapt to changing conditions of personal space. J. Adv. Comput. Intell. Intell. Inf. **24**(5), 621–629 (2020)
8. Fuse, Y., Ayedoun, E., Tokumaru, M.: Group norm-aware robot adaptively maintains suitable interpersonal distance in human-robot group. Int. J. Affect. Eng. **21**(3), 191–201 (2022)

A Telepresence Robot Partner for Remote Work: An Exploration into Design and Its Psychological Effect

Kunlin Jhang and Wei-Chi Chien[✉]

Department of Industrial Design, National Cheng Kung University, Tainan City, Taiwan (R.O.C.)
chien@xtdesign.org

Abstract. The COVID-19 pandemic significantly shifted the traditional workspace to the domestic environment. Social isolation inspires us to consider telepresence technologies to reshape our working experience. This study is inspired by the psychological concept of social facilitation and explores its implementation in telepresence robots. A telepresence robot representing somebody with minimal cues was designed and tested in our experiment on a puzzle task. We suspect a facilitative effect of the robot on the participants' work efficiency and self-efficacy through its social presence. To evaluate the design, different modalities of the "observer" were set up as different experiment conditions. The initial result shows no significant social facilitation effect. However, this study contributes to the ongoing debate on the effectiveness of robots in remote work environments.

Keywords: social facilitation · human-robot interaction · telepresence robot · social robot

1 Introduction

In the post-pandemic era, remote work has become increasingly prominent. The shift from traditional to home-based work environments has changed the work dynamics and has profound psychological impacts, particularly in the psychosocial demands. Social interaction in remote settings has evolved [1]. Face-to-face encounters are significantly reduced, while virtual videoconferencing and voice chats have surged [2–4]. This change led to decreased trust and increased social isolation, highlighting the importance of maintaining a sense of coworkers' presence for productivity and a positive working experience [2, 4].

By embodying the physical presence of remote individuals and merging mediated interaction with a human-like presence, telepresence robots offer the opportunity to bridge the socialization gap in remote work scenarios. The characterization of how to allow remote individuals to be present drives our research interests. Some recent studies suggested the potential design of telepresence robots in cooperative scenarios to enhance the quality of remote work [6]. From the sociopsychological perspective, we

M. Kurosu and A. Hashizume (Eds.): HCII 2024, LNCS 14685, pp. 105–115, 2024.
https://doi.org/10.1007/978-3-031-60412-6_8

are especially interested in the social facilitation theory. Social facilitation suggests that one person's performance can be promoted by the presence of other observers [7]. In this study, we prototyped a telepresence robot that conveys minimal information about the remote partner, such as ambient sound and behavioral cues, and conducted an explorative experiment.

Before we show our result, a review of related concepts and theories is presented as follows.

2 Background and Related Work

2.1 Telepresence Robot

Telepresence robots exemplify the concept of "tele-embodiment", offering a sense of presence in distant locations through processing sensory inputs, representing them, and merging avatars or robots [8, 9]. Recent studies have shown significant psychological and social impacts of telepresence robots. For instance, the study by Kristoffersson, Coradeschi, Eklundh, and Loutfiresearchers identified the social richness and a sense of real spatial presence when applying telepresence robots in the healthcare context [10].

The sense of presence strongly lies in the interactivity of the robot [11] and the strategy applied to represent the remote partner [12], such as a "promise" from a robot [8]. Almeida, Menezes, and Dias' [13] review of telepresence and co-presence robots follows the tradition of CMC and focuses on human-robot interaction in a pragmatic context and shows a wide range of discussion about the interaction strategies and functional principles. However, a more fundamental factor is the way we perceive robots.

The practices of how users interact with telepresence robots can be diverse – they can be human-like targets or machines. This difference has a further impact on the experience with the telepresence robots and determines whether sociopsychological mechanisms would involve [14, 15] and whether a humane "attitude" towards the robots is motivated [16]. In other words, the social presence of a robot is, therefore, not only fundamental but also the essential factor of its being [17].

2.2 Social Presence

Social presence refers to the perception of others' presence or the sense of connection with others from a long distance. Especially in the mediated and virtual context, social presence implies being in a shared 'virtual space' [18–20], allowing contextualized communication and complex interpretation of the remote partner [21, 22]. Another related concept is co-presence [23], which refers to the awareness that one is sharing or being in the same space with the remoted partner. While they exist physically in different locations, their interpersonal practice often follows or learns from their face-to-face experiences. Furthermore, their perception of each other's physical beings can be leveraged, which is why telepresence robots can contribute to remote social presence [13, 17].

As mentioned before, whether the virtual representation can be personified conditions users' interaction strategy to be social and interpersonal [24] and involves social-cultural practices [23, 25]. The degree of perceived social presence can be influenced by various factors, such as the appearance and behavior of agents, situational conditions, and individual psychological traits [26, 27]. Our social experience is, therefore, designable through the implemented telepresence agents. For example, adopting social agent robots could provide social connection, reducing loneliness [28]. To reduce social complexity or increase social distance, reducing social cues in the mediated human-agent interaction could avoid adverse effects, such as social anxiety and fear [14, 27]. By shaping the telepresence agents, we could also help remote workers develop unique social patterns, maintaining interaction and connection with the partners and thus improving work efficiency and satisfaction.

2.3 Social Facilitation

Social facilitation was first introduced by Triplett when explaining why people cycled faster when being watched [29]. The theory suggests that one person's performance can be affected by the presence of audiences, especially in simple or well-practiced tasks [7]. In contrast, if the task is perceived as unfamiliar and challenging, the audience's presence results in social inhibition and reduces efficiency [30]. Social facilitation is a complex phenomenon whose mechanism is not fully understood yet. Various hypotheses have been proposed. For example, researchers proposed four possible mechanisms of social facilitation: uncertainty, evaluation apprehension, self-awareness, and distraction-conflict [7, 22, 31–33], explained as follows:

Uncertainty Hypothesis. Zajonc's drive theory considers social facilitation as our born nature. When our organisms engage in threats in the social environment, they need to remain alerted to respond quickly to danger. As a result, our performance can be socially facilitated [7, 33].

Evaluation Apprehension Hypothesis. Cottrell's social evaluation theory asserts that people develop unconscious expectations of the future based on their social experiences in the past. Therefore, individuals concern themselves with others' evaluations, leading to changes in task efficiency and, subsequently, in the socialized context [30, 32].

Self-awareness Hypothesis. The presence of observers may also motivate individuals to align their current performance with an idealized image, thereby motivating a more qualitative behavior; however, only when the individual feels competent to accomplish the task [32, 34].

Distraction-Conflict Hypothesis. During the task, the concentration can be distracted by external factors, such as the presence of the audience, which forces the performer to pay more attention to the task. As a result, cognitive overload improves the quality of performance. This explanation also suggests that facilitation happens only in simple but not in complex tasks [31].

Despite the mechanisms, personality is another factor influencing the effects of social facilitation. Confident individuals are more likely to be affected by social facilitation, while anxious people get impaired when being observed in a task [22].

Social facilitation has extended to emerging areas of human-computer interaction and remote work. Although some studies suggest that social facilitation can be activated by telepresence or virtual agent, others found no difference in their experiments [35, 36]. So far, it is difficult to answer whether social facilitation exists in computer-mediated conditions [37].

3 Design: *PresencePeer*

In our experiment, we designed a robot, *PresencePeer* (Fig. 1) to simulate an audience in a work scenario. The core concept behind the robot's design was 'minimal information' to explore the idea of social facilitation. The robot operated autonomously, but we explained to participants that they were connected to the teleoperator via sensors on the robot.

The robot had an egg-like shape, with its head lifting from the shell to indicate an online remote observer. Its activation triggered various changes based on preset activity levels, expressed through sound and facial expressions. Office background noise was played as sound, increasing in volume with higher activity levels. Facial expressions were displayed on an OLED screen on its head, varying with activity: normal state with two round eyes, reading state with eyes scanning from left to right, thinking state with blinking eyes, and standby mode with half-open, half-closed eyes and minimal sound.

Fig. 1. PresencePeer: (left) off, (middle) active, (right) usage scenario

4 Evaluation Experiments

This study employed a controlled experiment to test the effects of different modalities of presence. Participants were required to complete jigsaw puzzles under three distinct modalities: camera surveillance, a telepresence robot, and a real person in the same room. We selected monochromatic puzzles in a single color and produced multiple puzzle sets using an online puzzle generator (*puzzle.telegnom.org*) with consistent parameters and random seeds to ensure the equal difficulty of each puzzle set.

Puzzles were chosen to test participants' working performance because they require shifting between different intelligent skills, such as spatial reasoning, pattern recognition [38], concentration on a complex process, and self-regulation to maintain one's patience [39–41]. The transfer between different skills could invite the impacts from the observer's presence. Besides, the outcome of the task is evident and observable to an audience.

The three modalities of the observer's presence were randomly ordered to reduce the learning bias. (1) Camera modality: Participants perform the task under observation via an iPad camera, conditioning the lowest level of the agent's presence. (2) Telepresence robot modality: The telepresence robot presented in the previous section is presented to the participants. We informed the participants that the robot was an agent of another participant in a remote space. (3) Real Person Modality: The first author was present and performing the same puzzle task in the same room next to the participants during the task. This modality was expected to have the highest level of presence (Fig. 2).

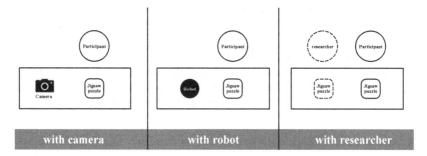

Fig. 2. Settings of the three experiment conditions

Our measurements include the quality of task performance, self-reported self-efficacy, and perceived social presence. The performance quality was calculated by the percentage of puzzle pieces connected to a second piece. For example, the total number of the jigsaw puzzle is 64. If the participants have assembled five and another three pieces, the score of the puzzle task is 12.5% (8/64).

We use the New General Self-Efficacy Scale (NGSE) [42] to measure the perceived performance quality and to understand the participants' confidence in completing tasks. The scale employs a quantitative method, rating each item on a Likert scale ranging from 1 to 5. Also, to evaluate the perceived presence of each modality, we used Biocca's [43] design and employed the two constructs, co-presence and behavioral engagement. Participants score on a Likert scale ranging from 1 to 5. Finally, a brief interview aimed at understanding participants' experiences across the three conditions was conducted after all the tests.

5   Result

A total of six participants (graduate students from the same college, two females and four males) were recruited in this experiment. The analyses are mainly based on descriptive methods due to the limited sample size and the unexpected complexity of psychological impacts by the different modalities.

5.1   General Comparison Between the Three Modalities

A general descriptive result of the scores is presented in Table 1 and Fig. 3. Under the camera surveillance condition, participants showed moderate task performance with an average correct rate of 40.36% (SD = 17.74%). In contrast, the telepresence robot condition seemed to facilitate a higher task completion rate, with participants achieving an average correct rate of 50% (SD = 9.63%). The presence of a real person in the room resulted in a task completion rate of 46.09% (SD = 12.61%), which is slightly lower than that of the telepresence robot but higher than the camera condition.

Interestingly, despite the minimal physical presence in this scenario, the social presence of the camera was perceived to be moderately high, with an average rating of 2.87 (SD = 0.56). The condition of a telepresence robot was reported to have the highest average social presence rating at 3.21 (SD = 0.34). The social presence score of a real person was only 2.96 (SD = 0.54), suggesting that a real human presence did not significantly enhance the feeling of social presence compared to the telepresence robot.

The self-reported self-efficacy of the camera modality among participants, with an average score of 3.00 (SD = 0.82). The self-efficacy scores of the telepresence robot were lower than the camera condition, averaging 2.60 (SD = 1.09). Real person condition had the highest average self-efficacy score at 3.31 (SD = 0.96), indicating that participants felt most confident about their performance in the presence of another human.

Table 1. Averages and standard deviations of task performance, self-efficacy, and social presence across the three conditions

Condition	Puzzle Performance		Social presence		Self-efficacy	
	M (%)	S.D. (%)	M	S.D	M	S.D
Camera	40.36	17.74	2.87	0.56	3.00	0.82
Robot	50.00	9.63	3.21	0.34	2.60	1.09
Real human	46.09	12.61	2.96	0.54	3.31	0.96

Across the three conditions, the highest average puzzle task scores were observed with the telepresence robot, while the lowest were under the surveillance camera condition. However, the result of three measures among the three modalities has no statistical difference. Considering that the perceived social presence can be highly personal, we analyzed the individual cases as follows.

5.2 Individual Differences

In our experiment, P3, P4, and P6 have similar experience profiles (Fig. 4). They have the highest puzzle performance scores among all participants but show rare differences between the three modalities (differences less than 5%). P3 and P4 also report the highest self-efficacy in the real human condition and the lowest in the robot. In these cases, social facilitation might exist in the human audience condition, although the actual performance remains the same. However, the perceived social presence is reported at a similar and moderate level in all modalities. Therefore, it is critical to advocate the social facilitation effect.

P5 performed significantly better in robot and real human conditions (Fig. 5). However, in the interview, the participant reported a potential learning curve during the

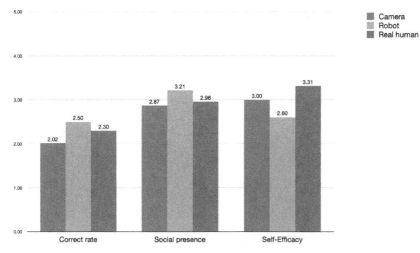

Fig. 3. Puzzle performance, social presence, and self-efficacy

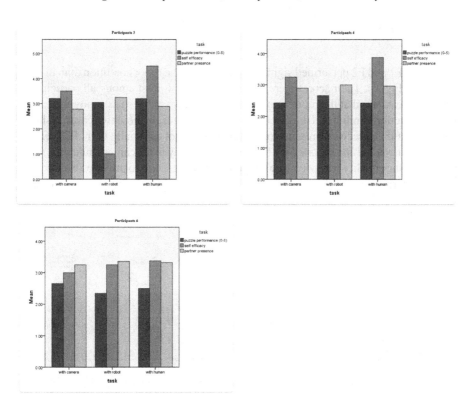

Fig. 4. Puzzle performance, self-efficacy, and perceived presence of P3, P4, and P6

experiment. This participant reported extremely high self-efficacy in the robot condition and found the noise produced by the robot very bothering during the test. This fits the explanation of the distraction conflict effect. However, the perceived social presence does not differ from other conditions.

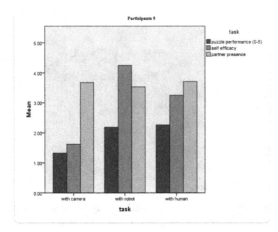

Fig. 5. Puzzle performance, self-efficacy, and perceived presence of P5

Finally, P1 and P2 performed significantly better in the robot condition than in other conditions (Fig. 6). Their scores were, noteworthily, the lowest among all participants. A possible reason is that the robot's noise, which they also reported as annoying, caused higher distraction conflict and the perceived social presence. In these two cases, it should be noted that the perceived presence of real humans is not especially high. P2 seems to prefer working alone and reported the highest self-efficacy in the camera modality, while the performance quality was poor. The telepresence robot seems to provide an alternative between interpersonal and personal conditions, through which the task performance benefits.

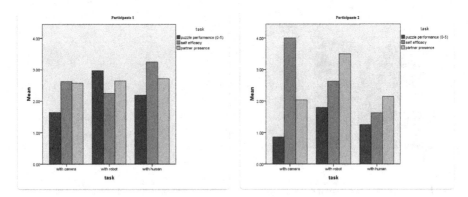

Fig. 6. Puzzle performance, self-efficacy, and perceived presence of P1 and P2

5.3 Summary

Overall, we may argue that social facilitation is not a generalizable phenomenon. Also, the facilitation effects on task performance and perceived working efficiency are different. In the current experiment, the measurement of social presence seems problematic. In most cases, the participants did not report differences between the modalities. Interpretation of the data becomes difficult.

Despite this, we can identify different experience profiles for further exploration of the social facilitation theory. In our cases, the telepresence robot was reported to be a noisy device that significantly drew participants' attention. The distraction conflict hypothesis could explain why some participants performed best in the robot condition. However, in some cases, this works only mentally without actual facilitation in the performance, especially for those who solved the puzzles with no difficulties. In other cases, the distraction conflicts increased the quality of performance; however, the perceived self-efficacy was low. Different patterns of facilitation are obvious. Besides, P2 was a case showing the potential of a telepresence robot providing a balanced condition to improve working performance.

6 Conclusion and Discussion

In this study, we presented our prototype of a telepresence robot to facilitate remote workers' working efficiency and experience and conducted an experiment to evaluate its effects compared to other social modalities.

Some limitations are obvious in our experiment. The small sample size limits the analyses and interpretation of our data. Besides, it may be inaccurate to evaluate the performance of jigsaw puzzles. Depending on the playing strategies, the difficulty curve may be different. The finished pieces may not be very representative of the performance quality. Also, the social presence of the different modalities did not seem to be appropriately measured. We explain that the experiment was conducted in the lab, and the task is decontextualized, while social facilitation might lie in a strong social context. Compared to other mechanisms, the distraction conflict theory involving less social context was easier to identify in our experiment.

This study explores the telepresence robot as a strategy to evoke social facilitation in the remote work context. The result of prototyping the robot and evaluating the user experience shows complex experiences, such as different performance quality and perceived self-efficacy when dealing with the different observers' modalities. In general, social facilitation was not significantly observed in our study. However, some issues remain undiscovered and require research in the future, for example, a contextualized field study of the telepresence robot or a different design strategy of the telepresence robot. We should also consider the different paths toward social facilitation. The perceived self-efficacy and the actual performance quality should also be distinguished.

Acknowledgment. This paper is funded by the National Science and Technology Council, R.O.C. Taiwan (NSTC112–2410-H-006–075-).

References

1. Van Zoonen, W., Sivunen, A.E.: The impact of remote work and mediated communication frequency on isolation and psychological distress. Eur. J. Work Organ. Psy. **31**, 610–621 (2022)
2. Augstein, M., Neumayr, T., Schönböck, J., Kovacs, C.: Remote persons are closer than they appear: home, team and a lockdown. In: Proceedings of CHI 2023 Conference on Human Factors in Computing Systems. ACM, New York (2023)
3. Bleakley, A., et al.: Bridging social distance during social distancing: exploring social talk and remote collegiality in video conferencing. Human-Comp. Interact. **37**, 404–432 (2022)
4. Miller, C., Rodeghero, P., Storey, M.-A., Ford, D., Zimmermann, T.: "How was your weekend?" Software development teams working from home during covid-19. In: Proceedings of ICSE 2021 International Conference on Software Engineering. IEEE, New York (2021)
5. Röcker, C.: Informal communication and awareness in virtual teams – why we need smart technologies to support distributed teamwork. Commun. Inf. Sci. Manage. Eng. **2**, 1–15 (2012)
6. Muratbekova-Touron, M., Leon, E.: "Is there anybody out there?" Using a telepresence robot to engage in face time at the office. Inf. Technol. People **36**, 48–65 (2023)
7. Guerin, B.: Social Facilitation. Cambridge University Press (1993)
8. Cominelli, L., et al.: Promises and trust in human–robot interaction. Sci. Rep. **11**, 9687 (2021)
9. Paulos, E., Canny, J.: Ubiquitous tele-embodiment: applications and implications. Int. J. Hum. Comput. Stud. **46**, 861–877 (1997)
10. Kristoffersson, A., Coradeschi, S., Severinson Eklundh, K., Loutfi, A.: Sense of presence in a robotic telepresence domain. In: Stephanidis, C. (ed.) Universal Access in Human-Computer Interaction. Users Diversity, pp. 479–487. Springer, Heidelberg (2011). https://doi.org/10.1007/978-3-642-21663-3_51
11. Sugiyama, J., Tsetserukou, D., Miura, J.: NAVIgoid: robot navigation with haptic vision. In: Proceedings of SA 2011 SIGGRAPH Asia. ACM. New York (2011)
12. Choi, J.J., Kwak, S.S.: You are my robot: the impact of synchronized motion cues on receivers. Int. J. Control Autom. **9**, 249–258 (2016)
13. Almeida, L., Menezes, P., Dias, J.: Telepresence social robotics towards co-presence: a review. Appl. Sci. **12**(11), 5557 (2022). https://doi.org/10.3390/app12115557
14. Hwang, A.H.-C., Won, A.S.: Ideabot: investigating social facilitation in human-machine team creativity. In: Proceedings of the CHI 2021 Conference on Human Factors in Computing Systems, pp. 1–16. ACM, New York (2021)
15. Spatola, N., Huguet, P.: Cognitive impact of anthropomorphized robot gaze: anthropomorphic gaze as social cues. J. Hum. Robot Interact. **10**, 1–14 (2021)
16. Lee, M.K., Takayama, L.: "Now, i have a body": uses and social norms for mobile remote presence in the workplace. In: Proceedings of CHI 2011 Conference on Human Factors in Computing Systems. ACM, New York (2011)
17. Schouten, A.P., Portegies, T.C., Withuis, I., Willemsen, L.M., Mazerant-Dubois, K.: Robomorphism: examining the effects of telepresence robots on between-student cooperation. Comp. Human Behav. **126**, 106980 (2022)
18. Biocca, F.: The cyborg's dilemma: Progressive embodiment in virtual environments. J. Comp.-Mediated Commun. 3(2), (1997)
19. Sheridan, T.B.: Musings on telepresence and virtual presence. Presence Teleoperators Virtual Environ. **1**, 120–126 (1992)
20. Steuer, J.: Defining virtual reality: dimensions determining telepresence. J. Commun. **42**, 73–93 (1992)
21. Allport, F.H.: The influence of the group upon association and thought. J. Exp. Psychol. **3**, 159–182 (1920)

22. Uziel, L.: Individual differences in the social facilitation effect: a review and meta-analysis. J. Res. Pers. **41**, 579–601 (2007)
23. Nowak, K., Biocca, F.: The effect of the agency and anthropomorphism on users' sense of telepresence, copresence, and social presence in virtual environments. Presence Teleop. Virt. **12**, 481–494 (2003)
24. Slater, M., Steed, A.: Meeting people virtually: experiments in shared virtual environments. In: Schroeder, R. (ed.) The Social Life of Avatars: Presence and Interaction in Shared Virtual Environments, pp. 146–171. Springer, London (2002). https://doi.org/10.1007/978-1-4471-0277-9_9
25. Slater, M.: Place illusion and plausibility can lead to realistic behaviour in immersive virtual environments. Philos. Trans. R. Soc. B Biol. Sci. **364**, 3549–3557 (2009)
26. Allmendinger, K.: Social presence in synchronous virtual learning situations: the role of nonverbal signals displayed by avatars. Educ. Psychol. Rev. **22**, 41–56 (2010)
27. Oh, C.S., Bailenson, J.N., Welch, G.F.: A systematic review of social presence: definition, antecedents, and implications. Front. Robot. AI **5**, 114 (2018)
28. Broadbent, E., Stafford, R., MacDonald, B.: Acceptance of healthcare robots for the older population: review and future directions. Int. J. Soc. Robot. **1**, 319–330 (2009)
29. Triplett, N.: The dynamogenic factors in pacemaking and competition. Am. J. Psychol. **9**, 507–533 (1898)
30. Zajonc, R.B.: Social facilitation. Science **149**, 269–274 (1965)
31. Baron, R.A.: Distraction-conflict theory: an integration of attention, arousal and expectancy. Psychol. Rev. **93**, 29–49 (1986)
32. Cottrell, N.B.: T. In: McClintock, C.G. (ed.) Experimental Social Psychology, pp. 185–236. Holt McDougal, New York (1972)
33. Zajonc, R.B.: Feeling and thinking: preferences need no inferences. Am. Psychol. **35**, 151–175 (1980)
34. Carver, C.S., Scheier, M.F.: Attention and self-regulation: a control-theory approach to human behavior. In: Harvey, J.H., Ickes, W.J., Kidd, R.F. (eds.) New directions in psychology: Vol. 1. Basic processes in self-control and motivation, pp. 1–30. Holt, Rinehart and Winston, New York (1981)
35. Koban, K., Haggadone, B.A., Banks, J.: The observant android: Limited social facilitation and inhibition from a copresent social robot. Technol. Mind Behav. **2** (2021)
36. Irfan, B., Kennedy, J., Lemaignan, S., Papadopoulos, F., Senft, E., Belpaeme, T.: Social psychology and human-robot interaction: an uneasy marriage. In: Proceedings of HRI 2018 International Conference on Human-Robot Interaction. ACM, New York (2018)
37. Sterna, R., Strojny, P., Rębilas, K.: Can virtual observers affect our behavior? Social facilitation in virtual environments: a mini-review. Soc. Psychol. Bull. (2019)
38. Lin, C.-H., Chen, C.: Developing spatial visualization and mental rotation with a digital puzzle game at primary school level. Comp. Human Behav. **57**, 23–30 (2016)
39. Chesham, A., et al.: Search and match task: development of a taskified match-3 puzzle game to assess and practice visual search. Serious Games 7, e13620 (2019)
40. Fissler, P., Küster, O., Laptinskaya, D., Loy, L., Arnim, C.V., von, Kolassa, I.: Jigsaw puzzling taps multiple cognitive abilities and is a potential protective factor for cognitive aging. Front. Aging Neurosci. **10**, 299 (2018)
41. Garcia, A.C.: An explorer in a cardboard land: emotion, memory, and the embodied experience of doing jigsaw puzzles. Int. J. Play. **5**, 166–180 (2016)
42. Chen, G., Gully, S.M., Eden, D.: Validation of a new general self-efficacy scale. Organ. Res. Methods **4**, 62–83 (2001)
43. Biocca, F., Harms, C., Gregg, J.: The networked minds measure of social presence: pilot test of the factor structure and concurrent validity. In: 4th annual International Workshop on Presence, Philadelphia (2001)

Exploring the Impact of a Playing Catch Task on the Impression of Interaction with Conversational Robots
-A Comparative Study with a Task Incorporating Only Turn-Taking Factor-

Ryuto Katsuki[✉], Masayuki Ando, Kouyou Otsu, and Tomoko Izumi

Ritsumeikan University, 1-1-1 Noji-Higashi, Kusatsu, Shiga, Japan
is0500ve@ed.ritsumei.ac.jp, {mandou,k-otsu,
izumi-t}@fc.ritsumei.ac.jp

Abstract. Communication robots are utilized in various conversational service fields, but it is suggested that there is a psychological barrier for users to interact with robots. In our previous study, we proposed focusing on a task performed during a conversation with a robot to create a conversational environment where the user would be willing to converse with the robot. In this paper, as a continuation of our previous study, we discuss the effects of incorporating a playful task of playing catch during conversations with a robot. Although previous research has shown that introducing a task to play catch effectively supported smooth turn-taking, it was not clear whether this effect was unique to the catch task or whether it was found in tasks that visualize conversational turns in general. Therefore, to verify the impact of the two aspects that the task of playing catch has on the motivation, enjoyment, and smoothness of an interaction with a communication robot, we conducted an experiment to compare it with a case using a simple device that only supports the visualization of turn-taking. Although the effect of improving the motivation to interact cannot be confirmed, we found that the ball exchange in the proposed task contributes to the visualization of the conversation exchange and improves both the smoothness of interaction and the sense of enjoyment for users.

Keywords: Human-robot interaction (HRI) · Turn-taking · Conversational interaction support · Collaborative task with a robot

1 Introduction

Communication robots are expected to support the provision of services as service providers interact with users in various fields, such as commercial stores and care facilities for the elderly [1, 2]. However, existing research on robots suggests that some people may feel psychological barriers to and discomfort with interacting with robots [3, 4], which can be one reason why users do not fully accept services using communication robots. Our research aims to find a conversational environment in which such users are more accepting and willing to converse with robots. Existing studies address the alleviation of awkwardness in talking to a robot and the enhancement of the willingness to interact with a robot by using nonverbal cues to clarify the robot's intentions [5] or by considering the conversation structure [4, 6, 7]. However, to create an environment where people would like to interact more with robots, it is also important to focus not only on the performance of a robot itself and the content of the conversation but also on the task being performed when talking to the robot. For example, in a face-to-face conversation between humans, playing games or sports in parallel with a conversation is a trigger for knowing each other and building trust. This fact suggests that the design of environments incorporating playful tasks into human-robot interactions could be a factor in motivating a user's willingness to converse with a robot. Therefore, designing such a conversational environment will trigger an expansion of the scope of applications for communication robots. This is a different approach from existing studies that focus on the interaction partner's appearance or the conversational content's design.

Against this background, we have been studying enjoyable tasks that can be performed during a conversation with a robot to motivate the willingness to converse with robots. In our previous study, we proposed a playful task of playing catch with a robot during a conversation (Fig. 1) and verified the effectiveness of its introduction [8]. This task is the exchange of a ball between a robot and a user during their conversation. From our previous study, it is found that the task of playing catch can contribute to creating an enjoyable conversational environment and clarifying turn-taking in the conversation. Playing catch is a well-known game that is often used in human interactions, and it can be played while conversing. Therefore, the task of playing catch is expected to be an effective and playful task that can enhance a sense of conversation in the context of human-robot interaction (HRI). Additionally, playing catch involves two roles: pitcher and catcher. Therefore, by doing it in conjunction with conversation, it can represent the switching of turns between the speaker and the listener. Considering the task of playing catch in the context of HRI suggests that the task is useful in clarifying turn-taking in conversational situations with robots. In particular, this task could potentially be used as a means to clarify the timing of speech transitions and improve the ease of interacting with robots. Therefore, the task of playing catch is expected to be an effective and playful task to help smooth turn-taking in conversation between robots and humans. In summary, the task of playing catch may encompass two aspects that can improve a user's motivation to interact with robots: (1) creating a sense of conversation together and (2) supporting smooth turn-taking.

The observed results in our previous experiments suggest that playing catch contributes to the two points. However, our previous experiment aimed to clarify the effectiveness of introducing playing catch by comparing its presence or absence during a conversation. In the previous experiment, the effect on supporting turn-taking was significantly observed, but it is not clear whether the effect is due to the unique features of the task of playing catch. In other words, it is possible that the effects could be equally observed for other tasks that support turn-taking in conversation.

In this study, we aim to clarify how the characteristics of playing catch may contribute to a user's motivation to interact with robots. To achieve this, we experimented with a conversational situation with a robot to compare the task of playing catch as a proposed

Fig. 1. Concept of the proposed method.

method with a system that functioned only to visualize the status of turn-taking by lighting lamps.

2   Related Research

Previous studies in the HRI field have considered effective interaction designs for motivating users to interact with robots. Many of these studies focus on the representation of information by the robot's appearance and the design of the content of the conversation with the robot. For example, Obo et al. [5] found that conventional robots have difficulty mimicking nonverbal turn-taking behavior, which can lead to communication breakdowns in human-robot interactions. Their study considered mounting an LED display on a robot to encourage nodding and responding in interactions with the robot. The robot displays a "heart symbol" while speaking and a "diamond symbol" while waiting for a response. From their experiment, it was confirmed that a case setting with a "diamond symbol" display time of two seconds enhances a user's response to nodding or giving a response to a robot. This result indicates that the visualization of turn-taking in conversation with a robot influences users' behaviors and attitudes toward the robot. In addition, Uchida et al. [6] proposed an approach to making a robot itself appear to have a sense of value to improve interaction motivation. In this system, a robot responds to a user's utterance by either affirming or denying it. The robot can adapt its sense of value by adjusting its ratio of affirmative to negative responses. From their experiment, it was suggested that a conversational design in which the robot expresses its attitudes based on a clear perspective is a motivating factor for users to interact with it.

These studies focus on mechanisms for robots' appearances and emotional expressions to improve the quality of conversational interactions. However, as mentioned at the beginning of this paper, to increase a user's willingness to talk with robots, it is important to not only provide assistance in conversation but also make the task of interacting with the robot itself seem enjoyable. Cooney et al. [9] mention a similar idea that robots should be capable of enjoyably interacting with people in order to be socially accepted. They proposed a mechanism to recognize playful human gestures toward a robot, such as hugging or moving it. Then, they proposed a playful robot design that performs gestures to encourage users to do such interactions and provides a reward if the users do it. From their experiment, it was found that clear and sustained play suggestions from the robot have a positive impact on interactions, and users found enjoyment in various styles of play with the robot and in "pleasing" the robot. This research mentions the possibility that incorporating a non-verbal play element into conversational interactions with robots may contribute to engagement with the robots.

Our research focuses on clarifying the effects of robots and humans performing playful tasks together and on how such tasks contribute to conversational assistance. Prior research [8] suggests the effects of playing with a robot; however, it addresses the effects of a robot and a human sharing the same playful experience together. In addition, such playing might be used as a means of assistance in conversation to support smooth turn-taking. Our research represents a step toward clarifying how playful tasks with robots can contribute to conversational assistance.

3 Materials and Methods

3.1 Experimental Method and Comparison Metrics

The purpose of this study is to clarify how the characteristics of the task of playing catch during a human-robot conversation may contribute to a human's motivation to interact with a robot. Our previous study [8] showed that the task contributes to two elements: (1) the creation of a sense of conversation together and (2) the ease of conversation. As mentioned in our previous study, these elements are considered components of a user's "motivation to interact." Therefore, in this study, these elements are also regarded as evaluation metrics, in addition to "motivation to interact."

To achieve this purpose, we experimented to compare three types of conversations:

- Playing Catch condition: Participants play catch with a robot while conversing.
- Lamp condition: Participants converse with a robot by using a device which visualizes the turn-taking.
- Baseline: Participants converse with a robot without any system.

These conditions are similar in that participants are asked to converse with a robot, but the Playing Catch and Lamp conditions differ from the Baseline condition in that participants are asked to converse using original devices prepared for each condition. In the following section, we describe the devices used in the experiment before explaining the details of the experiment.

3.2 The Task of Playing Catch and Its Implementation

The task of playing catch was proposed in a previous study [8], and it is a task involving the exchange of a ball between a robot and a user during a conversation. The speaker passes the ball to the other side when he/she finishes speaking, and the receiver receives the ball before starting to speak. Therefore, the conversation proceeds synchronously with the ball exchange.

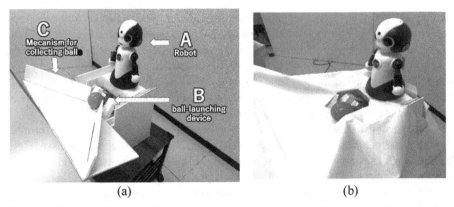

(a)   (b)

Fig. 2. (a) Configuration of the prototype system for playing catch with the robot. (b) Appearance of the system during the experiment (covered by the sheet).

In a previous study [8], we also developed a prototype system that can exchange a ball in conjunction with a conversation with a robot. In this previous system, a user throws a ball toward a robot, which is received by ramps on either side of the robot. In the experiments described below, we used a modified version of the prototype system from [8] to improve the stability of the ball ejection and to allow for the receipt of the ball in front of the robot. The newly developed system has the same basic equipment configuration as the previous system. The system consists of a communication robot (Sota, Vstone Inc., Fig. 2 (a)-A), a ball launcher (Fig. 2 (a)-B), and a mechanism for retrieving the ball returned by the user (Fig. 2(a)-C). In this system, the mechanism of the ball launching device was changed from the ejection mechanism based on movable bars that was introduced in [8] to one using rubber tension applied by pulling it with a motor. In addition, during the experiment, we covered the device with a cloth (Fig. 2(b)) so that the participants could not see the mechanical structure, making it appear as if the robot itself were throwing and receiving the ball.

3.3 Implementation of the Comparison Method

In this experiment, we set up a comparison case that only conveys information regarding the turn of speech by lighting a lamp during a conversation. In this section, we describe the details of the lamp system used in the Lamp condition.

Figure 3 shows the components of the lamp system. The system is equipped with LED lamps on each side (the user and robot side), and the light emission can be transitioned by each turn of speech. In addition, there is a button (C in Fig. 3) on the user's side, and the user can explicitly tell the robot that his/her speech has ended. The following is a simple use case for this system. For example, while the robot is speaking, the robot side's LED lamp (A in Fig. 3) turns on. Next, when the robot finishes its speech, the robot side's LED lamp turns off. Then, the user side's LED lamp (B in Fig. 3) turns on to indicate that the user's turn is coming. When it is the user's turn, the user starts speaking to the robot. Afterward, by pressing the button near the user's hand (C in Fig. 3), the user can turn off the user side's LED lamp and turn on the robot side's LED lamp. This procedure enables an expression of whose turn it is to speak by lighting a lamp.

The lamp system is implemented using an Arduino Uno microcontroller, LEDs, and a button. To realize the above procedure, each LED is set to switch automatically in conjunction with the robot's speech and the user's button operation. When the user presses the button while the user side's LED lamp is on, the user side's LED lamp turns off. Then, the robot side's LED lamp turns on, and the robot begins to speak. Conversely, when the robot has finished speaking, the robot side's LED lamp is set to automatically turn off, and the user side's LED lamp is set to automatically turn on.

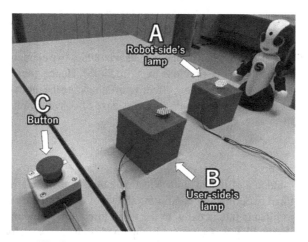

Fig. 3. System configuration of the lamp system.

4 Experiment

In this section, we describe the details of the experiment conducted using the system presented in Sect. 3.

4.1 Objectives and Hypotheses

As mentioned earlier, the experiment aims to consider whether the features of the task of playing catch led to increased motivation to interact, smoothness, and enjoyment of conversation for users. We set and tested the following three hypotheses in this experiment.

- H1: The clarification of turn-taking when interacting with the robot improves the ease of conversation.
- H2: Playing catch with the robot creates a sense of conversation together.
- H3: Playing catch with the robot enhances users' motivation to interact with the robot.

Hypothesis H1 is based on the possibility that the observed effect of turn-taking on the playing catch task in the previous study [8] was due to the clarification of turn-taking itself and not based on the feature of playing catch. The feature of the task of playing catch, such as the speaker being made visible by the shifting of the ball, may have contributed to the support of smooth turn-taking in the experiment from the previous study. However, this effect may also occur in other tasks that support turn-taking, such as the comparative method implemented in Sect. 3.3.

By contrast, we consider that the feature of the task of playing catch highly contributes to the user's sense of enjoying the conversation. Catch is played as a customary game by multiple people, so this task has the effect of creating a sense of shared enjoyment. However, the comparison method is a simple task of pushing a button, so this task is not considered to create a sense of shared enjoyment. For the above reasons, we set hypothesis H2.

In addition, the proposed method of playing catch includes two elements that motivate interaction from the results of our previous experiment [8]. Hence, there is a possibility that the task of playing catch may be more effective in enhancing the motivation to interact than the comparison method, which only provides ease of conversation. Therefore, we set hypothesis H3.

4.2 Settings

Thirty university students affiliated with Ritsumeikan University participated in this experiment. The three experimental conditions shown at the beginning of Sect. 3 were set up, and the participants interacted with the robot three times in total, once for each of the conditions. In the Playing Catch and Lamp conditions, the participants interacted with the robot using the corresponding devices described in Sects. 3.2 and 3.3. The order of the experimental conditions was randomized for each participant.

To make the robot appear to be talking and playing catch autonomously, the experiment was conducted in a setting based on the Wizard of Oz method [10]. Specifically, the experimenter checked the situation in the laboratory using a camera from a position invisible to the participants during the experiment, and the robot was manually controlled, according to the participant's responses.

4.3 Procedure

At the beginning of the experiment, we explained the outline of the experiment to the participants, and their consent was obtained. The experimental environment was different for each experimental condition. That is, the experiments were conducted in a total of three environments, where only the necessary equipment for each condition was installed. The experimental environment in the Playing Catch and Lamp conditions included a table with a robot and a system for each condition. The experimental environment in the Baseline condition consisted of only a robot on a table. The following paragraphs describe the procedure for each condition.

In the Playing Catch condition, the participants were instructed to throw a ball after speaking to the robot as a rule for playing catch within the experiment. Then, the participants were asked to practice catching the ball four times. After that, the experimenter

Table 1. An example of the speech content in a conversation between the robot and a participant in this experiment

ID	Question Category	Questions asked by the robot
(1)	The participant's name	Could you tell me your full name?
(2a)	Topics in the participant's daily life	Are you working part-time?
(2b)	Topics in the participant's daily life	What time did you go to bed yesterday?
(2c)	Topics in the participant's daily life	Do you like traveling?
(2d)	Topics in the participant's daily life	What's the most expensive thing you bought recently?
(2e)	Topics in the participant's daily life	Do you play sports?
(2f)	Topics in the participant's daily life	Do you like animals?
(3)	Closing greetings	I'm hungry, so I'm going to eat. See you next time!

moved out of sight of the participants and began the experiment by sending the first speech command to the robot. In this experiment, the participants were asked to proceed with the conversation while answering questions from the robot. At that time, they exchanged a ball with the robot using the system when the turn in the conversation was changed.

In the Lamp condition, the participants were instructed how to use the lamp system described in Sect. 3.3 while talking with the robot. As a rule, they were asked to press the button after responding to the robot. After the explanation, the experimenter moved and began the experiment, as in the Playing Catch condition. The participants then experienced the conversation with the robot using the lamp system.

In the Baseline condition, the participants were guided to a space with a robot on a tabletop without prototypes or comparison systems. Then, they were instructed to only respond to questions from the robot. After the explanation, the experimenter moved and began the experiment. The participants experienced conversations with the robot.

After the conversation in each condition, the participants were asked to respond to a questionnaire regarding their impressions of the robot. The participants repeated this procedure three times while the conditions changed.

4.4 Conversation Scenario

Regardless of the conditions, the conversation scenarios with the robot had a common structure. In the conversation scenario, nine exchanges were included when defining one exchange as the flow of the robot's speech and the participant's responses to the robot. Table 1 shows examples of the content of the robot's speech in the conversational scenario used in the experiment. To design the questions used in the scenario, we chose familiar and daily topics for Japanese university students. The scenarios were designed to allow a natural transition from one question to the next without relying on responses to each question. Specifically, to ensure that the speech would connect to all responses without discomfort, we either used generic content or took care to prepare multiple speeches according to the responses provided. If the speech content were the same in all conditions during the experiment, it may affect the impression of the robot. Thus, we prepared three patterns of speech scenarios, and each pattern was assigned in each condition for the experiment.

4.5 Evaluation Metrics

To verify hypotheses H1 to H3, we designed questions corresponding to these hypotheses and asked them in a questionnaire in the experiment. Table 2 shows the questionnaire items, where Q1 to Q3 correspond to hypothesis H1, Q4 to Q6 to hypothesis H2, and Q7 to Q10 to hypothesis H3. The participants answered the questions on the Visual Analog Scale (10 cm scale, with a 0 cm position set as "Strongly disagree" and a 10 cm position as "Strongly agree").

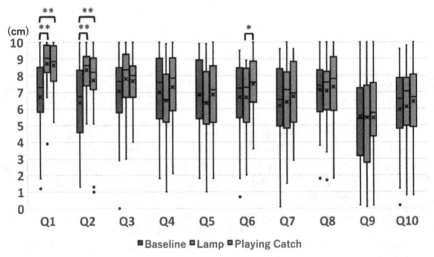

Fig. 4. Box-and-whisker plots of questions Q1-Q10 about the participants' impressions of the robots.

5 Experimental Results

5.1 Questionnaire Results on Impressions of Robots

For the questionnaire items in Table 2 that asked about impressions of the robot and the ease of conversation, a one-way analysis of variance (ANOVA) with repeated measures was performed to check for statistical significance ($p < 0.05$) in each question. Then, Bonferroni's multiple comparison test was performed to verify the statistical significance of the difference between each pair of conditions. Figure 4 shows box-and-whisker plots that describe the trends of results for each questionnaire item in each condition and the results of the multiple comparison test.

Table 2. Question items and results in the questionnaire. (N = 30)

ID	Question	Baseline	Lamp	Playing Catch	p-value
Q1	The interaction with the robot helped me understand when I should speak	6.72	8.72	8.62	**
Q2	The interaction with the robot allowed me to talk at a comfortable pace	6.36	8.33	7.71	**
Q3	I feel that the robot I was talking with was the ease of conversation	7.06	7.8	7.67	n.s
Q4	I feel that I had spent time with the robot	7.00	6.5	7.31	n.s
Q5	I feel that I had a coordinated conversation with the robot	6.88	6.33	6.86	n.s
Q6	I enjoyed interacting with the robot	6.70	6.68	7.49	*
Q7	I feel that I wanted to talk a little longer with the robot	6.18	6.4	6.75	n.s
Q8	I feel the robot is easy to talk to	7.14	7.08	7.32	n.s
Q9	I feel like talking to the robot from me	5.54	5.46	5.45	n.s
Q10	I feel like talking to the robot again in the future	5.95	6.11	6.44	n.s

**: $p < 0.05$, *: $p < 0.1$, n.s.: not significant5. Experimental Results

First, we describe the results of Q1 to Q3 about the ease of conversation with the robot. The mean scores for each condition range from high for the Lamp > Playing Catch > Baseline in all questions. The results of the ANOVA are significant for Q1 and Q2 but not for Q3. From the results of the multiple comparison tests of Q1 and Q2, significant differences are observed between the Playing Catch and Baseline conditions as well as between the Lamp and Baseline conditions. These results indicate that when talking to the robot, both playing catch and the lamp device are useful for understanding the timing of one's speech and creating a comfortable pace.

Next, we describe the results of Q4 to Q6, which ask about the creation of a sense of conversation. The mean scores for Q4 and Q6 range from high for Playing Catch > Baseline > Lamp. The mean values for Q5 range from high for Baseline > Playing Catch > Lamp. Therefore, the Lamp condition has the lowest mean score for all questions. From the results of the ANOVA for Q4 to Q6, a significant effect ($p < 0.05$) was not observed; however, the result of Q6 shows marginal significance ($p < .10$). In the multiple comparison test of Q6, the difference between the Playing Catch and the Lamp conditions is marginally significant ($p < .10$). These results indicate that playing catch with the robot may make an interaction with the robot more enjoyable than another form of conversation in which turn-taking is only made explicit like the lamp device.

Finally, we describe the results of Q7 to Q10, which ask about the motivation to interact with the robot. From the results of the ANOVA for Q7 to Q10, significant differences were not observed in all questions. In Q7, Q8, and Q10, the mean values in the Playing Catch condition are the highest. In contrast, the highest mean value for Q9 is in the Baseline condition. Thus, from the experimental results, we could not observe any effect of either the catch experience or the lamp device on the motivation to interact.

5.2 Discussion

First, we discuss hypothesis H1: "The clarification of turn-taking when interacting with the robot improves the ease of conversation." In the results of the related questions Q1 and Q2, the Lamp and Playing Catch conditions have significantly higher mean values than the Baseline condition. These results suggest that the participants could grasp their own speaking timing and converse at a comfortable pace when using either the lamp device or the playing catch system. In both conditions, the participants can recognize their turn to speak from either perceiving the emission of light or receiving a ball. In addition, they could control their turns to speak at their preferred timing by either pressing a button or throwing a ball. Therefore, these features may have made it easier for the participants to facilitate a conversation with a suitable pace. In Q3, which directly asked about the ease of conversation with the robot, the trend of the mean value is similar to that of Q1 and Q2. However, no significant difference is observed from the ANOVA. This result may be because both the Lamp and Playing Catch conditions require operating buttons and handling a ball before and after speaking, making the interaction with the robot more complicated for the participants.

Next, we discuss hypothesis H2: "Playing catch with the robot creates a sense of conversation together." In the results of the related questions Q4 to Q6, significant differences are observed only in Q6. In addition, the mean value for the Playing Catch condition is highest among the conditions. Although there is no statistical difference in Q4, "I feel that I had spent time with the robot," the mean value of the Playing Catch condition is highest, and the mean value of the Lamp condition is lowest. These results suggest that the participants may feel that playing catch is more enjoyable than using the lamp device when talking to the robot. These results are consistent with the aim of H2. However, for Q5, "I feel that I had a coordinated conversation with the robot," the mean for the Baseline condition was the highest and that for the Lamp condition was the lowest. From the results of this experiment, the collaborative task of playing catch is not suggested to affect the enhancement of the sense of cooperative conversation. By contrast, in Q4 to Q6, the mean values for the Lamp condition are lower than those for the other conditions. These results indicate the possibility that the mechanism for clarifying turn-taking with the lamp device decreases the sense of collaborative conversation with the robot.

Finally, we discuss hypothesis H3: "Playing catch with the robot enhances users' motivation to interact with the robot." No significant difference is observed for any question corresponding to hypothesis H3. Therefore, hypothesis H3 is not supported. In the experimental results, the significant effects of playing catch and the lamp device on the motivation to interact with the robot are not confirmed. However, for Q7 and Q10, which directly ask about the willingness of conversation, the mean values of the Playing Catch condition are higher than those of the other conditions. From this result, it is possible that the task of playing catch with the robot may positively influence the motivation to interact with the robot.

By contrast, the mean scores in Q9, "I feel like talking to the robot from me," are almost equal among the three conditions, with the differences between the means of all conditions being less than 1. Thus, it is considered that the robot's way of speaking and the conversational scenarios affect the results, regardless of the differences among experimental conditions. The experiment was conducted in a setting where the robot spoke a preset conversational scenario. Therefore, one possibility remains that different results will be observed when the user is conversing with a robot with a high response ability.

In summary, statistically significant results to support the hypotheses are not observed in all results from the questionnaire. However, it is suggested that playing catch with the robot supports the clarification of the conversational turn in the same manner as the lamp system, but it is perceived as more enjoyable than the experience of talking with a lamp. The results of this study suggest that considering the design of playful tasks during conversations with robots could both enhance the enjoyment of the conversation and support the conversation itself. Our study contributes by providing insights for designing HRI in terms of quantitatively demonstrating the possibility of playing catch as a conversational task that satisfies both properties.

6 Conclusions

In this study, as a continuation of a previous study, we discussed the effects of incorporating a playful task of playing catch during conversations with a robot. Prior research had shown that introducing the task of playing catch effectively supported smooth turn-taking. However, it was not clear whether this effect was unique to the task of playing catch or whether it could be found in other tasks that also visualize conversational turns. Therefore, in this study, we experimented with clarifying how the playing catch feature contributes to the motivation to interact as well as supports a sense of enjoyment in a conversation and smooth turn-taking, which can be interpreted as subcategories of the motivation to interact. In our experiment, we compared three conversational conditions with a robot: playing catch while talking, visualizing the turn in conversation using a lamp, and talking without using any system.

From the results of this experiment, it is not observed that playing catch via the proposed methods enhances the motivation of interaction compared with the lamp system and the baseline. However, these results establish the possibility that the proposed method can support the understanding of one's speech timing and facilitate a conversation at a suitable pace. Also, it can be considered that the proposed method not only contributes to the visualization of turn-taking but also enhances the enjoyment of playful interactions with the robot.

In future work, we will modify the conversational response model in the robot to consider the effectiveness of tasks in a conversational setting in which the robot can flexibly respond to a user's speech.

Acknowledgments. This work was supported in part by GMO Internet Foundation, KDDI Foundation, JSPS KAKENHI (Grant Number 22K21096) and Ritsumeikan Global Innovation Research Organization(R-GIRO), Ritsumeikan University.

References

1. Demir, K.A., Döven, G., Sezen, B.: Industry 5.0 and human-robot co-working. Procedia Comput. Sci. **158**, 688–695 (2019)
2. Calo, C.J., Hunt-Bull, N., Lewis, L., Metzler, T.: Ethical implications of using the paro robot, with a focus on dementia patient care. In Workshops at the 25th Conference on Artificial Intelligence AAAI'11, pp.20–24 (2011)
3. Nomura, T., Kanda, T., Suzuki, T., Kato, K.: Prediction of human behavior in human-robot interaction using psychological scales for anxiety and negative attitudes toward robots. IEEE Trans. Rob. **24**(2), 442–451 (2008)
4. Okafuji, Y., Mitsui, Y., Matsumura, K., Baba, J., Nakanishi, J.: Changes in embarrassment through repeated interactions with robots in public spaces. In 32nd IEEE International Conference on Robot and Human Interactive Communication, RO-MAN'23, pp. 2253–2258. IEEE (2023)
5. Obo, T., Takizawa, K.: Analysis of timing and effect of visual cue on turn-taking in human-robot interaction. J. Robot. Mechatron. **34**(1), 55–63 (2022)
6. Uchida, T., Minato, T., Ishiguro, H.: Does a conversational robot need to have its own values? A study of dialogue strategy to enhance people's motivation to use autonomous conversational robots. In: Proceedings of the 4th International Conference on Human Agent Interaction, HAI'16, pp.187–192 (2016)
7. Tae, M., Lee, J.: The effect of robot's ice-breaking humor on likeability and future contact intentions. In: Companion of the 2020 ACM/IEEE International Conference on Human-Robot Interaction, HRI'20, pp. 462–464 (2020)
8. Katsuki, R., Ando, M., Otsu, K., Izumi, T.: Introducing Playing Catch to Motivate Interaction with Communication Robots. In: Kurosu, M., Hashizume, A. (eds.) Human-Computer Interaction: Thematic Area, HCI 2023, Held as Part of the 25th HCI International Conference, HCII 2023, Copenhagen, Denmark, July 23–28, 2023, Proceedings, Part III, pp. 79–91. Springer Nature Switzerland, Cham (2023). https://doi.org/10.1007/978-3-031-35602-5_6
9. Cooney, M., Kanda, T., Alissandrakis, A., Ishiguro, H.: Designing enjoyable motion-based play interactions with a small humanoid robot. Int. J. Soc. Robot. **6**, 173–193 (2014)
10. Fraser, N.M., Gilbert, G.N.: Simulating speech systems. Comput. Speech Lang. **5**(1), 81–99 (1991)

Evolution of Mechanized Puppets in Animatronics: Unveiling the Transformative Journey from the 1960s to the Early 2000s

Si Jung Kim[1][✉], Silver Mendoza-Matute[1], Edison Smith[1], and Dong-Wook Lee[2]

[1] University of Nevada Las Vegas (UNLV), Las Vegas, NV 89154, USA
sj.kim@unlv.edu
[2] Korea Institute of Industrial Technology (KITECH), Ansan City, South Korea

Abstract. Animatronics involves the creation of mechanical puppets that utilize electronics and motors to create lifelike characteristics for various purposes such as entertainment, filming and simulation, and research. This paper explored the evolution and transformations of mechanized puppets utilized in the advancement of animatronics. It focused on the transition of animatronics from the beginning of modern animatronics in the 1960s till the first decade of the 2000s. The analysis was focused on identifying the characteristics of mechanized puppets from the perspectives of their embodiment, technological features and targets used as applications. The method used for the analysis was a qualitative analytical approach that broke down the literature review process into four steps and iterated them. The analysis with 33 animatronics found that 85% (28 of 33) of the animatronics surveyed are more geared toward entertainment venues such as theme parks and human-like animatronics are becoming increasingly more advanced and applications for animatronics in the theme park setting is becoming increasingly more prominent. As applications for animatronics, especially in theme park settings, continue to rise, this study contributes to the understanding of the ever-evolving landscape of animatronic technology.

Keywords: Animatronics · Mechanical puppets · Lifelike characteristics · Evolution · Transformation · Entertainment · Theme parks

1 Introduction

Beginning as a curiosity of the natural order of the world pushed the minds of many to find a mastery in the methods of recreating nature through science and technology. As the robotics industry leans heavily towards the next level, it prompts reflection on the broader consequences. What does this emphasis mean for other potential applications, such as theme parks and entertainment? Moreover, how might the saturation of humanoid and human-like animatronics affect societal perceptions and interactions with technology? Dating back to the 16th century to the first iteration of automata utilizing pneumatics and hydraulics [1, 2], animatronics continues to inspire and push a better understanding of the world with their semblance to the actions of animals and other creatures that populate it [3].

© The Author(s), under exclusive license to Springer Nature Switzerland AG 2024
M. Kurosu and A. Hashizume (Eds.): HCII 2024, LNCS 14685, pp. 129–138, 2024.
https://doi.org/10.1007/978-3-031-60412-6_10

Animatronics, as defined in literature [4], represent a fusion of animation and electronics, forming a mechanized puppet. Rooted in the principles of mechatronics and kinematic controls [5–7], animatronics leverages these technologies to engineer mechanical animations. This interdisciplinary approach finds diverse applications across entertainment, theme parks, cinema, and education [8–10], highlighting its versatility in bringing dynamic and lifelike movements to characters and figures in various settings. These are either computer programmed to act as an autonomous object or a remotely controlled object by human operators, otherwise known as tele-operational. With the advancement of sensors, telecommunications and manufacturing techniques, and electronics, animatronics today are more human-like, and their movements are becoming increasingly similar to the nature of human movement.

The central inquiry poised for exploration involves a meticulous analysis of the diverse categories of animatronics, with a specific focus on the foundational technology driving their operation and facilitating the generation of mechanical animations. The temporal parameter delineated for this examination spans from the 1960s to the first decade of the 2000s.

The overarching objective is to undertake an in-depth investigation into the evolutionary trajectory of animatronics during this chronological continuum. The scrutiny will delve into the nuanced characteristics of mechanized puppets, elucidating their embodiment, intricate technological features, and multifaceted applications. This comprehensive exploration seeks to unveil not only the technical advancements but also the contextual nuances that have shaped the landscape of animatronics over the designated time frame.

2 Methods

The chosen methodology for this comprehensive analysis adopts a qualitative approach, as outlined in the academic literature [11]. The approach encompasses a multifaceted strategy, combining an extensive literature review with active participation in a prominent theme park conference/expo. The literature review itself unfolds through a systematic, iterative process consisting of four key steps: initial data acquisition, the establishment of analysis criteria, data enrichment, and culminating in a rigorous analysis.

To augment this literary exploration, attendance at the International Association of Amusement Parks and Attractions (IAAPA) [12], renowned as one of the world's largest annual conferences and expos in the theme parks and entertainment domain, was undertaken. An independent coder was engaged for a thorough survey of existing animatronics, utilizing diverse academic databases and conducting a general search to capture applied usages and the progress of animatronics.

The qualitative analytical framework employed in this study entailed an initial literature review to formulate precise analysis criteria. Subsequently, data was methodically collected from an array of sources, including databases, online journal repositories, and on-site visits. Descriptive statistics were then applied to discern the salient features of mechanical puppets. Parameters such as the year of construction, character types, primary technological features, locations of development, installation, and application, as well as the sources of locomotion, were systematically identified and analyzed. This comprehensive approach aims to offer a nuanced understanding of the evolution of animatronics, drawing insights from both scholarly literature and real-world applications in the theme park industry.

3 Results and Discussions

3.1 Character Types

This exhaustive examination of mechanized puppets, conducted over an extensive year-long period of data collection and rigorous redundancy checks, meticulously identified and documented a total of 33 entities. The comprehensive breakdown provided is provided in Table 1.

An intriguing revelation emerged from this scrutiny: a significant majority, approximately 54.5% (18 of 33), exhibited a human-like configuration shown in Fig. 1. This substantial proportion underscores a prevalent trend within the dataset, indicating a significant inclination towards the creation of animatronic entities that mimic or embody human characteristics. The category included intricate variations, encompassing depictions ranging from human heads and full bodies to representations of fictional human characters, such as the iconic Elsa from Disney's Frozen.

In stark contrast, the remaining 45.5% (15 of 33) of these automata assumed the forms of animals or non-humanoid entities, excmplified by characters like Lightning McQueen from the Disney movie, Cars [13]. This diverse grouping extended to include an array of animal shapes, featuring dinosaurs, mythical monsters, and monkeys, as well as imaginative characters possessing animalistic traits, a notable example being the beloved alien "Stitch" from Disney's animated series, Lilo and Stitch [14]. This nuanced categorization not only offers a comprehensive overview of the diverse forms adopted by mechanized puppets but also serves as a valuable resource for scholars and enthusiasts delving into the intricate realm of robotic character design.

Among fictional characters, there exists the animatronic racoon of Rocket Racoon from the movie Guardians of the Galaxy directed by James Gunn at Disney California Adventure [15]. This audio animatronic begins its introduction by greeting the visitors of the attraction with instructions on a prison break and leads them through the attraction. Rocket displays an example of the strengths that audio animatronics have with its mechanical capabilities and ability to entertain an audience as not only the animatronic imitates gestures from a computer-generated-image (CGI) in a movie, but it adds another dynamic of stimulating the auditory senses alongside it. Rocket Racoon is just one example of the number of fictional characters who were once limited to onscreen appearances that have been given form for the enjoyment of the public.

3.2 Creations of Characters

Approximately 52% of the animatronic characters under consideration, specifically 17 out of the total 33, were brought to life during the 2000s. This notable period encompassed the creation of characters featured not only in Universal Studios but also in Walt Disney's theme parks located in Florida and California. An intriguing trend emerged

Table 1. A compilation of 33-character types.

No	Name	Character	Place Installed	Country	Year	No	Name	Character	Place Installed	Country	Year
1	Lucky Dinosaur		Natural History Museum of Los Angeles	USA	2003	17	Hopper & The Insects		Disney's Animal Kingdom	USA	1999
2	Kismet			USA	2000	18	Ursula		Disney California Adventure	USA	2011
3	ITU-1 Robot Head			USA	2004	19	Goblins		Universal Studios Florida	USA	2014
4	Yeti		Matterhorn Bobsleds at Disneyland	USA	2005	20	Stitch		Magic Kingdom	USA	2004
5	AnUon			UK	2001	21	Pirates and Wenches		Disneyland Park	USA	1967
6	SLA		Hospitals and other medical facilities	USA	2009	22	Abraham Lincoln		Disneyland Park	USA	1964
7	FR-1		Being developed Not yet installed	South Korea	2009	23	The Yeti		Disney's Animal Kingdom	USA	2006
8	Camptosaurus			USA	1991	24	Sinbad's Storybook Cast		Tokyo DisneySea	Japan	2001
9	Enchanted Tiki Birds		Disneyland Park, Enchanted Tiki Room	USA	1963	25	Seven Dwarfs		Magic Kingdom	USA	2014
10	The Dragon		La Taniere du Dragon Disneyland Paris	France	1992	26	Imhotep		Universal Studios Florida	USA	2004
11	Maleficent		Fantasmic Disneyland Park	USA		27	Davy Jones		Shanghai Disneyland	China	2016
12	Albert		Mystic Manor Hong Kong Disneyland	China	2013	28	Cars		Disney California Adventure	USA	2012
13	Rocket Raccoon		Disney California Adventure	USA	2017	29	Kong		Universal's Island of Adventure	USA	2016
14	T. Rex		Universal Studios Hollywood	USA	1998	30	Citizens of Arendelle		Epcot	USA	2016
15	Mr. Potato Head		Disney's Hollywood Studios	USA	2008	31	Olaf		Shanghai Disneyland	China	2016
16	Wicked Witch		Disney's Hollywood Studios	USA	1989	32	Shaman of songs		Disney's Animal Kingdom	USA	2017
						33	Lava Monster		Tokyo DisneySea	Japan	2001

during our analysis, revealing a distinctive characteristic shift in animatronic design. Characters predating the 2000s tended to be more inclined towards dinosaurs or monster-like figures, while those crafted post-2000 displayed a noteworthy transition. The newer animatronics exhibited a prevalence of human-like or child-friendly fictional characters from movies [16], signifying a perceptible evolution in the thematic and stylistic choices of animatronic creations over time (Fig. 2).

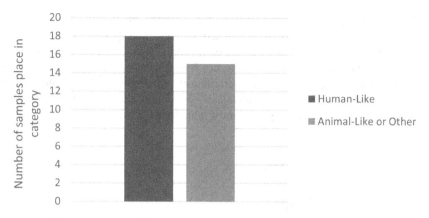

Fig. 1. Around 54.5% (18 of 33) exhibited a human-like configuration

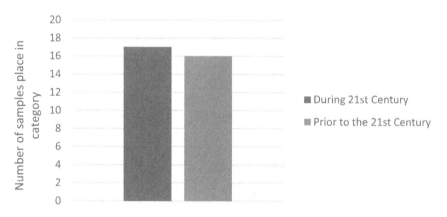

Fig. 2. Around 52% (17 of 33) were created during the 2000s.

3.3 Purposes

The overwhelming utilization of animatronic characters for entertainment, constituting approximately 85% (28 out of 33) underscores a deliberate emphasis on enhancing the theme park experience. These characters play pivotal roles, contributing to the immersive ambiance of theme parks by engaging visitors in interactive rides or serving as captivating side attractions [17, 18]. The design and deployment of these animatronics are intricately crafted to evoke awe, excitement, and amusement among theme park guests.

Conversely, the remaining 15% (5 of 33) of animatronic characters serve noble purposes in the realms of medicine and education. In these sectors, animatronics prove to be valuable tools for simulating medical scenarios or facilitating interactive educational experiences. Their lifelike movements and expressions enhance the effectiveness of training programs and medical simulations, providing a unique blend of realism and engagement.

The predilection for entertainment in the deployment of animatronics can be attributed to their innate ability to imitate and animate. This quality, coupled with the expressive medium of cartoonish characters, naturally aligns with the desire to create enchanting and visually appealing experiences for audiences. Drawing a historical parallel with traditional puppets used for entertainment, animatronics stands as the modern, electronically advanced successors, seamlessly continuing the tradition of captivating and entertaining audiences through the art of imitation (Fig. 3).

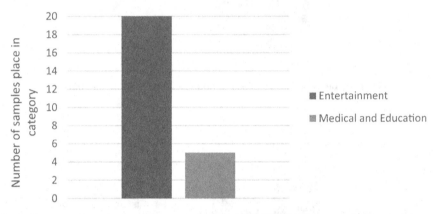

Fig. 3. Purposes for animatronic usage - Around 85% (28 of 33) are used for entertainment purposes.

3.4   Source of Animatronic Movement

When examining the mechanisms responsible for animating characters, a substantial majority, specifically 80% or 26 out of the total 33, relied on either pneumatics or hydraulics. The remaining implementations were built upon a foundation of direct current (DC), alternating current (AC), or servo motor-based actuators. This diversity in motion technologies underscores the adaptability and ingenuity applied in the field of animatronics. Consider, for instance, the exceptional craftsmanship showcased in the Abraham Lincoln audio animatronic—a masterpiece meticulously developed by the highly acclaimed Garner Holt Productions. This animatronic marvel stands as a testament to the convergence of artistic finesse and technological prowess, highlighting the industry's commitment to pushing the boundaries of creativity and engineering in character animation. This pioneering company not only takes pride in bringing historical figures to life but also stands as a key contributor to Disney's enchanting world of animatronics.

Garner Holt Productions consistently delivers unparalleled expertise, seamlessly blending artistry and cutting-edge technology to create captivating and lifelike animatronic experiences that transcend entertainment boundaries. Their illustrious portfolio includes an array of enchanting characters, making them an integral part of the magical tapestry that defines Disney's captivating storytelling. This particular animatronic is equipped with an impressive repertoire of 40 distinct gestures and expressions, each executed with such precision that the skin itself exhibits minute crinkles and wrinkles, mirroring the nuanced changes in facial expressions and speech.

The level of detail extends beyond mere movement, capturing the subtleties of human expression with exceptional accuracy. Moreover, to ensure a seamless and lifelike performance, this animatronic operates at an astounding 1,000 frames per second (fps). This remarkable frame rate not only enhances the fluidity of its motions but also contributes to an unparalleled level of realism, setting a new standard in the realm of animatronic technology.

3.5 Animatronics in a Theme Park Related Expo

The literature review conducted for this study relied on extensive internet searches and databases that predominantly sourced information from project websites, documents, and scholarly articles. However, it became evident that this approach did not adequately capture the current availability of animatronic characters in the market. To address this gap and gain a firsthand understanding of the contemporary landscape, a field trip was undertaken.

The choice of the International Association of Amusement Parks and Attractions (IAAPA) as the venue for the field trip was deliberate. Recognized as the largest convention and expo globally, the IAAPA event provided a comprehensive and unparalleled opportunity to observe and assess the latest animatronic characters available in the market. This strategic decision aimed to complement the findings from the literature review, ensuring a more holistic and up-to-date understanding of the animatronics industry.

During the International Association of Amusement Parks and Attractions (IAAPA) event, a massive gathering that drew approximately 32,000 visitors from 120 countries to explore the offerings of around 1,100 exhibitors, the landscape of animatronics-related industries stood out. Out of the multitude of exhibitors, onsite analysis revealed that 2.7% (30 out of 1,100) were specifically associated with animatronics. Within this subset of 30 animatronics-related exhibitors, a detailed breakdown revealed intriguing insights. Approximately 43% (13 out of 30) of these exhibitors showcased products directly related to animatronics. These could range from cutting-edge animatronic characters to advanced technologies designed to enhance the field. Further exploration into the animatronic projects unveiled a diverse range of focuses and specializations. Around 31% of these projects, representing 4 out of the total 13, were intricately managed using animal animatronics, with a predominant emphasis on the awe-inspiring world of dinosaurs. Another 23% of the projects, accounting for 3 out of the 13, demonstrated a high level of skill in execution through the utilization of sophisticated control systems and dedicated hardware.

Interestingly, only around 46% of the animatronic projects, constituting 6 out of the 13, showcased a comprehensive approach. These projects seamlessly integrated all aspects of the creative and technical fields involved, highlighting the nuanced and specialized nature of animatronic endeavors within this particular domain. This distribution underscores the multifaceted landscape of animatronic projects showcased at IAAPA, revealing a rich tapestry of creativity, technology, and specialization within the industry.

4 Conclusions and Future Works

The research explored existing animatronics and identified a total of 33 animatronic characters ranging from hyper realistic humanoid representations to vintage character fortune tellers and colorful animals. It presented a comprehensive exploration of animatronics, unraveling a tapestry of 33 characters that spans hyper-realistic humanoid representations, whimsical vintage character fortune tellers, and lively animals. A discernible trend surfaces as we scrutinize these characters: animatronics predominantly gravitates towards theme park entertainment. This animatronics, often humanoid or human-like, denote an ongoing trajectory towards heightened realism, showcasing the convergence of cutting-edge technology and artistic expression.

A closer examination of the 33 animatronics reveals a notable trend where pneumatic or hydraulic systems wield significant influence, especially in higher-end animatronic products. This prevalence suggests a deliberate choice in favor of these advanced systems, highlighting the technical intricacies and engineering excellence required to achieve fluid and lifelike movements in animatronic characters. The prominence of pneumatic or hydraulic mechanisms speaks to the sophistication of the machinery involved, transcending mere mechanization. It reflects a fusion of technology and artistry, where intricate engineering not only serves a functional purpose but also contributes to the creation of captivating and realistic movements. This intersection of cutting-edge technology and creative craftsmanship is a testament to the industry's commitment to pushing the boundaries of what is achievable in animatronic design. The reliance on these advanced systems not only underscores the technical prowess required but also emphasizes the industry's dedication to delivering immersive and awe-inspiring experiences. The intricate machinery powering these animatronics goes beyond functionality, evoking a sense of wonder at the seamless integration of technology and artistry, ultimately enhancing the overall impact and appeal of animatronic characters in various entertainment settings.

However, moving beyond surface-level observations, it is imperative to delve into the profound implications of these trends. A striking revelation emerges – a resounding 85% (28 of 33) of the surveyed animatronics are purposefully designed for theme park entertainment. This statistical dominance prompts critical questions about the overarching impact of this singular agenda on the animatronics industry's trajectory. Moreover, it invites contemplation of ethical considerations intertwined with the cognitive experiences of theme park visitors.

One noteworthy ethical issue in the field of animatronics revolves around the potential manipulation of emotions. As animatronics become increasingly sophisticated in mimicking human expressions and behaviors, there arises a concern about their capacity to evoke emotional responses. Theme Park visitors may form connections with animatronic characters, perceiving them as sentient beings. This blurring of the line between artificial and authentic emotions raises ethical questions about the responsibility of animatronic developers in managing and guiding these emotional engagements. As these creations become more adept at triggering emotional responses, considerations surrounding the potential impact on visitors' perceptions and well-being become paramount.

While the study offers valuable insights, it is essential to recognize its inherent limitations. One notable limitation stems from the reliance on a single independent coder for data collection, introducing an element of subjectivity into the analysis. The results could potentially vary with the involvement of multiple independent coders, highlighting the need for caution in interpreting findings.

Furthermore, the data collection method, primarily based on a random search, introduces a level of unpredictability and potential bias. A more structured approach, grounded in formal materials such as conference proceedings and dedicated journals focused on animatronics, could offer a more systematic and robust dataset. This shift towards a more formalized method would not only enhance the reliability of the information gathered but also provide a deeper and more nuanced understanding of the animatronics landscape. Acknowledging and addressing these limitations will contribute to a more comprehensive and reliable foundation for future research in the field, fostering a greater degree of confidence in the study's findings and conclusions.

Acknowledgments. This research was supported by the Ministry of Culture, Sports and Tourism (MCST) and Korea Creative Content Agency (KOCCA) in the Culture Technology (CT) Research & Program in South Korea.

References

1. Bissell, C.: A history of automatic control. In: Springer Handbook of Automation (2009).https://doi.org/10.1007/978-3-540-78831-7_4
2. Winterhalter, P.: Hydraulics and Pneumatics. MASCHINENMARKT (1987). https://doi.org/10.1016/c2013-0-01149-8
3. Wikipedia, F.: Walt Disney's Carousel of Progress. History (1975)
4. Holt, G.: MiceChat - Features, This Animatronic Life - Blurring the Mechanical Line: GHP's New Animatronic Head Offers a Glimpse Into the Future of Expressive Characters. MiceChat (2017)
5. Bishop, R.H.: Mechatronics: An Introduction (2017)
6. Kim, S., Kuc, T.: Kinematic Animation of Human Walking. Human-Computer Interaction Korea, pp. 251–257 (1998)
7. Kim, S., Kuc, T.: Goal-Directed Motion Control of 3D Human Characters. In: IEEE International Conference on Systems, Man, and Cybernetics, pp. 4334–4339 (1998)
8. Burns, B., Samanta, B.: Mechanical design and control calibration for an interactive animatronic system. In: ASME International Mechanical Engineering Congress and Exposition, Proceedings (IMECE) (2015).https://doi.org/10.1115/IMECE201552477
9. Madhani, A.J.: Bringing Physical Characters to Life (2009). https://doi.org/10.1145/1514095.1514096
10. Sempere, A.: Animatronics, Children, and Computation. In: Educational Technology and Society (2005)
11. Onwuegbuzie, A.J., Leech, N.L., Collins, K.M.T.: Qualitative Analysis Techniques for the Review of the Literature. Qual. Rep. (2012)
12. International Association of Amusement Parks and Attractions (IAAPA). https://www.iaapa.org
13. Zhang, W., Han, B., Hui, P., Gopalakrishnan, V., Zavesky, E., Qian, F.: CARS (2018). https://doi.org/10.1145/3177102.3177107
14. Walt Disney Pictures. Lilo and Stitch. United States of America: Buena Vista Home Entertainment (2013)

15. L.D.; produced by K.F.; written by J.G. and N.P.; directed by J.G. Marvel Studios presents a James Gunn film; co-producers, David J. Grant, Jonathan Schwartz; executive producers, Nik Korda, Stan Lee, Victoria Alonso, Jeremy Latcham, Alan Fine; Guardians of the Galaxy. United States of America (2014)

16. Krosnick, B.: The 25 Most Incredible Theme Park Animatronics On Earth|Theme Park Tourist (2014)

17. Schell, J., Shochet, J.: Designing Interactive Theme Park Rides Lessons Learned Creating Disney's Pirates of the Caribbean-Battle for the Buccaneer Gold. Game Dev. Conf. San Jose, CA (2001)

18. Jones, R.: The Most Realistic Robo-Lincoln Yet Proves the Future Is Going to Be Weird as Hell (2017)

Exploring Changes in Social Distance and Participant Discomfort with Virtual Robot Head and Visual Familiarity

Tomoya Minegishi[1]([✉]) and Hirotaka Osawa[1,2]

[1] University of Tsukuba, Tsukuba Ibaraki, Japan
s2130172@u.tsukuba.ac.jp
[2] Keio University, Yokohama, Kanagawa, Japan

Abstract. This paper investigates whether there exist social distances when interacting with human-like or animal-like 3D models displayed stereoscopically without wearable devices. While social robots with human-like bodies offer advantages in physical communication through gestures, they may be risks of harm to humans, leading to difficulties in maintaining appropriate social distances. To address these challenges, the authors propose employing a 3D display to present virtual robots, allowing observers to perceive their movements without physical actions. The study explores participants' impressions of virtual heads, categorized as either human-like or animal-like, through a survey conducted with 50 Japanese participants recruited via crowdsourcing. Results indicate that human-like heads were perceived as more physically present, whereas animal-like heads were deemed more familiar. These findings shed light on designing comfortable, effective long-term interactions between humans and robots, emphasizing the importance of considering appearance and approachability in social robot design. By leveraging non-verbal cues and alternative communication methods, such as virtual displays, researchers aim to enhance user experiences and optimize social interactions with robots in various settings, including homes and offices.

Keywords: Virtual Robot Head · Social Distance · Visual Familiarity

1 Introduction

In this paper, we examine whether there is a difference in social distance and psychological distance during communication with 3D models that is human-like or familiarity animal-like shown on the display that can be viewed stereoscopically without using any wearable devices. Through these conditions, we clarified the 3D model's appearance design to guide human's standing position. Social robots with human-like bodies are installed in human living spaces, such as residences and offices, and there are some studies to communicate with them comfortably [1–4]. Social robots have the advantage of being able to communicate with humans while performing physical movements, such as using non-verbal information through gestures. However, physical approaches by social robots may not be feasible due to the potential risk of harm to humans, for

© The Author(s), under exclusive license to Springer Nature Switzerland AG 2024
M. Kurosu and A. Hashizume (Eds.): HCII 2024, LNCS 14685, pp. 139–155, 2024.
https://doi.org/10.1007/978-3-031-60412-6_11

example the robots collide the humans when the robots raise its arms or lower its head to make a bow to humans, so social robots have the problem that they cannot perform proper physical movement while communicating with humans. There is a way to make the person to move away from the social robot by talking to them, but there is a study that shows that it did not help to get them to move away from the robots [5]. There is alternative method that making the person to imagine a physical presence to adjust the distance. This method is by getting close into the person's personal distance. The personal distance is the one of the social distances classified by Hall. Hall's social distances are classified four zones and taken by persons when they communicate according to their relationships. People take the personal distance when communicate with the close relationships, such as family and lovers. Therefore, people feel uncomfortable when someone they are not close relationships within their personal space, 0.15 m–0.45 m, and adjust distance between them. Social distances also applied between the social robots and people, and it is possible to user social distances to get people stay away from the robots [1, 2]. However, physical approaches by social robots may not be feasible due to the potential risk of harm to humans. There is a study that shows if social robots collide with persons, the persons reduce their trust in the robots [7]. Some method is desirable to encourage persons to move away from the social robots voluntarily, within avoiding physical harm.

To address the issues with the social robots, there is a solution which uses a flat screen and displaying the on-screen agents such as digital signage and PC. There are some studies to communicate with on-screen agents comfortably [8–10]. On-screen agents can express their body movements and facial expressions, so they have an advantage of reducing the risk of harming people. Furthermore, on-screen agents can be realized by preparing displays and computers that control 3D models and output them to displays, so another advantage is that it is easy to prepare the agents. However, because the on-screen agents do not have a physical body in real space, they cannot make humans imagine their physical presence and adjust their social distances.

To solve the social robots' and on-screen agents' problems, we developed "virtual head" using a 3D display that can be viewed stereoscopically without using any wearable devices [11, 12] (shown in Fig. 1). Because of the "virtual head" can be observed in 3D, people can feel physicality body presence, and they can maintain an appropriate social distance. It was found that when 3D virtual head shortened to the participants' personal distance, the participants moved away to their social distance. This result revealed that creating the agent's illusion body movements even without physical movements, people maintain an appropriate social distance.

When the virtual head changes its appearance, the impression the observers have of the virtual head, which may affect the social distance. Koda et al. [13] showed that when an on-screen agent using a flat display changes its appearance, it affects the impression of the observer has. The authors' previous research [11, 12], a 3D model with a human-like appearance was used as the virtual head, but it cannot be denied that interpersonal distance may have increased due to the influence of appearance. Furthermore, if the people's familiarity to the virtual head improves due to a change its appearance, the social distance might be decreased.

The purpose of this paper is to clarify whether changes in the virtual head's appearance affect the impression people have and affect the social distance between them. The authors asked the participants about their impression when observing the virtual head through an on-line questionnaire, and compared the results for the conditions, human-like and animal-like appearance. Based on the results obtained from the questionnaire survey, we investigated the social distance through an offline survey and clarify the effects of changes in appearance of the virtual head.

The chapter of this paper is as follows. Section 2 describes related research and describes research that investigated whether the social distance is applied to the social robots and the on-screen agents. Then discussing the problems of each study, the differences from this paper, and the points referenced in this paper. Section 3 describes the proposal of the virtual head and its implementations. Section 4 describes a questionnaire survey. We used crowdsourcing, and we clarify how the participants can imagine the body of a virtual head. Section 5 describes the face-to-face experiment that we conducted to clarify whether the virtual head's appearance effect the social distance between the virtual head and participants. Section 6 describes the findings obtained in this paper and discusses the limitations and contributions of this paper. Section 7 provides the conclusion.

Fig. 1. Human-like virtual head shown in the Looking Glass display.

2 Related Research

In this section describes the social distance in communication between people. After that, the next section describes some studies that tried to apply the social distance between people and the social robots or the on-screen agents.

2.1 Social Distance in Communication

The social distance is represented by the personal space classified by Hall [6]. When people communicate, they decide their social distance based on their relationships. Hall defined this personal space as the social distance. For example, people feel uncomfortable when someone who is not a family or lover comes within 0.45 m which is the personal distance of them. For people who are not close to each other to communicate comfortably, they need to be 1.2 m–3.6 m apart, which is classified as the social distance. On the other hand, Hayduk [14] showed that personal space is a distorted circle that is wide in front of oneself and narrow behind oneself. Bailenson et al. [15] showed that personal space is an ellipse that is wide in front and back and narrow in left and right. Gérin-Lajoie et al. [16] showed that the personal space on the dominant hand side becomes smaller when avoiding obstacles. Therefore, personal space may different from people, but in this study, we refer to Hall, who defines social distance as a range larger than the other studies [14–16].

2.2 Social Distance Between On-Screen Agent and Human

There are some studies that show the social distance in communication does not be applied between on-screen agents and humans. To solve problems of the social robots, there is a solution which uses a flat screen and displaying the on-screen agents [8–10], but it was shown that people get closer to on-screen agents than the lower limit of the social distance of 1.2 m. Hedayati et al. [8] investigated the social distance between people and on-screen agents when multiple people including on-screen agents discussion. They showed that when the on-screen agent was included, the distance between participants was significantly reduced. Therefore, it was found that the social distance is not applied between on-screen agents and humans. For the purposes of this study, on-screen agent displayed on a flat screen might be not suitable. Our past studies showed that people maintain an appropriate social distance with 3D virtual head [11, 12]. However, there are few studies on the social distance with on-screen agent considering appearance of it. The appearance of the on-screen agent might be increasing the social distance with people.

2.3 Controlling of the Social Distance by On-Screen Agents

On-screen agents might be able to manipulate the distance by changing the size of the 3D model they are displayed on. Aramaki et al. [17] investigated the size of agents displayed in augmented reality (AR) and the distance people take from them. They showed that the larger scale agent, the more people want to stay away from it. Jones et al. [18] showed that by projecting an agent operated by a remote person onto a telepresence robot, the agent was given the same level of presence as if the remote person were present, and the meeting could proceed. However, it is not clear whether it is possible to adjust the distance using an on-screen agent. Also, it is not clear how do the people gain a physical body sense of the on-screen agents. For example, the studies by Hedayati et al. [8] and Wachsmuth et al. [19] suggest that having a human-like virtual body affects the distance from people. It is not clear how the on-screen agent's appearance makes people to feel the agent's physical presence through display and maintain appropriate social distancing.

2.4 Social Distance Between Social Robot and Human

There are some studies that show Hall's social distance is applied between the social robots and humans. Also, the social robots can improve their impressions from people by maintaining an appropriate the social distance. Takayama et al. [2] investigated the effect of social robot's gaze behavior on the social distance. The women participants felt comfortable when the robot looked at their faces or looked further away than them, the men participants felt comfortable when the robot looked at their faces or looked at their feet. The participants who owned pets felt more comfortable shorter distance than those who did not. Mumm et al. [1] investigated the physical distance and psychological distance between the robot and participants. The participants who dislike robots maintain a larger distance from the robot when they are seen by the robot, but the participants who like robots maintain the same distance from the robot regardless of whether they are seen. Also, it was found that the participants who dislike robots did not disclose information about themselves to the robot and maintained larger distance from the robot. In the worst case, if social robots collide with persons, the persons reduce their trust in the robots and keep distance from it than before the collision [7]. These studies showed that the social distance classified by Hall [6] is applied between the social robots which has human-like physical body and humans. It also showed that social robots need to maintain appropriate social distance depend on their relationships. By maintaining appropriate social distance, the social robots can improve their impressions from people. However, there are few studies on the virtual head displayed on a stereoscopic display and the social distance. Also, these studies cannot consider to the effect of the social robot's appearance. Takayama et al. [2] showed that the gaze behavior of robots affects the social distance that people take. Therefore, these studies have a possibility that social distance can be increased by the social robot's appearance that allows estimation of its line of sight.

3 Virtual Head System

Display. In this study, we used Looking Glass [20] which is a stereoscopic display without any wearable devices (Fig. 1). This display has lenticular lenses and developed by Looking Glass Factory. Lenticular lenses are installed in front of a flat 4K display to deliver different images to viewers' left and right eyes. This allows the viewer to see stereoscopic images without any wearable devices. The Looking Glass has approximately 50° viewing angle and 45 viewing points. The display size is 15.6 inches, and the aspect ratio is 16:9. The minimum viewing distance is recommended to be 1ft (approximately 305 mm), and the maximum viewing distance is unlimited, but the drawback of the lenticular lens method is that the image becomes blurred further away from the screen, so we need to consider limiting the size of the experimental environment. The disadvantage of stereoscopic displays using lenticular lenses is that the number of pixels decreases as the number of viewpoints increases. However, the resolution of displays is now becoming higher, especially in Looking Glass, the reduction in the number of pixels is suppressed by using 4K (3840 × 2160 pixels) images. In Looking Glass, the depth can be set freely, but if the limit of expression is exceeded, the image will become blurred, so in this study, the expression area is from the screen border of 0 mm to a depth of 250 mm, and the movable area of the virtual head is 0 mm to 200 mm. In this paper, it is important to let the participants see the approaching movement without any physical movement, and it is especially important to be able to grasp the distance in the depth direction.

Software. Figure 2 shows a diagram of the virtual head system in this paper. The processing of the system as follows. The device input program monitors keyboard input and camera input. The experimenter determines what the virtual head do by inputting commands on the keyboard. The device input program passes the input commands to the main program. The main program determines its action according to the commands. Depending on determined action, the program issue instructions to the playing audio program and the body movement program. The playing audio program plays the audio files which are instructed by the main program, and outputs from the speaker installed at the back of the Looking Glass. Due to mouth movements are required during audio playback, the playing audio program returns True or False to the main program for each frame, if the audio file is playing, returns True, and if not playing, return False. The body movement program realizes the virtual head's body motion that corresponds to the given commands from the main program. For example, if the body movement program instructed to move closer to the participant, it changes the coordinates of the 3D model placed in virtual space to appear closer to the participant without any physical movements. In addition, the body movement program controls blinks predetermined number of times per a minute. Tsubota et al. [21] measured the number of blinks in people and showed that in an environment with a room temperature of 22.5 °C and humidity of 40%, people blink 22 ± 9 times/min in a relaxed state. In this virtual head, it blinks 20 times per minute. For Animal-like condition, we used "Mamehinata" 3D model designed by Mochiyama-kingyo[1].

---

[1] "Mamehinata" was designed and developed by Kameyama and Mochiyama-kingyo, https://mukumi.booth.pm.

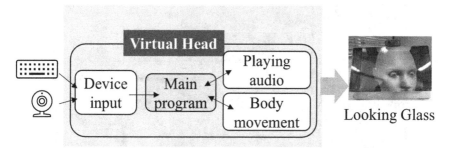

Fig. 2. Virtual head system developed with Unity.

Body Movement. The virtual head can move closer or further away from the participant. The position of the virtual head can be changed, and audio can be played back
by the experimenter. As explained in the previous sections, the virtual head operates
autonomously except for some operations. For parts that do not operate autonomously,
we use the Wizard of Oz method [22] to operate them. The WoZ is a method in which
humans operate the parts of the system that are not fully autonomous, making it appear
as if the system is operating completely autonomously to the observer.

After the experiment begins, the virtual head introduces itself and then explains about
the works exhibited in the museum. The content virtual robots read is shown in Table 1.

4 Online Survey

When the virtual head changes its appearance, the impression the observers have of the
virtual head, which may affect the social distance. Koda et al. [13] showed that when an
on-screen agent using a flat display changes its appearance, it affects the impression of the
observer has. Based on the above, it is possible that the impression the participants have
differ depending on the appearance of the 3D model, so we conducted an online survey
regarding on the virtual head's physicality and familiarity with a changed appearance.

We conducted a crowdsourcing survey on impressions of virtual heads with different
appearances. We prepared two types of appearance: Human-like condition (Fig. 3) and
Animal-like condition (Fig. 4). The previous studies showed that there is a difference
in the impression participant have between on-screen agent's appearance resembles like
a cartoon character and like a human, but it is not clear whether this will affect the
physicality of the virtual head. We used "Yahoo! Crowdsourcing (Japanese)" to recruit
50 participants. The participants were asked to watch a movie, then answer a survey.
The survey was conducted in Japanese. This survey was conducted with permission
from the Research Ethics Committee Secretariat, Institute of Systems and Information
Engineering, University of Tsukuba (Approval Number: 2023R811).

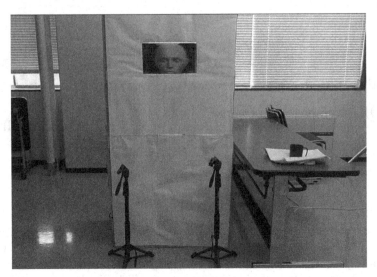

Fig. 3. Human-like condition virtual head.

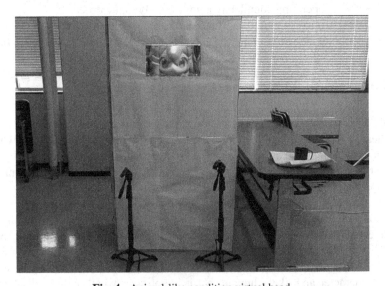

Fig. 4. Animal-like condition virtual head.

Table 1. Scenario contents (Japanese scenarios are shown below).

	Contents
1	I am an agent who will work in a museum. Today, I would like to ask you to help me with the scenario of introducing the pottery work. First, please stand about 10 cm in front of me. (in Japanese 私は美術館で働く予定のエージェントです．今日はあなたに，作品紹介の場面を想定したお手伝いをしてもらいたいと思います．最初に，私の前10cm程度に立ってください．)
2	Now, I'll start explaining the work placed next to me. You can go down as far as you want to hear the explanation. (in Japanese では早速，私の隣に置かれた作品について説明を始めます．あなたは，私の説明の途中で，説明を聞きたい場所まで好きなだけ下がってください．)
3	This work is a mug made by an American artist around in the 1800s. It was brought to Japan in around 1950 and has been kept at this museum until now. It is decorated by a manufacturing method that was rare at the time. It has been strictly managed and it is in a very good condition. (in Japanese この作品は，1800年頃，アメリカの美術家が作った，マグカップです．1950年頃日本に持ち込まれ，現在まで当美術館で保管しています．当時では珍しい製法により装飾されています．これまで厳重に管理されていて，とても良いコンディションを保っています．)
4	Are you sure about current position? If necessary, please come closer. (in Japanese その位置でよろしいですか．必要ならば下がったり，近づいたりしてください．)
5	Thank you very much. When I work in a museum, I'd like to explain in this distance. (in Japanese ありがとうございました．私が美術館で働く際は，この距離で説明したいと思います．)

4.1 Questionnaire Items

The items of the survey were based on Hoffman et al. [23] items. Hoffman et al. have created and verified items that can evaluate the embodiment and physicality of social robots and on-screen agents. As a result of the verification, items were shown that can evaluate the perception and interpretation of the on-screen agent's actions (Q1), interaction with objects (Q2), expression of nonverbal information (Q3), and physicality (Q4). We added items to evaluate the friendliness, based on [24–26]. Table 2 shows the contents of the questionnaire survey we conducted. This questionnaire survey was conducted in Japanese.

Table 2. Survey items (Japanese items are shown below).

	Survey Items
Q1	The virtual head is able to interpret my behaviors.
	バーチャルヘッドは、私の行動を予測できる。
Q2	The virtual head is able to touch objects.
	バーチャルヘッドは、物体に触ることができる。
Q3	The virtual head is unrestricted in its gestures.
	バーチャルヘッドの身体動作に制限はない。
Q4	The virtual head is real.
	バーチャルヘッドは、リアルだ。
Q5	The virtual head is approachable.
	バーチャルヘッドは、親しみやすい。

4.2 Survey Participants

We used "Yahoo! Crowdsourcing (Japanese)" [27] to recruit 50 participants whose native language is Japanese. All the participants were asked to watch a video of the virtual head in the Human-like condition, or the Animal-like condition giving a guiding tour of the museum and asked to answer the questionnaire. This survey was an online survey; all participants gave their consent by submitting their responses to the questionnaire. All participants were assigned to human-like or animal-like conditions, and the study was conducted in a between-participants design. Assignment is done using Google's Apps Script, which automatically and randomly issues a link to access the survey site. In the questionnaire after watching the video, the participants answered each item using 7-point Likert scale from 1 (strongly disagree) to 7 (strongly agree). The survey participants were 39 men and 11 women. The breakdown by age is as follows: 10s: 1, 20s: 1, 30s: 13, 40s: 18, 50s: 10, 60s: 7. The number of participants was 25 in both conditions.

4.3 Results

To compare the questionnaire answers between Human-like and Animal-like condition, we determined the corrected 5% significance level (.00714) by Bonferroni method, then performed multiple comparisons using the Wilcoxon rank sum test and judged based on the corrected 5% significance level (.00714). The R version used for analysis was 4.22. It was found that the question regarding physicality (Q4), the virtual head in the Human-like condition was rated significantly more physicality compared to the Animal-like condition ($p < .05$, Human-like: Mean = 4.60, SE = 0.38, Animal-like: Mean = 2.92, SE = 0.26, see Fig. 5. And it was found that the question regarding familiarity (Q5), the virtual head in the Animal-like condition was rated significantly more familiarly than in the Human-like condition ($p < .05$, Human-like: Mean = 3.00, SE = 0.23, Animal-like: Mean = 4.12, SE = 0.26, see Fig. 5). On the other hand, regarding other items, there are no significant differences between the Human-like and Animal-like conditions (Q1: Human-like: Mean = 4.00, SE = 0.20, Animal-like: Mean = 4.24, SE = 0.26,

Q2: Human-like: Mean = 1.84, SE = 0.19, Animal-like: Mean = 1.80, SE = 0.23, Q3: Human-like: Mean = 2.72, SE = 0.22, Animal-like: Mean = 3.16, SE = 0.38, see Fig. 5).

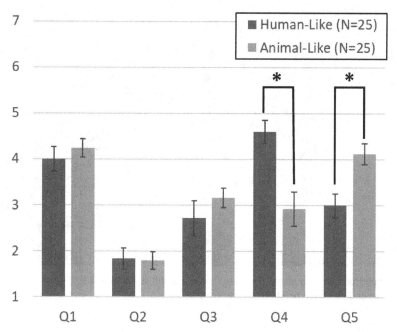

Fig. 5. The results of online survey, the error bar shows mean ± SE, and * shows $p < .05$.

5 Face-To-Face Experiment

We conducted a controlled laboratory experiment to verify whether changing the virtual head's appearance affects the social distance. In this study, we created a guided tour scenario regarding the introduction of exhibits at an art museum. The content of the scenario is shown in Table 1. In order to investigate the influence of the social distance it is important that the participants can move freely. To allow the participants to move around freely, we prepared the experiment environment that was larger than the area used in the museum tour. Figure 6 shows the experimental environment. This experiment was conducted with permission from the Research Ethics Committee Secretariat, Institute of Systems and Information Engineering, University of Tsukuba (Approval Number: 2020R439), and the Bioethics Committee, Faculty of Science and Technology, Keio University (Approval Number: 2023–143).

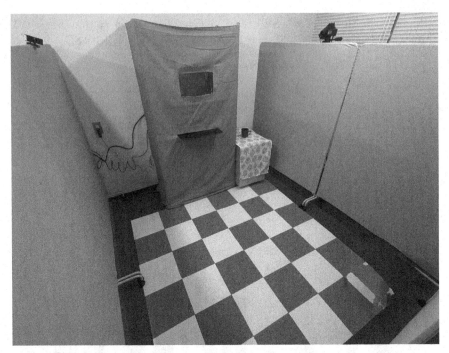

Fig. 6. Experiment environment. The virtual head's width is 750mm, and height is 1950mm – 2150mm depending on the height of the participant.

5.1 Procedure

In the scenario, the participants were asked to move to the location where they can listen to the explanation easily. The participants were instructed by experimenter to stand in a position about 500 mm from the virtual head before the start of the experiment and asked to wait there until experiment begin. The experimenter informs the participants that all the instructions of the experiment will be given from the virtual head. After beginning the experiment, the participants were instructed by the virtual head to approach the virtual head to about 100 mm in front of it. While the participants are receiving an explanation about the artwork placed next to the virtual head, they are instructed to move to a position where they can easily hear the explanation. As soon as the explanation begins, the virtual head reduces the distance until the participants' personal distance. At this time, the virtual head only displayed an image of approaching, and there is no physical approach. This allows us to measure the minimum distance that all participants feel comfortable from the distance that they feel uncomfortable, and this distance is compared for each condition.

5.2 Participants

The experiment participants were 22 Japanese people. There were no restrictions in recruiting participants. 10 people under the human-like condition (8 men, 2 women, age: Mean = 22.90, SD = 1.04), 12 people under the animal-like condition (5 men, 7 women, age: Mean = 23.75, SD = 2.31).

5.3 Hypothesis

We stetted up hypotheses for human and virtual robot head social distance based on the Hall's social distancing models and our earlier findings.

H1. Participants take more distance under Human-like condition.

We found that the human-like appearance is rated more physically through online survey. The physical body is an important element; people would take distance from the virtual head that looks like more human-like.

H2. Participants take more distance under 3D condition.

Our previous study has shown that participants take more distance from the virtual heads under 3D condition that the virtual head is displayed in stereotypical. Therefore, even if the virtual head's appearance changes, the participants take more distance from it.

5.4 Results

We conducted a mixed design two-way analysis of variance to compare the distance between the virtual head and the participants between the appearance factor, Human-like and Animal-like conditions, and the three-dimensional factor, 3D and 2D conditions. There is no significant difference between the appearance and the three-dimensionality $(F(1, 40) = .948, p = .336, \text{n.s.})$. Furthermore, there is no significant difference between 3D and 2D conditions $(F(1, 40) = 3.425, p = .072, \text{n.s.})$. However, there is a significant difference between Human-like and Animal-like conditions $(F(1, 40) = 9.312, p < .05)$. Based on the results, H1 is indicated, but H2 is rejected (Fig. 7).

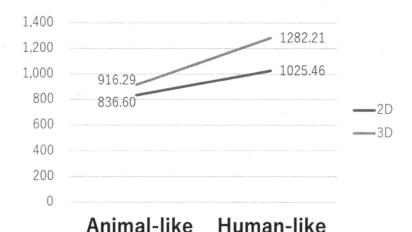

Fig. 7. Average of the social distance between participants and virtual robot head.

6 Discussion

When comparing the appearance of the virtual head displayed on a stereoscopic display between human-like appearance and animal-like appearance, we found that an animal-like appearance significantly increases the sense of familiarity. We also found that animal-like appearance significantly reduced the sense of physicality. Furthermore, we found that when the virtual head had an animal-like appearance, the social distance between it and the participants significantly decreased. It was found that people become closer to the virtual head its lack of physicality but become more familiar. In the interviews after the experiment, some participants said that the Human-like virtual head was "scary." This also shows that people determine their familiarity with others and their interpersonal distance based on their appearance. However, there is no significant difference between 3D and 2D conditions. The virtual head's appearance may have a significant impact on its familiarity and the social distance.

Contribution. The contribution of this study is that it is possible to compensate for the advantages and disadvantages of both on-screen agents, which have virtual bodies on the screen, and social robots, which have physical bodies but can cause harm to people through their actions by using the virtual head. The findings of this study will contribute to the new agent's development method that utilizes the advantages of both on-screen agents with virtual bodies and social robots with physical bodies. This study showed that animal-like appearance agents increase familiarity. On the other hand, physicality decreased, indicating that a sense of presence could not be obtained. These reductions showed that the social distance also decreased significantly. These findings can contribute to the development of on-screen agents that aim to evoke the feeling of being in the real world by displaying them 3D.

Limitation. This study did not consider cultural differences among participants. There are some studies shown that Hall's social distance vary depending on the culture of the people. Joos et al. [28]s showed that there are cultural differences in the social distance with social robots in China, the United States, and Argentina. In this study, we conducted a questionnaire survey and experiment using a virtual head with a changed appearance, but all the participants were Japanese. We should conduct future study that takes cultural differences into consideration.

The scenario of guiding exhibits in an art museum used in this research experiment was conducted for the one participant regarding the one artwork. There are also situations that communication is carried out by multiple people. In the future, we should consider the ways to explain to multiple people.

7 Conclusion

The purpose of this paper is to clarify whether changes in the virtual head's appearance affect the impression people have and affect the social distance between them. In our previous research, we developed the virtual head using a stereoscopic display without any wearable devices. In past studies, we showed that because the virtual head can be observed 3D, people feel physicality, gain a sense of body presence, and maintain an appropriate social distance. However, the effects of changes in appearance were not considered. There are some studies that shows there are differences in the impressions that observers have of on-screen agents depending on changes in their appearance, so this study investigated whether changes in appearance affect physicality and social distance. In this study, we compared the appearance of the virtual head displayed on a stereoscopic display between human-like appearance and animal-like appearance, we found that an animal-like appearance significantly increases the sense of familiarity. We also found that animal-like appearance significantly reduced the sense of physicality. Furthermore, we found that when the virtual head had an animal-like appearance, the social distance between it and the participants significantly decreased. These results showed that even the virtual bodies using stereoscopic displays, psychological distance and physical distance change depending on changes in appearance. Based on these results, we recommend that the virtual head with Human-like appearance should be used to guide people away from the virtual head, and the virtual head with Animal-like appearance should be used to guide people closer to the virtual head. However, there are some studies shown that Hall's social distance vary depending on the culture of the people. In this study, all the participants were Japanese, so we should conduct future study that takes cultural differences into consideration.

Acknowledgements. This work was supported by JSPS KAKENHI Grant Number JP21H03569, JP23H03896 and JST SPRING Grant Number JPMJSP2124.

References

1. Mumm, J., Mutlu, B.: Human-robot proxemics: physical and psychological distancing in human-robot interaction. In: HRI 2011 – Proceedings of 6th ACM/IEEE International Conference on Human Robot Interaction, pp. 331–338 (2011)
2. Takayama, L., Pantofaru, C.: Influences on proxemic behaviors in human-robot interaction. In: 2009 IEEE/RSJ International Conference on Intelligent Robots and Systems, IROS 2009 5495–5502 (2009)
3. Syrdal, D.S., Koay, K.L., Walters, M.L., Dautenhahn, K.: A personalized robot companion? - The role of individual differences on spatial preferences in HRI scenarios. In: Proceedings - IEEE International Workshop on Robot and Human Interactive Communication, pp. 1143–1148 (2007
4. Mitsunaga, N., Smith, C., Kanda, T., Ishiguro, H., Hagita, N.: Adapting robot behavior for human-robot interaction. IEEE Trans. Robot. **24**, 911–916 (2008)
5. Shiomi, M., Kanda, T., Koizumi, S., Ishiguro, H., Hagita, N.: Group attention control for communication robots with wizard of OZ approach. In: Proceedings of the ACM/IEEE International Conference on Human-Robot Interaction, pp. 121–128. ACM (2007)
6. Hall, E.T.: The Hidden Dimension. Doubleday, New York, vol. 6, no. 1 (1966)
7. Novikova, J., Watts, L., Inamura, T.: Emotionally expressive robot behavior improves human-robot collaboration. In: 2015 24th IEEE International Symposium on Robot and Human Interactive Communication (RO-MAN), pp. 7–12. IEEE (2015)
8. Hedayati, H., Szafir, D., Kennedy, J.: Comparing F-formations between humans and on-screen agents. In: Conference on Human Factors in Computing Systems – Proceedings, pp. 1–9. ACM (2020)

9. Komatsu, T., Kuki, N.: Investigating the contributing factors to make users react toward an on-screen agent as if they are reacting toward a robotic agent. In: RO-MAN 2009 - The 18th IEEE International Symposium on Robot and Human Interactive Communication, pp. 651–656. IEEE (2009)

10. Komatsu, T., Seki, Y.: Users' reactions toward an on-screen agent appearing on different media. In: 5th ACM/IEEE International Conference on Human-Robot Interaction, HRI 2010, pp. 163–164. ACM Press (2010)

11. Minegishi, T., Osawa, H.: Do you move unconsciously? Accuracy of social distance and line of sight between a virtual robot head and humans. In: 2020 29th IEEE International Conference on Robot and Human Interactive Communication (RO-MAN), 503–508. IEEE (2020)

12. Minegishi, T., Osawa, H.: Accuracy of interpersonal distance and line of sight between a virtual robot head and humans. J. Japan Soc. Fuzzy Theory Intell. Informatics **33**, 757–767 (2021). (Japanese)

13. Koda, T., Hirano, T., Ishioh, T.: Development and perception evaluation of culture-specific gaze behaviors of virtual agents. In: LNCS (including subseries Lecture Notes in Artificial Intelligence and Lecture Notes in Bioinformatics), vol. 10498 LNAI, pp. 213–222 (2017)https://doi.org/10.1007/978-3-319-67401-8_25

14. Hayduk, L.A.: The shape of personal space: an experimental investigation. Can. J. Behav. Sci./Rev. Can. des Sci. du Comport. **13**, 87–93 (1981)

15. Bailenson, J.N., Blascovich, J., Beall, A.C., Loomis, J.M.: Equilibrium theory revisited: mutual gaze and personal space in virtual environments. Presence Teleoperators Virtual Environ. **10**, 583–598 (2001)

16. Gérin-Lajoie, M., Richards, C.L., Fung, J., McFadyen, B.J.: Characteristics of personal space during obstacle circumvention in physical and virtual environments. Gait Posture **27**, 239–247 (2008)

17. Aramaki, R., Murakami, M.: Investigating appropriate spatial relationship between user and ar character agent for communication using AR WoZ system. In: Proceedings of the 15th ACM on International Conference on Multimodal Interaction, pp. 397–404. ACM (2013)

18. Jones, B., Zhang, Y., Wong, P.N.Y., Rintel, S.: VROOM: virtual robot overlay for online meetings. In: Extended Abstracts of the 2020 CHI Conference on Human Factors in Computing Systems, pp. 1–10. ACM (2020)

19. Wachsmuth, I., et al.: A virtual interface agent and its agency. In: Proceedings of the first international conference on Autonomous agents - AGENTS '97, pp. 516–517. ACM Press (1997)

20. Looking Glass Factory. https://lookingglassfactory.com. Accessed 21 Nov 2023

21. Tsubota, K., Nakamori, K.: Dry eyes and video display terminals. N. Engl. J. Med. **328**, 584 (1993)

22. Fraser, N.M., Gilbert, G.N.: Simulating speech systems. Comput. Speech Lang. **5**, 81–99 (1991)

23. Hoffmann, L., Bock, N., Rosenthal v.d. Pütten, A.M.: The peculiarities of robot embodiment (EmCorp-Scale). In: Proceedings of the 2018 ACM/IEEE International Conference on Human-Robot Interaction, pp. 370–378. ACM (2018)

24. Nittono, H.A.: Behavioral science framework for understanding kawaii. In: 3rd International Workshop on Kansei, pp. 80–83 (2010)

25. Ohkura, M., Jadram, N., Laohakangvalvit, T.: Comparison of positive feelings for motions of CG kawaii and cool robots. In: 2022 10th International Conference on Affective Computing and Intelligent Interaction Workshops and Demos, ACIIW 2022, pp. 1–6. IEEE (2022)

26. Seaborn, K., Rogers, K., Nam, S., Kojima, M.: Kawaii game vocalics: a preliminary model. In: CHI PLAY 2023 - Companion Proceedings of the Annual Symposium on Computer-Human Interaction in Play, pp. 202–208. ACM (2023)

27. Yahoo! Crowdsourcing. https://crowdsourcing.yahoo.co.jp. Accessed 14 Nov 2023 (Japanese)
28. Joosse, M.P., Poppe, R.W., Lohse, M., Evers, V.: Cultural differences in how an engagement-seeking robot should approach a group of people. In: Proceedings of the 5th ACM international conference on Collaboration across boundaries: Culture, Distance & Technology, pp. 121–130, ACM (2014)

NAO vs. Pepper: Speech Recognition Performance Assessment

Akshara Pande(✉) ⓘ, Deepti Mishra ⓘ, and Bhavana Nachenahalli Bhuthegowda ⓘ

Educational Technology Laboratory, Intelligent Systems and Analytics Group, Norwegian University of Science and Technology, Teknologivegen 22, 2815 Gjovik, Norway
{akshara.pande,deepti.mishra,bhavana.n.bhuthegowda}@ntnu.no

Abstract. Social robots are becoming increasingly popular due to their communication capabilities in various fields, such as schools, hospitals and other service industries. However, sometimes, it can be challenging to understand a person's voice due to background noise or auditory problems. To ensure effective communication, robots must have a good understanding of human speech. In order to evaluate their speech comprehension, an exploration of a speech recognition system is required. The present study focuses on the speech recognition system of two social robots, NAO and Pepper. The study aims to compare the robots' speech recognition systems and determine which performs the best. A speech-to-text conversion tool, Whisper, is integrated with robots' speech recognition systems to achieve this goal. Furthermore, evaluation measures such as WER, MER, WIL and CER are employed to determine the discrepancies between the original and the recorded speech by analyzing the corresponding text. The findings of the present paper suggest that both NAO and Pepper robot's speech recognition systems performed equally well, however, additional screen to display spoken words makes Pepper more valuable.

Keywords: Social Robot · NAO · Pepper · Speech Recognition · Whisper · Accuracy

1 Introduction

Communication is important for sharing individual thoughts, exchanging ideas, and expressing emotions. Effective communication skills are essential for encouraging healthy and positive relationships. Sometimes, understanding spoken words can be difficult due to varying accents, distinct speaking styles, and hearing impairments. The conversion of spoken words to written text would significantly enhance the capability to comprehend efficiently. The inclusion of social robots can provide an aid for establishing effective communication. Social robots are equipped with several sensors to perceive their environment and respond accordingly. These robots interact and offer several benefits that improve daily experiences in different domains with their specialized roles in personal assistance, teaching, healthcare and entertainment.

Social robots as personal assistants could help with household tasks [1], managing schedules [2], providing reminders [3] and many more. As teaching assistants, social

M. Kurosu and A. Hashizume (Eds.): HCII 2024, LNCS 14685, pp. 156–167, 2024.
https://doi.org/10.1007/978-3-031-60412-6_12

robots provide a collaborative [4] and engaging [5] environment to students, whereas social robots in healthcare can help persons in various ways, such as enhancing positivity and reducing stress [6]. Furthermore, social robots as entertainers can provide enjoyment and engagement [7]. NAO [8] and Pepper [9], developed by Softbank Robotics, have emerged as popular social robots employed by many studies. A few technical specifications (extracted from [10, 11]) of both robots are described in Table 1. They are humanoid robots capable of interacting with people using speech recognition. They both are equipped with microphones through which they can catch the person's voice. However, past studies suggested that there is a need for improvement in speech recognition system [12–14]. In order to conduct experiments that require the establishment of successful communication, it is highly important to accurately assess and select the most suitable robot. The careful selection of the robot depends on the effectiveness of the robot's speech recognition system to understand the person's voice. To the best of our knowledge, no such studies exist which compare the speech recognition capabilities of these social robots.

Table 1. Specification of NAO and Pepper robot [10, 11]

Specification		NAO	Pepper
Physical Information	Weight	5.48 kg	29.6 kg
	Size	22.6 X 12.2 X 10.8 in	55.1 X 22.8 X 22.8 in
Human Interaction		Audio, LEDs, 2D cameras, Cameras framerate	Screen and Audio, Flat imaging (2D), Depth and Stereo imaging, Touch Sensitive area, Buttons
Environment Sensors		Inertial Unit, Sonars, Force Sensitive Resistors (FSR)	Lasers, LEDs, Inertial Measurement Unit, IR Sensors, Sonars, Detection
Motion		Motors type, Motors position, Joint movement encoders	Degrees of freedom UP, Degrees of freedom DOWN, Displacement
Brain System	CPU	ATOM E3845	Quad core
	Cache memory	2 MB	-
	Clock speed	1.91 GHz	1.91 GHz
RAM		4GB DDR3	4 GB DDR3
Flash memory		32GB eMMC	32 GB eMMC
Battery Type		Lithium-Ion	Lithium-Ion

In order to evaluate speech recognition systems of robots, speech-to-text conversion can be one of the valuable tools. The text corresponding to original statements can be saved as referernce text. The matching of converted text with the reference text provides an idea about the accuracy of speech perceived by the robot. The accuracy can be measured by using error measures: Word Error Rate (WER), Match Error Rate (MER), Word Information Lost (WIL) and Character Error Rate (CER). The present study aims to evaluate the speech recognition systems of NAO and Pepper to identify the robot with a better speech recognition system. Furthermore, the aim is to integrate the speech-to-text conversion tool, Whisper, and assess the speech recognition capabilities of robots through evaluation metrics. The overall steps involved in the study have been illustrated in Fig. 1.

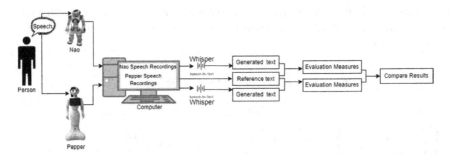

Fig. 1. Evaluation of speech recognition system of NAO and Pepper robot.

The structure of the paper is as follows: related works have been described in Sect. 2. The methodology is explained in Sect. 3. Section 4 contains the obtained results and discussions. Finally, conclusions and future works are discussed in Sect. 5.

2   Related Works

In recent years, various studies have been conducted on NAO and Pepper deployment in diverse settings, demonstrating their interaction with human beings. A speech recognition system is essential for establishing a successful interaction. Amirova et al. [15] reviewed the interaction between NAO and humans, focusing on the utilization and achievement of NAO. Both robots are frequently used in the education domain. Woo et al. [16] illustrated in their review that NAO and Pepper can be used in classrooms. Pandey et al. [13] showed the interaction between primary-grade students with NAO through quizzes. However, they found that there is a requirement for modification in the voice module of NAO. Pande et al. [17] suggested that the incorporation of Pepper with Whisper can be the potential solution for students who face challenges while understanding a teacher's accent. Gonzalez et al. [6] conducted a review on social robots in hospital settings and demonstrated that in most of the studies, the target population for social robots were children and older people. Blavette et al. [18] suggested that the inclusion of NAO could be an effective tool among elders for spreading precautionary measures for COVID-19. Betriana et al. [19] showed that Pepper was able to interact with schizophrenic patients effectively.

Past studies illustrated that NAO and Pepper robots play an important role as a companion. Mondal et al. [20] explored the possibility of using an NAO robot as a personal assistant using the Internet of Things (IoT) and proposed a prototype with various modules such as providing traffic situations, weather information, narrating stories, reading emails, and fetching news. Bertacchini et al. [21] incorporated machine learning techniques along with shopping companion NAO robot to recommend products to customers based on their preferences and availability of items in store. These machine learning algorithms were employed to identify the emotions of customers through facial expressions and speech sentiments. Carolis et al. [22] utilized Pepper's own voice and recorded human voice in Pepper to narrate stories to children, revealing that Pepper's voice had a better impact on their emotions. Pollmann et al. [23] compared the Pepper robot with a voice assistant (echo show device) in a game played via voice interaction. Further, their findings revealed that participants experienced higher enjoyment when they played with Pepper using voice interaction and its tablet, and enjoyment further increased when Pepper incorporated physical movements as well. Gauquier et al. [24] conducted an experiment comparing tablet kiosk and Pepper in which Pepper engaged with customers at Belgian chocolate shop situated at the airport using both its tablet and speech quizzes. Further, their findings suggest that Pepper had a positive impact on customers. However, they also mentioned that speech understanding was challenging because of noisy surroundings of airport.

The speech recognition system of both robots, NAO and Pepper, is affected by various factors, such as noise in the surroundings and the voices of children and elders. Kennedy et al. [12] demonstrated that the background noise can be influenced by varying distance from the NAO robot's microphone, with increased distance leading to decreased speech comprehension. Pande et al. [17] findings also suggested that the accuracy of speech recognition is highest when participants speak at a certain minimum distance from Pepper robot. Furthermore, Kennedy et al. [12] emphasized the importance of improving speech recognition for children, as it is challenging for NAO robot to understand their speech. Similarly, So et al. [14] also showed that NAO robot faced problems in perceiving children's utterances. Ekstorm et al. [25] noticed a problem with the speech recognition system of Pepper robot, which hinders interaction with children. Olde et al. [26] demonstrated that NAO faced problem associated with the voice of older adults. Furthermore, they also highlighted on concerns related with NAO's constrained speech library and its struggle with dialects. Carros et al. [27] illustrated that Pepper could not always understand elderly person's voice precisely.

Speech-to-text conversions are a beneficial way to observe recorded speech's efficacy and serve as a valuable tool for persons with hearing problems [28] and other disabilities [29]. Presently, there are several open-source tools for transcribing speech into text. Pande et al. [30] conducted a study to assess and compare numerous speech recognition tools, including Vosk, Google speech recognition, DeepSpeech, CMUSphinx, and Whisper. Their findings through evaluation metrics indicated that Whisper, which was created by OpenAI [31], revealed the highest accuracy out of all the tools.

3 Methodology

3.1 Experimental Setup

In this paper, experiments were performed to investigate the performance of the speech recognition system of the NAO and Pepper robots. The experiments took place at the Educational Technology Laboratory of NTNU Gjøvik in Norway, using a laptop with an 11th Gen Intel Core i5-1145G7 processor, 16 GB RAM, and Windows 10. The experiment was conducted using Python versions 2.7.16 and 3.9.13. Three participants were recruited for the experiment, and all were females. A sentence was selected from Wikipedia about the social robot and provided to the participants who spoke at less than 1 m from the robots. The experimental setup is shown in Fig. 2, where both robots captured the participant's voice at the same time.

Fig. 2. Experimental set-up to record the audio of a person through the speech recognition system of NAO and Pepper robots.

3.2 Pepper and Nao Audio Recordings and Transferring

ALAudioRecorder [32] service was utilized in both robots to record audio via their microphones. The recorded audios were stored in Waveform Audio File Format ('.wav' format). Python 2.7.16 was used to create the instance of this service utilizing the command 'ALProxy("ALAudioRecorder", pIp, PORT)', where "pIp" denoted Pepper's IP address, and "PORT" represented the port number. The recording was started with the "startMicrophoneRecording" method and ceased with the "stopMicrophoneRecording" method.

A Python library, Paramiko was installed to enable secure communication with remote servers through the SSH protocol [33]. To set up an SSH connection with NAO and Pepper, a transport object using 'paramiko.Transport(pIp, PORT)' was created. Subsequently, authentication was carried out in both the robots with their respective usernames and passwords. To establish the SSH connection, an SFTP client object was essential, which was obtained from the transport object ('t') through the paramiko.SFTPClient.from_transport(t)' method.

3.3 Speech-to-Text Conversion Using Whisper

Whisper [34] is an open-source speech recognition model that is versatile and can be used in various applications. It is trained on a vast audio dataset, can recognize multiple languages, and provides translation services. Whisper can help convert recorded audio files into text files, making it a perfect tool to integrate with audio recordings transferred from the NAO and the Pepper robots. Python 3.9.13 in conjunction with the Whisper library was utilized in the present study for implementation purposes. This library can be imported into Python code. The approach involved loading a pre-trained model called 'base,' which had undergone rigorous training on an enormous amount of audio data. This allowed the conversion of speech-to-text with remarkable efficiency using the transcribe () method.

3.4 Evaluation of Whisper-Generated Text Using Different Measures

In this study, four evaluation measures – WER, MER, WIL and CER were applied to measure the accuracy of recorded speech. Whisper-generated text was compared with the reference text using the above-mentioned measures. The Python library 'jiwer' was imported to calculate the error measures. The WER [35] is a metric that precisely estimates the number of word-level substitutions, deletions, and insertions essential to transform the identified text into the reference text. It can be done by dividing the total number of modifications in the predicted text by the total number of words in the reference text. MER [36] quantifies the possibility of an incorrect match between input and output words, presenting an idea of the proportion of inaccurate word matches. WIL [35] measures the ratio of erroneously predicted words when comparing reference statements to text generated by a speech recognition tool. CER [35] score reflects the percentage of incorrectly predicted characters.

4 Results and Discussions

The study involved instructing the participants to read a given statement (Fig. 3) while NAO and Pepper recorded their voices simultaneously. The audio files were transferred to a local system for further analysis after the recording. The description of files saved in the local system is illustrated in Fig. 4, and all the files were in '.wav' format.

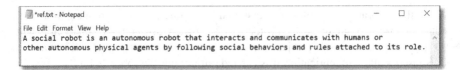

Fig. 3. Reference text which is provided to participants to state.

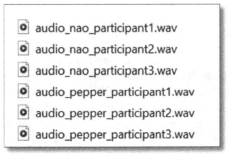

Fig. 4. Audio recordings captured by NAO and Pepper robots (after transferring to the local system).

Next, the recorded files were converted into text files with the help of Whisper. The saved text files in the local system were demonstrated in Fig. 5. The comparison of these Whisper-generated text files with reference files is essential to know how well the robots perceived the speech and which robot is the best among them.

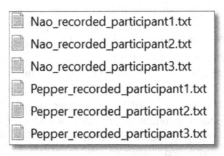

Fig. 5. Whisper-generated text files for audio recordings

A Python program was written to evaluate error measures from audio recordings of the NAO and the Pepper robot. For each participant, the text corresponding to their recorded speech was compared with reference text (Fig. 6). The result shows that WER, MER, WIL and CER scores are zero for participant 1 and participant 2. WER score of 0 means that the recognized speech is error-free and perfectly matches the reference transcription. Likewise, an MER score of 0 indicates that every match in the recognized speech perfectly aligns with the reference. A WIL score of 0 implies that no information in the recognized speech was lost with incorrect data compared to the reference. Finally, a CER score of 0 indicates that there are no errors at the character level in the recognized text. However, for participant 3, the error measures are varying. The findings suggest that for WER, 4% of words in generated text differ from reference text, and similarly for MER, there is a 4% error rate in matching words between predicted and reference text. Furthermore, the result shows a WIL score of 0.07, which implies a 7% loss in word information. It should be noted that the CER value is very low, 0.02, which suggests 2% of incorrect characters in the generated file.

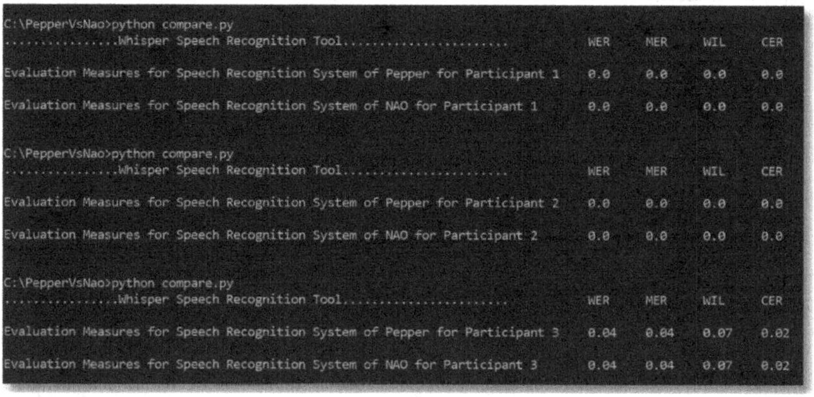

```
C:\PepperVsNao>python compare.py
...............Whisper Speech Recognition Tool.....................    WER    MER    WIL    CER

Evaluation Measures for Speech Recognition System of Pepper for Participant 1    0.0    0.0    0.0    0.0

Evaluation Measures for Speech Recognition System of NAO for Participant 1    0.0    0.0    0.0    0.0


C:\PepperVsNao>python compare.py
...............Whisper Speech Recognition Tool.....................    WER    MER    WIL    CER

Evaluation Measures for Speech Recognition System of Pepper for Participant 2    0.0    0.0    0.0    0.0

Evaluation Measures for Speech Recognition System of NAO for Participant 2    0.0    0.0    0.0    0.0


C:\PepperVsNao>python compare.py
...............Whisper Speech Recognition Tool.....................    WER    MER    WIL    CER

Evaluation Measures for Speech Recognition System of Pepper for Participant 3    0.04    0.04    0.07    0.02

Evaluation Measures for Speech Recognition System of NAO for Participant 3    0.04    0.04    0.07    0.02
```

Fig. 6. Assessment of captured speech recordings through evaluation metrics

The bar plots are shown in Fig. 7 for better visualisation purposes. There are four charts corresponding to WER, MER, WIL, and CER. X-axis presents the participant number, while the y-axis represents the error rate for each of the metrics. From four of the charts, it is evident that Participant 1 and 2 utterances were perfectly captured, whereas only for Participant 3 error measures were obtained. The interesting result is that the same values were achieved for evaluation measures for both NAO and Pepper robots. This finding suggests that the performance of both NAO and Pepper's speech recognition system is the same.

Further, to find the difference in reference text and generated text for participant 3, both files were manually analyzed (Fig. 8). The findings suggest that the audio recorded from both NAO and Pepper perceived the word 'humans' as 'women' for the participant 3, while the rest of the words were the same. Variations in speech patterns can contribute to the differences in recognition outcomes of a robot's speech recognition system. These patterns can vary with individual accents and pronunciation differences [37]. The other factors could be the participant's speaking style and pace of speech. Benzeghiba et al. [38] reviewed the impact of speech variability in automatic speech recognition. Shahre-babaki et al. [39] showed that the recognition of word spoken depends upon speaking rate. It is important to consider the energy levels of individuals during the experiment as they can impact their speech patterns, thereby affecting recognition outcomes. We only

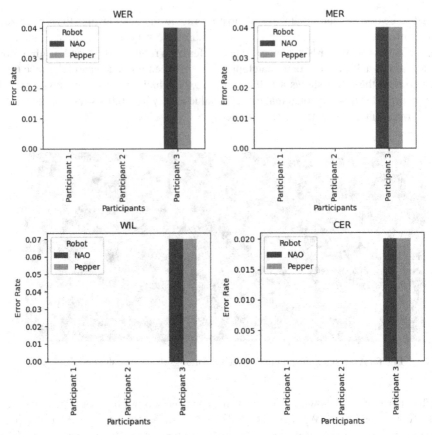

Fig. 7. Representation of evaluation metrics parameters for three participants

considered female participants for this study as some studies suggest that speech recognition performed well for female voices. Decker et al. [40] found that speech recognition was superior for females in English and French speech. It was important to select the appropriate participants group to minimize vocal issues of their speech which could help in identifying the limitations of speech recognition systems.

The distance between robots and participants were kept less than 1 m, as there are past studies which suggest that the proximity of speaker to the speech recognition system can play an important role in affecting the quality and accuracy of audio. Rodrigues et al. [41] highlighted the decrease in speech recognition performance as distance increased. Nematollahi et al. [42] proposed that more accurate speech recognition results from a smaller distance.

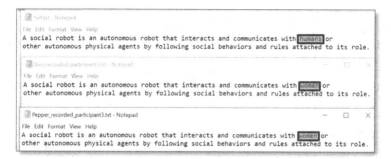

Fig. 8. Comparison of generated text (corresponding to participant 3) for NAO and Pepper robot with reference text

5 Conclusion and Future Work

The exploration of speech recognition systems is necessary to find the best between NAO robot and Pepper robot. In the present study, the statements were recorded using NAO and Pepper simultaneously, and the quality of recorded speech was evaluated with the integration of the speech-to-text conversion tool Whisper. The obtained evaluation metrics suggest an almost similar match between Whisper-generated text and the reference text when the participants were in proximity with robots. However, the evaluation measures are not the same for each participant, possibly due to variations in their speaking patterns. Additionally, sometimes robots are not able to understand complex words due to their limited vocabulary.

To ensure the generalizability of the results to select the best robot, it will be essential to expand the number of participants in the future. The present study was performed in an ideal laboratory setting; therefore, in future, the experiment can be conducted in real settings such as schools, hospitals and the service industry. If the performance of the speech recognition system of both the robots demonstrates similar accuracy, Pepper's screen for presenting transcribed text provides a distinct advantage. By integrating speech recognition tools with social robots, classrooms can become more inclusive and encourage participation. In healthcare, patient-doctor interactions can be transcribed for accurate record-keeping, while service industries can offer multilingual assistance to customers.

References

1. Leung, A.Y., et al.: Exploring the presence of humanoid social robots at home and capturing human-robot interactions with older adults: experiences from four case studies. In: Healthcare. MDPI (2022)
2. Cruz, E., et al.: Geoffrey: an automated schedule system on a social robot for the intellectually challenged. Comput. Intel. Neurosci. **2018** (2018)
3. Su, Z., et al.: Adaptation of a robotic dialog system for medication reminder in elderly care. Smart Health. **26**, 100346 (2022)
4. Rosenberg-Kima, R.B., Koren, Y., Gordon, G.: Robot-supported collaborative learning (RSCL): Social robots as teaching assistants for higher education small group facilitation. Front. Robot. AI. **6**, 148 (2020)

5. Mubin, O., et al.: Humanoid robots as teaching assistants in an Arab school. In: Proceedings of the 31st Australian Conference on Human-Computer-Interaction (2019)

6. González-González, C.S.V., Violant-Holz, V., Gil-Iranzo, R.M.: Social robots in hospitals: a systematic review. Appli. Sci. **11**(13), 5976 (2021)

7. Lytridis, C., et al.: Social robots as cyber-physical actors in entertainment and education. In: 2019 International Conference on Software, Telecommunications and Computer Networks (SoftCOM) (2019)

8. Nao webpage, https://www.aldebaran.com/en/nao, (Accessed 24 Oct 2023)

9. Pepper webpage, https://www.aldebaran.com/en/pepper, (Accessed 24 Oct 2023)

10. NAO Technical Specification, https://support.unitedrobotics.group/en/support/solutions/articles/80000959718-nao-technical-specifications, (Accessed 24 Oct 2023)

11. Pepper Technical Specification,https://support.aldebaran.com/support/solutions/articles/80000958735-pepper-technical-specifications, (Accessed 24 Oct 2023)

12. Kennedy, J., et al.: Child speech recognition in human-robot interaction: evaluations and recommendations. In: Proceedings of the 2017 ACM/IEEE International Conference on Human-Robot Interaction (2017)

13. Pandey, D., Subedi, A., Mishra. D.: Improving language skills and encouraging reading habits in primary education: A Pilot Study using NAO Robot. In: 2022 IEEE/SICE International Symposium on System Integration (SII). IEEE (2022)

14. So, S., Lee, N.: Pedagogical exploration and technological development of a humanoid robotic system for teaching to and learning in young children. Cogent Educ. **10**(1), 2179181 (2023)

15. Amirova, A., et al.: 10 years of human-nao interaction research: a scoping review. Front. Robot. AI **8**, 744526 (2021)

16. Woo, H., et al.: The use of social robots in classrooms: a review of field-based studies. Educ. Res. Rev. **33**, 100388 (2021)

17. Pande, A., Mishra, D.: The Synergy between a humanoid robot and whisper: bridging a gap in education. Electronics **12**(19), 3995 (2023)

18. Blavette, L., et al.: A robot-mediated activity using the nao robot to promote COVID-19 precautionary measures among older adults in geriatric facilities. Int. J. Environ. Res. Public Health **19**(9), 5222 (2022)

19. Betriana, F., et al.: Characteristics of interactive communication between Pepper robot, patients with schizophrenia, and healthy persons. Belitung Nursing J. **8**(2), 176–184 (2022)

20. Mondal S., N.C.G.: Personal robot: Towards developing a complete humanoid robot assistant using the Internet of Things. In: 2017 IEEE SmartWorld, Ubiquitous Intelligence & Computing, Advanced & Trusted Computed, Scalable Computing & Communications, Cloud & Big Data Computing, Internet of People and Smart City Innovation (SmartWorld/SCALCOM/UIC/ATC/CBDCom/IOP/SCI) (2017)

21. Bertacchini, F., Bilotta, E., Pantano, P.: Shopping with a robotic companion. Comput. Hum. Behav. **77**, 382–395 (2017)

22. De Carolis, B., D'Errico, F., Rossano, V.: Pepper as a storyteller: exploring the effect of human vs. Robot voice on children's emotional experience. In: Ardito, C., Lanzilotti, R., Malizia, A., Petrie, H., Piccinno, A., Desolda, G., Inkpen, K. (eds.) INTERACT 2021. LNCS, vol. 12933, pp. 471–480. Springer, Cham (2021). https://doi.org/10.1007/978-3-030-85616-8_27

23. Pollmann, K., et al.: Robot vs. voice assistant: is playing with pepper more fun than playing with alexa? In: Companion of the 2020 ACM/IEEE International Conference on Human-Robot Interaction (2020)

24. Gauquier De, C.L., et al.: Humanoid robot pepper at a Belgian chocolate shop. In: Companion of the 2018 ACM/IEEE International Conference on Human-robot Interaction (2018)

25. Ekström, S., Pareto, L.: The dual role of humanoid robots in education: As didactic tools and social actors. Educ. Inf. Technol. **27**(9), 12609–12644 (2022)

26. Olde Keizer, R.A., et al.: Using socially assistive robots for monitoring and preventing frailty among older adults: a study on usability and user experience challenges. Heal. Technol. **9**, 595–605 (2019)

27. Carros, F., et al.: Exploring human-robot interaction with the elderly: results from a ten-week case study in a care home. In: Proceedings of the 2020 CHI Conference on Human Factors in Computing Systems (2020)

28. Shezi, M., Ade-Ibijola, A.: Deaf chat: a speech-to-text communication aid for hearing deficiency. Adv. Sci. Technol. Eng. Syst. J. **5**(5), 826–833 (2020)

29. Debnath, S., et al., Audio-visual automatic speech recognition towards education for disabilities. J. Autism Developm. Disorders, 1–14 (2022)

30. Pande, A., et al.: A comparative analysis of real time open-source speech recognition tools for social robots. In: International Conference on Human-Computer Interaction. Springer (2023). https://doi.org/10.1007/978-3-031-35708-4_26

31. Radford, A., et al.: Robust speech recognition via large-scale weak supervision. In: International Conference on Machine Learning. PMLR (2023)

32. Naoqi API documentation - ALAudioRecorder. http://doc.aldebaran.com/2-5/naoqi/audio/alaudiorecorder.html, (Accessed 24 Oct 2023)

33. Paramiko documentation. https://www.paramiko.org/, (Accessed 24 Oct 2023)

34. OpenAI Whisper. https://openai.com/research/whisper, (Accessed 24 Oct 2023)

35. Pande, A., et al.: A comparative analysis of real time open-source speech recognition tools for social robots. in design, user experience, and usability. Springer Nature Switzerland, Cham (2023). https://doi.org/10.1007/978-3-031-35708-4_26

36. Filippidou, F., Moussiades, L.: A Benchmarking of IBM, google and wit automatic speech recognition systems. In: Maglogiannis, I., Iliadis, L., Pimenidis, E. (ed.) Artificial Intelligence Applications and Innovations: 16th IFIP WG 12.5 International Conference, AIAI 2020, 2020, Proceedings, Part I, pp. 73–82. Springer International Publishing, Cham (2020). https://doi.org/10.1007/978-3-030-49161-1_7

37. Braber, N., et al.: Assessing the specificity and accuracy of accent judgments by lay listeners. Lang. Speech **66**(2), 267–290 (2023)

38. Benzeghiba, M., et al.: Automatic speech recognition and speech variability: a review. Speech Commun. **49**(10–11), 763–786 (2007)

39. Shahrebabaki, A.S., Imran, A.S., Olfati, N., Svendsen, T.: Acoustic feature comparison for different speaking rates. In: Kurosu, M. (ed.) HCI 2018. LNCS, vol. 10903, pp. 176–189. Springer, Cham (2018). https://doi.org/10.1007/978-3-319-91250-9_14

40. Adda-Decker, M., Lamel, L.: Do speech recognizers prefer female speakers? In: Ninth European Conference on Speech Communication and Technology (2005)

41. Rodrigues, A., et al.: Analyzing the performance of ASR systems: the effects of noise, distance to the device, age and gender. In: Proceedings of the XX International Conference on Human Computer Interaction (2019)

42. Nematollahi, M.A., Al-Haddad, S.A.R.: Distant speaker recognition: an overview. Int. J. Humanoid Rob. **13**(02), 1550032 (2016)

Convenience vs. Reliability? Evaluation of Human-Robot Interaction Preferences in a Production Environment

Moritz Schmidt[(✉)] and Claudia Meitinger

Faculty of Electrical Engineering, Augsburg Technical University of Applied Sciences,
86161 Augsburg, Germany
{moritz.schmidt,claudia.meitinger}@tha.de

Abstract. This study examines the dynamics of human-robot interaction in an industry-related scenario, with a specific emphasis on how different error rates of a speech recognition system affect user preferences with respect to the kind of interface that is used for interaction. In modern production contexts, the growing number of collaborating robots (cobots) requires a thorough understanding of user interactions in order to build effective and user-friendly human-robot interaction approaches. This research is motivated by two important factors: (1) the continuous transformation of work due to automation, which leads to a shift in the responsibilities of human workers from manual labor to monitoring and directing, and (2) the lack of research that investigates the impact of speech interaction on trust in situations involving human-robot interaction. In consideration of this context, we conducted a user study using a closed wizard-of-oz design, in which users engage with a cobot that is fitted with a sanding end-effector in a noisy (75 dB) environment. The users could either use voice interaction or a robot teach panel to delegate tasks to a cobot while they had to complete a mental taxing task. The study evaluates the influence of different speech recognition error rates on user preferences by comparing the ease of use of voice-based interaction with the reliability of graphical user interfaces. Contrary to expectations, the findings contradict the predicted negative correlation between error rates and SUS scores. The use of the robot teach panel increases once speech recognition error rate exceeds 60%, indicating an overall preference of a convenient voice-based human-robot interaction even in noisy production facilities.

Keywords: Human-Robot Interaction · Cobots · SME · Task delegation

1 Introduction

The fourth industrial revolution had a significant impact on large-scale production and has resulted in a period of increased automation, digitization, and connectivity of production facilities. Notably, this shift is starting to have an impact on small and medium enterprises (SME) in addition to large industrial facilities. The use of collaborative robots (cobots) indicates a move toward automating single-unit production and small batch sizes. The task and responsibilities of human workers are going to change as the effectiveness and efficiency of such automation in SMEs becomes clear. In particular, it is expected that their duties are shifting from manual labor to monitoring, managing, and maximizing the operation of highly automated collaborative machines.

This shift in the workers' duties requires a development in task allocation, and more specifically, in task delegation, as teaching cobots is still a time consuming task usually making automated single-unit production unfeasible. Therefore, an efficient and effective interaction mechanism is required for the robot to be able to engage at the task-based abstraction level.

The choice to assign a task to a cobot could be influenced by several factors, for instance, trust, expected system capabilities, availability, and prior experience of the human worker with robotic system usage. Interaction methodology preferences among operators are not well understood due to the need to combine research on the preferred interaction modes for human-robot collaboration and trust in technical systems. People depend on system robustness, on the one hand, to boost their confidence in technical systems and increase automation reliance. On the other hand, with the increasing adoption of smart home gadgets such as voice assistants, increasing evidence [22,27] suggests people now prefer to interact with technical systems by speech. Considering voice-based interaction in a noisy environment, as is common in a production facility with robots, inevitably has some detrimental impacts on voice recognition, such as decreased accuracy of automatic speech recognition (ASR) and natual language processing (NLP) algorithms. As a result, the system's overall robustness could be decreased.

In this paper, we examine whether there is a noticeable error rate (ER) threshold, above which a dependable graphical user interface (GUI)-based interaction method is better than a more convenient voice-based one. Hence, the research question – individuals are expected to transition to the teach panel at a specific ER – is supported by the formulation of the following hypotheses: (H1) there is a negative correlation between ER and the system usability scale (SUS) score; (H2) participants are expected to switch to a teach panel following multiple consecutive voice control failures; and (H3) there is a specific ER at which participants choose to forego voice interaction and only use the teach panel.

To test these assumptions, in an experimental design, each participant will be given two tasks to complete in parallel: (1) completing as many steps of a mentally demanding Lego assembly instruction and (2) assigning various tasks to a robot via voice interaction or a state-of-the-art robot teach panel. Both tasks are executed not in close proximity to the robot to simulate future human worker duties like monitoring multiple robots in different locations. Hence, using the GUI is associated with increasing costs for walking to the teach panel.

2   Related Work

The research's theoretical foundation is derived from Muir's works, where automation robustness, automation reliance, and trust create a complex cycle [18,19]. Therefore, understanding the dependency of trust and system robustness is inevitable. Additionally, recent studies on voice-based interaction, for instance by Spille et al., evaluating the effectiveness of NLP algorithms in noisy environments [26], provide additional theoretical guidance. This research is also influenced by the kinds of jobs that shop floor employees may eventually be responsible for once automation technology properly steps in, thus, creating a close link between research and practice. Scholars anticipate that tasks will transition from dangerous, dull, and dirty [5] to monitoring and directing [6,7].

2.1   Trust and Trustworthiness

Establishing adequate trust in technical systems while avoiding overtrust or distrust is becoming increasingly important as a research field partially due to the rise of highly automated technical systems featuring various level of robot autonomy (LORA) [3] that could fail in an undefined behavior. Therefore, understanding the effects on trust from human operators towards automated systems is an essential piece to assess the differences of robust or convenient human-robot interaction (HRC) methods.

Lee and Moray conducted a study and reported that whether an operator confirms a task assignment either to automatic or manual control in complex systems is influenced by the "self-confidence in the ability to control the system manually" [14]. Furthermore, Lee and See provided a model to explain the relation of trust and trustworthiness and the concepts of overtrust and distrust based on a personal view [13].

In a study evaluating various effects on trust in robots Hancock et al. reported that the robot's performance is a major contributor to generating trust, consolidating the works of Muir et al. [9].

Xie et al. extended the definition of trust based on user study findings indicating that trust itself is no simple concept. Instead, humans use at least the capability and intention of the robot as parameters to create an extensive mental model [30].

Sapienza et al. developed a trust model where each interacting partner, machine or human, can have a trustee and trustor relationship. They define the trustworthiness to be a combination of competence and willingness of the interaction partner. They do not limit this to a human concept, but also to a machine-to-machine interaction [24].

In another study evaluating the effects of (un)reliable automation, the results indicate a reliable automation reduces workload but lowers the user's engagement, whereas the performance increases [17].

According to Roesler et al., non-anthropomorphic robots lead to increased trust and the type and timing of the error has a significant impact on trust towards robotic systems. In detail, errors during the information acquisition phase are considered to have a more negative impact on trust than errors in the acting phase of the automation procedure [23]. However, research by Urakami et al. argues that nonverbal cues are essential in human-to-human communication and give the robot a *aliveness* or *social agency* [28].

2.2   Voice Interaction

Contrary to the expectations of Strazdas et al., voice-based interaction appeared to be a favorable HRC methodology in a Wizard-of-Oz study despite the fact that industrial robots are usually operating in noisy environments [27].

According to Janicek et al., ASR recognition rates range from 68% to 98%. Longer commands result in higher recognition accuracy; one-word commands performed the worst [10]. Extensive studies on speech recognition performance have shown that, depending on the environment, the signal-to-noise ratio for the speech recognition threshold (SRT) is approximately 12 dB [26]. When the average word error rate (WER) is between 5% and 10%, a voice interaction system is considered to be of good quality [26]. However, not all test cases see the same level of performance between ASR algorithms and humans [29]. Pires et al. have previously suggested using a headset microphone in case voice-based interaction is required in a noisy environment. Unfortunately, no specific value for the background noise level is provided in the findings [21].

Halim et al. developed a multimodal interface based on voice interaction, micro and macro gestures, and an additional GUI as a fallback in case the voice base interaction is not working in a noisy setting. High ambient noise levels required voice-based interaction to be repeated frequently, which leads to the recommendation to adopt alternate input modalities [8]. In a parallel study, Ambadar [1] assesses the fusion of sensor data in a "speech-gesture multimodal interface" [1] and evaluates confidence intervals while continuously tracking ambient noise levels, leading to a multimodal mode that performs better than an unimodal mode [1].

When comparing the performance differences between multilayer GUI and voice interaction, Norda et al. discovered that, except the GUI's initial screen, voice interaction is typically faster than interacting with a GUI making it an efficient HRC methodology. During the tests, the ambient noise was intentionally not similar to that of a production facility [20].

Even though there is existing research on the issue of speech recognition in a production setting, the operator is typically situated close to the machine, and using a GUI has minimal associated costs (e.g. walking time to the robot) [1,8,20]. The purpose of our study is to determine the impact of higher expenses when choosing to utilize a teach panel that is not close to the operator's workstation.

3   Design of Experiment

The experimental setup involves a user study with an Universal Robots UR10e cobot equipped with an OnRobot Sander as the end-effector. The research context explained in [25], provides a foundation for this study. It explains the use case, challenges for SMEs, and the overall structure of delegated tasks. Shop floor workers are still occupied by completing dull and dirty tasks like sanding work pieces because cobot teaching technologies are not viable for single-unit or small batch size production.

(a) Participants workspace with robot, teach panel and wizard location in the background.

(b) The robot workspace.

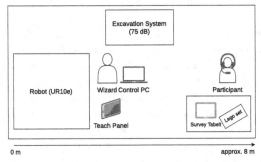

(c) Schematic setup of the user study with robot, workplace, excavation system, and wizard location.

Fig. 1. Setup of the user study.

Participants are tasked with delegating specific sanding tasks to the cobot, representing a typical process in finishing products for further production. The tasks and command texts are provided to participants including a checklist on their desk, cf. Fig. 1c, so remembering which tasks are delegated already is no mentally taxing task. Prior to the wizard experiment, participants delegated three test tasks via voice and teach panel to the robot to establish a sufficient understanding of the system.

A side task involving the completion of steps in a Lego instruction manual is introduced to simulate an increased mental workload. Only completed steps are counted. This additional goal aims to reflect the challenges individuals may face when simultaneously monitoring and directing multiple machines in an industrial setting once full automation also sets in SMEs. The inclusion of the side task serves a dual purpose: it increases the costs for users to control the robot via the teach pendant due to time constraints and simulates the heightened mental workload anticipated in an industry-ready scenario. Otherwise, there would be no limitation for participants to remain in close proximity of the robot to intervene any moment or use the teach panel making the voice interaction superfluous.

Participants in the study engage with the cobot by delegating tasks through different interaction methods. Two distinct approaches are provided for each participant: a less convenient GUI allowing task delegation by selecting a specific program, and a more convenient voice-based interaction imitated by ASR and NLP algorithms, for instance Fig. 2. The voice interaction is controlled by the wizard. The participants receive instructions that the choice of the interaction methodology is their decision without any restrictions. As a consequence, participants can neglect the voice interaction and only rely on teach panel interaction. Starting a task on the robot teach panel takes nine touch interactions.

ROBOT: System ready. Listening for a new task.
    Task x start time.
USER: Sand the object a.
    Wizard reject input. (invalid)
ROBOT: Command not understood.
USER: Sand the aluminium object a.
    Wizard acknowledge input. (valid)
    System determine acceptance (true)
ROBOT: Understood sand aluminium object a.
    Task x stop time.
    Robot performs task.
ROBOT: Task completed successfully. Listening for new task.
USER: *Delegates next task*
    . . .

Fig. 2. Task delegation dialogue as implemented in the user study.

The independent variable, the ER, varies among participants, randomly assigned by the study leader. The ERs range from 20% to 70%, representing the system's command recognition rate for valid inputs. In order to limit influences on dependent variables, for instance, trust in automation questionnaire (TiAQ) and SUS score, the robot always executes the delegated program and programs do not fail.

A closed Wizard-of-Oz study design is implemented, with the wizard controlling the cobot through short keyboard inputs. The wizard, disguised as the study leader, determines the validity of voice-based commands, ensuring a controlled environment. The distance between wizard and participant is intentional to catch unclear or quiet commands that might not be understood by an ASR algorithm. The excavation system with a sound pressure level of 75 dB is running during sanding tasks and due to the run-on time of the excavation system, commands are delegated while the excavation system is running.

In order to control for potential bias effects caused by individuals' preferences and preconceptions, participants were asked to complete a demographic questionnaire and express their attitude towards robots using the attitudes toward cooperative industrial robots questionnaire (ACIR-Q) by Leichtmann et al. [15] before the experiment. TiAQ [11,12] and SUS questionnaires [4] are completed after the Wizard-of-Oz study. The study leader's role as wizard is only revealed once the last part of the questionnaire is completed.

The ER, e, including both invalid commands and valid commands rejected by the wizard or the system, is computed as e_{total}, cf. Eq. 3, based on the number of attempts a. This is the ER that the participant experiences. The internal ER of the speech recognition system (e_{valid}, cf. Eq. 2) is calculated based on valid attempts, cf. Eq. 1, only. If a synonym or a shortened version of a material, object or process is used, the task delegation is considered to be valid. Furthermore, the order of process, object, and material does not matter. We want the interface to feel as natural and close to the shadowing conducted in crafts enterprises presented in [25]. The ERs are determined through a Bernoulli distribution, with the probability of generating a *true* determined by the assigned ER.

$$a_{valid} = a_{total} - a_{invalid} + a_{TeachPanel} \tag{1}$$

$$e_{study}^{valid} = \sum_{i=1}^{n=10} (a_{valid}^i - 1)/ \sum_{i=1}^{n=10} a_{valid}^i \tag{2}$$

$$e_{study}^{total} = \sum_{i=1}^{n=10} (a_{total}^i - 1 + a_{TeachPanel}^i)/ \sum_{i=1}^{n=10} a_{total}^i \tag{3}$$

4   Results

The study had 17 participants. One trial was canceled due to a severe robot error. Among the remaining 16 participants, people identified as male, female and diverse. Five individuals stated that they work with a robot at their workplace. The average age is 30.1 years (SD 10.5), with a range of 21–56 years. The majority of jobs are office-based. The initial ER set at the beginning of each experiment compared to the actual ER ($e_{total} - e_{initial}$: 4.53 (SD 12.27), $e_{valid} - e_{initial}$: -1.37 (SD 11.60)) provides evidence that the experiment setup and software work as intended.

The data point in Fig. 3 at $e_{total} \approx 83\%$ had a high amount of invalid attempts ($a_{invalid} = 10$). The ER of valid attempts $e_{valdi} = 74\%$.

The overall SUS score for the entire system consistently demonstrated high scores across the entire ER range, suggesting an overall satisfaction with the system considering a threshold for a favorable design based on SUS scores of 70 points [2].

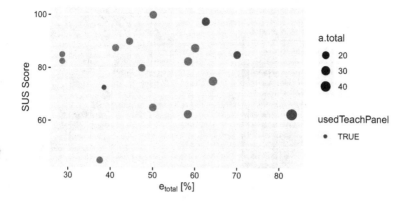

Fig. 3. e_{total} vs. SUS scaled by accumulated total attempts for each participant. Trials using the teach panel are colored in red. (Color figure online)

The ACIR-Q (5-point Likert scale) mean for affect is 4.36 (SD 0.60), social 3.94 (SD 0.73) and task 3.94 (SD 0.80). On a five-point Likert scale (1: do not agree; 5: agree), participants rated the Lego task as enjoyable (4.38, SD 0.81), more important than the robot task (2.13, SD 0.81), and distracted by the voice interaction (3.06, SD 1.29). The TiAQ (5-point Likert scale) yielded scores of 3.76 (SD 0.61) for competence, 2.53 (SD 1.47) for familiarity, 4.14 (SD 0.77) for understanding, 4.25 (SD 0.89) for developer intent, 3.12 (SD 0.58) for prosperity to trust, and 4.06 (SD 0.91) for trust in automation.

A total of 160 tasks were delegated from humans to the robot, accumulating to 343 task delegation attempts. Of these, 34 were invalid and 9 were via robot teach panel input. The teach panel was used after an average of 3.11 (SD 2.03) invalid attempts. Meanwhile, an average of 4.38 (SD 0.62) steps from the Lego instruction manual were completed. The average time for task delegation attempts was 12.38 (SD 5.93) seconds, with the first attempt taking 14.01 (SD 7.17) seconds. This was based on direct success without the use of the teach panel. The average time for successful delegation after two attempts was 11.41 (SD 4.76) seconds (excluding the teach panel). This is due to setup and task-switching times. The average time for task delegation without the teach panel is 12.26 (SD 6.01) seconds, compared to 14.42 (SD 4.10) seconds with the teach panel. These findings are consistent with [20], which found that voice interaction outperforms GUI interaction in speed.

The majority of robot tasks (8 out of 10) take around 30 s to complete, with the remaining tasks lasting nearly a minute. The average experiment time, excluding pre- and post-questionnaires, is 627.50 (SD 91.92) seconds.

Figure 4 depicts the correlation coefficient matrix across important measurements of the user study, also indicating significant correlations. The SUS score has an overall positive correlation with the TiAQ sub-scales except for the familiarity sub-scale. The significant strong positive correlation of ER and total trial time ($t.total$) also indicates a functional experiment setup since more repetitions due to an increased ER take more time.

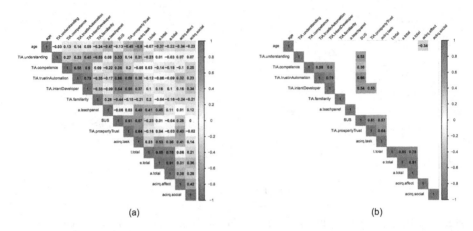

Fig. 4. Correlation coefficients; (a) all correlation coefficients; (b) filtered for the significance of p-Value < 0.05

5 Discussion

The study attempted to clarify the impact of ERs on user preferences in interacting with a cobot in an industry-related use case, taking into account the development of shop floor workers from completing tasks to monitoring and directing. The hypotheses proposed three key assertions, providing insights into the dynamics between ERs and user satisfaction measured via the SUS score.

The initial hypothesis suggested a negative correlation between the ERs and SUS scores. Surprisingly, and contrary to our expectations, we found no significant correlation between these variables. Participants appeared forgiving, perhaps attributing errors to the challenging environment of a manufacturing facility. While there is no correlation between SUS scores and ERs, the use of teach panels increases when the speech recognition ER exceeds 60%, as shown in Fig. 3. Other factors, such as the robot's never-failing performance, may have inflated SUS scores. Adding failing robot programs and incorrect task execution can improve realism in future user studies while also providing a means to measure awareness and engagement. Participants showed low engagement in the robot task, indicating competing goals with the Lego task, despite giving the Lego task lower priority on average. Participants expressed concerns about long-term system usability. This suggests the need for a longitudinal field study to better understand the cross-sectional laboratory-based user study results.

The data did not support the expectation that participants would switch to the teach panel after multiple voice control failures. In fact, despite voice control failures, only a fraction of participants chose the teach panel, demonstrating adaptability. In an unstructured interview, which was conducted at the end of the session, one participant explained that little frustration with multiple consecutive failures stemmed from the assumption of a learning speech recognition system. However, one participant quickly turned to the teach panel, but he was also working with the same robot on a regular basis indicating personal experience as an important factor.

The complexity of Lego set instructions probably hindered the measurement of significant differences in progress related to the ERs. Using a simpler set in the future could address this issue. Despite this, the Lego task was well-received, and rated as overall satisfying and fun. The approach ensures consistent effort, considering participants' previous experience with modular building block sets.

The hypothesis proposing a specific ER threshold for exclusive teach panel usage was not supported. Participants did not consistently converge on a particular ER threshold before resorting solely to the teach panel.

In summary, the overall conclusion regarding the trade-off between convenience and robustness, based on the hypotheses, favors the convenient HRC method. SUS scores across the range of ERs provide no data supporting the neglectance of voice-based interaction methodology and might be related to participants' interest in adopting and learning new technologies. A comparison with future user study results which also include shop floor workers would provide valuable insights between different groups while also reducing the limitations due to the small sample size of the study [16].

6   Conclusion

This study examines how HRC affects user preferences in an industry-related use case. The exploration aimed to provide valuable insights into how cobots might be used in real-world production environments.

Our findings showed no significant correlation between ERs and SUS scores, contradicting the initial hypothesis of a negative correlation. Although SUS scores were consistently high, the use of the teach panel increased when speech recognition errors exceeded 60%. We assume that robust robot programs affected the SUS, partially omitting the effect of unreliable speech recognition systems.

Only a small percentage of participants chose the teach panel after experiencing multiple voice control failures, demonstrating the preference for a more convenient HRC methodology. This challenges the assumption that users would always switch to the teach panel in such situations or even completely neglect voice-based interaction. Previous experiences using the same robot may influence user preferences for interaction methods.

The Lego task's complexity made it difficult to measure significant differences in progress with respect to ERs. Future studies could benefit from a simpler task to better capture participants' responses to different ERs.

In the future, we intend to replicate this study with craftsmen and craftswomen. This allows us to compare the results of a student-based survey with a study based on a target group with a different educational background.

In conclusion, the study explores the balance between convenience and robustness in HRC methodologies. The favorable SUS scores across varying ERs indicate that participants prioritize convenience over robustness in our study.

However, this conclusion is contingent on the specific conditions and tasks examined, and further research is needed to generalize these findings to broader contexts.

Acknowledgement. This publication was created as part of the AI Production Network Augsburg research project at the Augsburg Technical University of Applied Sciences. We want to thank Nina Hirsekorn and Rebecca Strohmeier[0000−0003−0297−6843] for their helpful remarks.

Disclosure of Interests. The authors have no competing interests to declare that are relevant to the content of this article.

References

1. Ambadar, F.F., Martinez, J.J.L.: Improving the performance of speech-gesture multimodal interface in non-ideal environments **216**, 587–596. https://doi.org/10.1016/j.procs.2022.12.173
2. Bangor, A., Kortum, P., Miller, J.: Determining what individual SUS scores mean: adding an adjective rating scale. J. Usability Stud. **4**(3), 114–123 (2009). https://doi.org/10.5555/2835587.2835589
3. Beer, J.M., Fisk, A.D., Rogers, W.A.: Toward a framework for levels of robot autonomy in human-robot interaction **3**(2), 74. https://doi.org/10.5898/jhri.3.2.beer
4. Brooke, J.: SUS - a quick and dirty usability scale **189**. https://www.researchgate.net/publication/228593520_SUS_A_quick_and_dirty_usability_scale
5. Engelberger, J.F.: Robotics in Practice. Springer, New York. https://doi.org/10.1007/978-1-4684-7120-5
6. Forster, N.: Hidden Digital Champions. Springer, Wiesbaden (2019). https://doi.org/10.1007/978-3-658-26724-7
7. Frey, C.B., Osborne, M.A.: The future of employment: how susceptible are jobs to computerisation? **114**, 254–280. https://doi.org/10.1016/j.techfore.2016.08.019
8. Halim, J., Eichler, P., Krusche, S., Bdiwi, M., Ihlenfeldt, S.: No-code robotic programming for agile production: a new markerless-approach for multimodal natural interaction in a human-robot collaboration context **9**. https://doi.org/10.3389/frobt.2022.1001955
9. Hancock, P.A., Billings, D.R., Schaefer, K.E., Chen, J.Y.C., de Visser, E.J., Parasuraman, R.: A meta-analysis of factors affecting trust in human-robot interaction **53**(5), 517–527. https://doi.org/10.1177/0018720811417254
10. Janíček, M., Ružarovský, R., Velíšek, K., Holubek, R.: Analysis of voice control of a collaborative robot **1781**(1), 012025. https://doi.org/10.1088/1742-6596/1781/1/012025
11. Körber, M.: Theoretical considerations and development of a questionnaire to measure trust in automation. In: Bagnara, S., Tartaglia, R., Albolino, S., Alexander, T., Fujita, Y. (eds.) IEA 2018. AISC, vol. 823, pp. 13–30. Springer, Cham (2019). https://doi.org/10.1007/978-3-319-96074-6_2. https://github.com/moritzkoerber/TiA_Trust_in_Automation_Questionnaire
12. Körber, M., Baseler, E., Bengler, K.: Introduction matters: manipulating trust in automation and reliance in automated driving **66**, 18–31. https://doi.org/10.1016/j.apergo.2017.07.006

13. Lee, J.D., See, K.A.: Trust in automation: designing for appropriate reliance **46**(1), 50–80. https://doi.org/10.1518/hfes.46.1.50_30392
14. Lee, J., Moray, N.: Trust, control strategies and allocation of function in human-machine systems **35**(10), 1243–1270. https://doi.org/10.1080/00140139208967392
15. Leichtmann, B., Hartung, J., Wilhelm, O., Nitsch, V.: New short scale to measure workers' attitudes toward the implementation of cooperative robots in industrial work settings: Instrument development and exploration of attitude structure. https://doi.org/10.31234/osf.io/tx3gy
16. Leichtmann, B., Nitsch, V., Mara, M.: Crisis ahead? Why human-robot interaction user studies may have replicability problems and directions for improvement **9**. https://doi.org/10.3389/frobt.2022.838116
17. Lin, T.C., Krishnan, A.U., Li, Z.: The impacts of unreliable autonomy in human-robot collaboration on shared and supervisory control for remote manipulation **8**(8), 4641–4648. https://doi.org/10.1109/lra.2023.3287039
18. Muir, B.: Trust in automation: Part I. Theoretical issues in the study of trust and human intervention in automated systems **37**(11), 1905–1922. https://doi.org/10.1080/00140139408964957
19. Muir, B., Neville, M.: Trust in automation. Part II. Experimental studies of trust and human intervention in a process control simulation **39**(3), 429–460. https://doi.org/10.1080/00140139608964474
20. Norda, M., Engel, C., Rennies, J., Appell, J.E., Lange, S.C., Hahn, A.: Evaluating the efficiency of voice control as human machine interface in production, pp. 1–12. https://doi.org/10.1109/tase.2023.3302951
21. Pires, J.N.: Robot-by-voice: experiments on commanding an industrial robot using the human voice **32**(6), 505–511. https://doi.org/10.1108/01439910510629244
22. Ray, C., Mondada, F., Siegwart, R.: What do people expect from robots? In: 2008 IEEE/RSJ International Conference on Intelligent Robots and Systems. IEEE. https://doi.org/10.1109/iros.2008.4650714
23. Roesler, E., Vollmann, M., Manzey, D., Onnasch, L.: The dynamics of human-robot trust attitude and behavior - exploring the effects of anthropomorphism and type of failure **150**, 108008. https://doi.org/10.1016/j.chb.2023.108008
24. Sapienza, A., Cantucci, F., Falcone, R.: Modeling interaction in human–machine systems: a trust and trustworthiness approach **3**(2), 242–257. https://doi.org/10.3390/automation3020012
25. Schmidt, M., Meitinger, C.: A Concept for User-Centered Delegation of Abstract High-Level Tasks to Cobots for Flexible Lot Sizes (2023). https://doi.org/10.48550/ARXIV.2311.01253
26. Spille, C., Kollmeier, B., Meyer, B.T.: Comparing human and automatic speech recognition in simple and complex acoustic scenes **52**, 123–140. https://doi.org/10.1016/j.csl.2018.04.003
27. Strazdas, D., Hintz, J., Felbberg, A.M., Al-Hamadi, A.: Robots and wizards: an investigation into natural human-robot interaction **8**, 207635–207642. https://doi.org/10.1109/access.2020.3037724
28. Urakami, J., Seaborn, K.: Nonverbal cues in human–robot interaction: a communication studies perspective **12**(2), 1–21. https://doi.org/10.1145/3570169
29. Weerts, L., Rosen, S., Clopath, C., Goodman, D.F.M.: The psychometrics of automatic speech recognition. https://doi.org/10.1101/2021.04.19.440438
30. Xie, Y., Bodala, I.P., Ong, D.C., Hsu, D., Soh, H.: Robot capability and intention in trust-based decisions across tasks. In: 2019 14th ACM/IEEE International Conference on Human-Robot Interaction (HRI). IEEE. https://doi.org/10.1109/hri.2019.8673084

Toward Intelligent Telepresence Robotics for Enhancing Elderly Healthcare in Smart Care Home

Syed Hammad Hussain Shah[1]([✉]) [ID], Abeer Badawy[2], Faisal Jamil[3] [ID], Tariq Alsboui[3] [ID], and Ibrahim A. Hameed[1] [ID]

[1] Department of ICT and Natural Sciences, Faculty of Information Technology and Electrical Engineering, Norwegian University of Science and Technology (NTNU), Larsgårdsvegen 2, Alesund 6009, Norway
{syed.h.h.shah,ibib}@ntnu.no
[2] Department of Health Sciences in Ålesund, Faculty of Medicine and Health Sciences, Norwegian University of Science and Technology, Larsgårdsvegen 2, 6009 Alesund, Norway
[3] Department of Computer Science, School of Computing and Engineering, University of Huddersfield, Queensgate, Huddersfield HD1 3DH, UK
{f.jamil,T.Alsboui}@hud.ac.uk

Abstract. Within the domain of smart care homes, where the well-being of the elderly is of the utmost importance, this article introduces a novel strategy that combines an AI-enhanced task-planning system with a transformer-based framework. The objective is to implement telepresence robots in a cost-effective manner so as to enable autonomous and sophisticated healthcare services. This innovative methodology enables the dynamic generation and self-regulating adjustment of a wide array of robotic behaviors in light of new information that arises throughout interactions. Our research demonstrates that the predicted performance of these machines is predicted with an exceptional degree of accuracy exceeding 97%. The efficiency, significance, and user-friendliness of the system are emphasized in participant feedback, which strongly indicates that such robotic assistance should be utilized in the Smart Care Home environment in the future. The aforementioned favorable results are a consequence of the system's diverse AI sub-components coordinating in a seamless fashion and its ability to swiftly adjust to changing interaction dynamics. The result underscores the potential of telepresence robotics to improve healthcare for the elderly in smart care homes.

Keywords: Telepresence Robotics · Elderly Healthcare · Autonomous Healthcare Services · AI-Enhanced Assistance · Smart Care Homes

1 Introduction

By 2022, the worldwide population of adults aged 65 or over had achieved a noteworthy milestone, amounting to 771 million. The projections indicate that this population will exceed 994 million by 2030 and a remarkable 1.6 billion by 2050 [1]. The increasing average life expectancy has heightened the need to provide comprehensive and efficient health and social care systems, with a particular focus on facilitating `aging in place`. This idea envisions people living in their own homes and communities in a secure, self-sufficient, and enjoyable manner, regardless of their age, income, or level of ability. Significant changes are required in the existing paradigms that control the monitoring and delivery of care to achieve this objective and provide efficient and cost-effective home-care services.

Research in the field of robot-based home-care systems has revealed the extensive capabilities of assistive and companion robots in supervising, interacting with, and reducing hazardous circumstances for elderly adults [2,3]. These robotic companions are also highly significant sources of assistance for both caregivers and healthcare professionals [4,5]. Telepresence robots have proven to be highly effective in enabling remote interactions in various fields, including remote education, enhancing museum visits, assisting older adults, and providing crucial aid to patients during the COVID-19 pandemic [6–11].

Nevertheless, despite notable advancements in creating robotic platforms [5], telepresence robots that are now on the market primarily provide fundamental telepresence functionalities, such as two-way audio and visual communication and the ability to be operated remotely. Their functionalities frequently lack autonomy in terms of robot capabilities. In addition, the available customization choices are restricted and mostly centered on features such as robot speed, color, height, and camera angle. There is minimal emphasis on the range of services they may provide. This limitation impedes the full practicality of telepresence robots for extended periods of use, especially in achieving the goal of `aging in place`. In addition, even when operating in teleoperated mode, telepresence robots can only partially alleviate the stress and mental burden faced by caregivers [12]. Complete relief is not achievable, as operators must simultaneously control the robot's reactive movements and closely monitor the well-being of elderly individuals. Moreover, the process of engaging with others by manually controlling a robot can be difficult, particularly when there are delays in communication. This challenge is much greater for those who are not familiar with this type of technology.

The absence of robust functionalities could potentially impact the long-term acceptance of incorporating robots into domestic settings. In practice, individuals often hold elevated expectations regarding the capabilities of social robots, anticipating them to display intelligent and adaptive behaviors tailored to the given context. Consequently, robots that fail to meet these expectations, unable to perform as users envision, may find themselves relegated to a corner once users lose motivation for their continued use [13].

Outlined below are the key contributions of our proposed intelligent healthcare framework

- Introduced an innovative approach by combining a transformer-based method with task-planning and AI sub-modules to empower the Pepper robot (a semi-humanoid robot) for telepresence, custom-tailored for Smart Care Homes.
- Enabled the Pepper robot to seamlessly connect with healthcare professionals and provide remote telehealth services, ensuring timely medical assistance and consultations for elderly residents within Smart Care Homes.
- Seamlessly integrated the ML Kit Pose Detection API with our autonomous robotic system, enhancing the Pepper robot's ability to monitor the health and well-being of elderly residents, even when caregivers are not present.
- Employed machine learning algorithms and the Pose Detection API to identify and alert healthcare personnel to any unusual or potentially risky movements or postures of elderly individuals.
- Implemented autonomous generation of robotic actions, enabling adaptability to dynamic and evolving interaction scenarios, ultimately contributing to the efficiency and effectiveness of healthcare services for elderly residents residing in Smart Care Homes.

The paper follows this organization: Section 2 explores prior research concerning telepresence and elderly care on healthcare platforms. Section 3 introduces our proposed framework utilizing ML Kit Pose Detection API for intelligent telepresence robotics for advanced elderly healthcare monitoring. Section 4 offers insight into the implementation environment and the processes it entails. Section 5 presents the proposed platform's implementation results. Lastly, Sect. 6 provides the paper's conclusion.

2   Literature Review

The Internet of Things has a transformative impact on healthcare by enabling remote monitoring and improving communication through telepresence, allowing for smooth engagement and connectivity. [14–21]. Telepresence technology has been thoroughly tested in controlled laboratory settings as well as in real-world residential scenarios. Numerous studies have been conducted to investigate the potential of these telepresence systems for remotely monitoring the well-being of older people. Cross-cultural research has consistently had positive results, particularly in terms of developing independence and autonomy [8,13,22–27]. Platforms such as GiraffPlus, SYMPARTNER, and ExCITE have dramatically improved older people's and their families' lives.

These technology solutions have effectively lessened social isolation among the elderly by permitting more engaging and participatory forms of connection that transcend the constraints of regular phone conversations. Simultaneously, family members have felt more involved and reassured since they can actively care for their loved ones without the limits of long-distance travel while preserving important ties [4]. Furthermore, in certain cases, these robotic devices have reduced the stress on formal caregivers, particularly after extensive training [28].

Prior research has demonstrated the use of advanced robotic assistive prototypes that go beyond simple telepresence. Examples of such studies are SERROGA, RAMCIPR, and SYMPARTNER [29,30]. The focus of these endeavors has mostly been on creating robotic devices specifically tailored to assist elderly people who are dealing with moderate cognitive impairments or dementia. These initiatives have utilized custom-made service robots equipped with advanced, durable, yet costly hardware and sensory equipment, which undeniably represent notable progress in the field of assistive robotics, especially in unstructured contexts. Nevertheless, despite the advancements made in science, these platforms have remained monetarily unattainable for widespread use in different home environments [31]. This paper proposes a novel approach by suggesting the use of cost-effective commercial robots that can independently carry out customized and situation-specific tasks. This technique deviates from the traditional method of depending on rule-based reasoning to govern robotic interactions. This change is due to the overwhelming complexity involved in handling a continuously growing range of unknown situations by depending on manually created rules.

Another crucial aspect revolves around the customization and flexibility of robot interactions, which have a substantial influence on user acceptability [32–34]. Unlike prior telepresence experiments, which mostly focused on modifying navigation and robotic movements (such as human tracking, fall detection, and goal attainment), our study adopts a unique method. It focuses on customizing interactions during cognitive and physical stimulation and discussions. This involves modifying the robot's actions, such as changing the length of time it does tasks, giving feedback, and molding conversations, all under the recognized conditions of the person and the surrounding environment.

The primary contribution of our model lies in the practical realization and deployment of a transformer-based three-tier architecture. This architectural model has been seamlessly adapted and integrated into the Pepper robot (a semi-humanoid robot) for telepresence, notable for its inherent limitations in computational resources. The central objective of this integration is to facilitate a wide range of cognitive and physical exercises, provide timely reminders, and engage users in meaningful and interactive dialogues.

An extensive series of tests and assessments were conducted to comprehensively evaluate the efficacy and practicality of the proposed architectural framework, along with the array of services it encompasses. These evaluations were not confined to the controlled laboratory environment but extended to real-world scenarios involving diverse participants. This real-world assessment aimed to gauge the framework's practical feasibility and potential for widespread applicability.

3   Proposed Intelligent Telepresence Robotics Framework For Enhancing Elderly Healthcare

In order to optimize healthcare for the elderly in smart care homes, the proposed model integrates an inventive fusion of transformer-based techniques, task-planning capabilities, and AI sub-modules into the Pepper robot. This integration enables continuous communication with healthcare professionals, thereby facilitating the delivery of telehealth services remotely and ensuring senior citizens receive timely medical assistance. Furthermore, the integration of the ML Kit Pose Detection API into the model enhances the robot's capability to remotely monitor the activities of patients when caregivers are not present. This is accomplished by employing machine learning algorithms that identify and alert healthcare personnel of any irregular movements or postures. Furthermore, the incorporation of autonomous robotic functions into Smart Care Homes improves the effectiveness and productivity of healthcare provisions for elderly users through the capability to adjust to ever-changing interaction situations.

3.1   Pepper Semi-humanoid Robot

Pepper, a humanoid robot known for its compact and user-friendly form, stands at approximately 1.2 m tall and has a width that is proportional to its size, enabling seamless interactions in various settings. Pepper is equipped with a robust central processing unit that powers its advanced features. This central processing unit enables the robot to process data from many sensors, with cameras being a crucial component. Pepper is equipped with a range of cameras, including high-definition head cameras that allow for precise evaluation of depth and object recognition, a chest camera for collecting user facial expressions and gestures, and sonar sensors for identifying obstructions. Collectively, these elements augment Pepper's comprehensive comprehension of its environment. Aside from its visual sensors, the device is also furnished with a collection of microphones for receiving speech commands and speakers for conveying emotions and messages. Pepper's mobility is facilitated by the inclusion of wheels on its base, allowing it to autonomously navigate and interact with people from different positions. Pepper is a highly versatile and engaging robot well-suited for various applications, such as healthcare, retail, education, and entertainment. It boasts advanced hardware, including a powerful processor, high-quality cameras, and excellent mobility. Moreover, Pepper seamlessly integrates and can be customized within the ROS ecosystem. Figure 1 displays the Pepper robot employed in the proposed model.

3.2   AI-Enhanced Personalized Interaction with Pepper Robot

This study focuses on creating services to promote active aging using the Pepper robot (a semi-humanoid robot). Pepper takes on the role of a proactive coach in this environment, capable of executing numerous responsibilities independently. To begin, it proposes cognitive and physical exercises that are suited to the individual's demands. Second, it provides clear instructions and motivational support to help people stick to their workout programs. Pepper also provides consumers real-time, individualized feedback, improving their overall performance. Recognizing the importance of cognitive ability maintenance, Pepper employs voice interaction to give personalized reminders, which aligns with findings from prior studies [29, 30, 33]. Aside from that, the telepresence Pepper

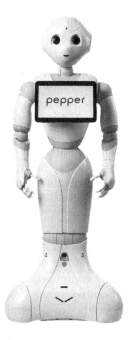

Fig. 1. Representation of Pepper robot in the proposed model at NTNU (Robotics-CPS Lab)

robot (a semi-humanoid robot) acts as a friendly companion, engaging people in meaningful conversations and exchanges that enrich their daily lives.

To achieve the desired services, we have addressed key prerequisites and obstacles. Our first objective was to develop a system that is easy for users to navigate and can dynamically gather user data for customized interactions following a short period of familiarization. Subsequently, our attention was directed towards effectively producing intelligent and flexible behaviors, even on hardware with limited performance capabilities. Finally, our objective was to streamline the process of characterizing interactions by employing machine learning techniques while ensuring meticulous control over the activities of the Pepper robot (a partially human-like robot) to guarantee uniformity.

The lack of individualized and automated behaviors in current commercial telepresence platforms posed a significant barrier, particularly in the absence of a Pepper robot, a semi-humanoid robot. To tackle this issue, our research expands upon the notion of **stories** in Pepper's framework, representing the data utilized for training conversational robots. These stories illustrate user conversations using advanced concepts like intentions (e.g., greetings), entities (e.g., location), and actions (e.g., answers from the Pepper robot, a semi-humanoid robot). By utilizing the Dual Intent and Entity Transformer (DIET) [35], a modular transformer architecture present in Pepper, we can carry out both intent classification and entity recognition in natural language utterances. This method guarantees adaptability and user-friendliness in generating the training dataset, even for individuals who are not proficient in programming, such as domain specialists.

Our approach, which stands in contrast to prior systems, utilizes the potential of **stories** to govern and extrapolate a wide range of robot behaviors. These behaviors extend beyond conversations and include actions such as robot movements, monitoring, user feedback facilitated by a dynamic tablet interface as depicted in Fig. 2, and the formation of assistive tasks customized to the user's present condition. As a result, cognitive and physical exercises, monitoring reminders, and dialogues are redesigned to incorporate intentions, entities, and actions, considering a range of variables, including user characteristics, performance indicators, and interaction results (including user reactions and possible misinterpretations).

The proposed flexible framework is predicated on a learned model that serves as a policy represented by $\pi(s) = a$, dictating the successive actions of the robot in accordance with the present state of the system s. Furthermore, the acquired policy integrates effortlessly with a component responsible for task planning in a three-tier architecture, as elaborated in the following section. The system is enabled by this architectural symbiosis to determine when and how to modify the robot's actions in accordance with the changing dynamics of interaction. The continuous interaction between a proficient task planner and the acquired policy, based on the narrative-based approach, guarantees that the robot's behaviors consistently correspond to the constantly evolving user context and surroundings.

3.3 Autonomous ROS-Based Three-Tier Architecture for Semi-humanoid Pepper Robot

To facilitate the operation of autonomous robots, we have addressed three fundamental prerequisites. The primary objective of our study was to develop a system that could efficiently execute goal-oriented behaviors by organizing a series of tasks in accordance with particular targets. Additionally, the system had to possess high adaptability, allowing for rapid modifications to predetermined duties in response to dynamic contextual shifts. Potential modifications may encompass task cancellations, task failures, task duration adjustments, or the introduction of additional tasks. Furthermore, we aimed to achieve contextual responsiveness from the system in real-time, enabling the robot to promptly perceive and react to dynamic changes that arise from its surroundings and user engagements. The ability to respond in real-time was of the utmost importance, both in the preparatory stage and when modifying existing strategies.

The autonomous ROS-based three-tier architecture that embodies the metaphor of thinking slowly, and thinking fast resulted from our methodology inspired by classical robotics principles. The architectural framework comprises three foundational elements, each fulfilling a unique function.

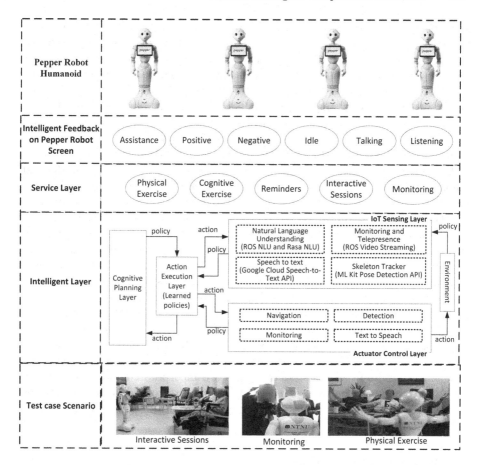

Fig. 2. Layerd architecture of proposed intelligent telepresence robotics framework for enhancing elderly healthcare

Central to the system is the Cognitive Planning Layer, which is tasked with the conception, implementation, and dynamic modification of plans. By utilizing semantic and causal reasoning, it guarantees that strategies are in accordance with the objectives of the automaton and can adapt dynamically as required. In the interim, action execution is the responsibility of the Action Execution Layer. A learned policy, denoted as $\pi(s)$, governs these actions and is contingent upon the system's present condition. In conclusion, the Actuator Control Layer acts as an intermediary between the sequencer tier's abstract actions and the low-level commands necessary to operate the actuators of the robot. It converts overarching directives into precise, implementable strategies for the bodily components of the robot, as shown in Fig. 2.

Considering the larger scope, this architectural design presents numerous benefits. The flexibility it provides in goal setting is manifested through the sequencing tier's ability to collaboratively generate goals with the user, request supplementary information for goal definition, or decline goals when necessary. Furthermore, in response to real-time changes, the sequencing stratum dynamically assesses and modifies execution plans; accepted activities are incorporated into the interaction context. This context aids in the interpretation of user input by considering ongoing operations and previous engagements.

The Cognitive Planning Layer efficiently generates solutions using heuristics and a timeline-based planner, which makes it compatible with hardware with limited resources. Moreover, it exhibits the capacity to modify strategies while in implementation, thereby guaranteeing adaptability. The operation of the Robot Operating System, a widely utilized middleware in robotics, is coordinated among all three layers. By leveraging modularity and an efficient communication infrastructure, this decision enhances the system's reproducibility across various robotic platforms. We have carefully developed frameworks that utilize Docker to achieve smooth integration with the Pepper robot, a semi-humanoid operating system-based robot. These frameworks establish a resilient interface with actuators and low-level libraries. The robot's camera records a comprehensive analysis of joint pose variations within the skeletal structure as part of our method for detecting physical exercise execution. In order to achieve this objective, we seamlessly integrate the Google ML Kit Pose Detection API, an intelligent artificial intelligence tool, into the Robot Operating System. By enabling precise identification and response to physical exercises, this function enhances the robot's awareness and perception of user movements. In addition, cognitive activities that engage users in substantive dialogues are incorporated into our methodology. Furthermore, the robot's graphical user interface and vocal interactions are seamlessly integrated during the configuration of reminders using a hybrid methodology.

4   Tool and Technologies

4.1   Implementation Environment

We performed a thorough evaluation of the robot's capacity to identify repetitions during physical activities, in addition to its primary functionalities. To accomplish this, we utilized a pre-existing activity recognition framework that is capable of analyzing crucial skeletal sites, notably those pertaining to the shoulder, elbow, and wrist of each arm. This framework efficiently classifies different actions into two main phases: outstretched arms and bent arms. Complex calculations that take into account the angles between the key joints and the coordination of arm motions determine the classification. Additionally, it verifies any changes in orientation that the sensors may have detected simultaneously, ensuring precise identification. We utilized the Google ML Kit Pose Detection API to track and record human volunteers during physical exercise to conduct a comparative analysis. Our system effortlessly integrated the ROS-based video streaming API, allowing seamless direct video hosting to any desired server in video telepresence. To improve the system's overall functionality and engagement, we utilized Google Cloud services to incorporate text-to-speech and speech-to-text capabilities, enhancing the user experience. Table 1 summarizes the tools and technologies used in the proposed framework.

Table 1. Implementation environment for proposed intelligent telepresence robotics framework for enhancing elderly healthcare

Tool and Technology	Description
Monitoring and Detection	Google ML Pose Detection API
TensorFlow	Open-source deep learning framework
Robot Operating System (ROS)	Support writing robot software
Docker	20.10 version
Google Cloud Services	Text-to-speech and speech-to-text API

4.2 Dataset

In this section, we introduce our recently compiled dataset, which includes a wide variety of comprehensive physical workouts specifically designed to meet the everyday requirements of older adults [36]. The data-collecting procedure utilized a built-in Pepper robot camera to capture RGB images from a single viewpoint at a constant rate of 30 frames per second. The camera's height and angle were carefully tuned to replicate the visual perspective of a ground robot. The dataset consists of a compilation of 19 exercises, carefully selected based on recommendations from physiotherapists working at a long-term care facility in Norway. It is important to emphasize that these exercises aim to improve overall mobility, facilitate rehabilitation evaluations, and encourage regular physical activity for older individuals rather than focusing on specific medical disorders. The data collection occurred exclusively in the Social Robots Lab at NTNU, with a sample size of 15 users ranging in age from 26 to 48 years.

4.3 Performance Metrics

During our study, we analyzed various important metrics to measure the system's performance. Initially, we assessed accuracy, which denotes the ratio of successful robot interactions to the total number of circumstances investigated. Another crucial aspect to consider was the system's robustness, which refers to its capacity to handle faults gracefully. The measure of responsiveness was determined by computing the duration between consecutive encounters. Also, we examine the user experience of a proposed framework in the Pepper robot via a custom questionnaire uncovers favorable impressions concerning ease of operation, responsiveness, utility, and inclination for future interaction, highlighting the framework's effectiveness in improving human-robot engagement. The measurements thoroughly assessed the system's operation and its influence on overall performance.

5 Experimental Results

Figure 3 illustrates the number of spoken interactions during human-robot contact and the distribution of time tasks across different categories. Upon analyzing the data depicted in the graphs, it is evident that the total number of interactions with Pepper robots covered interactions in four distinct categories: interactive sessions, cognitive exercises, physical exercises, and reminders. Meanwhile, human interactions were mostly comprised of cognitive exercises and reminders. The results highlight the model's ability to effectively and actively engage with elderly users across several interaction categories. The results in Fig. 4 show how the failure rates were calculated in the proposed framework for different types of services, like speech-to-text services, monitoring human action services, and Pepper robot actions. The data emphasizes that speech-to-text services have the highest rates of failure, whereas monitoring human action services demonstrate comparatively superior performance. Moreover, Pepper Robot Actions display different rates of failure depending on the particular sort of service, suggesting areas that should be enhanced. This research provides guidance for making further improvements to enhance the model's reliability and performance in delivering a range of services. A comprehensive research was undertaken to assess the efficacy of the proposed framework in improving user engagement. This analysis

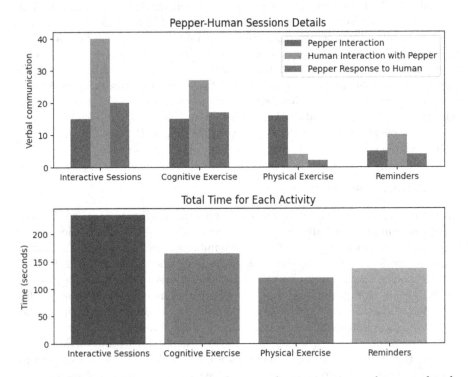

Fig. 3. Verbal interactions count during human-robot interaction and temporal task distribution.

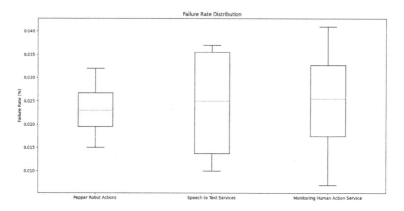

Fig. 4. Assessment of Failure Rates Across Services in the Proposed Model

was based on feedback received from 15 users. Each participant responded to a series of nine questions designed to assess their familiarity with the system. The questions encompassed a range of factors including the accessibility of information, comprehensibility of instructions, confidence in interactions, consistency with expectations, responsiveness, efficiency in completing tasks, support provided, and willingness to utilize the system in the future as presented in Table 2.

To accommodate the different levels of importance of these forms of interactions, distinct weights were allocated: cognitive exercise (weight = 0.24), physical exercise (weight = 0.26), interactive session (weight = 0.30), and reminders (weight = 0.20). The user experience index was obtained by calculating the weighted average of the mean scores for each interaction type across all users, which was then normalized by the total number of users=15. The objective function is mathematically formulated as:

$$
\begin{aligned}
\text{User Experience Index} = \frac{1}{15} &\times (0.24 \times \text{Average Score for Cognitive Exercise}) \\
&+ (0.26 \times \text{Average Score for Physical Exercise}) \\
&+ (0.30 \times \text{Average Score for Interactive Session}) \\
&+ (0.20 \times \text{Average Score for Reminders}) \quad (1)
\end{aligned}
$$

where the Average Score for each interaction type represents the proportion of positive responses (scored as 1) relative to the total number of responses for that type. This user experience index serves as a quantitative measure of the accuracy of the proposed model in improving various aspects of user interaction.

Table 2. User Interaction Survey for Pepper robot interaction

Category	Questions
Cognitive Exercise	
	– Were you sure about what to say or do with Pepper at every step?
	– Did Pepper act as you expected during your conversation?
	– Did Pepper help you with the task?
Physical Exercise	
	– Did the speed of talking with Pepper feel right to you?
	– Did Pepper sometimes take a bit too long to answer?
Interactive Session	
	– Was getting the information you needed from Pepper easy?
	– Was understanding what Pepper told you during your conversation simple?
	– Do you want to use Pepper again for tasks like this?
Reminders	
	– Did Pepper do the job well?

6   Conclusion

This study focuses on the complex task of delivering innovative and affordable services for elderly people using a Pepper robot that operates with restricted computational resources in smart care home settings. Our research gives technical proof that a collaborative approach that combines a new transformer-based method with a heuristic-based task planner and many AI-driven services works. The collaboration, as mentioned earlier, facilitates the independent administration and customization of exchanges, obviating the necessity for pre-established user models or specialized logical principles that exceed the constraints of the hardware.

It is imperative to recognize a constraint on this study, specifically the comparatively small number of participants, which could impede the ability to derive conclusive findings. However, our study was carefully planned to function as a preliminary assessment of the functionality and performance of the system in less controlled settings. This served as a precursor to further comprehensive inquiries into the effectiveness of the technology and the level of acceptability among users. Subsequent lines of inquiry will focus on investigating innovative learning methodologies to enable more personalized interactions, considering hardware limitations and other possible improvements.

References

1. Gaigbe-Togbe, V., Bassarsky, L., Gu, D., Spoorenberg, T., Zeifman, L.: World population prospects 2022. New York, NY, USA, Department of Economic and Social Affairs, Population Division (2022)
2. Mois, G., Beer, J.M.: The role of healthcare robotics in providing support to older adults: a socio-ecological perspective. Current Geriatrics Rep. **9**, 82–89 (2020)
3. Pollack, M.E.: Intelligent technology for an aging population: the use of ai to assist elders with cognitive impairment. AI Mag. **26**(2), 9–9 (2005)
4. Niemelä, M., Van Aerschot, L., Tammela, A., Aaltonen, I., Lammi, H.: Towards ethical guidelines of using telepresence robots in residential care. Int. J. Soc. Robot. **13**, 431–439 (2021)
5. Isabet, B., Pino, M., Lewis, M., Benveniste, S., Rigaud, A.-S.: Social telepresence robots: a narrative review of experiments involving older adults before and during the covid-19 pandemic. Int. J. Environ. Res. Public Health **18**(7), 3597 (2021)
6. Thompson, P., Chaivisit, S.: Telepresence robots in the classroom. J. Educ. Technol. Syst. **50**(2), 201–214 (2021)
7. Chang, E.: Museums for everyone: experiments and probabilities in telepresence robots. In: Exploring Digital Technologies for Art-Based Special Education, pp. 65–76. Routledge (2019)
8. Cesta, A., Cortellessa, G., Fracasso, F., Orlandini, A., Turno, M.: User needs and preferences on aal systems that support older adults and their carers. J. Ambient Intell. Smart Environ. **10**(1), 49–70 (2018)
9. Laniel, S., Létourneau, D., Grondin, F., Labbé, M., Ferland, F., Michaud, F.: Toward enhancing the autonomy of a telepresence mobile robot for remote home care assistance. Paladyn J. Behav. Robot. **12**(1), 214–237 (2021)
10. Winterstein, K., Keller, L., Huffstadt, K., Müller, N.H.: Acceptance of social and telepresence robot assistance in german households. In: Zaphiris, P., Ioannou, A. (eds.) HCII 2021. LNCS, vol. 12785, pp. 326–339. Springer, Cham (2021). https://doi.org/10.1007/978-3-030-77943-6_22
11. Esterwood, C., Robert, L.: Robots and covid-19: re-imagining human–robot collaborative work in terms of reducing risks to essential workers. Available at SSRN 3767609 (2021)
12. Pérez-Cruz, M., Parra-Anguita, L., López-Martínez, C., Moreno-Cámara, S., del Pino-Casado, R.: Burden and anxiety in family caregivers in the hospital that debut in caregiving. Int. J. Environ. Res. Public Health **16**(20), 3977 (2019)
13. Beer, J.M., Takayama, L.: Mobile remote presence systems for older adults: acceptance, benefits, and concerns. In: Proceedings of the 6th International Conference on Human-Robot Interaction, pp. 19–26 (2011)
14. Jamil, F., Hameed, I.A.: Toward intelligent open-ended questions evaluation based on predictive optimization. Expert Syst. Appli. 120640 (2023)
15. Jamil, H., Qayyum, F., Iqbal, N., Jamil, F., Kim, D.H.: Optimal ensemble scheme for human activity recognition and floor detection based on automl and weighted soft voting using smartphone sensors. IEEE Sensors J. **23**(3), 2878–2890 (2022)
16. Shahzad, A., et al.: Automated uterine fibroids detection in ultrasound images using deep convolutional neural networks. Healthcare **11**, 1493 (2023)
17. Jamil, F., Ahmad, S., Whangbo, T.K., Muthanna, A., Kim, D.-H.: Improving blockchain performance in clinical trials using intelligent optimal transaction traffic control mechanism in smart healthcare applications. Comput. Indust. Eng. **170**, 108327 (2022)

18. Ahmad, S., Khan, S., Jamil, F., Qayyum, F., Ali, A., Kim, D.H.: Design of a general complex problem-solving architecture based on task management and predictive optimization. Int. J. Distrib. Sens. Netw. **18**(6), 15501329221107868 (2022)

19. Qayyum, F., Jamil, F., Ahmad, S., Kim, D.-H.: Hybrid renewable energy resources management for optimal energy operation in nano-grid. Comput. Mater. Contin **71**, 2091–2105 (2022)

20. Jamil, F., Qayyum, F., Alhelaly, S., Javed, F., Muthanna, A.: Intelligent microservice based on blockchain for healthcare applications. Computers, Mater. Continua **69**(2), 22 (2021)

21. Jamil, F., Kim, D.H.: Enhanced kalman filter algorithm using fuzzy inference for improving position estimation in indoor navigation. J. Intell. Fuzzy Syst. **40**(5), 8991–9005 (2021)

22. Seelye, A.M., Wild, K.V., Larimer, N., Maxwell, S., Kearns, P., Kaye. J.A.: Reactions to a remote-controlled video-communication robot in seniors' homes: a pilot study of feasibility and acceptance. Telemed. e-Health **18**(10), 755–759 (2012)

23. Gonzalez-Jimenez, J., Galindo, C., Gutierrez-Castaneda, C.: Evaluation of a telepresence robot for the elderly: a Spanish experience. In: Ferrández Vicente, J.M., Álvarez Sánchez, J.R., de la Paz López, F., Toledo Moreo, F.J. (eds.) IWINAC 2013. LNCS, vol. 7930, pp. 141–150. Springer, Heidelberg (2013). https://doi.org/10.1007/978-3-642-38637-4_15

24. Shah, S.H.H., Karlsen, A.S.T., Solberg, M., Hameed, I.A.: A social vr-based collaborative exergame for rehabilitation: codesign, development and user study. Virt. Real. **27**(4), 3403–3420 (2023)

25. Shah, S.H.H., Hameed, I.A., Karlsen, A.S.T., Solberg, M.: Towards a social vr-based exergame for elderly users: An exploratory study of acceptance, experiences and design principles. In: International Conference on Human-computer Interaction

26. Shah, S.H.H., Steinnes, O.M.H., Gustafsson, E.G., Hameed, I.A.: Multi-agent robot system to monitor and enforce physical distancing constraints in large areas to combat covid-19 and future pandemics. Appli. Sci. **11**(16), 7200 (2021)

27. Aftab, H., Shah, S.H.H., Habli, I.: Classification of failures in the perception of conversational agents (cas) and their implications on patient safety (2021)

28. Fiorini, L., Sorrentino, A., Pistolesi, M., Becchimanzi, C., Tosi, F., Cavallo, F.: Living with a telepresence robot: results from a field-trial. IEEE Robot. Autom. Lett. **7**(2), 5405–5412 (2022)

29. Gross, H.-M., et al.: Robot companion for domestic health assistance: Implementation, test and case study under everyday conditions in private apartments. In: 2015 IEEE/RSJ International Conference on Intelligent Robots and Systems (IROS), pp. 5992–5999. IEEE (2015)

30. Gross, H.-M., Scheidig, A., Müller, S., Schütz, B., Fricke, C., Meyer, S.: Living with a mobile companion robot in your own apartment-final implementation and results of a 20-weeks field study with 20 seniors. In: 2019 International Conference on Robotics and Automation (ICRA), pp. 2253–2259. IEEE (2019)

31. Wang, M., Pan, C., Ray, P.K.: Technology entrepreneurship in developing countries: role of telepresence robots in healthcare. IEEE Eng. Manag. Rev. **49**(1), 20–26 (2021)

32. Moro, C., Nejat, G., Mihailidis, A.: Learning and personalizing socially assistive robot behaviors to aid with activities of daily living. ACM Trans. Hum.-Robot Interact. (THRI) **7**(2), 1–25 (2018)

33. Di Napoli, C., Ercolano, G., Rossi, S.: Personalized home-care support for the elderly: a field experience with a social robot at home. User Model. User-Adap. Inter. **33**(2), 405–440 (2023)
34. Umbrico, A., Cesta, A., Cortellessa, G., Orlandini, A.: A holistic approach to behavior adaptation for socially assistive robots. Int. J. Soc. Robot. **12**(3), 617–637 (2020)
35. Bunk, T., Varshneya, D., Vlasov, V., Nichol, A.: Diet: Lightweight language understanding for dialogue systems. arXiv preprint arXiv:2004.09936 (2020)
36. Shah, S.H.H., Karlsen, A.S.T., Solberg, M., Hameed, I.A.: An efficient and lightweight multiperson activity recognition framework for robot-assisted healthcare applications. Expert Syst. Appli. **241**, 122482 (2024)

A Path Planning Method Based on Deep Reinforcement Learning with Improved Prioritized Experience Replay for Human-Robot Collaboration

Deyu Sun, Jingqian Wen, Jingfei Wang, Xiaonan Yang[✉], and Yaoguang Hu

Industrial and Systems Engineering Laboratory, School of Mechanical Engineering, Beijing Institute of Technology, Beijing, China
yangxn@bit.edu.cn

Abstract. Owing to its ability to integrate human flexibility with robotic automation, human-robot collaboration possesses tremendous potential in intelligent manufacturing. A quintessential characteristic of this collaboration is the necessity for robotic arms to cooperate with humans in a dynamically changing environment, wherein humans could be considered as dynamic obstacles. One of the significant challenges in human-robot collaboration is the development of obstacle avoidance strategies for robotic path planning within dynamically changing environments. The inability of traditional two-dimensional path planning methods to handle high-dimensional spaces, therefore, many researchers have turned their attention to deep reinforcement learning, and many deep reinforcement learning methods have been applied to robotic arm path planning. However, most deep reinforcement learning models for robotic arm path planning require a significant amount of training time to achieve convergence. In this study, we introduce an algorithm that synergizes Soft Actor-Critic (SAC) with an improved version of Prioritized Experience Replay (PER)—SAC-iPER. We prioritizes experiences based on task-rewards, employing metrics such as time consumption and collision occurrences, in addition to task completion, to rank experiences. This reward-based ordering significantly boosts the learning process in both speed and quality. The results of this study significantly enhanced the training efficiency of deep reinforcement learning models for robotic arm path planning within human-robot collaboration, paving the way for the development of more efficient human-robot collaborative systems.

Keywords: human-robot collaboration · deep reinforcement learning · PER · SAC

1 Introduction

The existing automation systems have reached bottlenecks in handling various manufacturing tasks, such as the assembly or disassembly of complex products that frequently change [1]. In order to meet the people-centered needs under these working conditions, many researchers have turned their attention to the increasingly active field of

M. Kurosu and A. Hashizume (Eds.): HCII 2024, LNCS 14685, pp. 196–206, 2024.
https://doi.org/10.1007/978-3-031-60412-6_15

human-robot collaboration (HRC). Human-robot collaboration combines the strength, repeatability, and accuracy of robots with human cognitive flexibility to achieve high-level automation effects [2]. Human-robot collaboration is poised to be a predominant theme in the coming decades. Some even contend that the fifth industrial revolution will revolve around this synergy [3]. NIOSH researcher Larry Layne analyzed data from 1992 to 2017 and found that in the majority of worker fatalities related to robots, 78% of the accidents occurred due to robots striking workers [4]. The prevalence of accidents is attributed to the dynamically complex environment of human-robot collaboration. Hence, it necessitates the capability of robotic arms to dynamically plan and adjust their paths for obstacle avoidance to ensure human safety.

Existing traditional path planning methods, such as the teach pendant approach, have limitations in the context of robotic arm path planning. Demonstration method For manipulators in manufacturing, when given a specific task (e.g., moving an object), a human expert manually finds a collision-free path from the end-effector's start and target positions in order to perform the task and teach that path to the manipulator. Therefore, this process must be repeated if the start and target positions of the end-effector change due to task changes [5]. Other conventional methods such as A* [6, 7] have difficulty in constructing a cost function, Artificial Potential Field (APF) methods [8] are limited by the local optimization problem, and Fast Expanding Random Trees (FERT) methods [9] have difficulty in obtaining desirable motion trajectories in a narrow region, RRT (Rapidly-exploring Random Tree) [10], on the other hand, suffers from long computation times and requires a known environment, which is time-consuming when using RRT in a new environment that requires tedious engineering work in setting up parameters. Due to the limitations of traditional methods and the rapid advancement of deep reinforcement learning, scholars are increasingly applying deep reinforcement learning in the path planning of robotic arms. Evan Prianto, in an effort to accelerate the training speed of deep reinforcement learning models, combined the SAC with Hindsight Experience Replay (HER) to study obstacle avoidance path planning methods for robotic arms [5]. Xiaowei Cheng proposed a novel state space representation method suitable for robotic arms in dynamic environments and based on this, developed a deep reinforcement learning algorithm for dynamic obstacle avoidance planning for robotic arms [11]. Inspired by the concept of artificial potential fields, Wanxing Tang introduced a new reward and punishment function, utilizing deep reinforcement learning algorithms to enable robotic arms to approach patients on hospital beds without collisions in complex environments [12]. Quan Liu proposed an intrinsic reward function optimization method, which integrated with the Deep Deterministic Policy Gradient (DDPG) approach in deep reinforcement learning, facilitates real-time collision-free motion planning for industrial robots to achieve human-robot collaboration [13]. Evan Prianto leveraged the SAC algorithm combined with HER for multi-arm robot obstacle avoidance [14]. However, a major problem with deep reinforcement learning models arises in its training process. Deep reinforcement learning models consume a lot of training time to reach convergence [15]. Due to rapid changes in the environment, models often need to be retrained or optimized, which means that a significant investment of time and resources is required in order to deploy a new model or policy. This limitation has largely hindered the widespread adoption of deep reinforcement learning.

In the context of robotic arm path planning, SAC demonstrates faster convergence speeds and higher average rewards compared to other deep reinforcement learning algorithms such as DDPG and PPO. Additionally, PER [16] significantly enhances the convergence efficiency of deep reinforcement learning algorithms. Therefore, SAC combined with PER represents a highly effective approach in solving path planning challenges in the realm of deep reinforcement learning for robotic arms. In order to further improve the learning efficiency and effectiveness of deep reinforcement learning algorithms, and to advance the application of reinforcement learning methods to path planning methods, We present an algorithm that synergizes SAC with an improved version of PER, termed SAC-iPER, which substantially accelerates the training speed of deep reinforcement learning models. In contrast to the traditional TD-error based prioritization in PER, our method orders experiences based on task-rewards. Specifically, experiences are ranked according to metrics like time consumption and collision occurrences, coupled with task completion. This reward-based sorting significantly enhances the speed of the learning process. The introduced method was compared with SAC enhanced by the unmodified version of PER, and SAC alone. Experimental results indicate that the new model surpasses others in terms of convergence speed, laying a solid foundation for the future development of more advanced and safer human-robot collaborative systems.

2 Method

2.1 Action Space and Observation Space

In the specified training environment, the agent is tasked with operating an Auboi5L robotic arm, which is characterized by its six degrees of freedom. The agent's action space is defined as a 1×6 vector, corresponding to the joint angles of each of the robotic arm's six joints. These angles are confined within a range from $-\pi$ to π, affording the agent a broad and continuous spectrum of control over the robotic arm's movements.

The observation space of the environment is represented as a 14-dimensional vector, encompassing various critical aspects:

1. A 1×3 sub-vector detailing the x, y, and z coordinates of the target point, providing spatial information about the objective location.
2. Another 1×3 sub-vector for the x, y, and z coordinates of the obstacle, giving positional data about potential hindrances in the environment.
3. A single scalar element reflecting the Euclidean distance between the end effector of the robotic arm and the target point, crucial for gauging proximity to the objective.
4. A single scalar element indicating the distance between the end effector and the obstacle, essential for obstacle avoidance strategies.
5. 6 elements of the observation vector represent the current joint angles of the robotic arm, providing real-time data on its positional configuration.

Thus, this observation space effectively combines both the dynamic state of the robotic arm and vital environmental information, facilitating informed decision-making for task execution that involves both reaching the target and navigating around obstacles.

Figure 1 is the human-robot collaboration scenario targeted in this article, where a human and a robotic arm are at opposite ends of the table, collaborating to accomplish the task of assembling workpieces, and what the robotic arm needs to do in this task is to hand the workpieces that need to be assembled to the human, and at the same time not to collide with the human so as to injure the human.

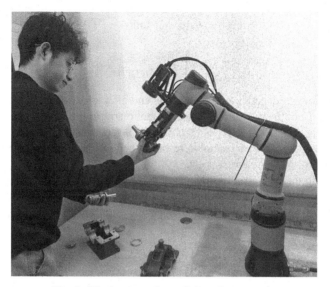

Fig. 1. The human-robot collaboration scenario

2.2 Reward Design

The reward should enable the Auboi5L robotic arm to successfully avoid obstacles and reach the target position while minimizing the time taken. The reward function is as follows:

$$r = r_{dist} + r_{reach} + r_{time} + r_{obs} \tag{1}$$

The computation for the distance reward is as follows:

$$r_{dist} = \begin{cases} 5 \times (d_n - d_c) \; if \; (d_n - d_c) > 0 \\ 0 \qquad\qquad otherwise \end{cases} \tag{2}$$

In this, d_n denotes the distance from the end-effector of the robotic arm to the target at the end of the previous step, and d_c denotes the same at the end of the current step. We use $(d_n - d_c)$ to compute the distance reward. If this value is positive, it implies that the end-effector of the robotic arm is approaching the target, and thus, we provide a positive reward. If this value is negative, it implies that the end-effector of the robotic arm is moving away from the target. However, since the robotic arm may execute backward joint movements to circumvent obstacles in close proximity, while still ultimately reaching the target, the reward function is structured to assign a zero reward in scenarios where the end-effector moves away. This design is implemented to prevent mistakenly penalizing the agent for engaging in backward movements as a means to avoid nearby obstacles, ensuring that the system does not inadvertently discourage such maneuvers that are essential for effective obstacle avoidance. This design aims to encourage the end-effector of the robotic arm to get as close as possible to the target.

The computation for the reach reward is as follows:

$$r_{reach} = \begin{cases} 50 \ if \ d_c < r_{ah} \\ 0 \ otherwise \end{cases} \tag{3}$$

The reach reward depends on whether the end effector reaches the target point. If the distance d_c from the end effector of the robotic arm to the target point is less than the threshold r_{ah}, it is considered as reaching the target point, a reward of 50 will be given. This is to provide a considerable reward when reaching the target to encourage the robotic arm to reach the target point.

In addition to the distance reward and reach reward, if the robotic arm collides with an obstacle, an obstacle penalty is introduced into the reward function to discourage the robotic arm from hitting obstacles. The computation for the obstacle penalty is as follows:

$$r_{obs} = \begin{cases} -60 \ if \ collide \\ 0 \ otherwise \end{cases} \tag{4}$$

Each collision with an obstacle incurs a significant penalty of -60, detracting from the total reward. The purpose is to urge the agent to avoid obstacles while trying to reach the target.

To promote efficiency in reaching the target, a time penalty is incorporated. The computation for the time penalty is:

$$r_{time} = -1 \tag{5}$$

Every step taken to reach the target incurs a penalty, which scales with the number of time steps taken. The longer the robotic arm takes, the greater the cumulative penalty, thus motivating faster target acquisition. This aims to encourage the agent to reach the targets as quickly as possible.

2.3 Network Structure

The proposed network architecture comprises:

As shown in Fig. 2, the Actor network receives a 14-dimensional state vector as input, representing the observation space. This includes the robotic arm's six joint angles, target coordinates, distance between the end effector and the target, obstacle coordinates, and distance between the end effector and the obstacle. The input is processed through two fully connected layers, each with 256 neurons, and employs ReLU activation functions. Subsequently, the network outputs a 6-dimensional vector representing the angles of the robotic arm's six joints.

The Critic network inputs a 20-dimensional vector, combining the 14-dimensional observation space and the 6-dimensional action vector produced by the Actor network. Structurally mirroring the Actor network, the Critic also processes inputs through two fully connected layers with 256 neurons each, utilizing ReLU activation functions. Unlike the Actor, however, the Critic outputs a singular value indicative of the expected return for enacting a specific action in the given state.

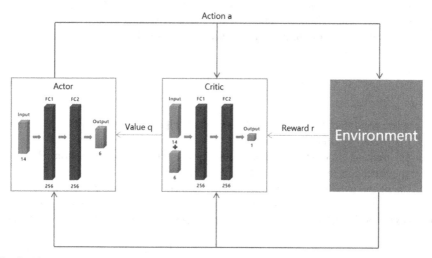

Fig. 2. The architecture of actor network and critic network and the flow chart of the algorithm

2.4 Improved PER

As opposed to traditional SAC, which picks events at random from a replay memory buffer, PER prioritises each experience according to how important it is to the agent's learning. The amount of the difference between the agent's predicted action and the actual reward received is taken into account in the approach used to determine this priority value. During training, PER selects events from the replay memory buffer based on the experiences' priority ratings. Higher priority events are selected more often, enabling the agent to gain more insight from the most crucial interactions. The priority values are also changed after each event is used for training in order for the algorithm to adapt to changing conditions and prioritise new experiences that are more important for the agent's learning process [16].

PER constitutes an enhanced mechanism for experience replay within the domain of reinforcement learning. In contrast to conventional Experience Replay, where agent-environment interactions—comprising states, actions, rewards, subsequent states, and termination flags—are aggregated in a data structure (typically a queue) and sampled uniformly for model training, PER introduces a distinct prioritization scheme.

In a canonical implementation of PER, the priority p(e) for a given experience e is predominantly computed based on Temporal Difference Error (TD − Error). Specifically, the TD-Error δ is given by the equation:

$$\delta = r + \gamma * V(s\prime) - V(s) \tag{6}$$

Here,

r represents the reward received,

γ is the discount factor,

$V(s)$ denotes the estimated value function of the current state s,

$V(s\prime)$ denotes the estimated value function of the next state s$\prime$.

The probability $P(e)$ of sampling an experience e is directly proportional to its priority $p(e)$:

$$P(e) = \frac{p(e)^\alpha}{\sum_k p(e_k)^\alpha} \tag{7}$$

where α is a parameter that lies within the range [0,1][0,1] and modulates the degree to which prioritization affects sampling.

In our training process, we initially employ TD-error for prioritization. However, once experiences in the experience pool that involve reaching the target comprise at least 10% of the experience replay buffer, we replace the original TD-error-based priority sorting method with our custom priority sorting function. This alternative method calculates the priority $P(e)$ based on whether the target is reached and the reward obtained:

$$P(e) = \begin{cases} 10^6 + reward & if\ d_c < r_{ah} \\ 10^4 - d_c & otherwise \end{cases} \tag{8}$$

This task reward-based experience prioritization method first divides experience into two parts, namely the experience of completing tasks and the experience of unfinished tasks, where the task refers to whether the target point has been reached. The priority of experience in completing tasks will be much higher than that of experience in unfinished tasks. Then, for the experience of unfinished tasks, priority sorting is performed based on the distance from the target point, so that the higher the attempt to approach the target point, the higher the priority of the experience. Finally, for the experience of completing tasks, the experience priority is ranked based on the reward value. Because rewards already include time rewards, collision rewards, and distance rewards, the experience of achieving the target point with fewer swings, shorter time, and fewer collisions will ultimately receive the highest priority. In this way, experiences that use less time and experience fewer collisions are prioritized higher, while experiences that have fewer collisions because they don't go near target points and obstacles are also prioritized lower, allowing for a scientific ranking of experiences that can drastically speed up training.

After each training iteration, priorities associated with each experience are updated in accordance with newly acquired data. This is accomplished by recalculating the priority based on rewards and the number of targets reached, followed by an update to the priority queue.

2.5   Training Details

In our study, we utilized PyBullet, a powerful physics simulation environment, to model a robotic arm, a human right arm, and the target points for the robotic arm. As depicted in Fig. 3, in this scenario, the red sphere represents the target point, and the blue cube symbolizes the right arm of a human collaborator. This setup is designed to simulate a scenario where the robotic arm passes an object to a human. The experiment is considered successful if the Auboi5L robotic arm can quickly reach the target point without colliding with the cube or the ground. The positions of the target point and obstacles randomly change with each event, as demonstrated in the figure, which shows several sets of random positions for the target points and cubes. These configurations create a dynamic and changing human-robot collaboration training environment for the agents.

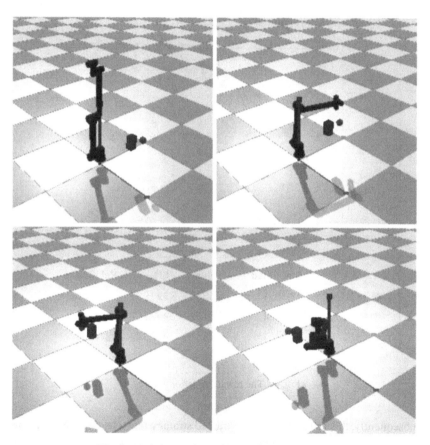

Fig. 3. Training environment for dynamic change

3   Results

3.1   Evaluation on Training of the Proposed Method

This article compares SAC, SAC-iPER, and SAC-PER. These three algorithms were trained using the same network architecture and reward function design over the same span of 1 million steps, with each episode containing a maximum of 500 steps. As depicted in Fig. 4, SAC converges at around 860,000 steps, SAC-PER at approximately 670,000 steps, while SAC-iPER converges around 450,000 steps, significantly faster than the other two methods. Therefore, the algorithm proposed in this article greatly accelerates the training speed of deep reinforcement learning models.

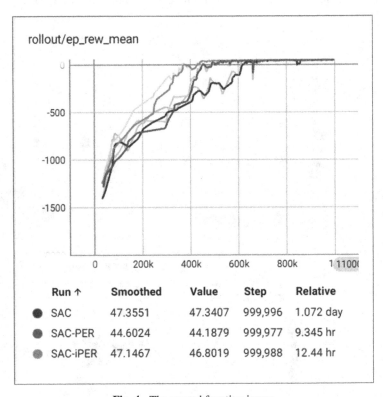

Fig. 4. The reward function image

Subsequently, this article imports the trained strategy into a testing environment for comparative analysis, primarily focusing on the completion of tasks, namely, the ability to reach the target point, the number of collisions with obstacles, and the number of steps required to reach the target point. As illustrated in Table 1, all three methods are capable of identifying paths that reach the target point without colliding with humans. In terms of the time required for decision-making, the SAC-iPER method is faster compared to the other two methods. SAC-iPER is faster than SAC-PER by an average of 2.1 steps per decision, approximately 8 ms; and faster than SAC by an average of 0.2 steps per decision, around 0.8 ms. Therefore, the solutions found by SAC-iPER are also relatively superior.

Table 1. Algorithm comparison for path planning

SAC	Obstacle Avoidance capability for reaching the target point	$\checkmark$
	Average Steps required for reaching the target point	8.22
SAC-PER	Obstacle Avoidance capability for reaching the target point	$\checkmark$
	Average Steps required for reaching the target point	10.12
SAC-iPER	Obstacle Avoidance capability for reaching the target point	$\checkmark$
	Average Steps required for reaching the target point	8.02

4   Discussion and Conclusion

This article presents an innovative framework that enhances the Priority PER method and integrates it with Soft Actor-Critic (SAC) algorithms. The SAC-iPER methodology enhances the training velocity of deep reinforcement learning models, facilitating swifter convergence. This advancement reduces the time required for model deployment in real-world industrial settings, offering a novel solution to the challenge of protracted training durations prevalent in human-robot collaboration scenarios within the deep reinforcement learning paradigm. This article also compares and analyzes SAC, SAC-PER, and the method proposed herein, demonstrating the latter's superiority in enhancing the training speed of deep reinforcement learning models. For future work, we plan to continue refining the prioritized experience replay (PER) mechanism, potentially involving more granular differentiation of experience prioritization levels.

Acknowledgement. The authors would like to thank the National Natural Science Foundation (52175451 and 52205513).

References

1. Wang, L.: A futuristic perspective on human-centric assembly. J. Manuf. Syst. **62**, 199–201 (2022). https://doi.org/10.1016/j.jmsy.2021.11.001
2. Wang, L., et al.: Symbiotic human-robot collaborative assembly. CIRP Ann. **68**(2), 701–726 (2019). https://doi.org/10.1016/j.cirp.2019.05.002
3. Baratta, A., Cimino, A., Gnoni, M.G., Longo, F.: Human robot collaboration in industry 4.0: a literature review. Procedia Comput. Sci. **217**, 1887–1895 (2023). https://doi.org/10.1016/j.procs.2022.12.389
4. Layne, L.A.: Robot-related fatalities at work in the United States, 1992–2017. Am. J. Ind. Med. **66**(6), 454–461 (2023). https://doi.org/10.1002/ajim.23470

5. Prianto, E., Kim, M., Park, J.-H., Bae, J.-H., Kim, J.-S.: Path planning for multi-arm manipulators using deep reinforcement learning: soft actor-critic with hindsight experience replay. Sensors **20**(20), 5911 (2020). https://doi.org/10.3390/s20205911

6. Kusuma, M., Riyanto., Machbub, C.: Humanoid robot path planning and rerouting using A-star search algorithm. In: 2019 IEEE International Conference on Signals and Systems (ICSigSys), Bandung, Indonesia, pp. 110–115. IEEE (2019). https://doi.org/10.1109/ICSIGSYS.2019.8811093

7. Xu, Z., Guo, S., Zhang, L.: A path planning method of 6-DOF robot for mirror therapy based on A* algorithm. Technol. Health Care **30**(1), 105–116 (2021). https://doi.org/10.3233/THC-202551

8. Liu, W., Zheng, X., Deng, Z.: Dynamic collision avoidance for cooperative fixed-wing UAV swarm based on normalized artificial potential field optimization. J. Cent. South Univ. **28**(10), 3159–3172 (2021). https://doi.org/10.1007/s11771-021-4840-5

9. Lee, S.-J., Baek, S.-H., Kim, J.-H.: Arm Trajectory Generation Based on RRT* for Humanoid Robot. In: Kim, J.-H., Yang, W., Jo, J., Sincak, P., Myung, H. (eds.) Robot Intelligence Technology and Applications 3. AISC, vol. 345, pp. 373–383. Springer, Cham (2015). https://doi.org/10.1007/978-3-319-16841-8_34

10. Bhuiyan, T., Kästner, L., Hu, Y., Kutschank, B., Lambrecht, J.: Deep-reinforcement-learning-based path planning for industrial robots using distance sensors as observation. In: 2023 8th International Conference on Control and Robotics Engineering (ICCRE), Niigata, Japan, pp. 204–210. IEEE (2023). https://doi.org/10.1109/ICCRE57112.2023.10155608

11. Cheng, X., Liu, S.: Dynamic obstacle avoidance algorithm for robot arm based on deep reinforcement learning. In: 2022 IEEE 11th Data Driven Control and Learning Systems Conference (DDCLS), Chengdu, China, pp. 1136–1141. IEEE (2022). https://doi.org/10.1109/DDCLS55054.2022.9858561

12. Tang, W., Cheng, C., Ai, H., Chen, L.: Dual-arm robot trajectory planning based on deep reinforcement learning under complex environment. Micromachines **13**(4), 564 (2022). https://doi.org/10.3390/mi13040564

13. Liu, Q., Liu, Z., Xiong, B., Xu, W., Liu, Y.: Deep reinforcement learning-based safe interaction for industrial human-robot collaboration using intrinsic reward function. Adv. Eng. Inform. **49**, 101360 (2021). https://doi.org/10.1016/j.aei.2021.101360

14. Prianto, E., Park, J.-H., Bae, J.-H., Kim, J.-S.: Deep reinforcement learning-based path planning for multi-arm manipulators with periodically moving obstacles. Appl. Sci. **11**(6), 2587 (2021). https://doi.org/10.3390/app11062587

15. Ren, J., Huang, X., Huang, R.N.: Efficient deep reinforcement learning for optimal path planning. Electronics **11**(21), 3628 (2022). https://doi.org/10.3390/electronics11213628

16. Joypriyanka, M., Surendran, R.: Priority experience replay DQN for training an agent in virtual reality game for kids with paraplegia. In: 2023 2nd International Conference on Applied Artificial Intelligence and Computing (ICAAIC), Salem, India, pp. 743–749. IEEE (2023). https://doi.org/10.1109/ICAAIC56838.2023.10141031

A Study of Human Proxemics on Social Robot Light Effects

Yajuan Su[✉] and Xinxin Sun

Nanjing University of Science and Technology, Nanjing 210000, China
15174733849@163.com

Abstract. The social interaction capability of social robots is crucial for user experience; therefore, social robots should be kept at an appropriate distance to enhance user comfort. User experience depends on various attributes of the robot, such as emotional state, noise level, and physical appearance. Therefore, it is crucial to better understand the robot attributes that affect human-robot proximity behavior. The purpose of this paper is to analyze the effect of robot light effects on the preference of human-robot proximity behavior including light effect position, light effect color, and light effect flashing mode. Analysis of the experimental data shows that the position and color of the robot light effect have a significant effect on the preference of human-robot proximity behavior. This result will help to design and develop light effects and human-robot proximity strategies for social robots to enhance social interaction.

Keywords: light effects · social robots · human-robot interaction · proxemics

1 Introduction

Social robots are widely used in healthcare, education and entertainment. Service robots should interact with humans in a way that users feel comfortable. Spatial relationality is the study of the interpretation, manipulation, and changes in spatial behavior during face-to-face social encounters. These changes are governed by socio-cultural norms that determine the overall sensory experience of social stimuli (language, gestures, etc.) for each interaction participant. In order to facilitate natural and efficient human-robot interaction (HRI), robots must interact with users through multimodality: speech, gesture, and vision, among others. This paper investigates how robot light effects affect HRI distance, including: do robot light effects change HRI distance? Do different users experience the same light effect in the same way? The role of light effects in the field of spatial relational science is further demonstrated through experiments.

X. Sun—This research was financially supported by MOE (Ministry of Education in China) Youth Project of Humanities and Social Sciences Fund, 2022. "Promote the multi-modal interaction and service system design research of social intelligence of elderly care robots" (No. 22YJCZH156).

M. Kurosu and A. Hashizume (Eds.): HCII 2024, LNCS 14685, pp. 207–220, 2024.
https://doi.org/10.1007/978-3-031-60412-6_16

2 Related Work

2.1 Proxemics in Social Life

Edward T. Hall [1] introduced the theory of proxemics, which is used for the personal space that people maintain around themselves, a space that varies depending on the social environment and cultural context. For people in different relationships, all cultures specify what kind of social distance is appropriate and what kind of social distance is inappropriate, and the difference between them lies in how appropriate and inappropriate are defined. Spatial relationality provides a systematic basis for the study of social and personal space among humans. Research has shown that social space largely reflects and influences social relationships and people's attitudes toward each other. Michael Argyle [2] proposed the Intimate Equilibrium Model, which links mutual gaze and proximity behavior [3]. This model illustrates how people respond to encroachment on their personal space by reducing mutual gazing or moving backwards. Human space is not only a physical buffer, but also a psychological buffer [4]. Violations of our personal space can be uncomfortable and unsettling. This disruption occurs when our intimate area (0.00 m to 0.45 m) is violated by someone who is not in an intimate relationship. The ideal zone for interpersonal interactions between good friends or family members is between 0.45 and 1.2, and the ideal zone for interpersonal interactions between acquaintances is between 1.2 and 2.1 m. These guidelines used in social psychology are based on human-human interactions, and it is only when we recognize that robots are viewed as social actors and comparable to humans that these guidelines [5] can be mapped to human-robot interactions [6]. However, humans and robots do not always interact in the same way that humans interact with each other [7] human beings. Previous research has shown that human-robot distance is reserved for close acquaintances or family members [9] which is considered to be within the intimacy zone. Assuming that this proximity behavior may also hold true in human-robot interaction (HRI) requires redefining a reasonable distance between users and robots. Social robots in human environments need to be able to reason about their physical environment when interacting with people. In addition, human proximate behavior around the robot can indicate how people perceive the robot and can inform the robot's personality and interaction design.

In human-robot interaction, there are many factors that can influence human approach behavior. Some of the factors are related to the robot, such as the robot's voice [9], appearance [10] speed [11] and height [12]. Other aspects are related to humans, such as age [13] personality [14], prior experience with robots [12] and gender [16] or social norms [2]. Therefore, it is crucial to understand which robot design decisions affect human behavior around the robot in order to enhance robot-human interactions.

2.2 Proxemics Applied to Social Robots

The American poet Frost once said, "A good fence makes a good neighbor." Boundary can be understood as "whether it is allowed", which is a means of self-defense, but also the most basic principles of human interaction. Social boundaries are divided into physical boundaries and psychological boundaries, physical boundaries refer to the interpersonal interaction according to the affinity relationship, the two sides of the external distance between the near and far. Psychological boundary (psychological boundary) refers to the boundaries of individual psychological space. Some scholars describe it as "the limit line of human psychological activities".

The user comfort of a social robot while interacting with a user depends on the robot's proximity, and the user's proximity preference depends on various attributes of the robot such as emotional state, voice and physical appearance. Proxemics/spatial relationality plays an important role when a social robot interacts with a user. Hall et al. (1959, 1966) [17] pointed out that there are four zones of space around us and all have different meanings in communication, and that spatial distance consists of four zones: intimate distance (15–46 cm), which usually produces physical contact and allows understanding of each other even without audible language; private distance (46–122 cm), which belongs to the distance between family members and close friends, and generally allows contact with each other when reaching out; social distance (120–370 cm), formal and informal distances of general social groups; and public distance (370 cm or more), distances that can be interacted with through great sound or movement.

Social robots are not just robots that can perform autonomous tasks, but also have complex human-like behaviors; for example, robots that can express emotional states have been developed [20], these robots use different modes of expression, such as interactive displays, sounds, and body movements, to communicate their emotional states to users. The different emotional states of the robots may change the user-robot interaction preferences, which also has implications for user-robot spatial relatology as well. Spatial relationality is the study of the spatial distances that individuals maintain in various social and interpersonal contexts. These distances depend on environmental or cultural factors. The term was originally coined by Hall [23] proposed to describe human management of space. Social interaction space can vary depending on the age, culture, type of relationship and environment of different users. Since cultural differences affect space-related behaviors (some cultures avoid physical contact, while others are more tolerant of it), at the same time, the metrics proposed by Hall in his study apply to U.S. citizens. In addition, Bar-Haim Y explored children's tolerance for interruptions [24] related to their sense of security with their mothers or caregivers.

Currently, research in human-robot distance focuses on how the overall physical distance of the robot from the user affects the interaction experience, e.g., a study by Iachini et al. (2014) found that humans are at a greater distance from a cylindrical object than from a humanoid object. A study by Wieser et al. argued that the gender of the robot influences the interpersonal distance between the user and the robot, i.e., people stay a greater distance from a male robots to maintain a greater distance. Meanwhile some studies have shown that females are biased to keep a greater distance from robots. According to Jin-Yu Lin et al. it was found that the relationship between robots and people is different from traditional proxemics in that the difference in distance does not affect the establishment of intimacy. In addition to the distance between objects, comprehensive elements such as vision, touch, and other senses need to be taken into account when robots and humans interact. Mejía et al. showed that touch interactions begin prior to physical contact; such pre-touch interactions are also associated with similar representations in humans. For example, in a range of distances prior to touch, humans respond by turning toward the approaching hand and maintaining a distance from it. Shiomi et al. (2018)

showed that humans preferred that the robot would respond to the approaching hand at a simulated comfortable distance based on pre-touch interactions between humans. In a VR study, Mejía et al. investigated the distance at which humans began to feel uncomfortable when a virtual hand approached their face (pre-touch response distance), which was measured in VR at a distance close to that measured in physical space. M. Dubois [25] et al. studied emotional actions and human-robot body position changes, but this study was limited to six facial emotions of happiness and sadness. E. Howarth [26] argued that human-robot approach behavior is influenced by the personality displayed by the robot: in the service industry, robots with extroverted traits are preferred. While M. Neff [27] et al. showed that social robots' language and rhythms, for example, can be used to demonstrate the robot's personality traits. Meanwhile, M. Y. Lim [28] et al. found that extroverted robots were favored and trusted more than introverted robots. The results of Moujahid et al. showed that different types of robot personalities, especially introversion and extroversion, can influence human proximate behavior. Participants kept a shorter distance from the introverted robot receptionist compared to the extroverted robot.

2.3 Proxemics in Nonverbal Behavior

Existing research has demonstrated that a robot's personality and interaction style affect the user's social interaction distance with a social robot, and that various attributes of a robot, such as appearance, sound, and haptics, all contribute to the user's perception of the robot's personality and interaction style, which in turn affects the human-robot social interaction distance. Meanwhile, in order to facilitate natural and efficient human-robot interactions, robots must often employ multimodal communication mechanisms similar to those used by humans, such as speech generation (via speaker), speech recognition (via microphone), gesture generation (via physical manifestation) and gesture recognition (via camera). Samarakoon [29] et al. proposed a system that is able to adapt the distance of human-robot social interaction based on the user's physical behavior. However, this system does not consider relevant attributes of the robot such as physical appearance or emotional state to adapt the social interaction distance. The most direct interaction between a social robot and a user is voice interaction, and the robot's voice consists of unconscious machine noise and desirable sounds such as voices or musical outputs [30]. In some cases, the robot's voice is critical to the user's [31] M.L. Walters [9] et al. investigated the effect of the gender of the robot's voice on the human-robot proximity distance, but vocal tones with emotions were not included in the study. G. Trovato [32] et al. presented a study to determine the spatial relativistic changes induced by robotic machine noise, investigating the path deviation according to the characterization of the machine noise when the user under test passes the robot on one side of a corridor. In this case, the passer-by did not intentionally interact with the robot. However, the study did not consider spatial relational changes in direct human-robot interaction scenarios. Therefore, the results may not be valid for the case of intentional human-robot interaction. Different appearances can likewise have different effects on the spatial relationality of human-robot interactions, D.S. Syrdal [33] et al. found that human-appearing robots and mechanical-appearing robots have different proximity distances for adult preferences. M.L. Walters [12] et al. attempted to get the effect of different heights of the robots on the comfort level of spatial relativity, but this study was not successful. The user's age, cultural background, and education also affect the social distance in human-robot interaction, Walters [34] et al. found that children tended to stand further away from the robot compared to adults. Mumm and Mutlu [35] found in a controlled experiment that participants who disliked the robot tended to stand at a greater distance from the robot when the user and the robot gazed at each other. Also, they found that participants' distance from the robot was influenced by participants' gender and whether they owned a pet. Robins [31] et al. showed that contextually rich environments can encourage users to actively interact with robots. Kanda [23] et al.'s field experiment results suggest that robots may be more successful in establishing common ground and influencing interaction distance when they have something in common with the user.

Currently, there are fewer studies related to the effect of light behavior on social distance in human-social robot interactions. Therefore, in this paper, we would like to investigate the effect of light behavior on the distance of human-robot interactions, as well as the effect of light behavior on human-robot spatial relationships with other channels such as facial expressions, gestures, and sounds. To address our research questions, the following hypotheses were formulated.

H1: There is a significant difference in the shortest distance between the different positions of the robot's light effect;

H2: There is a significant difference in the shortest distance between the different colors of the robotic light effect;

H3: Significant difference in shortest distance between different flicker modes for robotic light effects.

3   Executive Design and Setup

The humanoid robot was placed on a wall 420 cm away from the user, as shown in Figs. 1 and 2. At the beginning of the experiment, the user was located directly in front of the robot, and the robot emitted light effects of different positions, colors, and blinking frequencies, accompanied by the voice of "Attention, the robot is approaching you", and walked towards the user. When the user feels uncomfortable, the pause button is pressed to get the distance between the user and the robot. The height of the robot is 120 cm and its speed is 0.35 m/s. Different light effects appear randomly, and when the user presses the pause button, it automatically skips to the next video.

In the preliminary stage of this experiment, light behavior-related elements, facial expressions, eye gaze, personality traits, and body movements of 75 social robots on the market were collected through crowdsourcing, and the 75 social robots were classified into human-like (e.g., pepper), animal- or pet-like (e.g., sota), machine-like (e.g., vector), and a new type of human-like (e.g., jibo) according to their physical characteristics; Classification into assistant robots, therapeutic robots, tele/presence robots, companion robots and toy robots according to their functions and roles. The light behavior position shape, color dynamics, interaction mode and interaction distance of the robots with different shapes were made to get the variables of this experiment. The experiment was conducted using a humanoid robot, while the color (red, blue, color), position (head, torso, lower limbs) and flashing mode (fixed, 5 Hz flashing, fading) of the light effects

Fig. 1. Robot starting position.

Fig. 2. Robot stop position.

were used as the independent variables, and the distance between the user and the robot was used as the dependent variable to start the experiment.

Due to the large number of variables, we made provisions for other settings for each experiment:

1. Light effect color: The light effect position is directly in front of the robot's chest, without flickering;
2. Light effect position: Light effect color is red, no flicker;
3. Flashing mode: the light effect position is directly in front of the robot's chest, and the light effect color is red.

The experiment was a within-group experiment, no audio or video data were collected, and consent was obtained from participants for the demographic information collected.

In this study, 45 in participants were recruited by convenience sampling method, basically between the ages of 18–30 years old, of which 19 were males and 26 were females, 26 were undergraduates and 9 were graduate students, and the detailed demographic characteristics are shown in Table 1. The results of the questionnaire survey showed that 89% of the participants had had experience of the use of social robots, and 16% of the participants indicated that there were problems in the perception of the distance between the participants and the social robots problems.

4 Results

In this study, 45 in participants were recruited by convenience sampling method, basically between the ages of 18–30 years old, including 19 males and 26 females, 26 undergraduates and 9 postgraduates, and detailed demographic characteristics are shown in Table 1. The results of the questionnaire survey showed that 89% of the participants had experience of using social robots, and 16% of the participants indicated that the feeling of distance with social robots was a problem.

Table 1. Demographic characteristics

Statistical projects	hallmark	classifier for number of participants	percentage
distinguishing between the sexes	male	19	42%
	female	26	58%
age	18–30 years	39	86%
	31–50 years	4	9%
	51 years and over	2	5%
education	Junior high school and below	4	9%
	senior high school	3	7%
	specialized training school	3	7%
	undergraduate	26	57%
	Master's degree or above	9	20%
Experience with Social Bots	Never used	5	11%
	seldom used	12	26%
	occasional use	15	33%
	Sometimes use	11	25%
	regular use	2	5%
Distance perception of social robots	Too close for comfort	3	7%
	normalcy	28	62%
	Too far away to be inconvenienced	4	9%
	senseless	10	22%

4.1 The Effect of Social Robot Light Effect Position on User-Bot Distance

In this study, ANOVA analysis (also known as One-way Repeated Measures ANOVA analysis) was used in IBM SPSS version 27 to determine whether the robot light effect position would have an effect on the physical distance between the user and the robot. Judging by box plots, there were no outliers in the data; the Shapiro-Wilk test suggested that the data in each group obeyed a normal distribution; the sphericity test suggested that the assumption of sphericity was not met (W = 0.835, p = 0.021), and the multivariate test was used to analyze the data. The multivariate test yielded p = 0.022 (p < 0.05) which shows that there is a significant difference between the location of the robot's light effect (head, torso, and lower limbs) for the physical distance between the user and the robot, as shown in Tables 2 and 3. The mean values of the distances between the head, torso, and lower limbs of the robot were 1.23 ± 1.04, 1.06 ± 0.72, and 0.82 ± 0.69 m. Further two-by-two comparisons showed that the greatest difference in the mean values was found between the torso and the lower limbs of the robot, and this was statistically significant (p < 0.05). In summary, it can be seen that the location of the light effect has a greater impact on the physical distance between the user and the robot, and the distance is greater when the light effect is located on the torso.

Table 2. Multivariate tests

effect		value	F	Hypothesis df	Error df	Sig	Partial Eta Square
Location	Billet Tracks	0.162	4.151[b]	2	43	0.022	0.162
	Wilke Lambda	0.838	4.151[b]	2	43	0.022	0.162
	Höttling trajectory	0.193	4.151[b]	2	43	0.022	0.162
	Roy Biggest Root	0.193	4.151[b]	2	43	0.022	0.162

4.2 The Effect of Social Robot Light Effect Color on User-Bot Distance

In this study, ANOVA analysis (also known as One-way Repeated Measures ANOVA analysis) was used in IBM SPSS version 27 to determine whether the color of the robot's light effect would have an effect on the physical distance between the user and the robot. Judging by box plots, there were no outliers in the data; the Shapiro-Wilk test suggested that the data in each group obeyed a normal distribution; the sphericity test suggested that the assumption of sphericity was not met (W = 0.857, p = 0.036), and the multivariate test was used to analyze the data. The multivariate test yielded p < 0.001, which shows that there is a significant difference between the color of the robot's light effect (red,

Table 3. Pairwise Comparisons

(I) Location	(J) Location	mean Difference (I-J)	Std.Error	Sig.[b]	lower bound	Upper bound
1	2	0.174	0.117	0.432	−0.117	0.466
	3	0.412*	0.146	0.021	0.049	0.776
2	1	−0.174	0.117	0.432	−0.466	0.117
	3	0.238	0.104	0.082	−0.022	0.498
3	1	−0.412*	0.146	0.021	−0.776	-0.049
	2	−0.238	0.104	0.082	−0.498	0.022

blue, and colored) for the physical distance between the user and the robot, as shown in Tables 4 and 5. The mean values of distance for light effect color red, blue and color are 1.23 ± 1.04, 0.84 ± 0.66, and 0.56 ± 0.61 m. Further two-by-two comparisons show that the difference in the mean values is largest and statistically significant when the light effect color is red and color ($p < 0.05$). In conclusion, it can be seen that the light effect color has a greater effect on the physical distance between the user and the robot, and the distance is greater when the light effect is red.

Table 4. Multivariate tests

effect		value	F	Hypothesis df	Error df	Sig	Partial Eta Square
Color	Billet Tracks	0.354	11.764[b]	2	43	0.000	0.354
	Wilke Lambda	0.646	11.764[b]	2	43	0.000	0.354
	Höttling trajectory	0.547	11.764[b]	2	43	0.000	0.354
	Roy Biggest Root	0.547	11.764[b]	2	43	0.000	0.354

4.3 The Effect of Social Robot Light Effect Blinking Method on User-Bot Distance

In this study, ANOVA analysis (also known as One-way Repeated Measures ANOVA analysis) was used in IBM SPSS version 27 to determine whether the robot's light effect flashing method would have an effect on the physical distance between the user and the

Table 5. Pairwise Comparison

(I) Color	(J) Color	mean Difference (I-J)	Std.Error	Sig.[b]	lower bound	Upper bound
1	2	0.389*	0.123	0.009	0.083	0.695
	3	0.671*	0.138	0.000	0.328	1.014
2	1	−0.389*	0.123	0.009	−0.695	−0.083
	3	0.282*	0.097	0.018	0.040	0.525
3	1	−0.671*	0.138	0.000	−1.014	−0.328
	2	−0.282*	0.097	0.018	−0.525	−0.040

robot. Judging by box plots, there were no outliers in the data; the Shapiro-Wilk test suggested that the data in each group obeyed a normal distribution; the sphericity test suggested that the assumption of sphericity was not met ($W = 0.780$, $p = 0.024$), and the multivariate test was used to analyze the data. The multivariate test yielded $p = 0.625$, $p > 0.05$, which shows that there is no significant difference between the robot light effect blinking modes (fixed, 5 Hz blinking, and fading) for the physical distance between the user and the robot, as shown in Table 6. The mean values of the distances for the light effect flashing modes of fixed, 5 Hz flashing and fade-in are 0.9 ± 1.04, 0.97 ± 0.77, and 1.04 ± 0.62 m. In summary, it can be seen that there is no significant effect of the light effect flashing modes on the physical distances between the user and the robot.

Table 6. Multivariate tests

effect		value	F	Hypothesis df	Error df	Sig	Partial Eta Square
frequency variation	Billet Tracks	0.031	0.477[b]	2	30	0.625	0.031
	Wilke Lambda	0.969	0.477[b]	2	30	0.625	0.031
	Höttling trajectory	0.032	0.477[b]	2	30	0.625	0.031
	Roy Biggest Root	0.032	0.477[b]	2	30	0.625	0.031

5 Discussion

To validate H1, the experimental results show that the location of the social robot light effect significantly affects the physical distance between the user and the robot. In addition, the physical distance between the user and the robot is more likely to increase when the light effect is located in the torso of the robot than in the other two cases (head, lower limbs). Specifically, the height of the robot was 1.2 m, and the light effect location was essentially at the same level as the user's eyes. Therefore, the torso position is more likely to attract the user's attention than the light effect in the lower limb area. At the same time, there is no significant difference between the head light effect and the torso light effect, the torso part of the light effect is set with the robot's chest, and the closer distance between the two parts may be the reason for the lack of significant difference; and the head compared to the distance of the lower limbs, the physical distance between the user and the robot is farther away, which further suggests that the closer the location of the light effect is to the center of the human line of sight, the easier it is to attract the user's attention, and then the user will produce a sense of discomfort, and the user's social distance with the robot increases. The social distance between the user and the robot increases.

Second, the color of the light effect significantly affects the physical distance between the user and the robot. Compared to blue and colored light effects, red draws more attention to the user and increases the physical distance between the user and the robot, which is consistent with our everyday experience. In our culture, the color red often means "dangerous" and "need to be careful", so red light effects are more likely to make users alert and unconsciously distance themselves from "dangerous objects" than other colors. Therefore, compared with other colors, red light effects are more likely to make users alert and unconsciously distance themselves from "dangerous objects". In order to increase the intimacy between the robot and the user, the use of red light effects should be limited in the daily use of the robot's light effects. From the experimental results, we can also see that the acceptance of color light effects is higher than that of blue light effects. On the one hand, this can be attributed to the fact that users prefer color light effects, which leads to the shortening of the physical distance; on the other hand, in the process of the experiments, users inevitably feel bored, and the color light effects can be a very good way to alleviate the cognitive burden of the users.

Finally, the flashing mode did not significantly affect the physical distance between the user and the robot. This result is quite different from the original concept of the experiment team, which proved that there is no significant difference in the physical distance between the user and the robot in the three states of light effect fixed, 5 Hz flashing and fading in. First, the use of red as the color of the light effect here may have a psychological burden on the user, and the physical distances in all three cases are around 1 m. Second, "the red robot reminds me of the surveillance camera in the classroom" (Tested 23, Tested 24), and the different flashing modes of the red robot are given different meanings, adding extra decoding burden and thus cognitive load; finally, users are more sensitive to color under uncertainty, resulting in weaker blinking information.

6 Conclusion

In this study, we measured and compared the differences in light effects and human-robot physical distance among 45 participants by constructing a simulated human-social robot interaction experimental environment. The results show that the color and position of the social robot light effects significantly affect the human-robot interaction distance.

Overall, the range of human-robot interaction distances, regardless of the location of the light effect, was 0.9–2.5 m. The range of human-robot interaction distances with different colors of light effects was 0.6–3.6 m. The range of human-robot interaction distances with different flashing modes of the light effects was 0.8–1.5 m. This range overlapped between the social and the private areas of the human-robot interaction. These results suggest that the theory of spatial relationality does not map directly to human-robot interaction because humans interact with robots in a different way than humans interact with each other.

There are still some limitations in this study: firstly, the population in this study is small and age-concentrated, and the scope of the survey can be expanded to cover more age groups and cultural backgrounds; secondly, this study adopts watching videos as an experimental means, and social robots can be used as a further study to cover more tasks and more life-oriented scenarios.

Acknowledgements. This research was financially supported by MOE (Ministry of Education in China) Youth Project of Humanities and Social Sciences Fund, 2022. "Promote the multi-modal interaction and service system design research of social intelligence of elderly care robots" (No. 22YJCZH156).

References

1. Hall, E.T., Hall, E.T.: The hidden dimension. Anchor **609** (1966)
2. Argyle, M.: Bodily Communication. Routledge (2013)
3. Argyle, M., Dean, J.: Eye-contact, distance and affiliation. Sociometry, 289–304 (1965)
4. Dosey, M.A., Meisels, M.: Personal space and self-protection. J. Pers. Soc. Psychol. **11**(2), 93 (1969)
5. Reeves, B., Nass, C.: How people treat computers, television, and new media like real people and places (1996)
6. Nass, C., Steuer, J., Tauber, E.R.: Computers are social actors. In: Proceedings of the SIGCHI Conference on Human Factors in Computing Systems, pp. 72–78 (1994)
7. Mumm, J., Mutlu, B.: Human-robot proxemics: physical and psychological distancing in human-robot interaction. In: Proceedings of the 6th International Conference on Human-Robot Interaction, pp. 331–338 (2011)
8. Sardar, A., Joosse, M., Weiss, A., Evers, V.: Don't stand so close to me: users' attitudinal and behavioral responses to personal space invasion by robots. In: Proceedings of the Seventh Annual ACM/IEEE International Conference on Human-Robot Interaction, p. 229 230 (2012)
9. Walters, M.L., Syrdal, D.S., Koay, K.L., Dautenhahn, K., Te Boekhorst, R.: Human approach distances to a mechanical-looking robot with different robot voice styles. In: Proceedings of the RO-MAN 2008-The 17th IEEE International Symposium on Robot and Human Interactive Communication, pp. 707–712. IEEE (2008)
10. Syrdal, D.S., Dautenhahn, K., Walters, M.L., Koay, K.L.: Sharing spaces with robots in a home scenario-anthropomorphic attributions and their effect on proxemic expectations and evaluations in a live HRI trial. In: Proceedings of the AAAI Fall Symposium: AI in Eldercare: New Solutions to Old Problems, pp. 116–123 (2008)
11. Butler, J.T., Agah, A.: Psychological effects of behavior patterns of a mobile personal robot. Auton. Robot. **10**(2), 185–202 (2001)

12. Walters, M.L.: The design space for robot appearance and behavior for social robot companions. Ph.D. dissertation, University of Hertfordshire (2008)
13. Tokmurzina, D., Sagitzhan, N., Nurgaliyev, A., Sandygulova, A.: Exploring child-robot proxemics. In: Proceedings of the Companion of the 2018 ACM/IEEE International Conference on Human-Robot Interaction, pp. 257–258 (2018)
14. Syrdal, D.S., Dautenhahn, K., Woods, S., Walters, M.L., Koay, K.L.: 'Doing the right thing wrong'-personality and tolerance to uncomfortable robot approaches. In: Proceedings of the ROMAN 2006-The 15th IEEE International Symposium on Robot and Human Interactive Communication, pp. 183–188. IEEE (2006)
15. Walters, M.L.: The influence of subjects' personality traits on personal spatial zones in a human-robot interaction experiment. In: Proceedings of the ROMAN 2005. IEEE International Workshop on Robot and Human Interactive Communication, pp. 347–352. IEEE (2005)
16. Syrdal, D.S., Koay, K.L., Walters, M.L., Dautenhahn, K.: A personalized robot companion? The role of individual differences on spatial preferences in HRI scenarios. In: Proceedings of the RO-MAN 2007-The 16th IEEE International Symposium on Robot and Human Interactive Communication, pp. 1143–1148. IEEE (2007)
17. Hall, E.T.: The Hidden Dimension. Doubleday & Company Inc., Garden City, NY, USA (1966)
18. Bocardus, E.: Social distance and its origins. J. Appl. Sociol. 9 (1925)
19. Kaplan, K.J., Firestone, I.J., Klein, K.W., Sodikoff, C.: Distancing in dyads: a comparison of four models. Soc. Psychol. Q., 108–115 (1983)
20. Breazeal, C.: Social interactions in HRI: the robot view. IEEE Trans. Syst. Man Cybern. Part C (Appl. Rev.) 34(2), 181–186 (2004)
21. Bethel, L., Murphy, R.R.: Survey of non-facial/non-verbal affective expressions for appearance-constrained robots. IEEE Trans. Syst. Man Cybern. Part C (Appl. Rev.) 38(1), 83–92 (2008)
22. Moshkina, L., Arkin, R.C.: Human perspective on affective robotic behavior: a longitudinal study. In: 2005 IEEE/RSJ International Conference Intelligent Robots and Systems, pp. 1444–1451. IEEE (2005)
23. Hall, E.T.: The Hidden Dimension: Man's Use of Space in Public and Private. The Bodley Head Ltd., London (1966)
24. Bar-Haim, Y., Aviezer, O., Berson, Y., Sagi, A.: Attachment in infancy and personal space regulation in early adolescence. Attach. Hum. Dev. 4(1), 68–83 (2002)
25. Dubois, M., Claret, J.-A., Basañez, L., Venture, G.: Influence of emotional motions in human-robot interactions. In: Kulić, D., Nakamura, Y., Khatib, O., Venture, G. (eds.) 2016 International Symposium on Experimental Robotics. SPAR, vol. 1, pp. 799–808. Springer, Cham (2017). https://doi.org/10.1007/978-3-319-50115-4_69
26. Howarth, E.: Expectations concerning occupations in relation to extraversion-introversion. Psychol. Rep. 24(2), 415–418 (1969). pMID: 5809034
27. Neff, M., Wang, Y., Abbott, R., Walker, M.: Evaluating the effect of gesture and language on personality perception in conversational agents. In: Allbeck, J., Badler, N., Bickmore, T., Pelachaud, C., Safonova, A. (eds.) Intelligent Virtual Agents. LNCS (LNAI), vol. 6356, pp. 222–235. Springer, Heidelberg (2010). https://doi.org/10.1007/978-3-642-15892-6_24
28. Lim, M.Y.: We are all individuals: the role of robot personality and human traits in trustworthy interaction. In: Proceedings of the 2022 31st IEEE International Conference on Robot and Human Interactive Communication (RO-MAN), pp. 538–545. IEEE (2022)
29. Samarakoon, S.M.B.P., Sirithunge, H.P.C., Muthugala, M.A.V.J., Jayasekara, A.G.B.P.: Proxemics and approach evaluation by service robot based on user behavior in domestic environment. In: 2018 IEEE/RSJ International Conference on Intelligent Robots and Systems (IROS), pp. 8192–8199. IEEE (2018)

30. Moore, D., Ju, W.: Sound as implicit influence on human-robot interactions. In: Companion of the 2018 ACM/IEEE International Conference Human Robot Interaction, pp. 311–312. ACM (2018)

31. Sauppe, A., Mutlu, B.: The social impact of a robot co-worker in -industrial settings. In: Proceedings 33rd Annual ACM Conference on Human Factors in Computing Systems, pp. 3613–3622. ACM (2015)

32. Trovato, R., et al.: The sound or silence: investigating the influence of robot noise on proxemics. In: 2018 27th IEEE International Symposium on Robot and Human Interactive Communication (RO-MAN), pp. 713–718. IEEE (2018)

33. Syrdal, D.S., Dautenhahn, K., Walters, M.L., Koay, K.L.: Sharing spaces with robots in a home scenario-anthropomorphic attributions and their effect on proxemic expectations and evaluations in a live HRI trial. In: AAAI Fall Symposium: AI in Eldercare: New Solutions to Old AI in Eldercare: New Solutions to Old Problems, pp. 116–123 (2008)

34. Walters, M., et al.: Close encounters: spatial distances between people and a robot of mechanistic appearance. In: Proceedings Humanoids (2005)

35. Mumm, J., Mutlu, B.: Human-robot proxemics: physical and psychological distancing in human-robot interaction. In: Proceedings HRI (2011)

36. Robins, B., Dautenhahn, K., Nehaniv, C., Mirza, N., Francois, D., Olsson, L.: Sustaining interaction dynamics and engagement in dyadic child-robot interaction kinesics: lessons learnt from an exploratory study. In: Proceedings RO-MAN (2005)

37. Kanda, T., Hirano, T., Eaton, D., Ishiguro, H.: Interactive robots as social partners and peer tutors for children: a field trial. Hum. Comput. Interact. 19(1), 61–84 (2004)

"He Can Walk, He Just Doesn't Want To" - On Machine/Human-Likeness of Robots in Polish Children's Perception

Paulina Zguda[1]([⊠])[iD], Alicja Wróbel[2][iD], Paweł Gajewski[3][iD], and Bipin Indurkhya[2][iD]

[1] Doctoral School in the Humanities, Jagiellonian University, Kraków, Poland
paulina.zguda@doctoral.uj.edu.pl
[2] Jagiellonian University, Kraków, Poland
alka.wrobel@student.uj.edu.pl, bipin.indurkhya@uj.edu.pl
[3] AGH University of Krakow, Kraków, Poland
pgajewski@agh.edu.pl

Abstract. We explore the evolving perceptions of social robots among children, highlighting a shift from distinct categorizations of machine-like or human-like to a nuanced view where robots are recognized as mechanical entities with anthropomorphic features. Using Poland as a case study, we delve into the growing presence of social robots, exemplified by the 'Kerfuś' robot, which garnered attention for its cat-like appearance. Research conducted over five years reveals changing attitudes in children, with increased exposure to robots leading to a blend of lifelike and machinelike interpretations. Despite a growing understanding of robotic functionality, children, particularly younger ones, tend to anthropomorphize robots, attributing human or animal-like qualities. Age-related differences emerge in interactions with robots like Miro-E and NAO, showcasing a fluid cognitive development in perceiving these machines. We underscore the need to explore how increased robot presence shape children's evolving perceptions, ultimately emphasizing a trend toward attributing anthropomorphic features to robots while maintaining awareness of their mechanical nature.

Keywords: Social Robotics · Child-Robot Interaction · Human-Robot Interaction

1 Introduction

1.1 The Development of Social Robotics

Child-Robot Interaction (CRI) is a field of study that examines social encounters between children and humanoid robots. There are some important determinants influencing children's perception of robots. The youngest users of robots more easily attribute animated characteristics to them than adults, are more prone to anthropomorphize robots, and engage in play with a robot more eagerly [1].

© The Author(s), under exclusive license to Springer Nature Switzerland AG 2024
M. Kurosu and A. Hashizume (Eds.): HCII 2024, LNCS 14685, pp. 221–239, 2024.
https://doi.org/10.1007/978-3-031-60412-6_17

People from different backgrounds may have very different experiences and attitudes towards social robotics, especially given that some groups are more carefully researched than others [16]. This results in an interesting contrast. Over the past few years, GPT Chat has become an everyday programme for many pupils and students, and the SARS-19 pandemic has permanently changed the reality of education by pointing out the advantages and disadvantages of digitised learning and remote learning. Many households are assisted by technology (e.g. virtual assistants such as Alexa [2, 14]). Despite the increasing presence of social robots and the greater exposure of this topic in developing research areas, for many people, social robots may still seem like sci-fi machines. Rapid technological developments may be perceived diversely by particularly vulnerable groups, such as children.

Although children are recognised as a group characterised by exceptional curiosity [9], their positive attitude towards every new technology cannot be taken for granted — and needs to be verified in different circumstances. To this end, several studies have been carried out to address this issue. Particularly noteworthy, for example, is research into the use of social robots in reducing children's anxiety and stress in a hospital context. A systematic review of the methods used between 2009 and 2020 was presented by [13], pointing to the potential for the beneficial use of robots, while emphasising the pilot and unitary nature of the studies described. Still, the positive effect of social robots' usage was noted. Another systematic review aimed to determine to what extent communication with social robots influences how children develop empathy [15]. As promising, similar to the [13]'s work, the problem with the more coherent results was pointed out by the authors. There is a lack of long-term studies showing the development of empathy with the help of robots in more natural development, rather than in the form of brief, individual insights. Another important thread is the verification of the robot as a facilitator in the learning process. A remarkable example is also the 'learning by teaching' paradigm, where the robot — instead of the stereotypically assumed role of a teacher — takes on the role of a learner to be taught new skills by children while developing their own [8].

Nevertheless, robotics is still seen as a fledgling topic in some regions [22]. For instance, the analysis of [16] indicates that most reports of human-robot interaction correspond to the characteristics of WEIRD: Western, Educated, Industrialised, Rich, and Democratic societies. However, the situation is changing. Poland can serve as an example, where, over several years, the presence of social robots in everyday life has managed to increase significantly. When our research started in 2018, the number of studies on Polish participants was relatively low [7, 11, 12]. Recently, this number started to grow [10, 17, 18, 22].

1.2 Machine Vs Human-Likeness

Research suggests that to some extent anthropomorphism is desirable for robots. One of the important factors in the children's perception of robots as human-like agents is the robot's actions: an ability to perform tasks specific to humans [19]. Moreover, younger children (aged 4–8) in the UK expressed a lesser tendency to ascribe human-like qualities to social robots and the usage of the 'human' concept compared to older children and adults [4]. According to [5], younger children tend to perceive humanoid robots, especially those with lifelike facial features, as more person-like. This suggests that younger children may anthropomorphize robots, attributing human-like qualities to them. Older children, on the other hand, tend to classify the same humanoid robot as more machine-like. This indicates a developmental shift in how children categorize robots, with older children showing a reduced tendency to anthropomorphize. [3] claims that "children attribute more cognitive abilities to the robot and fewer mechanical properties over time". The question arises — can these two images, the robot as a machine and the robot read as a human, merge into one? Do the two paradigms only function disjointly? Another issue is the explosive growth of the internet and access to technology. Do children in 2024 have different attitudes towards social robots compared to their pre-pandemic peers?

1.3   Changing Perception of Social Robots

One of the more striking, unexpected examples may be the *Kerfuś* robot, which won the hearts of Polish internet users in the autumn of 2022 when it appeared in one of the supermarket chains. The robot, the design of which combined the appearance of a robotic waiter with features resembling a cat, quickly became the material for many memes, while also sparking a discussion about how contemporary robots can be perceived and how their original use can be altered through social, pop-cultural perception. However, this is a two-way street — in the case of Kerfuś, the robot waiter can become an internet sensation with whom internet users claim to want to interact sexually. Even if such declarations are absurd, they change our perception of this robot, and we will transfer newly acquired attributions towards robots in general to the next robots we encounter on our way. The Kerfuś case has helped to open up a wider discussion about the changing perception of the robot. In our research over several years, we have highlighted the increasing number of children who have had previous interaction with any robot, as well as the fact that the robot is anthropomorphised while maintaining the attribution of mechanical attribution.

Current research does not seem to provide a satisfactory answer to the question of whether it is possible for a robot — perceived as a machine — to still be anthropomorphised to some extent. The goal of this research was to examine how the children's perception of social robots changed over a few years. We are also interested in how the issue of human/lifelike and machinelikeness is addressed in children.

2   Methods

2.1   In-the-Wild Method

The research, conducted since 2018, combined Wizard-of-Oz and In-the-Wild methodologies. The choice of this methodology allowed the research to be conducted in a variety of contexts (most often the school environment, but also other spaces frequently visited by children, e.g. museums where extra-curricular activities took place), using diversified sets of activities that combined cross-modal elements (the use of different modalities, e.g. dancing and drawing) and allowed for a proactive attitude on the part of the children (by, for example, encouraging the children to carry out a series of questions and answers with the robots), and used literary works or songs familiar to the children to create an atmosphere of safe exploration. It is worth mentioning that our pilot studies started in 2018, however, here we elaborate only on some selected studies. Between 2020 to 2022 the studies were suspended because of the SARS-19 pandemic.

2.2 Study Designs

Interaction in Kindergarten, 2019. The event took place in kindergarten in Krakow, involving five groups of children, all in one day. Each group had 20–23 children aged 4–6.

Children interacted with a humanoid robot Pepper, presented in Fig. 1, controlled via the Wizard-of-Oz method. During the observation, the children had the opportunity to engage in the following activities: Greeting, Dancing, Reading, Drawing, Error activity, Free dialogue and Goodbye. All stages were initiated and 'controlled' by the robot (in fact, two researchers controlled Pepper from the back of the room). The 'error' activity was designed to test how the children would react to an unexpected action by the robot (e.g. making an unnatural pose and ceasing contact for one minute; after this time, the robot returns to its previous state and continues as usual.) The details of this study are presented in [22].

Interaction in a Museum, 2022. Our two-day study took place at Krakow's Museum of Contemporary Art in Poland, involving two groups of children, one per day. The first group had 8 children aged 6–7, and the second had 10 children aged 10–12, all familiar with the museum due to previous extracurricular activities. Each event was three hours long with a lunch break in the middle.

The study consisted of two segments for each group. Initially, children interacted with a robot: talking, asking questions, reading, and playing charades with a humanoid robot Nao (Fig. 2), controlled via the Wizard-of-Oz method. The second part involved a craft task where children drew their favorite moments from the interaction and crafted a book for the robot. Following these activities, semi-structured interviews were conducted to gather the children's feedback on their experiences. The details of this study are presented in [20, 21].

Interaction in School, 2023. In this excerpted part of a larger study, we examined interactions between 100 children (ages 7–9) from a local primary school and three different robots: Nao, Misty, and Miro-E, which are presented in Fig. 2, Fig. 3 and Fig. 4. The children, divided into four 25-member groups from the first grade, engaged in a uniform interaction pattern (detailed in the method section) with each robot. Conducted over two days, each of the four groups,

Fig. 1. Pepper robot

Fig. 2. Nao robot

two per day, participated in hour-long sessions. In small groups of 5–6, children rotated between activities with each robot, ensuring every child interacted with all four robots (the fourth being Pepper, but this part was not included into this analysis). The three mentioned activities with three different robots were as follows:

Fig. 3. Misty robot

Fig. 4. Miro-E robot

In the activity with NAO, the robot displayed emotions through body postures and LED colors, with children creating stories to explain these emotions. Emotions were triggered using a custom Python program, allowing a researcher to select and control them via a graphical interface. The activities, designed to maintain engagement, incorporated various modalities such as movement, manual skills, visual observation, and auditory learning. Each group experienced a unique flow due to task rotation, yet the interaction maintained a cohesive structure with a clear start and end.

In the activity with Misty, the children taught the robot a poem, 'Pomidor,' by Jan Brzechwa. A researcher introduced the task, while another discreetly controlled Misty, using pre-recorded phrases to interact and occasionally making mistakes in reciting the poem. After a few errors, Misty successfully learned and recited the poem, thanking the children. Misty was programmed through its onboard studio, enabling the visual composition of programs with command blocks and conditional statements. The controlling researcher, equipped with a variety of voice recordings, sat near the group to listen in without drawing attention.

In the activity with MiRo-E, children programmed the robot's movements using command sheets. After introducing the task and MiRo-E, the children selected and sequenced these commands. A researcher assisted in translating these sequences into the robot's programming via its web-based interface, MiRoCODE. The corresponding movements had been pre-programmed to match the command sheets. This process of converting paper algorithms to digital commands was done openly, allowing the children to observe and learn.

3 Analysis

The analyzed data consisted of video and audio recordings of children interacting with the robot and children's interviews by the researchers after the interaction from all three studies. The analysis included transcribing children's statements and coding them according to the scheme shown in Tables 1 and 2. Analysis was done by two researchers.

4 Results

Throughout their interactions with robots, children exhibited a range of behaviors that reflected their beliefs regarding the robot's perceived liveliness or mechanical nature.

4.1 Children 5–6 Interacting with Pepper Robot, 2019

Although the first pilot study already took place in 2018 (Pepper took the role of a co-leader of a workshop at the Museum of Contemporary Art in Krakow), this article will include research from 2019.

Table 1. Coding scheme of children treating the robot in lifelike/human-like terms

Treating the robot in lifelike/human-like terms	
Body features	Children refer to the robot's appearance using names of human/animal body features, e.g. "Look at his eyes!"
Autonomous movement	Children refer to the robot as moving autonomously, e.g. "Where is he going?"
Physiological functions	Children refer to the robot as having life functions, e.g. "He's sleeping!", "Can you eat?"
Responsiveness	Children show their belief in the robot's responsiveness by asking it questions and referring to it by its name, e.g. "Hello, Nao!", "Nao, do you like me?"
Emotions and mental states	Children refer to the robot using human/animal mental faculties, states of mind or emotions, e.g. "He's shy!", "He's tired", "Have you forgotten how to do that?", "Do you love us?"
Relationships	Children show their belief in robots having human-like relationships, by asking them questions about their parents, friends etc.
Human abilities and character features	Children refer to the robot as having human abilities, such as dancing, singing, mathematical abilities etc. They also show their belief that the robot can pose some character features such as having a favorite meal

Treating the Robot in Lifelike Terms. Studies show that children apply body awareness while interacting with a robot, which results in identifying the robot's body features with human body features [6]. Children accepted lifelike explanations for the robot's actions such as "I'm tired". Even though Pepper explained that its battery charge was low, Polish children still asked it human-like questions. In some cases, they even tried to be helpful, asking where is the charger (so they could help to plug it in). Polish children also sympathized with Pepper using soft expressions.

Pepper: I'm two years old.
Child: Sooo little.
Pepper: I don't have a wife.
Child: Poor robot.

They assumed Pepper had parents and asked about them, which is another sign of searching for human-like attributes in the robot.

Child: Do you have parents?
Child: If it was born, probably yes.

Treating the Robot in Machinelike Terms. Despite showing signs of humanizing the robot, Polish children also asked questions indicating that they saw it as a mechanical creature. Some children did not ask about the parental relationships of the robot but asked specifically about its creators.

Child: Who created you?
Child: He wasn't born, he was created!

They also made assumptions about the robot's life ("Robots never have birthdays") and asked questions that transcend human abilities or behaviours ("Can you change into something?").

Table 2. Coding scheme of children treating the robot in machinelike terms

Treating the robot in machinelike terms	
Mechanical components	Children refer to the robot as possessing mechanical components, such as cameras, speakers, integrated circuits etc.
Mechanical functions	Children refer to the robot as possessing mechanical functions, such as turning on/off, crushing, charging, driving on wheels etc.
Lack of human abilities	Children refer to the robot as not possessing human abilities like knowledge, reading etc., e.g. "He doesn't know everything because he doesn't know what people eat!"
Unhuman characteristics	Children show their belief that the robot possesses some unhuman characteristics like being created by another person

4.2   Children 6–7 yrs Interacting with NAO Robot, 2022

Treating the Robot in Lifelike Terms. Children aged 6–7 frequently anthropomorphized and animated the humanoid NAO robot, attributing it with human-like capabilities such as dancing, reading, and language learning.
Child: Please, NAO, dance!
Child: NAO will say that he can only read human languages.
Child: He knows human languages.
They also believed that NAO possesses mental faculties and emotions, including memory, forgetfulness, and the capacity to experience pleasure.
Child: Have you forgotten how to do that?
Child: NAO can recall his parents.
Child: NAO will be pleased.
When describing the robot, they often employed animal-like terms such as eating, sleeping, looking, and even feeling pain.
Child: Eat something!
Child: He's probably sleeping.
Child: He won't walk because his legs hurt.
These children had faith in the robot's responsiveness, engaging in conversations with it while expecting either answers or reactions.
Child: NAO! Please, come here! We have something to show you!
Child: Can you read for us?

Additionally, they were keenly aware of NAO's ability for autonomous movement.

```
Child: Where is he going?
```

Treating the Robot in Machinelike Terms. At the same time, these children displayed an awareness of the robot's mechanical nature. Some pondered the possibility that the robot might not possess the human-like abilities that others attributed to it, such as reading or understanding the human world.

```
Child: He can't read.
Child: NAO doesn't know everything! He doesn't know what people
eat, for example!
```

They described the robot's actions in terms of its mechanical functions, including references to it crashing, breaking down, or requiring charging.

```
Child: He crashed like a computer.
Child: This crystal makes sure that NAO doesn't break down.
Child: Charge yourself!
```

Furthermore, they were aware of the robot's mechanical components, such as integrated circuits, switches, and sensors.

```
Child: There is an integrated circuit inside.
Child: There is a switch, speaker, microphone, engine and sensors!
```

4.3   Children 10–12 yrs Interacting with NAO Robot, 2022

Treating the Robot in Lifelike Terms. Much like their younger counterparts, children aged 10–12 years old demonstrated a spectrum of behaviors that revealed their perception of the robot's liveliness. They were keen observers of the robot's human-like abilities, such as dancing and reading.

```
Child: The robot knows how to dance.
Child: He can read.
```

In their discussions, they ascribed mental and emotional attributes to the robot: attributing to it thoughts, desires, and the capacity for happiness or shyness.

```
Child: He's thinking.
Child: He can walk, he just doesn't want to.
Child: So, there is a robot and he's very happy...
He's just shy!
```

Their descriptions of the robot's actions often took on a vivid, lifelike quality, with references to hearing, sleeping, and even dying.

```
Child: The robot can hear.
Child: It's going to sleep.
Child: Is it like dying? *talking about robot turning off*
```

These children anticipated responsiveness from the robot, frequently demanding answers to their inquiries.

```
Child: Can you play Fortnite?
Child: Can you dance?
```

Additionally, they frequently commented on NAO's autonomous movements.

Child: He could sit. More of a crouch.
Child: He can walk.

Treating the Robot in Machinelike Terms. Older children also employed
mechanical terminology when referring to the robot. They delineated the robot's
mechanical functions, including concepts such as crashing, powering down, dis-
connecting, or undergoing programming.
Child: I'd like the robot not to crash.
Child: When you program a robot very well, it can do the same
things as people do.
Child: He's turning off.
Child: I think he's disconnected.
They also mentioned machine components like batteries.
Child: He has a battery.

These children treated the robot as a familiar technological entity, akin to the
voice assistants they routinely utilize in their everyday lives. Their interactions
with the robot were characterized by a sense of order, with each child taking
turns to communicate and displaying patience as they awaited responses. Their
determination to establish a connection with the robot was evident in their
persistence, as they frequently reiterated their questions and utilized simplified
language to ensure clear communication.

4.4 Children 7–9 yrs Interacting with Nao Robot, 2023

Treating the Robot in Lifelike Terms. Children 7–9 years mostly treated
Nao robot in lifelike terms. They believed in the robot's reactivity, by asking it
many questions, giving commands, greeting it and saying goodbye.
Child: Why are you called Nao?
Child: Nao, sit!
Child: A little robot! Hello!
Child: Bye, Nao!
They also treated the robot as if it possessed some biological features, like body
parts, gender, or motor abilities.
Researcher: What is most interesting about this robot?
Child: His eyes! His hand!
Child: He has 3 fingers!
Child: Are you a boy or a girl?
Child: Wave your hand for us!
Child: Can you sit?
Child: Can you run?

Children seemed to believe that the robot possesses some human abilities as
well, like playing ball, singing and dancing. They said Nao has a sense of humor
and a favorite color.
Child: Can you dance for us?
Child: Can you sing for us?

Child: Can you play ball?
Child: What is your favorite color?
Child: You have a great sense of humor!

Children seemed to believe that Nao has human emotions as well.

Child: Can you laugh?
Nao: Yes.
Child: Then I'll tell you a joke.
Child: He is crying!
Child: Do you like us?
Child: Do you love us?

They also were interested in robot relationships that resemble human relationships.

Child: Do you have a mom or a dad?
Nao: I don't.
Child: Oh!
Child: He's all alone!
Child: Do you have any cousins?
Child: How many cousins do you have?
Child: Do you like them?
Child: Do you have any pets?
Child: Do robots have their land?
Child: Do you have many friends?

Treating the Robot in Machinelike Terms. Children didn't display many behaviors of treating the robot in machinelike terms. However, they noticed it's machine features.

Child: He has a speaker in his head!
Child: Does he have cameras in his eyes?
Child: Turn off!

4.5 Children 7–9 yrs Interacting with Misty Robot, 2023

Treating the Robot in Lifelike Terms. These children displayed many behaviors where they treated Misty in lifelike terms. They treated Misty as if it was a pet, giving it commands such as 'high five' or 'give me your paw'.

Child: Can she put her hand up?
Child: Give me your paw!
Child: High five!
Child: He gave me a high five!

They also believed in the robot's responsiveness, engaging in conversations with it while expecting either answers or reactions.

Child: Hello, Misty!
Child: Misty, come here!
Child: Go forward!
Child: Move backwards a little bit, please!

Child: Misty, wake up!

Children even treated Misty in human-like terms, stating the robot has abilities like reading, possessing a language or learning poems.

Child: I'm answering in her language!

Child: Read for us!

Child: We are teaching her!

They also believed that the robot can possess human emotions like love.

Child: Do you love me?

Child: Misty loves us!

Children also reacted with patience to Misty's mistakes and tried to comfort the robot when it apologized for it's actions.

Misty: *accidentally almost hits a girl with its hand*

Researcher: Misty, you have to say sorry for almost hitting this girl.

Misty: *makes a sad face to say sorry, it does it for few seconds*

Child: Misty, it's okay. You said sorry, now we have to get back to the activity.

Misty: *said the poem with mistakes* I'm so sorry.

Child: Don't worry! Listen again and repeat!

Misty: *repeats correctly*

Child: Bravo!

Children also praised the robot after it has done it's task well.

Child: Good, Misty, you did great!

Child: You did it beautifully, Misty!

Child: You were very cool!

Treating the Robot in Machinelike Terms. These children displayed very little behaviors where they would treat the robot in machinelike terms. They noticed some machine functions of the robot.

Misty: *is plugged in*

Child: She is eating power!

Misty: *moves on it's wheels*

Child: It's driving!

They also had some knowledge about how the robots work

Child: Misty has artificial intelligence.

4.6   Children 7–9 yrs Interacting with Miro-E Robot, 2023

Treating the Robot in Lifelike Terms. Children engaged with the animal-resembling Miro-E robot frequently ascribed it to lifelike attributes. They portrayed its animal-like morphology by likening it to a dog or a donkey.

Child: He's cute.

Child: It's a little donkey.

Child: Maybe it's that little dog!

Descriptions of its behavior were framed in animal terms, including mentions of wagging tails, purring, or even yawning. Child: It's purring!
Child: Miro yawned! Yawned!
Child: Why isn't it wagging its tail at all?

Additionally, they referenced certain physiological characteristics typically associated with living organisms when describing Miro-E, including attributes like breathing, sleeping, looking, or even pooping.
Child: Is it sleeping?
Child: It's breathing!
Child: He's pooping.
Child: And he looked at me!

Intriguingly, they extended their perceptions beyond the realm of animals and also attributed to Miro-E certain human abilities such as singing, talking, and dancing, as well as human-like characteristics, like wanting. It's important to mention, that this robot wasn't talking, laughing, singing or dancing. It was only moving forwards and backwards, turning around, wagging it's tail, and producing sounds similar to squeaking.
Child: Oh, he's singing! He's laughing!
Child: It talks!
Child: Is it dancing?
Child: Maybe don't touch it when it wants to sleep.

Treating the Robot in Machinelike Terms. Simultaneously, children frequently characterized the robot in mechanical terms. Their discussions often revolved around the robot's machine functions, including actions like freezing, charging, and turning on.
Child: He froze.
Child: It's charging!
Child: Why isn't it working?
Child: Well, it's not turned on at all.

Furthermore, they compiled a list of the robot's components, referencing elements such as cameras, speakers, and wheels.
Child: Miro has cameras in his eyes, speakers in his ears, and something strange in his nose.
Child: It has wheels.
Child: It's made of plastic or metal.

5   Discussion

5.1   Children's Perception on Robot's Lifelikeness in 2019

In this study, the dual perceptions of children towards the humanoid robot Pepper — both lifelike and machinelike — offer intriguing insights into child-robot interactions. Children exhibited a strong tendency towards anthropomorphism, as evidenced by their application of body awareness, empathetic responses to

Pepper's lifelike statements, and inquiries about human-like experiences such as having parents. This inclination to humanize the robot, as noted in their sympathetic responses and assumptions about familial relationships, aligns with [6]'s findings on children identifying robot features with human characteristics. Simultaneously, there was a clear recognition of Pepper's mechanical nature, illustrated by queries about its creators and its inherent robotic capabilities, like transforming. This duality in perception suggests that while children are capable of and inclined to ascribe human-like attributes to robots, they also maintain an awareness of their mechanical and non-human essence. This blend of perspectives is critical for understanding how children conceptualize and interact with robots, potentially influencing how such technology is designed and utilized in educational or recreational settings for younger audiences.

5.2 Comparison of Younger and Older Children Reaction to Human-Like Robot NAO, 2022

The results from interactions with the NAO robot reveal distinct differences in how younger children (6–7 years old) and older children (10–12 years old) perceive and engage with technology designed to mimic lifelike and machinelike behaviors.

The younger children, aged 6–7, tended to anthropomorphize the NAO robot, endowing it with human-like capabilities and emotions. They believed the robot could dance, read, and even experience pleasure, using terms like "NAO will be pleased" to describe it. Additionally, they employed animal-like morphology when discussing the robot, attributing it to activities like eating and sleeping. These children engaged in conversations with the robot, expecting it to respond and even showed an awareness of NAO's autonomous movements.

In contrast, older children, aged 10–12, displayed a more balanced approach. They acknowledged both the lifelike and machinelike aspects of the robot. Like their younger counterparts, they believed the robot could dance and read, but they were also capable of perceiving the robot in mechanical terms, discussing concepts like crashing and turning off. These children referred to the robot's components, such as batteries, and treated it more as a familiar piece of technology, akin to voice assistants. They interacted with the robot in an organized and patient manner, reflecting a level of persistence in their attempts to establish effective communication.

Overall, this study highlights how children's perceptions of robotic technology evolve with age. While younger children tend to anthropomorphize and emphasize the lifelike aspects of the robot, older children exhibit a more nuanced understanding, recognizing both its human-like and mechanical qualities, as it was already suggested [5].

5.3 Comparison of Children's Reactions to Robots with Different Appearance, 2023

Comparing the interactions of children aged 7–9 with three different robots — Nao, Misty, and Miro-E — offers a nuanced view of how children perceive and interact with robotic technology from a lifelike versus machinelike perspective.

Nao. With the Nao robot, children displayed a strong inclination towards treating it on lifelike terms. They engaged in social behaviors such as asking questions, commanding actions, and initiating greetings, indicating they perceived Nao as a responsive, almost human-like entity. The children attributed not only physical but also emotional and social characteristics to Nao, including the ability to express emotions like laughing or crying and inquiries about its familial and social connections. While there was some acknowledgment of its mechanical aspects, such as speakers and cameras, these were not the focus of their interactions, suggesting a predominant view of Nao as a lifelike companion.

Misty. The children's interaction with Misty also leaned heavily towards a lifelike perception. They treated Misty akin to a pet or friend, engaging in conversation and attributing human-like abilities like reading, understanding language, and emotional responsiveness. The empathy and encouragement shown towards Misty's mistakes, and the praise for its achievements, further highlight this anthropomorphic treatment. The recognition of Misty's machine functions and artificial intelligence was present but less emphasized, indicating a stronger lean towards viewing Misty as a lifelike entity.

Miro-E. In the case of Miro-E, the children switched between lifelike and machinelike perceptions. They anthropomorphized Miro-E by likening it to animals and attributing it with human abilities like singing and dancing. Simultaneously, they also recognized and verbalized its mechanical aspects, such as charging and its component parts. It is important to mention that Miro was being programmed by children, what may have caused them to think of the robot more as a machine rather than alive being. Nevertheless, this suggests a more balanced view in their perception of Miro-E, fluidly navigating between seeing it as both a technological device and a lifelike companion.

Comparison of Three Robots. Across all three robots, children demonstrated a natural propensity to engage with robots in lifelike terms, attributing human or animal-like qualities and behaviors. This tendency aligns with the developmental stage of children aged 7–9, where imaginative play and anthropomorphism are common. However, there were differences in the extent and manner of lifelike treatment, which could be attributed to the design, capabilities, and interaction style of each robot. Nao and Misty were more often seen as human-like companions, with a focus on social and emotional attributes, whereas Miro-E elicited a more balanced view, with children readily acknowledging its mechanical and lifelike qualities. This suggests that while children are inclined to view robots in lifelike terms, their perceptions can be significantly influenced by the specific characteristics and interactions afforded by different robotic platforms and performed activities.

5.4   General Discussion: Evolution of Children's Perceptions of Robots

Over the years, the way children perceive robots has been a subject of extensive study, with each year bringing new insights. A comparative analysis of studies from 2019, 2022, and 2023 reveals an evolving understanding of how children interact with and conceptualize robots.

During the period covered in this study, from 2019 to 2023, we observed a clear trajectory in the understanding of child-robot interactions. Initially, children tended to oscillate between viewing robots as either lifelike or mechanical, as it was stated before [5]. As time progressed, studies revealed more nuanced perceptions - age-dependent differences and robot-specific reactions, expanding previous findings [4,5]. The trend suggests that children's perceptions are not static but evolve with age, exposure, and the nature of the robots they interact with. Additionally, contrary to the findings of [3], children seemed to ascribe more mechanical attributes over time, which can be caused by an increase in children's awareness of technology. More children engage in programming classes, have their own devices or are exposed to different technology in their everyday lives, making them less prone to be taken in by the Wizard-of-Oz paradigm. This evolution in perception has important implications for designing educational and recreational robot interactions for children, emphasizing the need for age-appropriate and robot-specific approaches.

Overall, these studies collectively underscore the complexity and dynamism in children's perceptions of robots, influenced by a myriad of factors including age, robot design, and the nature of interaction. This evolving understanding is crucial for the development of robotic technologies that effectively engage and appeal to children across different age groups and contexts.

6   Conclusions

In conclusion, this article presents the tendency to anthropomorphise robots regardless of their behaviour or appearance, while keeping children aware of the robot's functioning. The contribution also focuses on a new shift in the robot's perception — how the robots start to be seen as mechanical entities with anthropomorphic features, escaping the previous dichotomic categories of machinelike or human-like robots. In addressing the research questions, this study aimed to investigate the evolution of children's perceptions of social robots for several years. The primary focus was on understanding how the dynamics of perception, specifically the interplay between human/lifelike and machinelikeness, have transformed over time. The exploration of children's responses to humanoid robots like Pepper in 2019, age-dependent differences with the NAO robot in 2022, and varied reactions to robots with different appearances (Nao, Misty, Miro-E) in 2023 provided insights into the nuanced aspects of children's evolving perspectives. By delving into these distinct time points, the study contributes to a comprehensive understanding of how children conceptualize and engage with social robots, shedding light on the intricate balance between lifelike attributes and machinelike recognition in the younger demographic.

7   Future Directions

We are aware of certain limitations that have emerged in our research. One idea to address them is to expand the sample by including more children from different socio-economic backgrounds, particularly those not living in large cities. Another solution is to introduce robots with a different morphology, deviating from the standards maintained in CRI studies. Moreover, in future research, it is crucial to investigate the impact of emerging technologies, particularly social robots, in environments where parental supervision may be limited. As technology evolves autonomously, understanding how unsupervised exposure influences children's perceptions becomes pivotal. Exploring whether children, without parental oversight, tend to anthropomorphize or emphasize the mechanical nature of robots is essential. This inquiry into the ethical considerations surrounding unsupervised interactions aims to inform guidelines for safe and constructive engagement, emphasizing the complex interplay between evolving technologies, parental supervision, and children's perceptions in the dynamic landscape of human-robot interaction.

Acknowledgments. This research was supported in part by a grant from the National Science Centre, Poland, under the OPUS call in the Weave Programme under the project number K/NCN/000142.

The authors would like to thank Anna Kołota, Anna Grabowska, Zofia Samsel, Maria Kiraga, Maria Halesiak, Mateusz Jarosz, Filip Sondej, Takamune Izui, Maria Dziok, Wojciech Jędras, Gentiane Venture and Bartłomiej Śnieżyński for their help with conducting the studies over the years.

Disclosure of Interests. The authors have no competing interests to declare that are relevant to the content of this article.

References

1. Belpaeme, T., et al.: Child-robot interaction: perspectives and challenges. In: International Conference on Software Reuse (2013). https://api.semanticscholar.org/CorpusID:17712544
2. Beneteau, E., Boone, A., Wu, Y., Kientz, J.A., Yip, J., Hiniker, A.: Parenting with Alexa: exploring the introduction of smart speakers on family dynamics. In: Proceedings of the 2020 CHI Conference on Human Factors in Computing Systems, pp. 1–13 (2020)

3. van den Berghe, R., et al.: A toy or a friend? Children's anthropomorphic beliefs about robots and how these relate to second-language word learning. J. Comput. Assist. Learn. **37**(2), 396–410 (2021)

4. Burdett, E.R.R., Ikari, S., Nakawake, Y.: British children's and adults' perceptions of robots. Hum. Behav. Emerg. Technol., e3813820 (2022)

5. Cameron, D., et al.: You made him be alive: children's perceptions of animacy in a humanoid robot. In: Mangan, M., Cutkosky, M., Mura, A., Verschure, P.F.M.J., Prescott, T., Lepora, N. (eds.) Living Machines 2017. LNCS (LNAI), vol. 10384, pp. 73–85. Springer, Cham (2017). https://doi.org/10.1007/978-3-319-63537-8_7

6. Coninx, A., et al.: Towards long-term social child-robot interaction: using multi-activity switching to engage young users. J. Hum.-Rob. Interact. **5**(1), 32 (2015)

7. Dziergwa, M., Kaczmarek, M., Kaczmarek, P., Kędzierski, J., Wadas-Szydłowska, K.: Long-term cohabitation with a social robot: a case study of the influence of human attachment patterns. Int. J. Soc. Robot. **10**(1), 163–176 (2018)

8. Jamet, F., Masson, O., Jacquet, B., Stilgenbauer, J.L., Baratgin, J.: Learning by teaching with humanoid robot: a new powerful experimental tool to improve children's learning ability. J. Rob. **2018**, e4578762 (2018)

9. Jirout, J., Klahr, D.: Children's scientific curiosity: in search of an operational definition of an elusive concept. Dev. Rev. **32**(2), 125–160 (2012)

10. Kiraga, M., Samsel, Z., Indurkhya, B.: A field study on Polish customers' attitude towards a service robot in a cafe. In: Ali, A.A., et al. (eds.) LNCS, pp. 294–307. Springer, Singapore (2024). https://doi.org/10.1007/978-981-99-8718-4_26

11. Kędzierski, J., Kaczmarek, P., Dziergwa, M., Tchoń, K.: Design for a robotic companion. Int. J. Hum. Rob. **12**(01), 1550007 (2015)

12. Lewandowska-Tomaszczyk, B., Wilson, P.A.: Compassion, empathy and sympathy expression features in affective robotics. In: 2016 7th IEEE International Conference on Cognitive Infocommunications (CogInfoCom), pp. 000065–000070. IEEE, Wroclaw, Poland (2016)

13. Littler, B.K.M., Alessa, T., Dimitri, P., Smith, C., Witte, L.D.: Reducing negative emotions in children using social robots: systematic review. Arch. Dis. Child. **106**(11), 1095–1101 (2021)

14. Lopatovska, I., Williams, H.: Personification of the Amazon Alexa: BFF or a mindless companion. In: Proceedings of the 2018 Conference on Human Information Interaction & Retrieval - CHIIR 2018, pp. 265–268 (2018)

15. Pashevich, E.: Can communication with social robots influence how children develop empathy? Best-evidence synthesis. AI Soc. **37**(2), 579–589 (2022)

16. Seaborn, K., Barbareschi, G., Chandra, S.: Not only weird but "Uncanny"? A systematic review of diversity in human—robot interaction research. Int. J. Soc. Rob. **15**, 1841–1870 (2023)

17. Sienkiewicz, B., Indurkhya, B.: Is a humorous robot more trustworthy? In: Ali, A.A., et al. (eds.) Social Robotics. LNCS, Springer, Singapore (2024). https://doi.org/10.1007/978-981-99-8715-3_27

18. Szczepanowski, R., et al.: Education biases perception of social robots. Eur. Rev. Appl. Psychol. **70**(2), 100521 (2020)

19. Tan, H., Wang, D., Sabanovic, S.: Projecting life onto robots: the effects of cultural factors and design type on multi-level evaluations of robot anthropomorphism (2018)

20. Wróbel, A., Źróbek, K., Indurkhya, B., Schaper, M.M., Gunia, A., Zguda, P.M.: Are robots vegan? Unexpected behaviours in child-robot interactions and their design implications. In: Extended Abstracts of the CHI Conference on Human

Factors in Computing Systems, CHI EA 2023, pp. 1–7. Association for Computing Machinery, New York, NY, USA (2023)

21. Wróbel, A., Źróbek, K., Schaper, M.M., Zguda, P., Indurkhya, B.: Age-appropriate robot design: In-The-Wild Child-Robot Interaction Studies of Perseverance Styles and Robot's Unexpected Behavior. 32nd IEEE International Conference on Robot and Human Interactive Communication (RO-MAN), pp. 1451–1458 (2023)

22. Zguda, P., Kołota, A., Venture, G., Sniezynski, B., Indurkhya, B.: Exploring the role of trust and expectations in CRI using in-the-wild studies. Electronics **10**(3), 347 (2021)

Will You Participate? Exploring the Potential of Robotics Competitions on Human-Centric Topics

Yuchong Zhang[✉][ID], Miguel Vasco[ID], Mårten Björkman[ID],
and Danica Kragic[ID]

KTH Royal Institute of Technology, Stockholm, Sweden
{yuchongz,miguelsv,celle,dani}@kth.se

Abstract. This paper presents findings from an exploratory needfinding study investigating the research current status and potential participation of the competitions on the robotics community towards four human-centric topics: *safety, privacy, explainability,* and *federated learning*. We conducted a survey with 34 participants across three distinguished European robotics consortia, nearly 60% of whom possessed over five years of research experience in robotics. Our qualitative and quantitative analysis revealed that current mainstream robotic researchers prioritize *safety* and *explainability*, expressing a greater willingness to invest in further research in these areas. Conversely, our results indicate that *privacy* and *federated learning* garner less attention and are perceived to have lower potential. Additionally, the study suggests a lack of enthusiasm within the robotics community for participating in competitions related to these topics. Based on these findings, we recommend targeting other communities, such as the machine learning community, for future competitions related to these four human-centric topics.

Keywords: Robotics · federated learning · privacy · safety · explainability · needfinding · survey

1 Introduction

Robotics-themed competitions have been successfully initiated and consistently held spanning several decades, along with numerous prestigious conference venues like ICRA, IROS, NeurIPS, HRI, etc [6]. The topics of the competitions are diverse across a wide array of application domains. In recent years, the focus of robotics competitions has gradually evolved beyond purely pragmatic techniques to incorporate human-centric perspectives [20], including some aspects of human-robot proxemics [23]. This paper aims to gain a comprehensive understanding of the potential impact of four specific and widespread human-centered topics – *safety, privacy, explainability,* and *federated learning* – on robotics competitions as shown in Fig. 1. These topics were determined in line with a Europe-wide project – (ELSA) European Lighthouse on Secure and Safe AI

© The Author(s), under exclusive license to Springer Nature Switzerland AG 2024
M. Kurosu and A. Hashizume (Eds.): HCII 2024, LNCS 14685, pp. 240–255, 2024.
https://doi.org/10.1007/978-3-031-60412-6_18

Fig. 1. The four human-centric topics identified in this paper. a : Federated learning; b : Privacy; c : Safety; d : Explainability.

(https://benchmarks.elsa-ai.eu/?ch=5&com=introduction). We conducted the first (to our knowledge) exploratory study to assess the current status, underlying interests, and future prospects of these topics within the perspectives of robotics/human-robot interaction (HRI) communities. Through a needfinding study [4,5,29], we sought to gather the feedback and insights and from robotics researchers and practitioners regarding these four specialized topics, so as to offer inspiration and guidance for future competitions.

Safety is a fundamental consideration when designing robotic systems, in particular for interaction scenarios with humans. These systems have the potential to inflict physical harm on humans, due to the forces exerted on humans during direct contact with the robot, and psychological harm, due to repeated violation of social norms and conventions during interaction with the robot [12]. This risk has lead to significant efforts to develop international safety standards, specifically for human-robot collaboration, which define quantitative biomechanical limits on the forces exerted on different parts of the human body and monitoring tools for robot motion [10]. In literature, safety can be achieved through different methods: through control, developing methods that limit the velocity and motion of the robot prior to and post collision with the human user; through motion planning, developing methods to plan safe robot paths and motions that avoid potential collisions with humans; though prediction, developing methods that either predict human actions and motions to anticipate potential collisions; and through considering psychological factors, developing methods to monitor the quality of the interaction and identifying which factors influence the perceived safety of the robot [12].

Privacy is another emerging topic in HRI research, due to their increasing appearance in multiple social contexts with humans. In particular, the majority of literature has focused on three particular privacy phenomena of the interaction with social robots [14]. The first concerns the surveillance capabilities of social robots, due to their potential autonomous mobility, that can affect the physical privacy of human users (e.g., entering autonomously a private room). The second concerns the social bonding capabilities of social robots, that may lead the human users to disclose private information. Finally, the third phenomena concerns the opacity of the processing and data collection capabilities of social robots, which may be misunderstood by the human user.

Explainability is a traversal topic to AI that attempts to build systems that are able to find human-interpretable interpretations for complex pattern recognition models. In the context of autonomous social robots, the goal is build systems that are able to explain its actions to human users while interacting in a shared space [22]. To achieve this goal, four steps have been proposed [22]: designing or learning a robot decision-making space that is interpretable by a human; estimating the human decision-making space and its planning algorithm, which allows the generation of personalized explanations; extracting information that is important for communicating plans; converting explanatory factors into an efficient medium (either speech of visual information).

Federated learning (also referred to as collaborative learning), unlike the conventional machine learning, is an advanced machine learning methodology that involves training an algorithm through numerous independent sessions, each utilizing its distinct dataset [9]. Having garnered significant attention in recent years, this methodology diverges from traditional centralized machine learning approaches where local datasets are amalgamated into a single training session, and it differs from methods assuming identical distribution of local data samples. Federated learning empowers multiple participants to collaboratively develop a shared and resilient machine learning model without the need to disclose individual datasets. This approach effectively tackles crucial concerns, including data privacy, data security, and data access rights [13]. Yet, data privacy is the most prevailing topic associated with federated learning since it allows building personalized models without violating sensitive information, complying with ethical principles [21,26,27]. Aligning with the common acknowledgement of human-computer interaction (HCI): It aims to design a seamless connection between users and machines for required services, optimizing performance in terms of quality and efficiency [11]. Therefore, federated learning exhibits a notable connection with HCI where this intersection becomes imperative in line with the human-centric design considerations and ethical implications in privacy-preserving machine learning systems [3]. Specifically, federated learning has already been employed for improved distributed learning in HRI scenarios [7].

We employed a method known as 'needfinding', derived originally from the research process product design [1]. The objective of this methodology is to pinpoint the essential user needs that a product is intended to fulfill towards the specific group. The general needfinding process is outlined in Fig. 2 [19]. It commences by fostering empathy for the user group (via interviews, surveys, or other media) and subsequently the outcomes from this steps will be extracted and presented in frameworks, for instance, graphical representations. Then, the design implications are formulated from the framework while the ultimate solutions are fabricated. In our paper, the empathy stands for designing a goal-oriented survey targeted for the robotics community, while the frameworks represent the

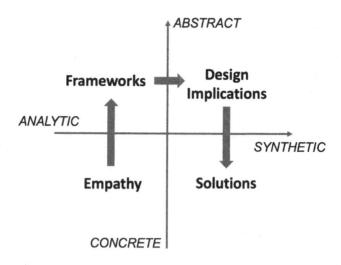

Fig. 2. The general overview of a needfinding process.

extracted results from the survey. Specifically, the approaches we used for obtaining the outcomes combined both qualitative and quantitative approaches. In the qualitative phase, we summarized and coded the responses we've gathered to assess the prevailing circumstances, future aspirations, and the envisioned benefits reported by participants. This qualitative analytics provided valuable insights into the perspectives to be used by the robotics/HRI community towards the four topics in future robotics competitions. In the quantitative analysis, we conducted statistical significance tests on select survey variables that are expressed on mathematical scales. By employing these statistical methods, we aimed to uncover patterns, trends, and the importance of different factors related, thus providing a second viewpoint which is objective data-driven understanding of the surveyed results. The design implications are revealed as findings with insights formulated from the results, employed as guidelines (solutions) for future considerations in robotics competitions related to these human-centric topics. In our paper, we affirmed the lack of a strong inclination within the robotics community to participate in these competitions. We also suggest the potential for a shift of the target group, such as the machine learning community.

The organization of this paper is as follows. Section 1 introduces the basic background and emphasizes the principles of needfinding of out study. Section 2 presents the related work while Sect. 4 delineates the employed methodology, including the design strategy of our questionnaire. The results, comprising both quantitative and qualitative analyses are displayed in Sect. 5, followed by an in-depth discussion presented in Sect. 6. Section 7 concludes the paper.

2   Related Work

A literature review was conducted, revealing that needfinding (usually in the form of surveys, interviews, workshops, etc.) has been extensively used in exploring the needs of target users within a broad field of robotics and HRI research [15,18,30]. Chung et al. [4] designed four case studies including survey and interview to probe the potential usage of physical robots in collecting feedback in hotels. Especially, they were aware of the privacy of guests during the interaction with the service robots. O'Brien et al. [17] employed a comprehensive needfinding process in prototyping a therapeutic robot for children, where involved a detailed literature crawling, an ethical analysis, and interviews and pediatric experts. Similarly in designing a robotic system for children, Bejarano et al. [2] executed a semi-structured needfinding interview with local experts in children's hospital to identify the requirements of robots to be empathetic and emotionally supportive. Vatsal et al. [25] engaged a needfinding contextual inquiry to generate guidance before designing specific capabilities for a wearable robotic forearm. Apparently, the utilization of needfinding has been proven its efficacy in gathering early-stage feedback and requirements before delving into the practical artifacts. However, no prior work, to our knowledge, has investigated the correlation of human-centric topics with robotic competitions, which formed the motivation of our paper.

3   Research Question

Our study aims to assess the present research landscape and the potential of competition participation aligned with the four human-centric topics on the robotics community. Our objective is to disclose the current and prospective interests of the engagement of robotics competitions so as to formulate the guidelines of hosting future events for researchers and practitioners. The research questions addressed in this paper are listed below:

- What are the current interests situated in robotics research on *safety, privacy, explainability,* and *federated learning* in terms of the robotics/HRI community?
- What are the willingness of the robotics/HRI community in participating robotics competitions related to *safety, privacy, explainability,* and *federated learning* and the potential benefits or drawbacks brought afterwards?

To address these questions, we conducted a survey study in the form of a crafted questionnaire containing both closed and open-ended questions targeted for the robotics community. By concentrating on this distinct group, our aim is to derive valuable insights and draw conclusions regarding the intent and willingness of robotics researchers/practitioners to participate in competitions centered around the four topics.

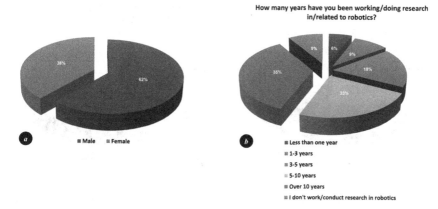

Fig. 3. Background information of participants. *a* : Gender information. *b* : Academic background of participants.

4   Method

In this section, we introduce the approach used in our paper, including the participants recruited and the specification of the survey designed.

4.1   Participants

We conducted our survey study with a questionnaire including a number of curated questions which were oriented exclusively for the robotics community. We invited 34 participants (21 self-identified males and 13 self-identified females) by emailing from three distinct and reputable robotics consortia: (1) a distinguished Europe-wide project community euRobin (https://www.eurobin-project.eu/) specializing in advanced and reproducible research in robotics and (2) the local academic division (including faculty members, research fellows, PhD students, research engineers) of robotics of the authors' university and (3) the renowned robotics company PAL Robotics (https://pal-robotics.com/) to complete the survey. Their ages ranged from 23 to 54 (mean = 35.68, SD = 8.43). As shown in Fig. 3.*b*, nearly 60% of participants possess hands-on experience in research or work within the field of robotics, spanning over a noteworthy period of more than 5 years. Furthermore, the highest proportion (35.3%) is observed among those with an extensive background, surpassing 10 years of experience in robotics. All participants approved a consent that all of the collected data (no private and sensitive information) from the survey will be kept confidential and merely used for research.

4.2   Questionnaire

The questionnaire was rigorously crafted through numerous iterative discussions among the authors, ensuring its representative nature. First, we extracted basic

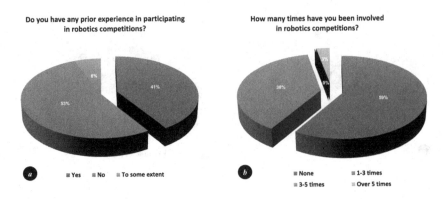

Fig. 4. Prior information of participants' past involvement in robotics competitions.

demographic information, including gender, age, and years of experience. Then we investigated information about the prior experience of robotics completions. A shown in Fig. 4.*a*, over half of participants have zero experience in robotics competitions (52.9%). Specifically, 5.9% of participants reported that they have been involved in robotics competitions "to some extent", from that we believe this signifies informal involvement in certain aspects of the competition procedure, rather than any deliberate, structured participation. Interesting, this complied with the information that 41.2% of participants indicated preceding involvement with robotics competitions on at least one occasion (Fig. 4.*b*). Next, we concentrated on identifying the current research landscape, the future possibilities, and the perceived importance of the four topics in robotics and competitions as far as the community concerned. As depicted in Table 5, we presented a set of questions to gauge the extent and intent of exploration within the robotics community regarding the four tested topics. These queries were formulated using a 7-point Likert scale to quantitatively assess the perceived responses. Finally, we provided a few objective and open-ended questions, aiming to gather the opinions of the participants towards these four topics. Some extra short follow-up interview sessions were complemented as needed. Finally, we verified that all responses from the 34 participants were deemed valid (Table 1).

5   Results

In this section, we present the results obtained, including the quantitative and qualitative outcomes.

Table 1. The questions (*Q1–Q5*) quantified by 7-point Likert sale.

	Questions	Scale: 1–7
Q1	To what extent do you explore Federated Learning, Privacy, Safety, and Explainability in your research?	Very inactive–Very active
Q2	Do members of your research group or lab or division explore the topics of Federated Learning, Privacy, Safety, and Explainability in Robotics?	Very unlikely–Very likely
Q3	Are Federated Learning, Privacy, Safety, and Explainability in robotics potential research fields that you would like to explore in your future research?	Very unlikely–Very likely
Q4	Would you have interest in participating in a robotics competition focused on the topics of Federated Learning, Privacy, Safety, and Explainability?	Very unlikely–Very likely
Q5	How do you rate the importance of Federated Learning, Privacy, Safety, and Explainability in robotics?	Very unimportant–Very important

5.1   Quantitative Analysis

To conduct the statistical analysis on the data obtained from the quantified scales, we performed the necessary normal distribution tests. The results confirmed that the data from *Q1–Q5* all exhibited a normal distribution. Therefore, to examine the significant effects, the one-way repeated-measures analysis of variance (rmANOVA) [28] was implemented for the answers from these questions. If any statistically significant effects ($p < 0.05$) disclosed, the Bonferroni-corrected post hoc tests were then performed to determine which pairs of the four topics were significantly different. All of the analysis was performed through IBM SPSS Statistics. Figure 5 displays the descriptive results (mean, SD) and significance representation with 95% confidence intervals (CI).

For *Q1*, the results of the one-way rmANOVA with a Greenhouse-Geisser correction determined a significant main effect of the extent our participants' exploration among the four topics ($F(2.572, 82.296) = 27.722, p < 0.001$). Moreover, Post hoc analysis with a Bonferroni adjustment revealed that statistical significance was eve found in some pairwise comparisons (Fig. 5). For example, it indicates the extent that participants devoted towards *federated learning* is significantly much less than that on *safety*. Likewise, the rmAVONA a Sphericity Assumed correction showed that the significance is also found in the likelihood of the ambient colleagues explore the four topics (*Q2*) ($F(3, 66) = 20.989, p < 0.001$). It is noteworthy some pairs of the topics again possessed significance through the Bonferroni post hoc tests. For instance, our participants' colleagues show a higher likelihood of exploring explainability compared

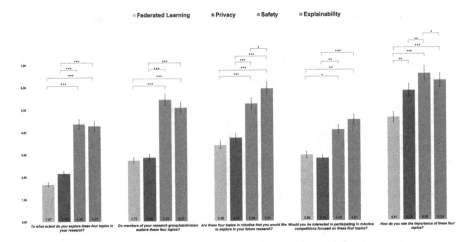

Fig. 5. Results of collected responses from the questions using Likert scale (*Q1–Q5*). Pairwise significance is displayed on the top. $*: p < 0.05; **: p < 0.005; ***: p < 0.001$.

to privacy, and this difference is statistically significant. Noteworthily, our observation indicates that the intent for future exploration of the four topics was quantified with relatively high values (*Q3*). Also, the rmANOVA with a Sphericity Assumed correction showed the significance was identified among the topics ($F(3, 96) = 23.072, p < 0.001$), with more pairwise comparisons being significant (safety-explainability here) after the post hoc test. However, we found that the future interest (*Q4*) in participating in robotics competitions received the lowest scores, showing a distinct decline across each topic compared to other questions. *Federated learning* and *privacy* gained particularly negative assessments, while *safety* and *explainability* elicited slightly more positive responses, although the average values merely approached neutrality (Scale: 4). Still, the rmANOVA with a Greenhouse-Geisser correction determined the existence of significance on the topics ($F(2.551, 81.640) = 13.820, p < 0.001$), with some pairwise significance via the post hoc measurement. Through *Q5*, we obtained an overview into how mainstream robotics researchers/practitioners perceive the four tested topics. *Safety* received the highest score, while *federated learning* was rated as the least important. Similarly, significance was identified from the rmANOVA with a Sphericity Assumed correction ($F(3, 96) = 27.235, p < 0.001$), while post hoc pairwise comparison showed *safety* was significantly deemed to be of more importance than explainability.

5.2 Qualitative Results

In this section, we present the qualitative responses from our survey study involving 34 participants. These insights, gleaned from the narratives and perspectives of our diverse participant pool, provide the opportunity for better understanding the perspectives regarding the four human-centric topics which are of interest to the mainstream robotics/HRI community. Beyond statistical analysis, the qualitative findings displayed here offer an additional deep and textured understanding that informs the public about the future exploration of essential design considerations in relevant competitions.

Safety is Widely Acknowledged for Its Paramount Significance

It emerged from our collected results that *safety* is the most prioritized topics manifested either in the current research landscape or future research considerations in terms of the robotics community. One participant commented: *"For embodied robots, the safety issue needs to be considered from the outset."* Most of the robotics researchers/practitioners in our study expressed the desire of prioritizing the human-robot safety so as to avoid any unwanted consequences, for instance, a collision which might jeopardize the human health. Similarly, another participant exemplified the navigation problem: *"Safety applies to navigation as well. Instances such as abrupt stops or prolonged delays can pose challenges, especially in environments where people anticipate human-like behaviors."* One participant indicated the necessity of *safety* in competitions, that it might be resolved by problem changing by time: *"In competitions, it is crucial that problems evolve or broaden annually to prevent a competition from becoming a benchmark-focused pursuit that diverges from addressing real-world problems."*

Explainability May Be Overlooked, But We Are Aware of Its Significance and Difficulties

As displayed in the quantitative results, *explainability* has gained less attention compared to *safety* pertaining to the current research status, however, it was more recognized with respect to future explorations (Fig. 5). One participant pointed out: *"Explainability, from my perspective, is an underappreciated aspect, and any initiative to highlight its importance is commendable. This becomes especially crucial in the current trajectory towards a black-box AI environment."* We found that the awareness and recognition of this topic is being noticed with the emergence of explainable AI [8]. Another two comments we received (*"I would anticipate that more researchers will delve into this explainability in the future."* and *"The explainability will be intriguing in the exploration of comprehending agency in HRI."*) also imply that the acknowledge of this topic rooted with human centrism. In the meantime, our findings revealed that there are challenges and obstacles. One participant reported: *"Achieving excellence in explainability appears to be challenging, given its reliance on human comprehension of the explanations."*, which reflects that making explanations accessible needs to be considered and prioritized. In addition, one participant posed the concerns of engaging parallel topics to obtain desirable explainability: *"Besides, transparency should also be incorporated at the same time."*

Privacy Is Important, But Yet Hard to Realize It

Similarity has been identified between qualitative reasoning and quantitative analysis regarding privacy, that it receives considerably less recognition within both the present research community and prospective explorations in contrast of *safety* and explainability. Many participants reported that *privacy* should be

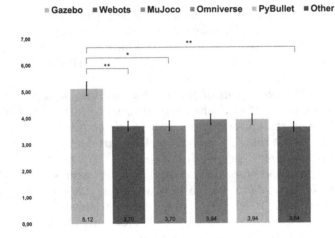

Fig. 6. The comparison of participant's preferences on robotic simulators.

valued since it relates with ethical issues, for example, one commented: *"I think privacy holds considerable importance for robots due to that there would be multitude of sensors equipped with. It is imperative to establish explicit guidelines for data flow and ownership."* Nonetheless, the most common issue appeared was the tremendous difficulties including lack of prior knowledge which hinder successful exploitation of privacy in robotics and prospective competitions. *"Privacy consistently ranks as one of the foremost concerns; however, addressing it in a robotics competition necessitates a thoughtful setup to imbue it with meaningful contexts"*, stated by one participant, similar to another: *"I have no ability to envision its viability and feasibility within a competition setting."* Moreover, one specifically concerned about the limited generalizability which would be formidable: *"This topic is more broadly associated with AI as a whole, extending beyond the scope of just robotics."*

Federated Learning Is Not Popular, and Should Not Be Separated From Privacy

Through our results, we disclosed that so far, *federated learning* has the least attention among the robotics community (also refer to Fig. 5). Most of the qualitative feedback we received showed that besides the unpopularity, the infeasibility of federated learning in a robotics competition is the moat influential factor (*"At first glance, implementing authentic federated learning in a competitive environment appears very challenging."*; *"From my perspective, I'm skeptical about its practicality within the context of a robotics competition."*). Furthermore, we recognized the inherent association of federated learning with privacy, emphasizing the importance of maintaining this connection rather than detachment, in terms of the robotics community. For example, one participant *"believes that federated learning cannot and should not be disentangled from privacy considerations"*. The finding coincides with what we mentioned in Sect. 1: as an advanced machine learning mechanism, federated learning is privacy-preserving in order to achieve no inference in sensitive information.

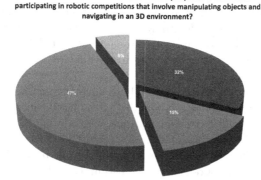

Fig. 7. Participants' preferences on high/low level control in robotics competitions.

5.3   Robotic Control and Simulators

In addition, we analyzed both the preference over the type of robotic simulator employed in robotic competitions and the level of control of the robotic agent in simulation. We considered five different robotic simulators, widely used by the community: Gazebo, an open-source simulator based on the ROS platform; Webots [16], an open-source 3D simulator; MuJoco [24], an open-source physics simulator; Omniverse, a proprietary robotic simulator; and PyBullet, an open-source and python-based physics engine. The results are presented in Fig. 6. The results show a clear preference for the Gazebo platform, a more established platform, over more recent platforms such as MuJoco. This insight is expected given the experience level of the participants in the study.

In addition, the participants were also asked about their preferred level of control of the robot agent in the simulation environment. The participants could select low-level control, in which the roboticist can have control over the low-level joint and motor sensors of the robot, high-level control, in which roboticist can only control high-level actions of the robotic platform (e.g., move to a specified position, pick up an object), or both. Moreover, the participants could also select they had no preference over the level of control. The results, shown in Fig. 7, show a preference for high-level or both level of control, in comparison to low-level control.

6   Discussion

6.1   Insights

We conducted a needfinding study to initially identify the current research landscape of the robotics community towards four human-centric topics – *safety*, *privacy, explainability,* and *federated learning.* Moreover, we sought to probe the intention of robotics researchers/practitioners in participating these four themed competitions. A questionnaire was then formulated and answered by 34 recruited participants from three renowned robotics consortia across Europe. Close to 60% of the participants possess over five years of experience in robotics and related fields, which renders our sample group representative and compelling. The findings suggest that the mainstream robotics community holds distinct viewpoints on the four topics, along with varying attitudes toward participating in competitions related to each topic.

What do we learn from the study? In both current research status and future research agenda, *safety* and *explainability* elicit significantly greater concern compared to *privacy* and federated learning. On one hand, *safety* emerges as a more prevalent focus in current robotics research exploration. On the other hand, *explainability* is regarded as a more favored topic in future research directions. This trend is attributed to the constant consideration of safety as an imperative issue in the design of robotic/HRI systems, as reported by participants. Additionally, our results highlighted an increasing focus on anticipating robotic behaviors to be explainable, marking it as a central concentration in the past years. In comparison, *privacy* and *federated learning* are much less noticed at present and less possible being considered in the future research. Particularly, *federated learning* has the least exposure among the four topics. This could be summarized to two main factors: (1) Persistent challenges in delving into privacy-related areas due to the sensitivity of data; (2) The mainstream community has not yet universally embraced federated learning.

An evident quantification decrease was observed from our results regarding the interest in participating the four themed robotics competitions. In a word, this reveals a lack of strong enthusiasm within the robotics community for participating in future competitions focused on these four human-centric topics. This may because of the deficiency of the previous experience in similar competitions (Fig. 4.*b*). In addition, the uncertainty and unforeseen risk of participating a robotic competition can be another obstacle, since substantial dedication of effort is frequently required in such a context where real robots might be needed. For example, testing practical robots may demand precision and a considerable amount of endeavour, making it a time-consuming process. An intriguing fact is that despite a low willingness for competition participation, *explainability* was ranked as the most desired topic, whereas *privacy* was treated as the least favored. We believe this can be ascribed to: (1) The growing interest in researching explainable AI; (2) Lack of robotics competitions focusing on privacy, as the authors conducted a comprehensive search and found no such competitions held in prestigious robotics venues so far. As these four topics are all closely relevant to AI, we expect that the target group can be shifted towards the machine learning/AI community.

6.2 Limitations

We acknowledge the presence of some certain limitations in our study Firstly, the survey was mostly implemented online, while physical interaction with more constructed interviews might provide more in-depth insights and feedback. Secondly, the questions we designed for the users may not incorporate a sufficiently comprehensive scope to thoroughly examine the attitudes of the robotics community, potentially impacting the depth of the results. Last but not least, the participants in our study were exclusively based in Europe, which may deviate from the inclusive principles commonly employed in defining sample groups in user study design.

7 Conclusion

In this paper, we proposed a needfinding study to investigate the prospective enthusiasm of the mainstream robotics community towards the participation in future competitions themed with four human-centric topics. We found that a low level of willingness was observed according to the results, implicating the possible change of the target community. We envision the needfinding study presented in this paper to be as an informative reference for robotic researchers/practitioners to learn the exploratory space and get inspired prior to participating or holding the pertinent robotics competitions. We hope our investigation can offer advisable guidance for the robotics/HRI community in advancing the new frontiers of the related research, especially future competitions considerations in *safety, privacy, explainability*, and *robust federated learning*.

Acknowledgment. This work was funded by the HORIZON-CL4-2021-HUMAN-01 ELSA project and the Swedish Foundation for Strategic Research (SSF) grant FUS21-0067.

References

1. Beckman, S.L., Barry, M.: Innovation as a learning process: embedding design thinking. Calif. Manage. Rev. **50**(1), 25–56 (2007)
2. Bejarano, A., Lomax, O., Scherschel, P., Williams, T.: Designing for perceived robot empathy for children in long-term care. In: Li, H., et al. (eds.) ICSR 2021. LNCS (LNAI), vol. 13086, pp. 743–748. Springer, Cham (2021). https://doi.org/10.1007/978-3-030-90525-5_65
3. Chhikara, P., Singh, P., Tekchandani, R., Kumar, N., Guizani, M.: Federated learning meets human emotions: a decentralized framework for human-computer interaction for IoT applications. IEEE Internet Things J. **8**(8), 6949–6962 (2020)
4. Chung, M.J.Y., Cakmak, M.: Exploring the use of robots for gathering customer feedback in the hospitality industry. In: HRI Workshop on Social Robots in the Wild (2018)
5. Chung, M.J.Y., Cakmak, M.: "How was your stay?": exploring the use of robots for gathering customer feedback in the hospitality industry. In: 2018 27th IEEE International Symposium on Robot and Human Interactive Communication (RO-MAN), pp. 947–954. IEEE (2018)

6. Dias, J., Althoefer, K., Lima, P.U.: Robot competitions: what did we learn? [competitions]. IEEE Rob. Autom. Mag. **23**(1), 16–18 (2016)

7. Gamboa-Montero, J.J., Alonso-Martin, F., Marques-Villarroya, S., Sequeira, J., Salichs, M.A.: Asynchronous federated learning system for human-robot touch interaction. Expert Syst. Appl. **211**, 118510 (2023)

8. Gunning, D., Stefik, M., Choi, J., Miller, T., Stumpf, S., Yang, G.Z.: XAI-explainable artificial intelligence. Sci. Rob. **4**(37), eaay7120 (2019)

9. He, J., Cao, T., Duffy, V.G.: Machine learning techniques and privacy concerns in human-computer interactions: a systematic review. In: Degen, H., Ntoa, S., Moallem, A. (eds.) HCI International 2023 - Late Breaking Papers, pp. 373–389. Springer, Cham (2023). https://doi.org/10.1007/978-3-031-48057-7_23

10. ISO: Robots and robotic devices-collaborative robots (ISO-15066: 2016). International Organization for Standardization (2016)

11. Karray, F., Alemzadeh, M., Abou Saleh, J., Arab, M.N.: Human-computer interaction: overview on state of the art. Int. J. Smart Sens. Intell. Syst. **1**(1), 137–159 (2008)

12. Lasota, P.A., Fong, T., Shah, J.A., et al.: A survey of methods for safe human-robot interaction. Found. Trends® Robo. **5**(4), 261–349 (2017)

13. Li, L., Fan, Y., Tse, M., Lin, K.Y.: A review of applications in federated learning. Comput. Ind. Eng. **149**, 106854 (2020)

14. Lutz, C., Schöttler, M., Hoffmann, C.P.: The privacy implications of social robots: scoping review and expert interviews. Mob. Media Commun. **7**(3), 412–434 (2019)

15. Martelaro, N., Ju, W.: DJ Bot: needfinding machines for improved music recommendations. In: 2017 AAAI Spring Symposium Series (2017)

16. Michel, O.: Cyberbotics Ltd. Webots™: professional mobile robot simulation. Int. J. Adv. Rob. Syst. **1**(1), 5 (2004)

17. O'Brien, C., O'Mara, M., Issartel, J., McGinn, C.: Exploring the design space of therapeutic robot companions for children. In: Proceedings of the 2021 ACM/IEEE International Conference on Human-Robot Interaction, pp. 243–251 (2021)

18. Pantofaru, C., Takayama, L.: Need finding: a tool for directing robotics research and development. In: RSS 2011 Workshop on Perspectives and Contributions to Robotics from the Human Sciences (2011)

19. Pantofaru, C., Takayama, L., Foote, T., Soto, B.: Exploring the role of robots in home organization. In: Proceedings of the Seventh Annual ACM/IEEE International Conference on Human-Robot Interaction, pp. 327–334 (2012)

20. Parreira, M.T., Gillet, S., Winkle, K., Leite, I.: How did we miss this? A case study on unintended biases in robot social behavior. In: Companion of the 2023 ACM/IEEE International Conference on Human-Robot Interaction, pp. 11–20 (2023)

21. Rieke, N., et al.: The future of digital health with federated learning. NPJ Digit. Med. **3**(1), 119 (2020)

22. Sakai, T., Nagai, T.: Explainable autonomous robots: a survey and perspective. Adv. Robot. **36**(5–6), 219–238 (2022)

23. Samarakoon, S.B.P., Muthugala, M.V.J., Jayasekara, A.B.P.: A review on human-robot proxemics. Electronics **11**(16), 2490 (2022)

24. Todorov, E., Erez, T., Tassa, Y.: MuJoCo: a physics engine for model-based control. In: 2012 IEEE/RSJ International Conference on Intelligent Robots and Systems, pp. 5026–5033. IEEE (2012)

25. Vatsal, V., Hoffman, G.: Wearing your arm on your sleeve: studying usage contexts for a wearable robotic forearm. In: 2017 26th IEEE International Symposium on Robot and Human Interactive Communication (RO-MAN), pp. 974–980. IEEE (2017)
26. Xu, J., Glicksberg, B.S., Su, C., Walker, P., Bian, J., Wang, F.: Federated learning for healthcare informatics. J. Healthcare Inf. Res. **5**, 1–19 (2021)
27. Zhang, C., Xie, Y., Bai, H., Yu, B., Li, W., Gao, Y.: A survey on federated learning. Knowl.-Based Syst. **216**, 106775 (2021)
28. Zhang, Y., Fjeld, M., Fratarcangeli, M., Said, A., Zhao, S.: Affective colormap design for accurate visual comprehension in industrial tomography. Sensors **21**(14), 4766 (2021)
29. Zhang, Y., Nowak, A., Rao, G., Romanowski, A., Fjeld, M.: Is industrial tomography ready for augmented reality? A need-finding study of how augmented reality can be adopted by industrial tomography experts. In: Chen, J.Y.C., Fragomeni, G. (eds.) HCII 2023. LNCS, vol. 14027, pp. 523–535. Springer, Cham (2023). https://doi.org/10.1007/978-3-031-35634-6_37
30. Zubrycki, I., Granosik, G.: Understanding therapists' needs and attitudes towards robotic support. The roboterapia project. Int. J. Soc. Rob. **8**, 553–563 (2016)

Child-Computer Interaction

Imagination in Enactive Interactions with Aquarela Virtual: Case Study in a Remote Socioenactive Setting

Maria Jêsca Nobre de Queiroz[1]([✉]) [ID], Emanuel Felipe Duarte[1] [ID],
and Julio Cesar dos Reis[1,2] [ID]

[1] Instituto de Computação, Universidade Estadual de Campinas (UNICAMP),
Campinas, Brazil
`jescanobre@gmail.com`, {`emanuel,jreis`}`@ic.unicamp.br`
[2] NIED, Universidade Estadual de Campinas (UNICAMP), Campinas, Brazil

Abstract. With computers being everywhere, used for virtually infinite purposes, and by many people, new interaction possibilities emerge. However, the intersubjective aspect of these new interactions is often neglected, especially the role of imagination in interaction design. With an enactivist perspective, we characterize imagination as a process of coordination that integrates current and past experiences with perceived possible future actions. This article investigates how imagination occurs in the Aquarela Virtual system, designed and developed during the COVID-19 pandemic to allow children to interact remotely, simultaneously, and collaboratively with elements and audiovisual animations inspired by the popular Brazilian song Aquarela. We conducted a thematic analysis of the video transcribed actions of one 5-year-old child interacting with two remotely situated colleagues through the system. As a result, we identified three main themes: 1) Interaction, 2) Identification, and 3) Embodied Imagination. We found that imagination was manifested during the interaction mainly through an active engagement of the body that is present and constantly in movement, manipulating physical objects that are part of the system. As implications for design, our results suggest freedom to explore possibilities of interaction and action, as well as emergent playfulness, made it possible to observe the phenomenon of embodied imagination.

Keywords: Imagination · Enaction · Embodiment · Socioenactive Systems · Remote Interaction · Thematic Analysis

1 Introduction

The evolution of computational technology leads to new interaction possibilities. Computers are now embedded in a diversity of everyday objects and even the human body, used for virtually infinite purposes everywhere and by many people. These developments align with the concept of ubiquitous computing as proposed

M. Kurosu and A. Hashizume (Eds.): HCII 2024, LNCS 14685, pp. 259–274, 2024.
https://doi.org/10.1007/978-3-031-60412-6_19

by Weiser [15]. However, the intersubjective aspect of these new interactions is often neglected, especially the role of imagination in interaction design.

Imagination is a characteristic inherent to human beings in various life stages, though it is most commonly associated with childhood. Imagining introduces new senses and meanings and can enhance participants' engagement with interactive installations [2]. In this study, we adopt an enactivist [14] perspective on imagination. According to Gallagher [8], the enactivist vision of imagination is tightly related to a concept with long-standing research within the field of Human-Computer Interaction (HCI), which is the concept of affordances. The author argues that affordances can be interpreted as opportunities for interaction that emerge from the relationship between someone and an object, whether abstract or concrete [9]. In summary, imagination is not a predetermined state within an organism. On the contrary, it is part of a process of coordination that integrates current and past experiences with perceived possible future actions; it is imagination in action.

Inserted in this context of ubiquitous computing and with a fundamental enactivist background [6,8,14], this investigation is part of a six-year thematic project titled "Socioenactive Systems: Investigating new dimensions in the design of interaction mediated by information and communication technologies". Socioenactive systems are examples of the application of ubiquitous computing with an emphasis on the social aspect of technology. These systems promote a coupled interaction between the physical, digital, and social dimensions. In socioenactive scenarios, human and technological aspects become intertwined in a cycle of perceptually guided actions as people interact with physical environment elements and each other through a digital system. Socioenactive systems are a suitable context for investigating imagination because they address not only the digital but also the physical and social aspects of interaction, emphasizing experience and perceptually guided action.

This article aims to investigate how imagination may occur in socioenactive systems. To this end, the socioenactive system we study is Aquarela Virtual [4], designed and developed during the Covid-19 pandemic. Aquarela Virtual allows children to interact remotely, simultaneously, and collaboratively with elements and audiovisual animations inspired by the popular Brazilian song Aquarela [11]. The interaction happens mainly through manipulating the physical objects and emojis with embedded QR codes. With this system in mind, our research question reads as follows:

How does Aquarela Virtual's design contribute to expressing imagination through interaction with the system?

We conducted a thematic analysis [1] of the video transcribed actions of one 5-year-old child interacting with two remotely situated colleagues through the Aquarela Virtual system. This method allows us to identify, analyze, and present patterns (or themes) in the transcription related to the presence and physical manifestation of imagination through action. Our methodology included the following steps: 1) familiarization with the data; 2) creation of codes; 3) search for themes; 4) revision of the themes; 5) definition and naming of the themes; and 6) reporting of the results through the writing of this paper.

As a result of the interaction of a child with the system, we identified the three main themes (and subthemes) of 1) Interaction, 2) Identification (Of Yourself, Of Another), and 3) Embodied Imagination (Exploration, Enactive Metaphor, Playfulness). We exemplified each theme and subtheme with direct excerpts from the interaction transcription. We thoroughly discussed them concerning the design decisions of the Aquarela Virtual system.

This study found that imagination was manifested during the interaction with the system, mainly through an active engagement of the body that is present and constantly in movement. At the same time, this engaged body manipulates the physical objects that are part of the system. As implications for design, our results demonstrated the presence of embodied imagination through the freedom to explore possibilities of interaction and action, as well as the emerging playfulness of it.

Our thematic analysis showed how embodiment and imagination are interconnected: the interactions with the Aquarela Virtual system depend on physical, tangible actions, and these actions, in turn, modulate the way that embodied imagination emerges during the experience of exploring the system. This results from how the Aquarela Virtual system was designed to allow interactions beyond well-defined and task-oriented objectives. The children can freely explore the system and its tangible objects, constantly choosing which objects they want to interact with and how. In summary, the children are free to make sense of the objects and the interaction on their terms. They are free to roleplay with the selection of objects available to them and how the system reacts to each of these objects. We highlight that our qualitative method of Thematic Analysis is not particularly concerned with sample size. We understand that a single instance is enough to illustrate the occurrence of a particular phenomenon, which can be better understood and described with an analysis grounded by the collected data. We further discuss such aspects in this work.

The remainder of this article is organized as follows: Section 2 presents a theoretical and methodological background, along with a selection of related studies; Sect. 3 presents the Aquarela Virtual system and the case study conducted with the system; Sect. 4 presents the results of our original thematic analysis of the interactions with Aquarela Virtual remotely situated; Sect. 5 presents a discussion of our findings with the thematic analysis and its implications for design; lastly, Sect. 6 presents our conclusions and directions for future investigations.

2 Background

In this section, we first present the theoretical foundations of our investigation and then proceed to present a selection of related studies.

2.1   Theoretical Foundations

Imagination is commonly seen as an activity of representation, as something already pre-determined in our subconscious, intangible, and unrelated to our physical bodies [12]. Even in enactive theory, some enactivists understand imagination as a cognitive state that reenacts some aspects of original perceptual processes, as in a kind of simulation in which processes are reenacted. For example, for Thompson [13], imagination involves a presentational activity that brings into presence something absent. For this reason, for him, imagination involves visualizing something, mentally staging a possible visual experience of it. Thus, imagination involves a simulated or emulated "offline" sensory experience. However, the enactivist perspective on imagination emphasizes the notion that imagining is an activity or action. When we remember or imagine something, we are engaged in some form of action to solve a problem or immerse ourselves in a situation of aesthetic pleasure, gathering information, or constructing something.

In the enactive framework for cognitive science [14], the concept of action guided by perception contains an inherent aspect of imagination. According to Gallagher [8], the enactivist view of imagination is related to affordances, which can be interpreted as opportunities for interaction that arise from the relationship between someone and an object, be it abstract or concrete [9]. Therefore, imagination is not considered a predetermined state within the individual's organism, emerging from a history of interactional activities to cause a new action. Instead, it is a constitutive part of a coordination process that integrates experiences with the broader context in which the individual is involved and with the possibilities of future activities available.

Imagining involves a multiplicity of different practices, some of which are explicitly embodied, involving manipulation of parts of the environment, and others when we imagine something through the manipulation of concepts thoughts, or images. These cases have in common that in any of them, imaginative practice may involve affective and kinesthetic aspects of embodiment [8]. Even in the case of more abstract practices of imagination, we are still dealing with affordances. Concepts or thoughts can be considered resources that offer us or communicate with us possibilities to follow one path or another as we engage with thought. Thus, imaginative practice is about manipulating concepts, thoughts, and images. Making a parallel with the pretend game, we can take these concepts and play with them, remodel them, and assign new meanings to be able to solve a problem, for example.

In this study, our understanding of imagination aligns with Gallagher's view, as we perceive objects or events in terms of the possibilities they offer, we think of this phenomenon as imagination in action.

2.2   Related Work

As related studies, we raised three investigations from scientific literature: Galindo *et al.* [7], Loke *et al.* [10] and Erkut *et al.* [5], which address the presence of imagination in interactive installations. These three studies were selected from the results of a previous systematic literature review that we conducted on the subject of imagination in interactive installations [2].

Titled "Embodied Imagination", Galindo *et al.* [7] presented an embodied interaction approach through body movements such as arms, legs, *etc.* The authors studied the concept that users could place themselves in imagined places and situations through the movements captured by a Kinect and the visual feedback offered by an application. Interaction through movements allowed users to embody their fantasies and explore their imaginations while telling their narratives. When observing the interaction of workshop participants with the application, the authors indicated that most participants moved around the space and used their entire bodies to embody fantasies. Qualitative assessments suggested that this process successfully stimulated embodied imagination.

The study by Loke *et al.* [10], titled "Bodily Experience and Imagination", emphasized the perception and performance of bodily processes (*e.g.*, breathing and heartbeats). Most interaction with the installation occurs through participants' physiological data. The data are captured by sensors and amplified through digital soundscapes. According to the authors, the interactions developed in the installation were designed to draw attention to the links between felt bodily experience and processes of imaginative exploration, where the boundaries between self and the world are reinvented through scale and metaphor. In their study, imagination was directly linked to the use of the body, where breathing and pulse are part of the "narrative" constructed throughout the experience. The authors used the term "embodied imagination" to refer to the intertwining of human imaginative capacities and the felt experience of the body. During participation in the performance at different moments, participants were led to imagine themselves as parts of a whale's body, escalating their sense of identity beyond their physical skin. During participation in the performance at different times, participants were led to imagine themselves as parts of a whale's body, scaling their sense of identity beyond their physical skin.

Lastly, in "Design and Evaluation of Interactive Musical Fruit", Erkut *et al.* [5] presented an application that had as inspiration the concept of embodied interaction as proposed by [3]. The interaction with the installation involved manipulating fruits placed on a tree to produce sounds and control characteristics of that medium, such as volume, using the body in a natural and significant way. As for imagination, the authors used enactive metaphors to enable children's understanding of musical expressions and concepts. Enactive metaphors, in this context, stands for metaphors that bring something new into existence only through our action on a certain object or idea. In this case, children produce and manipulate sound characteristics by manipulating musical fruits, effectively bringing something new into existence.

All these studies provided important contributions to a better understanding the relationship between body and imagination. They also exemplified practical applications involving sensing body movements, physiological signals, and manipulating objects. However, given the context of social isolation caused by the COVID-19 pandemic, we highlight the need to investigate ways to encourage bodily involvement during compulsorily remote interactions. Thus, this investigation studies how imagination emerges in a remote socioenactive experience, which still encourages meaningful use of the body despite social restrictions.

3   Exploring Aquarela Virtual as a Case Study

This section presents the Aquarela Virtual system and the workshop conducted with it, detailing who the participants were, how the workshop took place, what data was collected, and how it was analyzed. We disclaim that the design and development of the Aquarela Virtual system and the planning and con- duction of the workshops presented here are part of the Socioenactive Systems project. Therefore, both these activities also involved other researchers besides the authors of this article. Consequently, the Aquarela Virtual system and its workshops also addressed other objectives and research questions beyond what is presented in this paper. Figure 1 illustrates the methodology of this study, starting with the key purpose of our work (Imagination in Enactive Interactions investigation)[1], and the planning and conduction of the workshop.

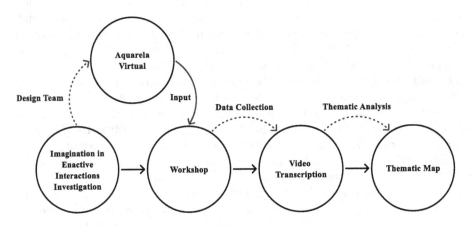

Fig. 1. Overview of the methodology employed in this study.

3.1   Aquarela Virtual System

The Aquarela Virtual system allows remotely situated children to interact socially through excerpts and elements of the Brazilian song "Aquarela" by singer and songwriter Toquinho [4]. The interaction takes place primarily through physical objects embedded with QR codes, which are recognized by the computer's camera, digitally translating the children's actions into the sys- tem. For example, a paper airplane with a QR code attached to it allows a child, by displaying the code to the computer's webcam, to interact with an animation

---

[1] Master's Thesis of the first author in this paper (who also participated in the design and development team of Aquarela Virtual).

of the fifth stanza of the song, which mentions a pink and maroon airplane that appears flying between the clouds.

From the song's stanzas, some nouns were highlighted as physical objects with which children could interact, and the system could generate some form of feedback. For the first version of Aquarela, six objects were selected: 1) sun, 2) castle, 3) seagull, 4) paint drop, 5) sailboat, and 6) airplane. With these objects chosen, children can use toys they already have or build toys with recycled materials and crafts that represent the song's objects. In addition to interacting with the toys, children can also express affective states using a set of emojis attached to sticks with QR codes on their backs.

When the system detects a QR code, an action on the interface is activated. If the code of an object is recognized, a segment of the song and an animation related to the object are activated. In this animation, the object the child displays is highlighted in a way; for example, the sun increases in size and "rises" on the horizon. On the other hand, if the QR code of an emoji is detected, the system generates animations with emojis rising on the screen, referring to the affective state. When multiple children show the same object from a specific stanza currently being played, their avatars are displayed together in the animation. Figure 2 presents a participant's screen with the sailboat animation. In the same figure, two avatars are blowing on the sailboat, corresponding to users who displayed the sailboat QR code.

Fig. 2. Aquarela Virtual system interface.

The interaction proposal in Aquarela Virtual goes beyond task-oriented activities, as children have the freedom to explore and choose how and with which objects to interact. The design intention is for children to have the autonomy to make sense of objects and interactions on their own, according to their embodied experience. They are also free to interpret in their way roles based on the objects and responses that the system offers.

3.2   Participants

Eleven children participated in workshops held with Aquarela Virtual - six girls and five boys - with children aged between 4 and 6 years old[2]. These children were currently experiencing a remote teaching context due to the Covid-19 pandemic. The children were organized into four groups (groups A, B and C containing three children, and class D containing two children). To preserve anonymity, we use fictitious names to refer to these children. For this case study in particular, we selected data from a single child's participation in the workshop with Aquarela Virtual, Ana (fictitious name), from group C.

Along with the children, two Human-Computer Interaction researchers, Ph.D. candidates in Computer Science who were part of the Socioenactive Systems project, and two teachers from the school were at the site. In addition, other project researchers were present remotely.

3.3   Workshops

The Aquarela Virtual system was used in workshops held at the Centro de Convivência Infantil (CECI) (Children's Community Center, in free translation), in partnership with the *Divisão de Educação Infantil e Complementar* (DEdIC) (Division of Early Childhood and Complementary Education, in free translation). This is a structure within the *Universidade Estadual de Campinas* (UNICAMP) campus, which receives and cares for children of professors, employees, and students of the university. The workshops were held on November 4th and 5th, 2021, and were filmed for later analysis.

Before the workshops and the children's interaction with the Aquarela Virtual system, teachers conducted activities at school with the theme of the song Aquarela and emotional states. The objects from the song (airplane, boat, castle, seagull, *etc.*) used in the workshops were built freely by the children with scrap material, partly during these activities and partly with the help of their caregivers. The creation of these objects involved different materials and forms of presentation, each being unique. Figure 3 presents some objects created and used by the children during the Aquarela activity. Later, these objects were associated with specific QR codes provided on adhesive paper by the research group responsible for the activity. The QR codes were then attached to the respective objects by the teachers. The researchers also provided kits with six printed emojis attached to popsicle sticks featuring QR codes on the back to be used during the workshop for effective expression and feedback.

During the workshops, the Aquarela Virtual system was used in parallel with Google Meet to support communication between participants and between them and the activity mediators. This communication, however, happened through voice only as Google Meet was left open as a background window to allow Aquarela Virtual to be at the forefront as the focus of the activity.

---

[2] All children signed consent forms appropriate to their ages, as well as their guardians signed the free and informed consent form. This research was approved by a Research Ethics Committee (CAAE 72413817.3.0000.5404).

Fig. 3. Children and artifacts used during the workshop.

The workshops took place in sessions that lasted an average of 30 min and occupied the morning shift. Each session was made up of groups of three or two children chosen by the class teacher. During the workshop, each participating child stayed in a different room prepared for the activity. The environment consisted of a table with a laptop, the child's objects/toys, the emojis, and a camera. Each child was accompanied by an adult, either a class teacher or one of the two project researchers who were present at the site. The sessions were organized as follows:

1. First, there was a brief presentation between the children and the researchers who were participating remotely through Google Meet;
2. Then, the children accessed the Aquarela Virtual system and, with the help of the accompanying adult, filled in their name and chose an avatar to represent them during the interaction;
3. After logging in, children interacted freely with the system and the surrounding physical artifacts for an average of 15 min;
4. Lastly, after the end of the interaction, a brief closing conversation was held for approximately 10 min.

3.4   Thematic Analysis

To analyze Ana's interaction with Aquarela Virtual and to assess whether and how imagination emerged from it, we conducted a thematic analysis. This qualitative method was chosen for its ability to allow a detailed exploration of data and to be useful in identifying, analyzing, and presenting patterns present in data [1], even in the circumstance of the analysis of data related to a single participant, as is the case of our study. We followed the proposed process and conducted the following activities:

1. **Familiarization with the Data:** We transcribed a video excerpt of Ana's interaction with Aquarela Virtual from the free exploration phase. The video was 28 min and 14 s long, of which we analyzed the first 16 min and 45 s, corresponding with the free exploration of Aquarela Virtual. All verbal or

physical expressions, speeches, gestures, and movements recorded on video were meticulously transcribed to obtain an overview of the content, analyze it, count it, categorize it, and begin to identify initial patterns.

2. **Code Generation:** Based on some observed patterns in the data, initial codes were generated to concisely describe the transcribed excerpts. The first author generated the codes, and they were reviewed by the other authors, dispensing with the need for inter-rater reliability measurements, which are not mandatory in thematic analysis.

3. **Theme Search:** The generated codes were compared to identify similarities, differences, and patterns. They were then grouped and categorized into potential themes. This task was conducted by the first author and revised by the other authors.

4. **Theme Review:** The identified themes were reviewed and refined, producing a set of themes intrinsically related to the dataset, and connections between these themes were established through means of a hierarchy of themes and sub-themes. This task was conducted by the first author, with brainstorming and contributions from the other authors.

5. **Definition and Naming of Themes:** Each theme was defined with meaningful names, described in terms of content and context, and aligned with the theoretical foundations presented in Sect. 2.1. A thematic map, illustrated in Fig. 4, was drawn using the consolidated themes.

6. **Report Production:** The final stage of thematic analysis involves formally relating and describing the findings, providing illustrative examples from the data to support the analysis. As presented here, this article is the materialization of this final stage. Section 4 presents the obtained results.

4   Results

In this section, we present the results of our thematic analysis. We start by presenting details of the transcription and respective codings (cf. Subsect. 4.1) and then present and exemplify themes and the final thematic map (cf. Subsect. 4.2).

4.1   Transcription and Codes

The transcription resulted in 139 lines corresponding to approximately one line every 7 s of video. Table 1 presents a complete list of the assigned codes in alphabetical order and the specifics of these codes. The following excerpt illustrates a transcribed line and the codes assigned to it[3]

[01:11] Ana takes the happy emoji (yellow) and shows it to the computer while making a low/high-pitched sound and turning her head to her left, as if she was 'posing' when showing the emoji to her colleagues who are in

---

[3] All excerpts presented in this article are free translations to English provided by the authors, as the original transcription was in Brazilian Portuguese.

the videoconference, still looking at the computer.

Identified codes:

- Object manipulation - emoji;
- Affective expression - emoji;
- Interaction with the system - webcam;
- Local verbal communication - expression;
- Body language - pose

Table 1. Transcription codes and their specifics.

Code	Specifics
Autonomy	
Local non-verbal communication	pointing, nodding
Local verbal communication	comment, conversation, expression, inaudible, instruction, question, question and answer, sounds
Remote verbal communication Context	comment, question, question and answer
Exploration with the body	movement
Exploration with objects	emoji, sheet with QR codes, color palette
Affective expression	hug, emoji, speech, clap, laughter
Interaction with the system	mouse, keyboard, webcam
Body language	gesture, metaphor, movement, pose, posture
Object manipulation	cards, castle, emoji, sheet with QR codes, color palette
Look towards the camera	
Look at someone else	
Perception of yourself in the system	
Perception of the remote other	

4.2 Themes and Thematic Map

After a process of review, refinement, definition of names, and visual design, the grouping and categorization of these codes resulted in the following themes and subthemes (indicated in parentheses), as illustrated in Fig. 4: **Interaction**, **Identification** (Self, Other), **Embodied Imagination** (Exploration, Enactive Metaphor, Playfulness).

The **Interaction** theme expresses direct actions in the Aquarela Virtual system. This interaction involved 62 instances of interaction through the *webcam*, which included displaying objects, *emojis*, poses and taking photos. In addition, there were 12 instances of interaction through mouse manipulation, allowing the cursor to move and the "take photo" button to be clicked. Examples of excerpts related to **Interaction**:

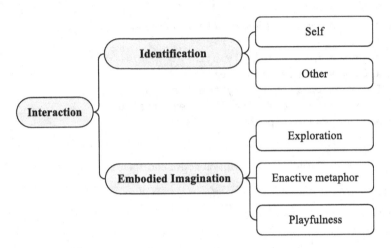

Fig. 4. Thematic map

[03:31] Ana takes the color palette and shows the QR Code for the webcam; the teacher points to the computer screen and says "Hey, did you choose which animal?"; Ana continues showing the color palette and rotates it slightly to the sides.

[06:51] The teacher asks: "Do you want to take a photo?"; Ana already had her hand on the mouse and, while holding the happy emoji (yellow) next to her face, she presses the left mouse button; The teacher says in an excited tone "eeeee, how cool"; Ana claps her hands, gives a brief laugh and says "I took a photo" before putting away the emoji she had in her hands.

The **Identification** theme is composed of two subthemes **Of self** and **Of the other**, which is related to the perception that Aquarela Virtual is a collaborative system in which several people interact together. This theme illustrates the perception of herself (Ana) in the system and that of others; it is related to Ana's possibility of imagining herself within the system and her colleagues. The excerpt that begins at [05:11] illustrates the perception of herself within the system; after showing the plane and seeing the animation in the system, Ana imagines herself inside the plane that is appearing. Regarding the perception of the other, the excerpt starting at 08:28 describes Ana perceiving the affective state expressed by Gabriel, a remote colleague, and showing the QR code of the same affective state and perceiving the action mirrored in her avatar in the system.

[05:11] The teacher says 'Oh, you can take a photo too, okay?', when she takes the computer mouse, she adds: 'Oh, you come here... (moves the mouse) oh'; Ana interrupts: 'I want to take a photo on the plane!'

[08:28] Ana comments 'Gabriel has a question' (referring to her interpre-
tation of an emoji, not visible in the video, next to Gabriel's avatar); and
then she takes the calm emoji (green), shows it to the computer and adds:
'I also have a question'

The **Embodied Imagination** theme with the three subthemes **Exploration**, **Enactive Metaphor** and **Playfulness**, refers to the embodied way in
which imagination emerges during the experience with Aquarela Virtual. Expressions, speeches, postures, poses, and body metaphors, with 40 occurrences, gave
rise to this theme and its subthemes.

- The subtheme **Exploration** is connected to the theme **Embodied Imagination** because the active interaction with physical objects and exploration
  with them and body movements allowed Ana to acquire information and
  experiences that fueled her imaginative capacity.
- The subtheme **Enactive metaphor** refers to how Ana's action on an idea
  brought something new into existence. In this context, creating a metaphor
  means enacting it, thus being an embodied process. In the section that begins
  at 05:03, Ana incorporates and stages the plane's movement by raising both
  arms as if gliding in the air.
- As for the **Playfulness** subtheme, it is connected to playful interactions that
  appeared during Ana's interaction with Aquarela Virtual. In the excerpt that
  begins at 02:55, while exploring the emojis that were at her disposal, Ana
  demonstrates a playful response; she shows the emoji of fear to the *webcam*
  and says *"I'm scared"*, but says it in a cheerful tone. Just like in the section
  that starts at 08:03 where Ana shows the angry *emoji* to the webcam and
  says: "I'm mad" and puts her hands on her hips, making a serious expression.

We present some excerpts related to **Embodied Imagination, Exploration**, **Enactive Metaphor** and **Playfulness**, respectively:

[00:20] Ana holds the sad (blue) emoji with her right hand, while with her
left hand she holds the happy (yellow) emoji, showing both to the computer
at the same time. Initially, Ana moves the emojis quickly up and down,
and then holds them crossed, still showing them to the computer.

[05:03] Ana quickly points to the computer screen and exclaims: 'Look! The
airplane!'; The teacher responds, 'Theeere, Ana's plane'; Ana opens both
arms and imitates the flight of an airplane

[02:55] Ana brings the fear emoji (black) a few centimeters closer to the
webcam, and the teacher says "Not too close, further away"; Ana moves
the emoji away a little, and after a few moments she hears a beep; The
teacher says "There, did you see the little face there?"; Ana responds with
a light laugh, in a joking tone "I'm scared", and saves the emoji. The
teacher seems to imitate the sound of a ghost.

[08:03] Ana takes the anger emoji (red) and holds it in front of her face for a few seconds, and then turns it so that the QR code is facing the computer. Ana returns the anger emoji (red) and expresses it out loud, placing her hands on her hips: "I'm angry!"

5 Discussion

Imagining goes beyond something that happens to us. As discussed by Gallagher [8], imagination is not just an abstract mental activity but also rooted in our bodily experiences and interaction with the world around us, and our active participation is required for it to emerge. Our imagination tends to be naturally sparked by the situations and opportunities we encounter and the narratives we process. Body movement contributes to the imaginative process by imagining new possibilities. This understanding of imagination as an embodied phenomenon is crucial for our investigation into the expression of imagination during interaction with the Aquarela Virtual.

In this paper, we followed a rigorous methodological approach based on the well-established qualitative method of Thematic Analysis [1]. This methodological approach enabled us to explore how bodily experiences and interaction with the system contribute to the physical manifestation of children's imagination. Although we only explored data from a single child interacting with the Aquarela Virtual system, the chosen method is not particularly concerned with sample size, as a single instance is enough to illustrate the occurrence of a particular phenomenon. The phenomenon in case, the physical manifestation of children's imagination, is now better understood and described with an analysis grounded by the collected data, as presented in Sect. 4.

Returning to the research question *"How does Aquarela Virtual's design contribute to the expression of imagination through interaction with the system?"* it is possible to say that the design of both the system and the workshop allowed children to express their imagination mainly through active engagement. In this regard, the themes from the thematic analysis highlight some key aspects that contribute to the emergence of imagination during the interaction with Aquarela Virtual. Furthermore, the analysis highlights how embodied aspects and imagination are connected: interactions with Aquarela Virtual depend on physical, tangible actions, and these actions modulate how embodied imagination emerges while exploring the system.

Further discussing the thematic map, the theme **Interaction** mediates the themes **Identification** and **Embodied Imagination**; during the interaction with Aquarela Virtual, a child's actions are mirrored in the system and communicated to all participants, enabling **Identification** of oneself as well as others. Identification is also linked to imagination when the child can imagine themselves inside Aquarela Virtual with their peers, and opportunities for playful interactions and narrative creations arise.

Our thematic map also shows that the design enabled **Embodied Imagination** through freedom for exploration, enactive metaphors, and playful interactions. Interaction with Aquarela Virtual happens through the physical manipulation of objects, whether they are elements of Aquarela music or the emojis provided. We argue that imagination is incorporated in its essence, but this relationship is more evident when it appears through movements, gestures, postures, and poses. It is through exploring the available opportunities that it is possible to form meaning and engage in enactive metaphors, as when Ana imitates the plane's movement with her body, raising both arms and moving them as if she were gliding in the air.

In essence, incorporating imagination into interaction with Aquarela Virtual not only increases the expressive potential of the system. It also deepens children's engagement with their imaginative creations. By inserting embedded aspects into the design, Aquarela Virtual offers a rich platform for children to explore, express, and embody their imaginative ideas dynamically and interactively. By recognizing the influence of embodied imagination in interacting with systems like Aquarela Virtual, designers of interactive systems can incorporate elements that encourage (promote) embodied imagination, providing opportunities for children to fully integrate their physical and mental experiences while interacting with the system.

6 Conclusion

Promoting imagination in user experience interactions is a challenging endeavor, but some design guidance scan be provided. In this study, the Aquarela Virtual and the workshop allowed children, being geographically distributed in a context of social isolation, to express their imagination through tangible and embodied interaction. We aimed to understand how the design of the Aquarela workshop helped children express their imagination. The results indicate that the freedom to explore possibilities of interaction and action and its emerging playfulness made it possible to observe the emergent embodied imagination.

Future work includes expanding the analysis of data from the workshops, encompassing a broader and more in-depth analysis that encompasses data from more participants and including other data collected in addition to the recordings. By carrying further thematic analyses, it will be possible to investigate more specific research questions and provide recommendations for design improvements with a focus on imagination.

Acknowledgments. This study was financially supported by the São Paulo Research Foundation (FAPESP) through grants #2015/16528-0 and #2020/04242-2, and by the Coordenação de Aperfeiçoamento de Pessoal de Nível Superior - Brasil (CAPES) - Finance Code 001.

Disclosure of Interests. The authors have no competing interests to declare that are relevant to the content of this article.

References

1. Braun, V., Clarke, V.: Using thematic analysis in psychology. Qual. Res. Psychol. **3**(2), 77–101 (2006)
2. De Queiroz, M.J.N., Duarte, E.F., Dos Reis, J.C., Pimenta, J.R.D.O.G.: Imagination on interactive installations: a systematic literature review. In: ICEIS, no. (2), pp. 223–234 (2022)
3. Dourish, P.: Where the Action Is: The Foundations of Embodied Interaction. MIT Press, Cambridge, USA (2001)
4. Duarte, E.F., Mendoza, Y.L.M., de Queiroz, M.J.N., Baranauskas, M.C.C.: Aquarela virtual: Design e desenvolvimento de um sistema socioenativo em contexto de isolamento social. Technical report, IC-22-01, Institute of Computing, University of Campinas, February 2022
5. Erkut, C., et al.: Design and evaluation of interactive musical fruit. In: Proceedings of the 2014 Conference on Interaction Design and Children, IDC 2014, ACM, New York, USA (2014). https://doi.org/10.1145/2593968.2610451
6. Fuchs, T.: Ecology of the Brain: The Phenomenology and Biology of the Embodied Mind. Oxford University Press (2017)
7. Galindo Esparza, R.P., Healey, P.G.T., Weaver, L., Delbridge, M.: Embodied imagination: an approach to stroke recovery combining participatory performance and interactive technology. In: Proceedings of the 2019 CHI Conference on Human Factors in Computing Systems, pp. 1–12. ACM, New York, USA (2019). https://doi.org/10.1145/3290605.3300735
8. Gallagher, S.: Enactivist Interventions: Rethinking the Mind. Oxford University Press (2017)
9. Gibson, J.J.: The Ecological Approach to Visual Perception. Houghton Mifflin (1979)
10. Loke, L., Khut, G.P., Kocaballi, A.B.: Bodily experience and imagination: designing ritual interactions for participatory live-art contexts. In: Proceedings of the Designing Interactive Systems Conference, DIS 2012, pp. 779–788. ACM, New York, USA (2012). https://doi.org/10.1145/2317956.2318073
11. de Moraes, V., Toquinho, Morra, G., Fabrizio, M.: Aquarela (1983)
12. Rucińska, Z.: Enactive Imagination: Its Roots and Contemporary Horizons, p. 1–256. Bloomsbury Publishing (2014)
13. Thompson, E.: Mind in Life. Harvard University Press (2010)
14. Varela, F.J., Thompson, E., Rosch, E.: The Embodied Mind: Cognitive Science and Human Experience. MIT Press (2016)
15. Weiser, M.: The computer for the 21st century. Sci. Am. **265**(3), 94–104 (1991)

Play and Gender Expression: A Critical Design Exhibition to Generate and Measure Awareness About Gender Differences Within the Context of Children and Toys

Alakesh Dhibar(✉) [ID], Eduardo Gonçalves [ID], and António Gorgel [ID]

UNIDCOM/IADE, Unidade de Investigação em Design e Comunicação, Av. D. Carlos I, 4, 1200-649 Lisbon, Portugal

`alakeshisavailable@gmail.com`, {`eduardo.goncalves,`
`antonio.gorgel`}`@universidadeeuropeia.pt`

Abstract. The paper focuses on the exhibition, 'Play and Gender Expression', which showcases Critical Design artifacts to generate awareness regarding gender differences within children's play experience through the objects of play, such as toys. It covers the methodology behind recording participants' responses in physical space and digital mediums like a website and proposes a comprehensive analysis to measure the change in perception and knowledge. The exhibition addresses the problem of gender stereotypes and how they limit children's early play experiences and may impact their skills and abilities. Several sociocultural factors, such as education, economy, politics, religion, rights, social duties, sexual expressions, and cultural belief systems, are touched through diverse mediums, from physical and digital products to t-shirts and photographs, to encourage open discussions. Additionally, it asks the participants to summarize their experiences by recording their responses in a closed voting system. The exhibition attempted to break the limitation of visual interactions in design speculation and critical approaches by effectively implementing perceptual understanding of the participants and translating into tacit knowledge. It was directed towards the public in a Portuguese academic setting in a physical space for a limited time. Further, a website is designed to extend the reach towards more participants by adopting physical data collection techniques. It aims to add a new dimension to the traditional qualitative approaches using digital interactions within the diverse mediums of exhibitions. The paper demonstrates the research and insights regarding gender-inclusive awareness by comparing human interactions in physical and digital platforms.

Keywords: Critical Design Exhibition · Gender Inclusive Awareness · Inclusive Play Framework

1 Introduction

The paper focuses on the exhibition, 'Play and Gender Expression', which showcases Critical Design artifacts to generate awareness regarding the problem of gender differences focusing on children and one of the most prominent objects of play, such as

M. Kurosu and A. Hashizume (Eds.): HCII 2024, LNCS 14685, pp. 275–294, 2024.
https://doi.org/10.1007/978-3-031-60412-6_20

toys. It covers the methodology behind recording participants' responses within the engagement in the exhibition scenarios through a physical space and digital mediums like a website. Currently, the issue of gender discrimination in our society has grown increasingly problematic. The socio-political implications of gender vary across cultures, geographies, and demographics, which makes it more severe and complex [1]. The study focuses on the effect of gender differences in the context of children's play experience and available objects of play. The problem is examined from various fields of study, including biology, psychology, and social science, and it is established that gendered trends apparent in children's toy interests can narrow their early play experience. The resulting gendered play patterns and repeated exposure to gender stereotypes during children's formative years raise concerns about the potential impact on their skills and abilities [2–4]. Addressing the complexity, a substantial number of sociocultural factors, such as education, economic background, political climate, religion, parental relationship, peer pressure, product ethics, governmental policies, fundamental rights, social duties, sexual expressions, and belief systems indicate a need of inclusive understanding of gender within a culture-specific environment [5–7]. Further, the vast array of human agents related to the problem [8–10], including parents, siblings, other family members, peers, educators, toy designers, and advertising directors among others, emphasizes the need for a holistic medium of promoting awareness towards adults.

To address the issue, the exhibition attempted to utilize Critical Design artifacts to promote diversity in perception and knowledge towards changing behavior. It was directed towards the general public including students, professors, and staff within a university environment addressing Portuguese culture and beyond. The exhibition enabled a diverse range of mediums from physical and digital products to t-shirts, and photographs to initiate open discussions and provocations among the viewers. Specifically, the exhibition stimulated the participants with daily life actions and decisions, which can sometimes lead to conscious or unconscious gender dichotomy and recorded their knowledge and perceptions through a qualitative data collection method. After experiencing and reading about each of the artifacts, the participants were asked to prioritize a response through a closed voting system. Apart from the three-day physical exhibition, a website was designed to increase the reach of more participants and the data collection techniques were adopted with virtual forms and polls, extending the experience into human-computer digital interactions. In contemporary times, the applications of design speculation and critical approaches are mostly limited to the forms of art exhibitions, displays, installations and other mediums of visual communication [11]. 'Play and Gender Expression' was an attempt to use conceptual design to gather qualitative data by implementing perceptual understanding of the participants and translating in the form of tacit knowledge [12]. It aimed to utilize the website as an instrument for gathering primary data [13], focusing on technology as an added way to traditional qualitative approaches to address awareness through digital experiences.

2 Background Research

The exhibition is part of a larger research plan from the doctorate in design, named 'Social Awareness and Cultural Significance in Designing (Non) Gendered Toys' [14]. The Critical Design artifacts from the exhibition were designed and developed within the different phases of the study as integral parts of the Inclusive Play Framework. With three levels - Identify, Diversify, and Inclusify, the framework uses Design for Behavior Change [15] and Inclusive Design [16] with the objective to promote and measure gender-inclusive awareness. Focusing on the role of adults, the framework is applicable to three adult clusters, including parents, educators, and designers with different levels of complexity. The study focuses on the fundamental cluster of Parents-Children with the primary objective of finding a more holistic solution to improve the awareness of parents of gender-inclusive play, which can increase the possibility of providing children with a better environment to grow up. It emphasizes children between the ages of four and seven, which covers a diverse range of agents crucial to addressing the multidimensional issue of gender differentiation [17]. The framework has been tested through its integration into semi-structured card games and a board game and implemented via workshop activities, co-creating with families from Portugal within distinct scenarios through parent-child play interactions [18]. It attempted to determine, measure, and compare the 'state' of gender-inclusive awareness through different iterations of the workshop activities. The study focuses on sociocultural variables within the Portuguese context to understand the origin of enigmatic aspects that can cause gender differences. Despite government initiatives in Portugal with the organizations like CIG - Comissão para a Cidadania e a Igualdade de Género (Committee for Citizenship and Gender Equality) [19], the movement for gender equality is a progressive aspect including economic, social, and political levels [20, 21] and the parameters such as work, money, knowledge, time, power, health, and violence. The issue of gender-inclusive awareness in Portugal includes family dynamics [22, 23], the role of education [24–26], and available objects of play and related industry [27].

The exhibition, 'Play and Gender Expression' employed current Critical Design philosophies like Speculative Design [28] and Discursive Design [29] within the Inclusive Play Framework. The diverse mediums of the exhibition artifacts attempted to create an immersive experience utilizing different modes of interactions, such as visual, audial and touch interactions. The digital version of the exhibition, the website, attempted the same with the available technical support in a virtual platform. Both the exhibition scenarios included a qualitative data collection approach, which asks the viewer to prioritize and determine a specific response after experiencing each of the artifacts exhibited. There were three questions strategically aligned with three levels of the Inclusive Play Framework, Identify, Diversify and Inclusify, to give the participants three different contexts in the form of choices. Finally, with diverse mediums, including physical space and digital website, the exhibition attempted to find dynamic applications of human interactions by providing a critical space to analyze and measure the change in perception and knowledge, laying the foundation of gender-inclusive awareness within a culture-specific setting.

3   Literature Review

The literature covered in this paper addresses the implementation of the Inclusive Play Framework in the context of an exhibition scenario. The primary literature related to the formation of the Inclusive Play Framework consists of various theories in the field of Design for Behavior Change [15]. The levels of the framework are designed by combining the tools, theories, and frameworks like augmented theory of interpersonal behavior [30], practice-oriented design [31], and social learning theory [32], to understand the underlying concepts behind human perception, knowledge construction and awareness through changing behavior. Further, Inclusive Design aids with the process of recognizing exclusion with holistic implementation. For example, the method of persona spectrum [16] synthesizes the extension of a design solution towards a broader population by understanding the feasibility of the solution in permanent, temporary, and situational conditions. This leads towards different inferences within the levels of the Inclusive Play Framework by implementing the core principles like equitable use, flexibility, simplicity, intuitiveness, open-endedness, accessibility, and adaptability [33]. Additionally, several literatures, such as classification of toys [34], and genetic epistemology [35] were utilized to understand the feasibility of the Inclusive Play Framework by analyzing the interaction between children and different objects of play, such as toys towards diverse opportunities and inclusive development. Finally, various theories from judgement, cognition, and psychology, like decision-making [36], interpersonal perception [37], and cross-cultural psychology [38], were addressed to visualize the problem under investigation through a dynamic lens beyond the scope of the traditional discipline of Design.

Connecting with the abstract ideas from different levels of the framework, the artifacts in the exhibition are designed through various theories from Speculative Design and Discursive Design. For example, the concept of scenario building through utopia and dystopia [28] from Speculative Design helped to understand the role of design fiction by providing diverse imaginary realities. It motivated the fundamental idea behind the exhibition artifact, 'What did I do wrong?', where a toy is speculated to wearing a rainbow dress representing Pride and supporting the LGBT + movement. Again, Discursive Design advanced with several discourse techniques such as reminding, informing, provoking, inspiring and persuading, to apply the framework in making the exhibition artifacts. For example, the concept of provoking emotions [29] from Discursive Design was connected with the application of cognitive dissonance [39] to design the touch-sensitive toy, 'Blob' for the exhibition.

Finally, the conceptual ideas and themes behind the exhibition artifacts are developed from the primary observations and design ethnography within Portugal [18]. The process involved communications with notable people from academia, research, crafts, toy shops, toy companies, public libraries, and other organizations, such as different toy museums from all over Portugal. For example, the temporary exhibition 'Brinquedos Sem Género' (Nongendered Toys) at Museu do Brinquedo Português, Ponte de Lima [40] leads to the justification behind the need of an exhibition in raising gender inclusive awareness through different objects of play. Furthermore, it provided adequate observations and communications to strengthen the study and its application. For example, the relevance of Pride month within the LGBT + movement in Lisboa with the initiatives from organizations like ILGA Portugal [41]. Although it was beyond the scope of the design ethnography in Portugal, it is essential to mention the relevance of the television advertisement in India from 2021, which impacted the formation of the interactive sculpture in the exhibition artifact 'The Family'. Finally, the diverse mediums for the exhibition artifacts were required to revise diverse literature, such as P5 creative coding [42] for the interactive touchscreen installation in 'Child's Dream' and basic electronics through Arduino coding [43] for developing the interactive toy, 'Blob'.

4 Inclusive Play Framework

The fundamental idea of the Inclusive Play Framework suggests a medium of alternative perception to link the abstract form of recognizing the gender associations with different objects of play. The framework is applicable for three user clusters, Parents-Children, Educators-Children, and Designers-Children, with varying degrees of complexity. Figure 1 represents the initial formation of the framework with its levels of intervention, Identify, Diversify, and Inclusify. The outcome of Identify progressively enables the recognition of elements in gender discrimination; Diversify attempts to generate motivation towards diverse perspectives; and Inclusify promotes the transmission of inclusive knowledge through reconfiguring beliefs and practices. The articulated compilation of different tools, theories, other literature, and opportunity areas from the design ethnography in Portugal through deductive, inductive, and abductive reasoning emerges into different inferences within the steps of the framework. More precisely, the study utilizes primary observations through design ethnography in Portugal, which leads to inductive inferences, such as, recognizing problems, and understanding exclusion. Several theories within the field of play-interaction design and gender studies have been analyzed in the form of deductive inferences, such as, human abilities, adaptability, and accessibility. Similarly, the complexity of awareness and behavior change speculates into probable conclusions, resulting in abductive inferences, such as, reconfiguration, intrinsic motivation, and maintenance.

Beyond the two iterations of the workshop activities targeted to Parents-Children [44], the exhibition, 'Play and Gender Expression' aims at the academic setting inviting diverse participants, exceeding the first user cluster. The closed voting system within the exhibition asks the participants to record their responses after experiencing, interacting, and reading about each of the artifacts. The format of the questions from the voting system follows the abstract ideas behind three levels of the framework. For example, the question for Identify focuses on the context of observation and identification. Whereas the question for Diversify aims on the context of diverse perspectives through collaboration. And finally, the question for Inclusify directs towards incorporating the understanding with children. The participants were asked to prioritize and determine a specific option out of these three by putting tokens in the most appropriate ballot box with each of the artifacts. Adopting the same, the website employed virtual forms and polls after the digital experiences of the artifacts.

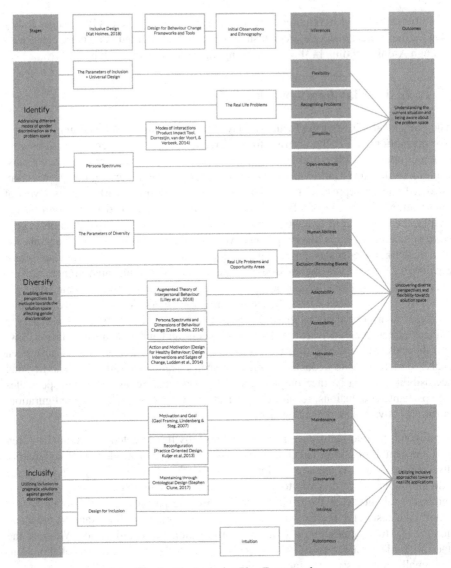

Fig. 1. The Inclusive Play Framework.

5   The Exhibition

'Play and Gender Expression' was held for three days at IADE - Creative University, an art and design college in Lisboa, Portugal. The exhibition had the time allocated between 10am and 6pm, in the auditorium attached to the lounge area on the ground floor. The exhibition area was designed for an autonomous and self-instructed experience assigning arrows on the floor. At the entrance, two panels were placed to welcome the participants and describe the study with instructions about the voting system. Each of the artifacts was supported with a panel of dialogue explaining the context. The space was presented with adequate lights and sound complementing the overall experience. In Fig. 2, we can see the instructions and some pictures taken with the author in the physical space of the exhibition. After three days of the physical exhibition, a website [45] was developed to extend the time by supplementing the experience in the digital platform. Adopting the instructions with virtual forms and polls (see Fig. 3), the data gathered with the website includes three months before documenting the results.

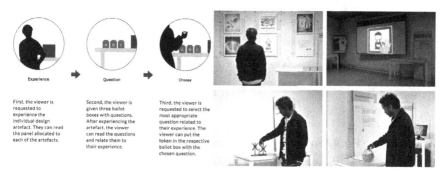

Fig. 2. Instructions about the voting mechanism and some pictures from the exhibition.

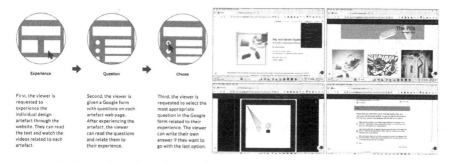

Fig. 3. Instructions about the experience and some screenshots from the website.

6 Design Artifacts from the Exhibition

Altogether, six Critical Design artifacts with diverse mediums were in the exhibition. Below is the description of each of the artifacts.

6.1   The Pills

The artifact 'The Pills' was a series of pictures and illustrations (see Fig. 4), developed through screen printing and digital editing, to convey societal biases related to different genders in the form of a drug.

Fig. 4.   Some images and illustrations used in 'The Pills'.

The Dialogue to Explain the Artifact.   A drug is generally used to cure and control a disease, but what if we were born with a disease caused by some kind of drug? 'The Pills' is a form of Critical Design artifact to address our biases related to different genders caused consciously and unconsciously. It also questions the viewer to identify these pills in their daily life activities. It would probably help us to understand how and when the universal phenomenon of gender differences transforms into gender discrimination.

6.2   'What Did I Do Wrong?'

The artifact 'What did I do wrong?' was a speculation about a toy wearing a dress representing Pride (LGBT +) in rainbow colors to reflect the problem behind categorizing and limiting toys in terms of gender (see Fig. 5). The digital illustration is printed on cotton t-shirts.

Fig. 5.   The illustration and t-shirts used in 'What did I do wrong?'.

The Dialogue to Explain the Artifact. What if a toy can become part of the LGBT + movement? The illustration and t-shirts are an attempt to relate the issue of gender discrimination through toys with the contemporary movement of the LGBT + community. The metaphorical speculation imagines a toy wearing a dress representing Pride in rainbow colors. It stimulates the problem behind categorizing toys in terms of gender and specifying them with biased societal colors, pink and blue. In this vision, the toy, as a living being, supports the fight for freedom, identity, and expression. The t-shirts were used to support the Pride celebrations in Lisbon in 2023, which initiated some interesting discussions with different people. For example, the relevance and opportunities to initiate campaigns like Let Toys be Toys [46], which was designed to persuade retailers to stop categorizing toys by gender in the United Kingdom.

6.3 Child's Dream

The artifact 'Child's Dream' was a touchscreen video installation, developed by digital illustrations and P5 creative coding, to empower children's imagination and inspiration over societal stereotypes (see Fig. 6). The video on the screen looped several job opportunities for children, and it will stop on a specific profession if the participant decides to touch the screen, being a metaphor for rigid societal beliefs.

Fig. 6. Some images of the interactive screen (Without touch and with touch).

The Dialogue to Explain the Artifact. Can we touch and stop a dream?! 'Child's Dream' is an interactive art installation where the viewer perceives a dreamland with several possible job professions playing over the screen. Touching over one specific profession stops the flow of the dream, and the possibilities continue to change if the viewer decides not to touch the screen. The screen and the video represent the endless possibilities for a child to become in the future. The viewer is the metaphor for a specific society where the possibilities and opportunities are limited and divided in terms of rigid beliefs and cultural differences. The installation is an attempt to promote awareness towards empowering a child's imagination and inspiration raising over societal rules and stereotypes addressing gender, race, class, and so on.

6.4 The Family

The artifact 'The Family' was inspired by a television advertisement as a sculpture to explore the possible roles of a mother and a father in a family beyond the human values of love and strength (see Fig. 7). The sculpture is developed using wood and metal.

Fig. 7. The sculpture used in 'The Family'.

The Dialogue to Explain the Artifact. 'Mummy ka Pyar aur Papa ki Shakti' (Mothers' love and father's strength), the message on an Indian television advertisement. In 2021, one of the most common advertisements on Indian television promoting a health drink had a child actor as the main character. The overtly family advertisement ended with the dialogue from the child actor, saying that if somebody consumes the drink, they will be protected by the mother's love and the father's strength. The Family' is a critical viewpoint to address one of the unconscious biases related to gender differences present in our society in contemporary times. It asks the question of exploring other probable perspectives within the context through the abstraction of a sculpture. The sculpture illustrates the structure of a family with the possible roles of a mother and father through the rotation of metaphorical limbs. It attempts to provoke the viewer towards how unconscious biases can affect long-term conscious gender differences with varying skills and abilities.

6.5 The Soul

With a video and voice over, developed with Adobe After Effects and Adobe Premier Pro, the artifact 'The Soul' questions the participant to find a universal form of toys without being limited by functions and properties such as size, shape, color and sometimes gender (see Fig. 8).

The Dialogue to Explain the Artifact. What is the purpose of a toy? 'The Soul' is a Critical Design artifact to consider a toy from the core perspective of play. It attempts to trigger a thought in the form of questions to find the universal form of toys, which is not limited by any functions and properties such as size, shape, color and so on. More specifically, it focuses on the intangible idea behind categorizing toys and the limitations of the categorization parameters influenced by human stereotypes, such as gender.

Fig. 8. Some screenshots from the video used in 'The Soul'.

The Voice-over used in the Video. Some cultures believe a soul is a spiritual and immaterial part of being. It is here portrayed as the core of identity with the fundamental aspects of existence and purpose. The forms can vary according to individual functions, yet the definitions carry the elemental essence. What is a toy? Is it something to take up the slack of a boring and lonely afternoon? Something that keeps the child busy and out of the way? Something to have fun with? Something to fan the spark of creativity? What are we looking for when we choose a toy for our child? Are we choosing it with the child in mind, or is it the child in our grown-up bodies with adult consciousness choosing? Can we answer the question of whether toys have their souls embedded within them?

6.6   Blob - the Toy with a Question

The artifact 'Blob - The toy with a question' tried to provoke the participant with two possible interactions signifying social biases related to females and males (see Fig. 9). Pressing the toy softly makes it pink, whereas putting force transforms it into blue. The interactive part of the toy is developed with 3D printing using polyethylene fibers and Arduino coding with LEDs.

Fig. 9. Some images of the product used in 'Blob – The toy with a question'.

The Dialogue to Explain the Artifact. 'Why are there only pink and blue!?' Can interacting with an object initiate discrimination? 'Blob' is a Critical Design artifact to provoke a question in viewers' minds. There are only two possible ways the viewer can interact with the toy: press it softly or with force. The toy becomes pink in the first case and blue in the second. The deliberate design ideas behind the interactions aim to signify different gender roles within a biased societal scenario. Gently touching is associated with love and care toward female gender stereotypes, and putting force relates to strength and protection, which are male stereotypes. The central idea behind the artifact is an attempt to design a question to trigger a thought, whereas playing with the toy can be perceived as the secondary objective.

7 Discussion and Analysis

The responses of the participants from both exhibition scenarios were collected in the form of tokens in the respective ballot boxes and digital feedback through Google Forms. The initial plan aimed to invite 100 participants for the three-day exhibition, but the final count surpassed expectations, with a total of 123 participants. This number was the average of all the collected tokens from the six exhibition artifacts. During the engagement of the physical exhibition, the participants were given a set of rules to take only six tokens at the beginning that they could put in the respective ballot boxes provided with the artifacts. They were also asked to skip voting for any artifact if they thought that their response was not aligned with any of the questions provided. This was the reason behind the difference in total collected tokens for different exhibition artifacts. This fact was taken into consideration when developing the website to give the participants more space and flexibility to express themselves. In the virtual forms, there was an extra option for the participants to write their responses without selecting any of the three given questions. For the website, there was no intended total number of participants and the process of collecting data is still ongoing. Yet, the total number of responses recorded was 13 till the time of writing this paper. This number is again the average of the total number of responses recorded from six exhibition artifacts. It implies that some of the participants only went through fewer artifacts than the total of six exhibits on the website. Figure 10 illustrates the comparison between the actual number of collected responses related to different design artifacts in the physical exhibition and through the exhibition website.

The evaluation phase, along with the analysis and synthesis, provides several insights regarding the semantic analysis to understand the effect of the exhibition over gender inclusion. The examples of three questions related to three levels of the Inclusive Play Framework are: for Identify, 'After experiencing The Family, do you think you generally see the message in your daily life?'; for Diversify, 'After experiencing The Family, do you think you generally talk about the message with others?'; for Inclusify, 'After experiencing The Family, do you think you generally consider the message while talking to children?'. The formation of these questions included the abstract ideas behind each of the levels from the Inclusive Play Framework. Specifically, the questions were designed with simplified syntaxes in the form of understandable language which is meaningful, and context driven. The level Identify attempts the user to enable recognition of elements related to gender differences through behavior change mechanics like information processing, and connecting through association, guidance, and persuasion. It was attempted to simplify by using verbs like 'see' in the formation of the question related to Identify. The level Diversify tries to generate diverse perspectives related to the elements of gender differences through behavior change mechanics like facilitating conditions,

Physical Exhibition		Exhibition Website		
Design artefacts	Total number of tokens collected	Design artefacts	Number of written answers from the participants	Total number of responses recorded
'The Pills'	130	'The Pills'	1	17
'What did I do wrong?'	123	'What did I do wrong?'	1	20
'Child's Dream'	119	'Child's Dream'	1	11
'The Family'	123	'The Family'	0	10
'The Soul'	122	'The Soul'	0	7
'Blob - The toy with a question'	118	'Blob - The toy with a question'	0	11

Fig. 10. Total number of responses from the physical exhibition and the exhibition website.

and collaboration with others to change perceived consequences. This was attempted to simplify by using verbs like *'talk about'* in the making of the question related to Diversify. Following the same, the level Inclusify attempts to include the context of children related to the elements of gender differences through behavior change mechanics like reconfiguration of knowledge, confrontation, and intrinsic motivations. Again, it was attempted to simplify by using verbs like *'consider'* and in the making of the question related to Inclusify. Finally, the space for writing the answers on the exhibition website asks, *'You can go with the fourth option and write your answer if you disagree with the first three options.'*

Figure 11 represents the data gathered by the voting system in the physical exhibition and by the virtual forms on the exhibition website. The graphs for the exhibition website also include the number of written responses from the participants. If we follow the patterns from the data visualization from both the scenarios, we can find the insights below,

- The highest number of responses in the physical exhibition is in the domain of Diversify, gradually decreasing in Identify and Inclusify. This illustrates the presence of flexibility and space for varying perspectives through collaborating with others. It also initiates the idea behind further interventions where the participants can be part of the design process of the exhibits through a participatory approach [47].
- The highest number of responses on the exhibition website is in the domain of Identify, gradually decreasing in Diversify and Inclusify. This illustrates the presence of identification of the issue and the need for diverse perspectives and inclusion of knowledge within the context of child development. Considering the previous data visualization from the physical exhibition, we can see a difference here. The difference between the human-exhibit interactions may be dependent on the presence of other participants while experiencing and understanding [48]. It was observed that the participants mostly appeared in groups in the physical exhibition scenario, but the participants went through the exhibition website individually through their personal devices like laptops or mobile phones.

- Considering the total number of participants in both scenarios, the number of responses is very high in the physical exhibition compared with the exhibition website. Again, the highest number of responses in the physical exhibition comes under Diversify, whereas in the case of the website, it falls into Identify. If we attempt to connect these facts, we may speculate that there is a relation between the number of participants attended and their choices. This may lead to the conclusion that increasing the number of participants in this research methodology affects the cumulative 'state' of awareness as a form of education [49] in a closed setting.

- Although three levels of the Inclusive Play Framework are situated independently, there is a varying degree of complexity in the 'state' of perception leading towards the desired change in behavior. The fundamental ideas behind these levels are again complex with different steps involved. The schematic representations of these levels with different questions work in a way that we can see the differences in the responses of the participants. Through the process of abstraction and simplification, the questions use three different contexts, which are 'your daily life', 'with others', and 'talking to children'. This may result in the fact that there is a connection between context and choices.

- Again, according to the fundamental ideas behind the levels of the Inclusive Play Framework, each level is situated in a specific position within the process of changing behavior. The highest number of responses in the physical exhibition is under Diversify and it falls under Identify in the case of the website. This may lead to the connection between the medium of the exhibition and the desired 'state' of perception in the context of gender inclusive awareness. The physical exhibition was more effective than the website considering the methodology of the data gathering with different contexts and choices [50].

- The Inclusive Play Framework attempts to generate awareness resulting in a change in one's perspective, the complexity and sensitivity behind gender inclusion could take a longer time to be implemented, sometimes maybe generations. Here, the parameter of time is one of the most important factors while raising awareness. The investigation through exhibition is unable to analyze this fact as the results are focusing on the current 'state' of awareness and not on the difference on before and after experiencing the artifacts. This leads to the opportunity of a refined data collection technique within the exhibition scenarios [51].

- Again, following the parameter of time, the physical exhibition was open for three days where the data gathered through the website includes three months. Yet, the total number of responses on the website is far less than the physical exhibition. This may lead to the conclusion that there is a connection between the motivation to attend an exhibition and the medium of the exhibition, considering the process of promoting the event. More specifically, most of the artifacts in the exhibition were interactive where the participants can touch the artifacts within an immersive environment. The website could not provide the same experience where the digital interactions were limited to visual and audial senses.

- 'Child's Dream' and 'The Soul' received the most responses in the physical exhibition under Inclusify. The artifacts explored scenarios highlighting factors influencing gender differences, aligning with the study's focus on understanding children's formative years. While 'Child's Dream' and 'The Soul' directly related to children and toys, the other four artifacts had more passive connections. For instance, 'What did I do wrong?' addressed gender-inclusive knowledge about the LGBT + community, loosely connecting it to children. Similarly, 'The Family' explored diverse human skills within families but lacked a direct link to the influence of parental roles on children. This emphasizes the need for more direct contexts in raising awareness. We are unable to justify this fact with the website as we need more responses to analyze the same further.

- 'The Pills,' 'What did I do wrong?' and 'Child's Dream' relied on visual interactions, with 'Child's Dream' being presented as a video due to the absence of a touch screen. 'The Soul' incorporated both visual and audial interactions. 'The Family' and 'Blob' included touch interactions along with visual perceptions. Analyzing these differences in alignment with responses, no clear pattern emerged regarding the impact of interactions on perception and awareness in the physical exhibition. However, website responses, predominantly under 'Identify,' utilized only visual and audial interactions through digital media. It suggests that the additional touch interaction in the physical exhibition yielded dynamic results aligning with the objective of the study.

- The exhibition website provided a better way of identifying the participants by asking them to write their nationality or culture, age, and profession. This provides more parameters for the process of analysis. Yet, it may lead to a smaller number of responses if we consider the complexity and privacy of the participants behind recording their responses.

- The additional option to write responses on the website provided an extra layer in the collected data, but at the same time increases the complexity of the analysis process. The written answers from the website: *'After seeing the artifact I question why there is only two options both of which come with exhausting expectations, I also would say I do all that is mentioned in options above'*, for the artifact, 'The Pills'; *'After experiencing, I more than ever see how the "LGBT + " movement is a brain washing movement that is getting into our society and destroying the naturally and innocence of our children and teens'*, for the artifact 'What did I do wrong?'; and, *'I think the issue raised by the Child's Dream design artifact is less gendered than in previous artifacts given that the society is more open to equal access at the professional level, despite lots of stereotypes remain in sociocultural values limiting equality in professions and trades'*, for the artifact, 'Child's Dream'. Although the number of written responses is too few to recognize any patterns, we can say that it gave the participants a space to critique and express diverse perspectives. This fact is aligned with cultural variability, and we may say that if we continue the process, it can substantially support the study with finding cultural relevance in gender-inclusive awareness.

The exhibition 'Play and Gender Expression' sparked discussions and provocation on gender differences in child development and toys in the Portuguese cultural context. During the physical exhibition, the author engaged in discussions, extending the experience toward the broader goal of gender-inclusive knowledge. Responses covered women's empowerment, childhood memories, and the transgender community in Portugal. For example, 'The Family,' featuring an Indian television advertisement, connected participants with family dynamics and cultural values in Portugal. A professor from

Fig. 11. Visualization of the data gathered in the physical exhibition and the exhibition website.

Germany invited her students to experience the artifacts and intervene with their own topics during the course of design process. After experiencing the artefacts, the groups of students had small discussions with the author, focusing on the inspiration for the ideas, different behavior change techniques, and the material used in prototyping. Out of six artifacts, three were designed and developed using digital technology, where the user interaction was directly influenced by the technology. The concept behind 'Child's Dream' speculated an interactive touchscreen, but it could not be implemented due to lack of economic and technical support. However, the human interaction with the motion graphics and voice over in 'The Soul' and the interactive touch-sensitive toy 'Blob', is majorly focused on the technical interventions. These design artifacts attempted to signify the role of technology as diverse mediums for human interactions to generate awareness for large-scale social issues such as gender discrimination. Finally, the exhibition website is currently working as a tool for gathering qualitative data by adopting the process of the physical exhibition, removing the limitation of parameters like time and space constraints, and extending the experience with a larger audience with participants from places outside of Portugal, such as Brazil, Spain, the United States of America, Belarus, the Netherlands, and India.

8   Critical Success Factors

Awareness is the ability to directly know and perceive, to feel, or to be cognizant of events. More broadly, it is the state of being conscious of something [52]. Yet it is a complex concept which is difficult to measure, leading to a shift in one's perspective. Again, gender knowledge, a sensitive topic for different people, increases the difficulty of measuring the change in understanding. The medium of the exhibition was strategically decided to target a larger group of adults beyond the first user cluster, Parents-Children, following the core objective of gender-inclusive awareness. Yet, there is a need to understand the effect of the same in the longer duration. The exhibition attempts to address the complex concept of societal change. It focuses on trying to measure the perceptions of the participant groups through the local scale with small steps within the larger research plan. The concept of society itself is vast and complex, and it is important to understand the specificity of the local regions where the exhibition would be most appropriate with its best intentions. Although the first iteration of the exhibition includes the dynamics behind testing the artifacts within a safe space, the vital significance relies on the consecutive iterations of the exhibition from secluded places like local villages to big cities all over Portugal. Finaly, the exhibition, with its relevance in doctorate study, critically explores the connections between fundamental phenomena such as objects of play, gender-inclusive development and the concept of awareness for future studies.

9   Conclusion

The exhibition, 'Play and Gender Expression', aims to utilize human interactions to provide a distinct and comprehensive understanding of the implementation of gender knowledge to achieve the holistic development of children. With its multiple mediums and immersive experience, it attempts to motivate the participants towards a space to critique and analyze the connection between multi-layered affordances behind the objects of play, such as toys, and the modes of expression for children [53, 54]. The interventions with Critical Design along with the support of the Inclusive Play Framework take advantage of diverse themes towards the goal of changing and improving perceptions. The implementation of the qualitative data collection technique supports the evaluation phase of the research. The exhibition helps to synthesize insights into the future application of the Inclusive Play Framework, where the core study attempts to measure the qualitative phenomena of gender awareness by quantitative implementation of a gender awareness scale. Finally, the exhibition attempts to conclude by addressing the complexity of gender discrimination, with all of its social, cultural, economic, historical, and political aspects towards an inclusive human cognition [55], which is aware of the long-term consequences behind the betterment of our future generations [56].

Acknowledgments. The research is part of the doctorate (PhD in Design) investigation: 'Social Awareness and Cultural Significance in Designing (Non) Gendered Toys' from UNID-COM/IADE - Unidade de Investigação em Design e Comunicação, with the funding reference no. UIDB/0711/2020. The research project is funded by Fundação para a Ciência e a Tecnologia (FCT) with reference no. UI/BD/152261/2021.

References

1. O'Brien, K., Fitzsimmons, T.W., Crane, M., Head, B.: Workplace gender inequality as a wicked problem: Implications for research and practice. Acad. Manag. Proc. **2017**(1), 14717 (2017). https://doi.org/10.5465/ambpp.2017.14717abstract
2. Li, R.Y., Wong, W.I.: Gender-typed play and social abilities in boys and girls: are they related? Sex Roles **74**(9–10), 399–410 (2016). https://doi.org/10.1007/s11199-016-0580-7
3. Liben, L.S., Schroeder, K.M., Borriello, G.A., Weisgram, E.S.: Cognitive consequences of gendered toy play. Gender typing of children's toys: how early play experiences impact development 213–255 (2018). https://doi.org/10.1037/0000077-011
4. Weisgram, E.S., Dinella, L.M.: Gender typing of children's toys: How early play experiences impact development (2018). https://doi.org/10.1037/0000077-000
5. Holmes, R.: Children's play and culture. Scholarpedia **8**(6), 31016 (2013). https://doi.org/10.4249/scholarpedia.31016
6. Huang, C., Lamb, M.E.: Are Chinese children more compliant? Examination of the cultural difference in observed maternal control and child compliance. J. Cross Cult. Psychol. **45**(4), 507–533 (2013). https://doi.org/10.1177/0022022113513652
7. Brown, C.S., Stone, E.A.: Environmental and social contributions to children's gender-typed toy play: the role of family, peers, and media. Gender typing of children's toys: how early play experiences impact development. 121–140 (2018). https://doi.org/10.1037/0000077-007
8. Boe, J.L., Woods, R.J.: Parents' influence on infants' gender-typed toy preferences. Sex Roles **79**(5–6), 358–373 (2017). https://doi.org/10.1007/s11199-017-0858-4
9. Kollmayer, M., Schultes, M., Schober, B., Hodosi, T., Spiel, C.: Parents' judgments about the desirability of toys for their children: associations with gender role attitudes, gender-typing of toys, and demographics. Sex Roles **79**(5–6), 329–341 (2018). https://doi.org/10.1007/s11199-017-0882-4
10. Weisgram, E.S., Bruun, S.T.: Predictors of gender-typed toy purchases by prospective parents and mothers: the roles of childhood experiences and gender attitudes. Sex Roles **79**(5–6), 342–357 (2018). https://doi.org/10.1007/s11199-018-0928-2
11. Mitrović, I., Auger, J., Hanna, J., Helgason, I.: Beyond speculative design: past, present – Future (2021)
12. Herriott, R.: What kind of research is research through design? (2019)
13. Rich, M.: Student research in a web 2 world: learning to use new technology to gather primary data. Electron. J. Bus. Res. Methods **9**(1), 78–86 (2011)
14. Dhibar, A., Gonçalves, E., Gorgel, A.: Social awareness and cultural significance in designing (Non) gendered toys. In: Proceedings of Senses and Sensibility Conference (2021)
15. Niedderer, K., Clune, S., Ludden, G.: Design for Behaviour Change: Theories and Practices of Designing for Change. Routledge, London (2017)
16. Holmes, K.: Mismatch: How Inclusion Shapes Design. MIT Press, Cambridge (2020)
17. Martin, C.L., Ruble, D.N.: Patterns of Gender Development. PMC (2013). https://doi.org/10.1146/annurev.psych.093008.100511
18. Dhibar, A., Gonçalves, E., Gorgel, A.: Inclusive play framework for children and parents: a tool to promote awareness about gender neutral play through toys. In: International Toy Research Association (ITRA) Conference (2023)
19. Portugal mais Igual. CIG, 22 August 2023. https://www.cig.gov.pt/estrategia-nacional-para-a-igualdade-e-a-nao-discriminacao-2018-2030-portugal-igual/
20. Gender equality index 2020: Portugal. (n.d.). European Institute for Gender Equality. https://eige.europa.eu/publications-resources/publications/gender-equality-index-2020-portugal
21. Gender equality index 2022: The COVID-19 pandemic and care. (n.d.). European Institute for Gender Equality. https://eige.europa.eu/publications/gender-equality-index-2022-covid-19-pandemic-and-care

22. Schouten, M.: Undoing gender inequalities: Insights from the Portuguese perspective (2019)
23. Brito, R., Dias, P., Oliveira, G.: Young children, digital media and smart toys: How perceptions shape adoption and domestication. Br. J. Edu. Technol. **49**(5), 807–820 (2018). https://doi.org/10.1111/bjet.12655
24. Cardoso, A.P., Correia, L., Rodrigues, P., Felizardo, S., Lopes, A.: Traditional toys and student motivation and commitment in technological education. In: European Proceedings of Social & Behavioural Sciences (2016). https://doi.org/10.15405/epsbs.2016.11.6
25. Cordazzo, S., Vieira, M., & Almeida, A. (2012). PORTUGUESE AND BRAZILIAN CHILDREN'S PLAY IN SCHOOL
26. Mind the gap: Step up for gender equality. APF, 5 September 2023. https://apf.pt/atuacao/projetos/mind-the-gap-step-up-for-gender-equality/
27. Portugal: Most purchased toys 2022. Statista, 20 September 2022. https://www.statista.com/statistics/1337985/portugal-most-purchased-toys/
28. Dunne, A., Raby, F.: Speculative Everything: Design, Fiction, and Social Dreaming. MIT Press, Cambridge (2013)
29. Tharp, B.M., Tharp, S.M.: Discursive Design: Critical, Speculative, and Alternative Things. MIT Press, Cambridge (2019)
30. Lilley, D., Wilson, G., Bhamra, T., Hanratty, M., Tang, T.: Design interventions for sustainable behaviour. Des. Behav. Change. 40–57 (2017). https://doi.org/10.4324/9781315576602-5
31. Kuijer, L.: Practices-oriented design. In: Niedderer, K., Clune, S., Ludden, G. (eds.), Design for behaviour change: Theories and practices of designing for change, pp. 116–127. (Design for social responsibility). Taylor and Francis Ltd. (2017). https://doi.org/10.4324/9781315576602-10
32. Bandura, A.: Social learning theory. Encyclopedia of Criminological Theory (2010). https://doi.org/10.4135/9781412959193.n17
33. Dhibar, A., Gonçalves, E., Gorgel, A.: Inclusive play framework: an approach to promote awareness about gender neutral play in Portuguese Context. In: Design Principles and Practices Conference (2023)
34. Kawin, E.: The wise choice of toys (1965)
35. Piaget, J., Hutchings, M.J., Mays, W.: The principles of genetic epistemology. Philos. Q. **24**(94), 87 (1974). https://doi.org/10.2307/2218298
36. Eysenck, M.W., Keane, M.T.: Cognitive psychology (2020). https://doi.org/10.4324/9781351058513
37. Hinton, P.R.: The psychology of interpersonal perception (1993)
38. Shiraev, E.B., Levy, D.A.: Cross-cultural psychology: critical thinking and contemporary applications (6th ed.). Taylor & Francis (2016)
39. Vaidis, D.C., Bran, A.: Cognitive dissonance theory. Psychology (2014). https://doi.org/10.1093/obo/9780199828340-0156
40. Museu do Brinquedo Português. (n.d.). CM Ponte de Lima. https://www.cm-pontedelima.pt/pages/400
41. ILGA Portugal. ILGA Portugal | Intervenção Lésbica, Gay, Bissexual, Trans e Intersexo Portugal, 15 December 2023. https://ilga-portugal.pt/
42. Arduino. (n.d.). Arduino - Home. https://www.arduino.cc/
43. P5. (n.d.). home | p5.js. https://p5js.org/
44. Dhibar, A., Gonçalves, E., Gorgel, A.: Connect-collaborate-confront: an approach to address and measure gender-neutral awareness through workshop activities. In: Senses and Sensibility Conference (2023)
45. Artifacts. (n.d.). Play and Gender Expression. https://sites.google.com/view/play-and-gender-expression/artifacts?authuser=0
46. Let toys be toys. Let Toys Be Toys, 5 December 2020. https://www.lettoysbetoys.org.uk/

47. Simon, N.: The participatory Museum. Museum 2.0 (2010)
48. Parry, R.: Museums in a Digital Age. Routledge, Milton Park (2013)
49. Evemuseos. Museos para el Aprendizaje Y Educación. EVE Museos + Innovación, August 2024. https://evemuseografia.com/2022/02/24/museos-para-el-aprendizaje-y-educacion/
50. Cómo se comunican los museos, Biblioteca Nacional de España – Eve Museos e Innovación, Spain, ISSN: 3020–1179 (2024). https://evemuseografia.com/2024/02/08/como-se-comunican-los-museos/
51. Griffin, J., Kelly, L., Savage, G., Hatherly, J.: Museums actively researching visitor experiences and learning (MARVEL): a methodological study. Open Museum J. **7** (2005). https://media.australian.museum/media/dd/Uploads/Documents/12718/JGriffin-Paper.718dc80.pdf
52. Chalmers, D.J.: The Conscious Mind. In Search of a Fundamental Theory. Oxford Paperbacks, Oxford, United Kingdom (1997)
53. Weida, C.L.: Gender, Aesthetics, and sexuality in play: uneasy lessons from girls' dolls, action figures, and television programs. J. Soc. Theor. Art Educ. **31** (2011)
54. Gosso, Y., Carvalho, A.M.: Play and cultural context. Encyclopedia on early childhood development (2013). https://www.child-encyclopedia.com/play/according-experts/play-and-cultural-context
55. Norman, D.A.: Design for a Better World: Meaningful, Sustainable, Humanity Centered. MIT Press, Cambridge (2023)
56. The 17 goals. (n.d.). Sustainable development. https://sdgs.un.org/goals

A Study on Tangible Interaction Design for Children Cooperative Learning

Haiyan Li$^{(\boxtimes)}$ ⓘ, Zhuoqing Jiang, Zhonghe Ruan ⓘ, and Min Fan ⓘ

School of Animation and Digital Arts, Communication University of China, Beijing, China
hyli@cuc.edu.cn

Abstract. Cooperative learning is a crucial aspect of children's socio-emotional development. Currently, traditional teacher-guided methods dominate children's cooperative learning, lacking timely and comprehensive feedback and relying on teacher's organization and guidance, while digital applications, constrained by their medium, are of limited help for children's cooperative learning. Tangible User Interfaces (TUI) and intelligent physical objects present new possibilities for children's cooperative learning. We constructed a design model for children's cooperative learning tangible interaction system, proposing corresponding design suggestions to address the previously mentioned issues. Guided by this model, we have developed a tangible interaction-based cooperative learning application for Chinese character learning in children. The system focuses on addressing learning difficulties faced by early readers and the challenges of deliberate cultivation of cooperative learning. Finally, comparative experiment was used to validate the effectiveness of the design recommendations and model, demonstrating that tangible interaction has a more positive impact on children's cooperative behavior and learning outcomes compared to traditional offline learning activities.

Keywords: child · tangible user interface · tangible interaction · cooperative learning

1 Introduction

Cooperative learning is an instructional form where 2–8 students form groups to engage in interactive learning and collectively complete assigned tasks [1]. Cooperative learning is a crucial aspect of children's socio-emotional development. Jean Piaget explicitly points out the facilitative role of cooperative activities among children in cognitive development. From an intellectual perspective, cooperative interactions among children can foster genuine exchange of thoughts and aid in the development of higher-order thinking skills [2]. Cooperative learning is a creative and effective instructional theory and strategy system widely adopted in many countries worldwide. In cooperative learning, individuals learn to empathize, establish personal responsibility, and develop a sense of collective honor, resulting in significant effectiveness in improving the social-psychological atmosphere in classrooms, enhancing students' academic performance, and promoting the formation of positive non-cognitive qualities [1]. As a skill acquired

M. Kurosu and A. Hashizume (Eds.): HCII 2024, LNCS 14685, pp. 295–311, 2024.
https://doi.org/10.1007/978-3-031-60412-6_21

through postnatal learning, cooperative learning in children requires deliberate cultivation through specific educational activities and content. Currently, the cultivation of children's cooperative learning is limited to traditional educational methods, relying on the teacher's instructional level and guidance capabilities, with limited scalability and a lack of real-time feedback and effective data recording methods.

Building on theories related to tangible interaction design and children's cooperative learning, we have constructed a design model for a tangible interaction system for children's cooperative learning. We divided children's learning space into action space and cooperative space, proposing corresponding design suggestions to address the previously mentioned issues. Guided by this model, we developed a tangible interaction-based cooperative learning application for Chinese character learning in children, named Good Friends. The system focuses on addressing difficulties faced by early readers and challenges that can be addressed through cooperative learning. In this paper, we present a comparative experiment involving groups using the tangible interaction-based children's Chinese character learning application Good Friends and traditional learning groups using Chinese character learning cards. Data collection and behavioral analysis were conducted to investigate whether the tangible interaction system has a promoting effect on children's cooperation and learning outcomes. The results indicate that the interactive system using Tangible User Interfaces (TUI) and intelligent physical objects has a more positive impact on children's cooperative behavior and learning outcomes compared to traditional offline learning activities.

2 Background

2.1 Cooperative Learning Theory

Cooperative learning emerged in the early 1970s in the United States and made substantial progress from the mid-1970s to the mid-1980s, being recognized as a creative and effective instructional theory and strategy. Renowned American education commentator Ellis referred to it as one of the greatest contemporary educational reforms. In 2001, the Decision on Reform and Development of Basic Education issued by the State Council of China encouraged cooperative learning, promoting mutual communication and common development among students, fostering mutual growth between teachers and students [3].

According to Piaget, in the cognitive development of children, those aged 2–7 are in the preoperational stage, where thinking is egocentric. It is only in the later stage of this period that children begin to consider others' thoughts. From 7 to 11 years old, logical thinking begins to appear but is still primarily connected to specific events rather than abstract concepts [2]. The transition from the preoperational stage to the operational stage requires deliberate cultivation of children's cooperative learning abilities through specific educational activities and content.

Cooperative learning is considered by Chinese educators, including Wang Tan, as an activity and strategy system guided by teaching goals, organized around heterogeneous groups, and driven by the interactive collaboration of various dynamic factors in teaching, with group achievement as the basis for rewards. Unlike simply grouping students for learning, cooperative learning emphasizes interaction and collaboration among students, allows students to assume individual responsibility while depending on each other through the allocation of the roles, resources, etc. [4]. Traditional teaching evaluation focuses on the individual's position within the overall ranking, emphasizing score-based competition. Cooperative learning strives to establish a new paradigm of "intra-group cooperation, inter-group competition," shifting the focus of evaluation from encouraging individual competition to promoting cooperative achievement.

Tangible User Interfaces offer the potential to facilitate cooperative learning. Schneider investigated how a Tangible User Interface could influence the performance of groups in a problem-solving task with Tinker, a learning environment developed for apprentices in logistics [5]. Results showed that tangibility helped groups perform the task better and achieve a higher learning gain. Compared to groups using multitouch interfaces, groups using the tangible interface collaborated better. Through the similar logistics learning task, Son investigated the effects of a TUI in Collaborative Learning of a classroom setting [6]. The study compared a tangible user interface against the traditional way of studying using paper and pens in terms of task performance and learning outcomes. The tangible condition resulted in better task performance.

2.2 Researches on Tangible Interaction Design for Child Learning

Tangible interaction is built on physical manipulation, providing rich opportunities for action and embodying the concept of embodied cognition. Combining the cognitive and behavioral characteristics of children with the features of tangible interaction reveals a high degree of compatibility between them. Tangible interaction emphasizes natural and simple interaction methods, bodily engagement in cognitive processes, and contextualization. Natural interaction reduces cognitive load for children while increasing their familiarity with the system, enabling quicker immersion in content learning. Multisensory interaction allows children to perceive through their bodies, combining knowledge with specific perceptual contexts to aid understanding and memory.

In enhancing learning abilities-aimed tangible interaction products, the goal is often to help children understand abstract concepts and symbols through the concretization and tangibility of entities. For instance, PhonoBlocks utilizes a multisensory teaching approach linking visual, auditory, tactile, and kinesthetic representations to assist children with dyslexia in learning phonics [7]. By embodying tangible letters that children can touch, it provides a more concrete cognitive understanding of letter shapes. The built-in light changes also indicate alterations in letter pronunciation, helping children distinguish easily confused letters. Researchers extended this concept to Chinese character learning, designing cards with grooves and corresponding colors(such as making the " ⺿"in green, whcih represent the grass) to assist children in recognizing and memorizing characters through touch [8].

The inherent graspable nature of entities naturally facilitates collaboration in tangible interaction. StretchyStars requires children to move stars on elastic fabric based on game conditions, using explicit cooperative prompts to guide collaboration. For example, requiring two distant stars to move simultaneously to a specified location encourages children to strategize for a common goal [9]. Topobo, an extension of LEGO, adds a driving device, encouraging cooperative assembly and activation to make the toy move [10].

More blocks encourage collaboration among children, prompting them to pass blocks to each other, thinking about how to make an object stand, and contemplate the reasons behind its movement, promoting basic programming and physics concepts. Narrative-based tangible interaction devices encourage children to collaboratively create stories [11]. Different children placing entities with RFID recognition led to corresponding elements on the screen, promoting real-time collaborative storytelling and enhancing language expression, as well as oral and written skills. In 2018, Microsoft's Zanzibar also supported cooperative learning, displaying real-time movements and stacking of objects with recognition on a mat [12]. GrouPen, a TUI prototype integrated into a regular pen, facilitated intuitive interaction for remote collaborative learning, enhanced learning connectedness and engagement across different learning phases [13].

Antle's Child Tangible Interaction Framework (CTI Framework) categorizes existing tangible interactions for children under 12 based on tangible and spatial interaction system features, abstracting into action space and friend space [14]. In another study, Antle emphasized factors in TUI design related to learning activities, constructing the Tangible Learning Design Framework to associate learners, learner behaviors with tangible interaction systems, and learning behaviors [15]. The framework includes taxonomy and corresponding guidelines.

3 Tangible Interaction System Design Model for Children's Cooperative Learning

Following Gill et al.'s classification of children's states during playing TUI games [16], we categorize children using TUI systems for cooperative learning into two groups: participants and collaborators. In the context of children's cooperative learning, we have developed a TUI design model for children's cooperative learning (as illustrated in Fig. 1). It includes:

1. Collaborators, Participants: Collaborators are children actively engaging in tangible interactions, altering the state of the current tangible device through physical manipulation. Participants are children who observe the actions of collaborators, contemplating the relationships between different elements in the scenario through observation and dialogue.
2. Tangible Representation, Digital Representation, Digital Model Processing: Tangible representation involves physically graspable entities representing digital information, establishing a corresponding mapping relationship with digital representation. Digital representation is a non-physical, ungraspable form of representing digital information, offering a flexible and dynamic dimension of information for children, compensating for the physical limitations of tangible representation. Digital model processing refers to the underlying algorithms of the tangible interaction device, determining the coupling and presentation methods between digital and tangible representations.
3. Tangible Feedback: Tangible Feedback 1 and Tangible Feedback 2 are immediate sensory feedback provided by tangible representation after collaborators manipulate the tangible entities, such as changes in physical attributes (position, orientation) visually and tactile feedback. Tangible Feedback 3 represents immediate feedback provided by tangible representation to participants; when collaborators manipulate

the tangible entities, participants simultaneously observe the changes in physical attributes of tangible representation from their own perspective.

4. Digital Feedback: Non-tangible feedback provided by digital representation to both collaborators and participants, which may include audio, video, and other multi-channel feedback methods.

5. Action Space: The scenario where children engage in physical and cognitive actions constitutes the action space. The action space encompasses the tangible interaction device, presented in the model as including tangible representation, digital representation, and the connection between the two. As children's interactions may be related to other children in the same action.

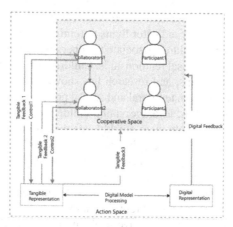

Fig. 1. Tangible Interface Design Model for Children's Cooperative Learning

4   Design Recommendations

Combining the requirement of Cooperative Learning, the cognitive and behavioral characteristics of children, we propose design recommendations for children's cooperative learning tangible interaction systems, as below:

- Configure a safe and easily operable action space and tangible representation. Ensure that the action space is suitable for children.
- Configure an appropriate amount of independently operable tangible inputs. Considering the egocentric cognitive characteristics of young children, setting an appropriate amount of independently operable tangible inputs ensures that each child has an individual tangible input, avoiding unnecessary conflicts and ensuring that each child has the possibility of participating in collaboration. The inclusion of multiple input ports allows the system to support multiple children simultaneously, encouraging children to actively engage in cooperative situations.

- Configure physical attribute design and physical constraints to guide children in corresponding actions. Use physical attributes such as shape and material to guide children in performing corresponding actions with tangible objects. Different input ports with different shapes or colors for physical operations help children understand the relationships between various input ports. Simultaneously, the physical constraints of tangible objects support interaction between children, such as stacking or arranging, assisting children in exploring potential tangible interactions.
- Configure visually readable multi-channel digital feedback and interrelated tangible feedback. Digital representations should use expressions that children can understand, avoiding the use of obscure text. Utilize visually intuitive images, vivid animations, and sound that corresponds to visual content to provide feedback. This helps children perceive digital information from different dimensions and comprehensively understand digital feedback. In situations where multiple children are operating simultaneously, use sound effects or indicator lights to remind others to pay attention to the current operator, helping children associate the operator with the system's feedback.
- Design simple and direct causal relationships. Children often use temporal proximity to judge causal relationships, and research has shown that the causal judgment of young children relies more on temporal and spatial priority than on substantial causal relationships [17]. In design, leverage young children's sensitivity to time by providing instant feedback to help them quickly establish connections between actions and results. Also, due to the developing stage of children's abstract thinking abilities, they cannot handle complex causal reasoning. Therefore, in design, use clear and explicit feedback results to help children understand the relationship between their actions and the system's results, establishing the mapping relationship between actions, tangible objects, and digital representations.
- Design a simple and visually reflective evaluation system. Considering that language expression abilities are not yet fluent in young children, evaluation methods should use a simple and visually accessible approach. Design graphical, interesting evaluation forms, stickers, etc., de-emphasizing the concept of scores, encouraging children to self-evaluate and evaluate others, while maintaining the self-esteem and self-confidence of the evaluated individuals.
- Design enjoyable and collaborative gamified cooperation that downplays failure. In social behavior, symbolic role-playing games are crucial. Use tangible symbols (such as badges, dolls, etc.) and digital identifiers (corresponding to tangible symbols) to assign and set roles for each child participating in collaboration. This allows children to enter cooperative scenarios with role identities. Timely incentives, rewards after challenges, etc., increase children's interest, enhance their enjoyment, and encourage them to take subsequent actions. Depending on the age of participating children, provide encouraging forms of feedback in gamified collaboration. Avoid directly informing children of behavioral errors, downplay failure by setting special achievements, etc., maintaining children's self-esteem, preventing mutual complaints among group members in heterogeneous groups, and encouraging children to participate and experiment continuously.

5   Empirical Study

We applied the previously mentioned design methods to practical design to validate their effectiveness. We developed a tangible interaction-based Chinese character learning application system for cooperative learning among children. Chinese character learning is a crucial aspect of early education for Chinese children. It is essential to cultivate their interest in learning characters alongside the actual learning process. This approach helps prevent children from developing anxiety due to the abstract nature of Chinese characters during the initial learning stages, which is a problem worth exploring. The radical structure of Chinese characters provides a foundation for collaboration. Through tangible interaction and cooperative learning, children can not only stimulate their interest in learning but also utilize multisensory methods to memorize characters. In collaboration with peers, children reinforce knowledge through cooperation, help each other learn new characters, and reduce dependence on adults, fostering children's abilities for independent and cooperative learning.

5.1   Design Requirements Analysis

After analyzing existing offline Chinese character learning tools, such as "Magic Chinese Characters" cards, and online Chinese character learning apps like "Hongen Literacy" designed for children aged 3 to 8, we identified the requirements of children's cooperative character recognition learning as follow:

- Chinese characters Learning: The primary function is to ensure that children learn the meaning, pronunciation, and word composition of Chinese characters.
- Mutual evaluation: The evaluation system reflects the cooperative situation among children. By guiding children to review their own and others' actions, it helps them consolidate learned characters and encourages reflection on oneself and understanding of others.
- Encourage collaboration: Cooperative learning encourages children to learn through positive interaction with peers. By providing cooperative guidance and explicit cooperation requirements, children engage in cooperative behaviors, progress together with peers, and develop social skills.

Based on the above design requirements, we designed the " Good Friends" tangible interaction application for cooperative character recognition using a spelling approach. This application allows children with individual character to find friends for combined character, while also encouraging children themselves to become friends through collaboration. The application consists of several left-right structured parts of Chinese characters, corresponding recognizers, LED lights for tangible feedback, and a display screen for digital feedback.

5.2 Application Functional Module Design

There are four modules in Good Friends:

1. Character combination: Children can find good friends for the physical characters in the application by combining in pairs. The natural way of splitting characters for combination naturally provides possibilities for cooperation. Meanwhile, different characters may have one or more correct combination methods, helping children explore continuously in cooperation.

2. Cooperative challenges: Design gamified levels that require different team sizes to promote cooperation among children, which helps children progressively learn new knowledge during the game and encourages them to interact with multiple children, fostering their social development.

3. Character interpretation: When a child places any tangible character on the recognizer, the corresponding meaning image will be displayed on the screen. If the correct character is formed, the interpretation picture of the corresponding combined character will be displayed at the same time. The images are mainly of figurative things to ensure that children can quickly understand the meanings.

4. Evaluation and review system: Design guidance for self and peer evaluations to help children reflect on the behavior process. Mutual evaluation guides children to pay attention to others' behaviors. Through reflection, children can review the characters they have learned and assess their learning effectiveness.

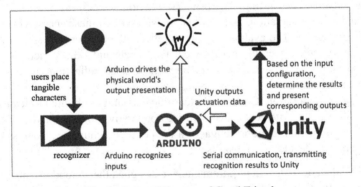

Fig. 2. System Diagram of Good Friends

The system diagram is shown in Fig. 2, where users place tangible characters on the recognizer, and the corresponding content is displayed on the screen. The dashed box represents the physical part of the system, and the screen content is the digital part. The connection between the physical part and the digital part is achieved using the Arduino microcontroller, and the digital display part is implemented using Unity3D.

5.3   Design and Implementation of Tangible User Interface

Tangible user Interface Design involves the design of tangible Chinese characters and insertion devices. In tangible interface design, it is crucial to focus on specific design recommendations that leverage the characteristics of tangible elements, enabling children to engage in cooperative learning through natural interaction.

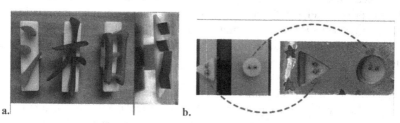

Fig. 3. (a)Tangible and Colored Chinese Character Left Radical, (b) Base Encapsulation and Grooves

1. Configuration of Safe, User-friendly, and Independently Operable Tangible Chinese Characters

   In the design of tangible components, tangible Chinese character components that are easy to grip for children are designed, and interaction is facilitated by placing them in corresponding grooves. Multiple left and right radicals are designed. Children can to observe and try operating the tangible Chinese character components in their hands, thereby reducing cognitive load in subsequent cooperative activities caused by the operation itself. In terms of groove design, four access points are provided as technical support for simultaneous operation by four children, ensuring the possibility of collaboration. The tangible Chinese character components and groove devices, designed and handled for safety and robustness, are depicted in the illustration in Fig. 3.

   Configuring Physical Constraints to Guide Children's Operations and Understanding.To express certain meanings on tangible Chinese characters as much as possible, colors representing meanings are applied to left radicals such as the water radical, wood radical, and sun radical. As shown in the front view of the left radical in Fig. 3(a), the water radical is colored blue to represent the lake, the wood radical is colored green to represent the tree, and the sun radical is colored red to represent the sun. This provides children with a more intuitive radical interpretation, helping them understand the meaning of the characters.

   Different-shaped bases are designed to guide operations, indicating that children should place bases of different shapes in corresponding grooves, as shown in Fig. 3(b). The specific angle of the triangular base acts like an arrow, providing children with guidance to align the groove and place the base correctly. The triangular base also implies a certain association between the left and right of the radical, helping children understand that compound characters result from the combination of radicals.

2. Configuring Tangible Devices for Offline Reflection and Review

Allowing children to freely combine tangible Chinese characters offline helps them autonomously review previous compound character learning experiences. This encourages children to reflect on their behavior and complete knowledge reviews. Children can continue to place tangible characters in the grooves, facilitating shape characteristic review and enabling them to predict results based on previous learning experiences (when the light will illuminate or when digital feedback will appear). This thinking process helps children deepen the establishment of mapping relationships.

3. Configuring Visual Evaluation Using Tangible Stickers

Considering the limited expressive abilities of children learning Chinese characters, star stickers are used as a visual means for self-evaluation and peer evaluation.

4. Configuring Physical Constraints to Guide Chinese Character Combinations

Physical constraints using different base shapes and the width of Chinese characters guide cooperative behavior among children. Two different shapes of bases imply that children must find another child holding a base of a different shape to form a Chinese character. Additionally, bases with different widths provide an intuitive classification of Chinese character radicals, visually guiding the differentiation between left and right components. The groove device also guides cooperation through physical constraints. As shown in Fig. 4, each group of triangular grooves points to circular grooves, indicating that these two grooves belong to the same group and guiding children in the same group to combine Chinese characters. Visually, groupings are indicated through embellishments and front-side LED lights, helping children establish the relationship between lights and characters.

5. Configure tangible feedback associated with digital feedback.

LED lights are placed on the front side of each group's groove. When children successfully piece together a compound character, the light turns on. If the compound character is not successfully formed, or if only one character is placed in the groove, the light will flash, prompting children to continue the process. The illumination and flashing of the lights correspond to the output in the digital interface. This also provides a clearer and more visible indication for children, both as collaborators and participants, to perceive the results of others' actions.

Fig. 4. The grooves

5.4   Design and Implementation of Digital Interface

The design of the digital interface includes feedback design and level description design. The digital interface provides children with richer information, supplementing the tangible Chinese characters with more diverse and dynamic information beyond the character form through a multi-channel feedback format.

Fig. 5. The Interface for Character Meaning

1. Configure visually readable digital representations

    The interface design for digital presentation should intuitively display the most important content—character meanings, minimizing the frequency of text and using graphic images that are understandable to children, as shown in Fig. 5. The images on the left and right sides of the interface correspond to the arrangement of tangible objects, and the yellow pattern below the characters in the image corresponds to the shape of the tangible Chinese characters. This deepens children's impressions, offering them a "what you see is what you get" digital feedback, helping them establish an intuitive mapping relationship between tangible objects and numbers.

2. Configure audio interpretation and multi-channel digital feedback for images.

    Multi-channel digital feedback engages children's multisensory connections, helping them concentrate. Considering that children are novices in learning characters, not having the ability to rapidly read and comprehend sentences and paragraphs, the digital feedback should be designed based on children's concrete thinking. It should primarily consist of images and videos with audio as a supplementary element for level instructions and character meanings, allowing children to understand from both visual and auditory perspectives.

3. Establish a rich reflection and evaluation system.

    After completing a level, a trophy animation is displayed to remind children of their accomplishment, encouraging them to reward their team members with stars for mutual encouragement. In the second level, introduce levels titled "Think about it" and "Praise each other" are introduced as a diverse evaluation system to help children conduct reviews and mutual evaluations. This not only helps children solidify knowledge, but also reminds them to pay attention to others' behavior in cooperation, fostering more positive interactions in the next collaboration.

4. Design levels with different cooperation rules and special error prompt methods.

    The application consists of two levels: the first level involves pairs of two, and the second level involves groups of three, utilizing various team formations to motivate children and also. When a child makes a spelling mistake, considering the establishment of children's self-esteem, the error prompt is designed as an encouraging interface. It presents a silver medal interface indicating the attainment of the "Little Inventor Award" and uses audio to explain to the child that the combination of characters does not exist, encouraging them to continue trying and cooperatively create the correct combination.

6 Preliminary Evaluation

To test whether the tangible interaction application implemented following design recommendations, has a promoting effect on children's cooperation and learning outcomes, three research questions were formulated and validated through a controlled experiment:

- RQ1.Does the tangible interaction application improve children's learning outcomes compared to traditional games?
- RQ2.Does the tangible interaction application increase children's engagement compared to traditional games?
- RQ3.Do children learning through the tangible interaction application exhibit richer cooperative behavior?

Experimental data were collected through video recordings, observation, pen-and-paper records, and user interviews. After analysis, experimental results are derived. The experiment involved two groups: the tangible interaction system learning group (experimental group - Group A) and the card game learning group (control group - Group B).

6.1 Experimental Design

1. Participants

As a preliminary evaluation, 16 participants were selected from the senior class of a public kindergarten, aged 5–6 years, including 4 boys and 12 girls. Before the experiment, the children's general character recognition abilities were assessed through inquiries with teachers.

The grouping of test members is as follows: Group A, the experimental group, divided into two subgroups (A1 and A2), each consisted of 4 children engaging in the tangible interaction game; Group B, the control group, divided into two subgroups (B1 and B2), each consisted of 4 children participating in the card game. For easy recording, test members were sequentially numbered. The member information includes three aspects: gender-age-character recognition ability. L0 represented relatively weaker character recognition ability, while L1 represented relatively stronger character recognition ability. See Table 1 for specific details.

2. Procedure

The experiment started with the card game learning Subgroup B1, and Subgroup B2 repeating the experiment.; then Subgroup A1 engaged in the tangible interaction system, while Subgroup A2 repeated it.

Table 1. Identification Numbers and Character Recognition Abilities of the Children

Group A1	A1–1	A1–2	A1–3	A1–4
Member Information	Boy-5-L0	girl-6-L1	Girl-6-L1	Girl-5-L0
Group A2	A2–1	A2–2	A2–3	A2–4
Member Information	Boy-5.5-L0	girl-5.5-L1	girl-5.5-L0	girl-5.5-L0
Group B1	B1–1	B1–2	B1–3	B1–4
Member Information	Boy-5-L0	girl-6-L1	Girl-6-L1	Girl-6-L0
Group B2	B2–1	B2–2	B2–3	B2–4
Member Information	Boy-5-L0	girl-6-L0	Girl-6-L1	Girl-5-L1

Each experimental session for 4 subgroups lasted approximately 60 min: 5 min for a brief introduction and explanation of the game, 15 min for the first level, 5 min for evaluation, 20 min for the second level, another 5 min for evaluation and 10 min for the final review.

Group B: Initially,4 children chose either left- or right-radical cards, 2 children each selected one left-radical card from "氵" and "木," and 2 children each selected one right-radical card from "每" and "青." and the teacher read the character on each card aloud. Then, a child holding a left-radical card stepped forward and asked the other children, "Who is my good friend?". If the others believed that the two could combine a character, they responded with "I am your good friend," and they went to the teacher for verification. If correct, the next child continues. Completing two characters represented the completion of the first level, and the children rewarded their successfully paired teammates with star stickers. Subsequently, in the second level, 2 additional left-radical cards "日" and "亻" and right-radical cards "目" and "白" were added. Children freely asked and found 4 different Chinese characters to complete the task. After completing the second level or when the 20-min timer expired, the review phase began. The children were asked about the character combinations they had just learned. Five minutes later, they entered the mutual evaluation phase, where they evaluated their own and others' behavior.

Group A: The 4 children chose either "left-radical" or "right-radical" 3D tangible characters. After the teacher read each child's tangible character, the first level began. The children watched an instructional video for the first level and placed the tangible characters into the corresponding grooves. After completing the matching of two characters, they rewarded their successfully paired teammates with stickers and proceeded to the second level. Successfully combining four characters in the second level represented completing the challenge. Following this, they entered the "think about it" phase for review, asking the children if they remembered the characters from earlier. Five minutes later, they entered the "praise" phase, where the children evaluated their own and others' behavior.

3. Data Collection and Analysis

To address the research questions, the completion time for each level was timed, and data on the number and content of characters remembered by each child were recorded. For Group A, the number of tangible characters placed, and for Group B, the number of inquiries made to others, were recorded as indicators of children's engagement. For evaluating children's cooperative behaviors, we utilized video recordings and observation notes to collect data on their cooperative actions.

6.2 Result

1. The tangible interactive cooperative literacy application effectively helps children improve learning effectiveness: The experimental timing results show that children in Group A completed the two levels faster than those in Group B. Group A had an average completion time of 1 min for the first level and 4 min for the second level, while Group B had an average completion time of 4 min seconds for the first level and 7 min for the second level. After the two levels, the teacher inquired about each group's children's learning of characters. It was found that 87.5% of the children in Group A recognized the characters they assembled, while 50% of the children in Group B did. 75% of the children in Group A recognized the characters assembled by the other two members in the group, while this percentage was 25% for Group B. This indicates that children in Group A not only focused on the tangible characters in their hands but also showed interest in characters assembled by other children in the group.

2. Tangible interactive applications have a positive effect on increasing children's engagement: During the two cooperative learning phases, Group A children continuously attempted to place their radicals in the device's grooves, confirming the results by watching the displayed digital content on the screen. In two rounds of experiments, the average placement frequency for the eight children was 5.75 times. In contrast, Group B children confirmed the results by asking the teacher after completing the spelling, with an average inquiry frequency of 2.75 times for eight children.

    In Subgroup B1, child B1–1 took away the card of B1–2 for character combination. Child B1–2 was left isolated outside the subgroup and did not attempt to re-enter the subgroup. Throughout the process, B1–2 only observed from a distance, as shown in Fig. 6. In Subgroup B2, four children were observed engaging in quiet discussions among themselves, hesitating to approach the teacher. It required multiple prompts to encourage these children to approach and inquire from the teacher.

    After completing the first level, A1–2 and A1–3, two children with higher character recognition ability in Subgroup A1 actively requested to proceed to the next level, showing high enthusiasm.

3. Children exhibit richer cooperative behavior in the process of learning through tangible interactive applications: Cooperative behaviors were categorized into help, mutual task completion, negotiation. We selected Subgroups A1 and B1 for video observation. The observation and records showed that Subgroup A1 exhibited more cooperative behaviors than Subgroup B1.

    Subgroup A1 visited in sequence and engaged in verbal and action-based negotiation, which was absent in Subgroup B1. Both groups exhibited helping behaviors, but in Subgroup A1, children assisted each other with actions and verbal reminders, likely due to the novelty of tangible interactive applications, encouraging various attempts, and richer feedback.

Both subgroup s exhibited behaviors in mutual task completion. In Subgroup A1, children were eager to place their characters and were not concerned about physical obstacles caused by their positions, thus successfully completing compound characters. As shown in Fig. 7, three children were operating simultaneously but were not concerned about physical obstacles. In the second level, A1–4 actively inquired about completing the second level, demonstrating high attention to level goals. In contrast, Subgroup B1, with B1–3 taking the lead, primarily had B3 searching for the possibility of combining characters. Other children were more detached and needed multiple prompts to participate.

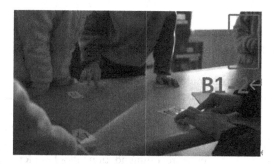

Fig. 6. B1–2 was outside the subgroup and did not attempt to re-enter the subgroup

Fig. 7. In Subgroup A1, three children were operating simultaneously

Combining this observation with the analysis of children's learning outcomes, it is evident that due to the poor learning outcomes of Subgroup B, lacking proficiency in recognizing their own characters, they showed reluctance in actively participating in character combinations. This made it more challenging for them in the second level, where they had to judge four characters. In contrast, Subgroup A, having the experience of placing characters in grooves and receiving feedback, deepened the impression of their peers in the cooperative character placement process.

7 Conclusion

Through the validation of those three research questions, it is evident that the application of tangible interactive cooperative learning does indeed have a positive impact on children's cooperative behavior and learning outcomes. Moreover, children using the application are able to establish a mapping relationship between the tangible and the digital, understand the causal relationship between actions and feedback.

We proposed a design model for a tangible interactive system for children's cooperative learning and provided design recommendations. Based on this, we guided the development of a tangible interactive cooperative learning system for children's Chinese character learning. Our system focuses on addressing the difficulties faced by beginners in character recognition and the challenges of cooperative learning training. The results of our case study indicate that the system is beneficial in improving children's learning outcomes, engaging their participation, and effectively promoting cooperation among children. These findings revealed that Tangible User Interface (TUI) design has a positive impact on children learning Chinese characters at an early stage.

We have only conducted preliminary experiments, and the selected sample size is relatively small. The experimental results cannot yet be considered as comprehensive conclusions. However, we have observed some interesting phenomena, providing valuable insights for future in-depth research. In our upcoming studies, we plan to increase the sample size for experiments and conduct larger-scale controlled experiments to validate the effectiveness of the system. The next steps involve verifying the proposed tangible user interface (TUI) design recommendations in a broader range of children's cooperative learning scenarios and exploring their effectiveness in specific contexts.

Acknowledgements. This work was supported by National Social Science Fund of China under grant [22BG137].

References

1. Liu, J., Wang, T.: The basic principles of cooperative learning (Part One). J. Public Educ. (2004)
2. Piaget, J.: Educational science and child psychology (1981)
3. The decision on reform and development of basic education issued by the state council of China (2001)
4. Wang. T.: On the basic concepts of cooperative learning. J. Educ. Res. (2) (2002)
5. Schneider, B., Jermann, P., et al.: Benefits of a tangible interface for collaborative learning and interaction. IEEE Trans. Learn. Technol. 4(3), (2011)
6. Do-Lenh, S., Jermann, P., et al.: Task performance vs. learning outcomes: a study of a tangible user interface in the classroom. In: EC-TEL 2010: Sustaining TEL: From Innovation to Learning and Practice, pp. 78–92 (2010)
7. Fan, M., Antle, A.N., et al.: Why tangibility matters: a design case study of at-risk children learning to read and spell. In: Proceedings of the 2017 CHI Conference on Human Factors in Computing Systems (CHI 2017), pp. 1805–1816 (2017)
8. Fan, M., et al.: Character alive. CHI EA 2019, pp. 1–6 (2019)

9. Vazquez, V., Cibrian, F.L., Tentori, M.: StretchyStars: a multitouch elastic display to support cooperative play among preschoolers. In: Personal and Ubiquitous Computing (2018)
10. Raffle, H.S., Parkes, A.J., Ishii, H.: Topobo: a constructive assembly system with kinetic memory. In: Proceedings of the CHI Conference on Human Factors in Computing Systems (CHI 2004), pp. 647–654 (2004)
11. Sylla, C., et al.: Investigating the use of digital manipulatives for storytelling in pre-school. Int. J. Child-Comput. Interact. **06**, 39–48 (2015)
12. Villar, N., Cletheroe, D., Saul, G., et.al.: Project zanzibar: a portable and flexible tangible interaction platform. In: Proceedings of the 2018 the CHI Conference on Human Factors in Computing Systems (CHI 2018), pp. 1–13 (2018)
13. Li, Y., Sun, Y., Lu, T.: GrouPen: a tangible user interface to support remote collaborative learning. In: IFIP Conference on Human-Computer Interaction (2021)
14. Antle, A.N.: The CTI framework: informing the design of tangible systems for children. In: Proceedings of Conference Tangible and Embedded Interaction, pp. 195–202 (2007)
15. Antle, A.N., Wise, A.F.: Getting down to details: using theories of cognition and learning to inform TUI design. Interact. Comput. **12**(06), 1–20 (2013)
16. Francis, et al.: Do tangible user interfaces promote social behaviour during free play? A Comparison of autistic and typically-developing children playing with passive and digital construction toys. Res. Autism Spect. Disord. **58**, 68–82 (2019)
17. Li, H., et al.: The influence of inference direction and rule dimension on children's causal reasoning. Acta Psychologica (05) 550–557 (2004)

Exploring the Integration of Light and Music in Artistic Furniture Design: A Study in Interaction Design Informed by Children's Climbing Behavior

Minyu Li[1] 📷, Yuanhan Zhang[2] 📷, and Ao Qi[3](✉) 📷

[1] Chongqing University, No. 174 Shazheng Road, Shapingba District, Chongqing, China
[2] Soochow University, No.1 Shizi Street, Gusu District, Suzhou, China
[3] South China Normal University, No. 55, West Zhongshan Avenue, Tianhe District, Guangzhou, China
18588456977@163.com

Abstract. In the context of ongoing physical and cognitive development, the motor skills of children exhibit a continual enhancement. Notably, climbing behavior emerges as a prevalent learning activity among children aged 9 to 24 months, contributing significantly to the development of various muscle groups. However, owing to the inherent limitations in safety awareness and behavioral capabilities of children, conventional children's furniture often falls short in addressing the imperative of facilitating safe climbing and play. This deficiency renders young children susceptible to potential injuries and hinders their interactive experiences during climbing endeavors. To address this gap, our study introduces an innovative approach in the form of interactive children's climbing furniture equipped with light and sound elements. This design aims to create a secure environment where children can engage in climbing activities while fostering interaction through dynamic elements such as light and sound. The paramount objective remains to ensure the safety of the children throughout these interactive experiences. In a controlled trial involving 11 infants aged 9–24 months, we sought to gauge the acceptance and behavioral responses of children towards this interactive climbing furniture. Comprehensive observations were conducted to analyze and synthesize the outcomes of the trial. The experimental results demonstrated a notable increase in the duration of children's engagement with the interactive furniture, indicating a heightened willingness to accept and joyfully participate in this novel form of interaction. These findings underscore the potential of the proposed design to enhance both safety and enjoyment in children's climbing experiences.

Keywords: Childhood Climbing Behavior · Furniture Design · Interaction Design

1 Introduction

Climbing behavior represents a fundamental motor skill that children progressively master throughout the course of their growth and development. Through a sequence of actions involving "climbing, supporting, pulling, and climbing," children effectively engage various muscle groups, including the back, waist, and abdomen. This not only fosters physical growth but also serves as a catalyst for the stimulation of cognitive abilities in the developing brain. Empirical evidence from pertinent studies underscores the significance of appropriately designed climbing equipment in facilitating safe and controlled play experiences for children. Cao Yanru's investigation into life-oriented movement resources within children's environments revealed that children can interact with soft and comfortable materials, leveraging their senses, perception, and motor abilities [1]. Likewise, Hu Yijun and Wang Danqin's exploration of climbing walls in German kindergartens highlighted their capacity to kindle children's interest in climbing [2].

In the domestic setting, children frequently engage in a spectrum of activities, encompassing "climbing, supporting, pulling, and climbing," utilizing basic furnishings like infant beds, low tables, and chairs. Positioned in the early stages of learning, children undertake a gradual process of acquiring and assimilating pertinent information, subsequently deploying it for the prospective control of actions (Adolph, 2000). This developmental trajectory, marked by a blend of safety and risk, introduces an inherent degree of unpredictability [3]. Consequently, traditional furniture design often falls short in comprehensively addressing the safety considerations paramount to children in both design and material selection. When employed by children to explore their surroundings and engage in climbing activities, traditional furniture inadequately aligns with the physiological demands of such activities, thereby posing inherent risks.

Moreover, the utilitarian aspects of conventional children's furniture tend to be rudimentary, primarily fulfilling basic life requirements but offering limited avenues for interactive engagement. This limitation extends to the inability to cultivate children's curiosity and play desires at the level of interest. In a departure from conventional approaches, Theofanopoulou et al. (2019) devised an intervention strategy underpinned by technology. Smart toys, seamlessly integrated into children's emotional regulation practices, interact with them during moments of seeking relaxation or tranquility. This symbiotic relationship fosters a profound emotional connection between children and smart toys, resulting in satisfaction derived from these interactive experiences [4]. Nevertheless, the landscape of existing interactive toys for children, as critiqued by Lynne Hall and other scholars, reveals a dichotomy. Despite claims of high playability and educational value [5], many interactive toys exhibit inherent limitations in terms of user experience and functionality. This inherent constraint often leads to a reduction in playtime once children master the prescribed play methods. This nuanced evaluation underscores the need for a more comprehensive understanding of design principles that not only prioritize safety but also extend the interactive potential of furnishings, thereby enriching children's cognitive and emotional development.

Given the inadequacies observed in conventional furniture with regards to fulfilling the physical and cognitive requisites of children, our endeavor is to amalgamate the fundamental attributes of children's toys to address the ensuing concerns. In this scholarly pursuit, we intend to delve into the subsequent inquiries:

How can the safety of children's climbing furniture be assured during the design phase?

What methodologies can be employed to intertwine interactive experiences with children's furniture to evoke their innate proclivity for climbing?

What are the discernible behavioral patterns exhibited by children of varying age groups when engaging with interactive climbing furniture?

Hence, anchored in the inherent propensity of children towards climbing, this investigation delineates the conceptualization and development of luminous and melodically interactive children's furniture. Its principal objective is to harness and nurture the latent potential for enhancing children's climbing capabilities while concurrently ensuring the safety and manageability of their climbing endeavors. Furthermore, the integration of a network of interactive lighting conduits within the furniture's framework enables real-time detection of children's movements during climbing activities, facilitating adaptive color alterations that serve to heighten engagement and provide directional cues. Moreover, a suite of musical modules has been meticulously crafted to deliver responsive auditory feedback contingent upon the spatial distribution and intensity of the child's climbing actions. By attending to the dual imperatives of climbing safety and experiential enrichment, the synergistic interplay of light and sound augments the enjoyment derived from the climbing process, thereby fostering enhanced cognitive development and holistic growth in children.

2 Related Work

2.1 Safety Considerations in Children's Furniture

The safety of children's furniture is a critical concern, given the evolving nature of children's body proportions, strength levels, and balance abilities. In the familial context, the movement behaviors of children are notably challenging to control, often manifesting in creative and unpredictable ways. Furthermore, their perception of environmental cues, particularly availability, is not as precise as that of older children, rendering them more prone to opting for riskier behaviors [3].

In a pivotal research experiment conducted by Ulrich, Thelen, and Niles (1990), infants with an average age of 13.3 ± 2.24 months and toddlers with an average age of 20.5 ± 2.30 months were selected. The study focused on observing climbing behaviors across three sets of stairs with varying heights—3 in., 6 in., and 12 in., respectively. The findings revealed that 41% of younger infants opted to climb directly to the top, contrasting with only 16% of older infants who made a similar choice. The remaining participants engaged in diverse actions within the stair intervals [6]. Consequently, the nuanced behaviors exhibited by infants and toddlers are contingent not merely on their physical size but more significantly on their cognitive experiences. Considering that infants often lack specific experiences within the home environment, their behaviors tend to carry a heightened probability of being potentially dangerous and unsafe. Unfortunately, traditional home environment designs frequently overlook crucial factors essential for ensuring the safety of children. This underscores the imperative for a comprehensive exploration of design elements that account for the cognitive experiences of infants and toddlers, thereby fostering environments that prioritize both safety and developmental needs.

2.2   Material Selection for Children's Furniture

The cognitive development of children's brains is situated in the primary stage, accompanied by inherent limitations in cognitive abilities. In their daily interactions with the environment, children commonly employ their mouths and hands to explore and perceive objects. Consequently, a paramount consideration in the realm of children's furniture design is to ensure the safety of materials used. Everyday items such as furniture and toys, integral to children's routines, predominantly employ materials like plastic, fabric, cloth, glue (rubber, latex, silicone), and wood. Within the category of plastics, while many offer advantages such as easy cleaning and disinfection compared to alternative materials, some plastics may pose potential harm to children [7].

Furthermore, Ani N. Shabazian and Caroline Li Soga emphasize that the functionality of materials and their corresponding tactile attributes are fundamental considerations in the design process [8]. For instance, materials like wood and plush fabrics serve the basic function of attenuating environmental noise to a certain extent. In terms of tactile experience, considering plush toys as an exemplar, diverse textures in hair or fabric can evoke rich tactile sensations in children, contributing to the cultivation of their perceptual abilities. Actions like holding, pinching, and fiddling during play are conducive to muscular development. Therefore, it becomes evident that leveraging the functional and tactile characteristics of materials in the design of children's furniture is crucial, facilitating an enhanced user experience for children while concurrently ensuring their safety. This dual consideration underscores the necessity of a meticulous approach to material selection and design in the context of human-computer interaction, particularly within the domain of children's furniture.

2.3   Interactive Constraints in Children's Toys

Toys that facilitate interaction with children serve as essential mediums for their worldly experiences, skill development, and cognitive training. Conventional toys for children encompass items such as soft books, large blocks, plush toys, and simple puzzles. Basic toys enable guardians to engage in uncomplicated interactive activities with children. A notable example is Gabriel Guyton's examination of building block toys, where children employ manual dexterity to stack them vertically or arrange them horizontally, fostering an initial exploration and comprehension of spatial relationships [9]. Doris Pierce et al.'s investigation into infant growth and development revealed that, by the age of 9 months, children exhibit a keen interest in adult technologies, such as the auditory stimuli produced by cabinet switches, television sounds, and telephones [10]. Furthermore, young children often seek comfort in plush blankets when fatigued or distressed. Consequently, the design of children's furniture should meticulously consider the mobility of sound, material attributes, and interactive modalities catering to children's sensory experiences.

Given the inherent curiosity and exploratory nature of children, their behaviors manifest in considerably unpredictable ways. Conventional furniture designs, prevalent today, often fall short of meeting the safety requirements associated with children's activities. Additionally, the selection of materials for children's furniture assumes critical significance, as it is imperative to eschew substances potentially harmful to the human body, ensuring that the furniture poses no threat to the safety of children. In tandem, the functional aspects of materials must be factored into the design considerations for children's furniture. The design process should also meticulously account for the mobility of sound, material characteristics, and interactive modalities to cater to the dynamic needs of children.

3   User Interview

Table 1. User interview record form.

	Problem	Parent evaluation
1	In the family's daily routines, which pieces of furniture does the baby engage with most frequently?	The majority of interviewed parents highlighted that the primary furniture facilitating their babies' interactions consists of cribs and walkers. This preference is attributed to the vibrant assortment of toys typically accompanying these items, including hanging toys that produce sound upon touch
2	Could you describe the preferred behavior exhibited by the baby when using specific baby furniture?	As babies transition into the phase of walking adeptly, parents noted a proclivity for exploring walking and climbing activities, particularly navigating the space between low tables and cabinets. Some infants exhibit an inclination to ascend and descend staircases, utilizing the strength of their limbs. Additionally, parents mentioned their babies' curiosity regarding areas illuminated by sunlight and the soft glow of night lights. Apart from their luminosity, night lights featuring musical functionalities garnered heightened interest among infants
3	How would you characterize the emotional state of the baby during these interactions with furniture?	Emotionally, parents identified pleasure and curiosity as prevalent responses observed during their babies' interactions with furniture. A subset of parents also noted that contact with soft furniture elicited feelings of comfort and security, especially during sleepy moments

(continued)

Table 1. (*continued*)

	Problem	Parent evaluation
4	When it comes to selecting furniture for children, what factors are of primary concern to you?	Given the developmental stage of infants, characterized by limited mobility and increased vulnerability, parents unanimously emphasized the paramount importance of safety in children's furniture. Functionality ranked as the second crucial consideration, with parents expressing a desire for furniture that captivates their babies, fostering meaningful interactions
5	Are there any additional insights or suggestions you'd like to share regarding the interaction between baby furniture and children?	several parents expressed a collective aspiration for children's furniture to encompass a diverse range of functions, thereby sustaining the baby's attention for more extended periods. Notably, seven parents articulated the desire for furniture to possess educational significance, playing a positive and guiding role in the baby's overall growth and development

To enhance the congruence of design with the developmental requisites and preferences of children, the present study engaged in interviews with 11 parents having infants within the age range of 9–24 months. The primary objective of these interviews was to elucidate the nature of interaction between children and commonplace furniture within their domestic milieu. Prior to the interviews, a comprehensive overview of the interview's purpose and intent was provided to the participants, followed by individualized 15-min interviews. The ensuing section encapsulates the consolidated assessment articulated by the participants in response to the posed inquiries (Table 1):

The interview synthesis elucidates that baby cribs and walkers emerge as the predominant choices in the realm of children's interactive furniture, characterized by a diverse array of colors and auditory stimuli. The incorporation of musical functions consistently proves efficacious in enticing infants to engage in playful activities. Primary infant behaviors observed encompass crawling, standing, and navigating vertical spaces, aligning with the distinct stages of physical development. Emotionally, the predominant states manifested by infants are characterized by pleasure and curiosity, indicative of the inherent appeal of the interactive furniture under scrutiny. Safety and functionality stand out as the paramount criteria influencing the decision-making process among respondents. In terms of prospective developments in children's furniture, the majority of participants express a collective aspiration for heightened functionality, coupled with a pronounced emphasis on the educational and guiding dimensions. Respondents envision children's furniture as not merely utilitarian but as instrumental tools in stimulating the curiosity of infants and fostering their holistic physical and mental development.

4 Product Design

4.1 Contour Design

The aesthetic inspiration for the interactive children's climbing furniture with light and sound draws from the Taihu stone featured in classical works from the Northern Song Dynasty. Taihu stone, a natural outcome of rock extrusion, cracks, and extensive weathering, is predominantly found in the Taihu region of Jiangsu Province, China (see Fig. 1). Renowned for its naturally formed landscape images on the surface, Taihu stone has been traditionally employed in the ornamentation of garden landscapes within Chinese garden designs. Leveraging the visual cues from Taihu stone, the designed climbing furniture incorporates features such as multiple folds, facilitating ease of grip and ascent.

Fig. 1. Schematic diagram of Taihu stone morphology.

The entire furniture unit comprises carpet and climbing components. In the realm of color design, the incorporation of natural elements aims to provide children with an immersive encounter with nature and enhance their overall perception. The climbing section is adorned in the hues reminiscent of Taihu stone, while the carpet section reflects the verdant shades of grass. Structurally, the entrance climbing segment features three entrances and four decorative climbing doors. The carpet, predominantly crafted from natural latex and short plush, combines the softness afforded by latex with the tactile richness of short plush, contributing to a sensorially engaging experience for children. Upon entering designated areas, the carpet responds with a warm ambient glow and emits natural sounds like running water and rustling leaves, synchronizing with the children's footsteps, creating an engaging and captivating ambiance (see Fig. 2).

Concerning the wall design, we meticulously mitigate the original protrusions of Taihu stone, eliminating sharp edges. Retaining the stone's characteristic features, we introduce contoured blocks to the surface, minimizing the risk of bumps and injuries for children. Additionally, on the rear sides of the wall, we incorporate gentle slopes without gaps, accompanied by climbing handles spaced at approximately 17 cm intervals, catering to the varied physical abilities of children. These handles enable larger children to climb and play, while the lowest handle facilitates assistance for smaller children in standing and walking.

4.2 Security Guarantee

In the context of shape design, a rounded corner approach is implemented at the pivotal junctions between each block surface to mitigate the likelihood of injury to children caused by the sharp edges commonly found in conventional household corners.

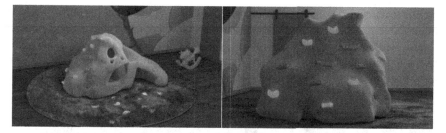

Fig. 2. Product renderings and side views.

Concerning size and positioning considerations, the access hole nearest to the ground is designated with a diameter ranging between 38 and 42 cm. This positioning guarantees the safety of children as they crawl into the furniture, while the specified size ensures that children of various dimensions do not encounter difficulties or entrapment during play. The dimensions of the four decorative holes at higher levels are confined within the range of 3–16 cm, a measure intended to prevent situations where children might inadvertently drill into confined spaces or experience accidental falls post-drilling. Additionally, the carpet, featuring a prototype diameter of 310 cm, is instrumental in enabling young children to mitigate impact forces across a broad spectrum of movements, contributing to a safer play environment (see Fig. 3).

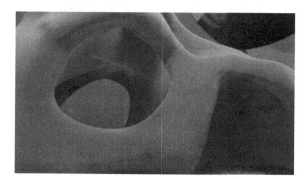

Fig. 3. Furniture entrance design.

The material selection process is primarily bifurcated into two components. In the realm of carpet materials, our preference leans towards short plush fabric as the direct contact surface for children. This choice is driven by its superior ability to mitigate the risk of aspiration and ingestion compared to traditional plush materials, while also offering enhanced convenience for parental cleaning routines. Beneath the contact surface, a 2.5 cm thick layer of natural latex is positioned to serve as a shock-absorbing barrier, providing protective cushioning in scenarios where children may inadvertently fall or trip.

Regarding the climbing elements and handle design, polyethylene and polypropylene are identified as the primary internal materials. The carpet surface is equipped with a short pile to dampen the impact of young children's movements. These materials exhibit commendable resistance to both impact and tension, meeting stringent environmental standards while maintaining structural integrity even amidst vigorous play. This robust construction not only prioritizes safety but also fosters an environment conducive to healthy play for children (Fig. 4).

Fig. 4. Carpet and handle design.

4.3 Interactive Programming

To ensure a rich experiential environment for children of all ages, we have implemented an interactive design involving light and sound within the carpet component. LED beads, pressure sensors, sound modules, and wiring are strategically positioned within the spaces between the carpet latex and pile layer, encapsulated within silicone sleeves designed to accommodate various footprint shapes while safeguarding the internal electronics. When a child steps on the carpet, the pressure sensor detects the footprint's location and transmits the signal via wiring to the controller. Upon receipt, the controller executes programmed responses by activating specific LED clusters and corresponding sound effects. For instance, when a child steps on a designated area, the controller triggers the corresponding LED beads to illuminate and emit a specific sound effect.

Moreover, installation entails positioning a controller in one corner of the carpet, linking the controller's input port to the pressure sensor lead and its output port to the LED light bank and sound module leads. To maintain aesthetic integrity, wiring is neatly secured beneath the carpet using appropriate fixtures. A power supply is installed in another corner, with its lead connected to the controller's power port. A concealed wire trough is established beneath the carpet to safely house all wiring. Through this meticulous design and layout, our footprint sensing carpet system seamlessly fulfills its function, delivering an engaging experience for young children.

5 Evaluation and Results

5.1 Participants

To evaluate the interaction and behavior of children aged 9 to 24 months with interactive climbing furniture, the researchers employed a controlled trial assessment methodology. Two controlled experiments were conducted, involving a total of 11 children recruited from Chongqing, spanning the age range of 9 to 24 months. The distribution included 3 infants aged 9–12 months, 3 infants aged 13–16 months, 3 infants aged 17–20 months, and 2 infants aged 21–24 months. All participants were in good physical and mental health and encountered the luminous sound of baby furniture for the first time.The study aimed to observe and compare the behavioral responses of children while using conventional furniture (toddler bed, toddler table and chair, toddler sofa) and the interactive climbing furniture under investigation. Additionally, the study examined the duration of their interaction with the respective furniture setups.

5.2 Controlled Trial Evaluation Process

Eleven children, aged 9 to 24 months, underwent a comprehensive controlled trial evaluation process, encompassing the interactive encounters between children and furniture, along with subsequent behavior documentation. Prior to the experiment, researchers engaged in discussions with parents to ensure the appropriateness of the children's physical and mental conditions for their participation in the furniture experience, providing them with a fundamental overview. The specific testing procedure unfolded as follows (Tables 2 and 3):

1. Parents received a basic introduction to the test's purpose, interaction method, and the furniture involved.
2. Parents positioned the child in ordinary child furniture.
3. Commencement of video recording and timer activation to capture time and behavior.
4. When children voluntarily ceased interaction or engaged in alternative behaviors, they were relocated for a 15-min rest period.
5. Subsequently, parents placed the child in the luminous sound-emitting child furniture.
6. Resumption of video recording and timer activation to document time and behavior.
7. Following the child's active disengagement, the experiment concluded with the child being relocated.
8. Video replay ensued, allowing for the observation of children's interaction behavior, modes, and time, culminating in a comprehensive summary.

5.3 Results

The findings elucidate that during the developmental phase of their motor skills, young children exhibit a proclivity towards actively exploring novel avenues. Comparative analysis between conventional children's furniture and interactive counterparts revealed no statistically significant variance in the duration of play engagement among young children. Moreover, minimal alterations were observed in their climbing behaviors across the two furniture types. Notably, children with a greater developmental age exhibited prolonged engagement with interactive furniture, accompanied by a discernible augmentation in behavioral diversity.

Within this cohort, children demonstrated heightened interest in interactive furniture that responded to their actions, particularly favoring interactive features facilitating visual (light) and auditory (sound) engagement. Furthermore, contrasting with their older counterparts, children at an earlier developmental stage exhibited a preference for

Table 2. Children's climbing time record.

	Age (unit: month)	Time spent using ordinary furniture (unit: minutes)	Use interactive furniture for time (unit: minutes)
01	9	7	9
02	9	5	8
03	11	8	5
04	14	5	10
05	15	6	6
06	16	9	14
07	18	5	10
08	20	13	11
09	20	6	10
10	22	5	11
11	24	3	7

individual furniture components, displaying a propensity for localized attention. Correspondingly, their overall engagement in climbing activities was relatively subdued. Conversely, older children displayed a more comprehensive observational approach, engaging in multifarious behaviors characterized by reciprocal play interactions and manifesting a heightened level of concentration.

6   Discussion

In this study, we prioritize the safety of children's use through meticulous material selection, the seamless design of block surfaces, and detailed size considerations. Regarding interactive functionalities, we have devised links involving light, sound, and child engagement. Drawing inspiration from nature enhances children's sensory experiences during play. Simultaneously, the uncomplicated interaction mode facilitates children's familiarity and acceptance. Furthermore, we observed the interactive climbing behavior of children aged 9–24 months with furniture, noting that older children displayed a preference for interactive climbing furniture due to their enhanced climbing abilities. However, the limited sample size constrains the comprehensiveness of our experimental results. Additionally, the richness of interactive links in the proposed design of children's climbing furniture requires refinement. Future endeavors will involve expanding the sample size while augmenting the interactive function design to enhance the degree of interaction. This approach aims to deepen our understanding of climbing furniture design and explore the relationship between children's climbing behavior and interactive furniture.

Table 3. Child behavior record sheet.

	The act of using ordinary furniture	The act of using interactive furniture
01	Initiating mobility by using the guardrail near the baby's bed, taking a few steps, pausing intermittently, and attentively surveying the surroundings	Engaging consistently with the illuminated footprint area through tactile exploration
02	Exploring beneath the baby table, sitting briefly, suddenly standing up, accidentally colliding with the head, followed by an emotional response of tears	Expressing excitement by clapping hands in response to the auditory stimuli of running water
03	Attempting to ascend the guardrail of the baby bed, encountering a fall onto the bed, persisting in efforts to stand after turning over despite previous unsuccessful attempts	Demonstrating forward movement without a specific focus on the environment, relying on hands for support
04	Engaging in a repetitive effort to ascend and transport baby chairs, occasionally stumbling and concluding with a seated position on the floor	Demonstrating exploratory behavior by probing furniture, slapping walls, and moving about the space
05	Maneuvering on the toddler couch, traversing back and forth, experiencing occasional falls, ascending and attempting to scale the rear of the couch	Attempting to ascend, experiencing a fall to the ground without exhibiting distress, followed by further exploration involving furniture
06	Navigating between a bench, table, and children's table, involving interactions with toys, climbing down, and subsequently ascending a chair to engage in seated play	Utilizing a handle for climbing, reaching about one-third of the landing's end, and experimenting with walking between two climbing walls
07	Transporting a baby chair in both directions, utilizing the chair to access the table, orchestrating toy swings to the ground, and engaging in rhythmic interactions with the table's surface	Exploring the tactile qualities of the wall structure, interacting with a handle, and stepping onto footprints to produce auditory feedback
08	Successfully traversing the guardrail from the baby bed to the baby table and chair, followed by a transition to the sofa	Continuing exploratory behavior by drilling into furniture, climbing walls with hand support, reaching two-thirds of a stationary surface
09	Ascending onto the sofa, engaging in dynamic movements and play for a duration	Executing controlled ascents and descents along the vertical plane with the aid of a handle

(continued)

Table 3. (*continued*)

	The act of using ordinary furniture	The act of using interactive furniture
10	Climbing onto a dining chair upon discovering a preferred toy, engaging in play while seated on the chair	Engaging in a playful combination of foot-trotting on carpeted surfaces and vertical exploration by climbing walls using manual dexterity
11	Ascending to the pinnacle of the baby sofa, descending from the high back of the sofa, and subsequently repeating the climbing and sliding sequence	Pursuing dynamic interaction by actively chasing after and responding to luminous footprints in a back-and-forth manner

7 Conclusion and Future Work

We have developed a secure and interactive climbing apparatus tailored to the developmental needs of children aged 9–24 months. This apparatus incorporates illuminative features, including carpet footprints and handles, fostering a spectrum of interactive encounters for children. Simultaneously, the interactive sessions are enriched by ambient sounds mimicking natural elements such as running water and rustling leaves. This augmentation enhances the auditory experiences of children, thereby facilitating improved climbing abilities and fostering holistic physical and cognitive development. Based on the comprehensive analysis of behavioral feedback obtained from the experimental cohort, it was evident that a substantial majority of children exhibited heightened interest and happiness while engaging with the interactive climbing apparatus. Subsequent research endeavors will strategically concentrate on establishing collaborative partnerships with nurseries, early education centers, and allied institutions. This collaborative approach aims to afford a broader demographic of children the opportunity to engage with our interactive climbing apparatus. Through this outreach, we aspire to systematically observe and document the diverse array of climbing behaviors exhibited by children, substantiating the efficacy of our product in promoting and influencing positive climbing behaviors in this demographic.

References

1. Cao, Y.: On the guiding strategies of climbing activities for children aged 30–36 months. Tutoring World **000**(007), 61–62 (2020)
2. Hu, Y., et al.: Sports kindergarten in Germany. Early Childhood Educ. (Educ. Sci. Ed.) **12**, 48–51 (2008)
3. de Matos, R.C.: Environment perception and child safety. Universidade Tecnica de Lisboa (Portugal) (2010)
4. Theofanopoulou, N., et al.: A smart toy intervention to promote emotion regulation in middle childhood: feasibility study. JMIR Mental Health **6**(8), 40–49 (2019)
5. Hall, L., et al.: Still looking for new ways to play and learn…Expert perspectives and expectations for interactive toys. Int. J. Child-Comput. Interact. **31**, 100361 (2022)
6. Ulrich, B.D., et al.: Perceptual determinants of action: stair-climbing choices of infants and toddlers. Adv. Motor Dev. Res. **3**, 1–15 (1990)

7. Wargo, J., et al.: Plastics that may be harmful to children and reproductive health. North Haven, CT: environment and Human Health, Inc. (2008). www.ehhi.org/reports/plastics/ehhi_plastics_report_2008.pdf
8. Shabazian, A.N., et al.: Infants and toddlers: making the right choice simple: selecting materials for infants and toddlers. YC Young Children **69**(3), 60–65 (2014)
9. Guyton, G.: Using toys to support infant-toddler learning and development (2011)
10. Pierce, D., et al.: Informing early intervention through an occupational science description of infant–toddler interactions with home space. Am. J. Occup. Ther. **63**(3), 273–287 (2009)
11. Artemova, L., et al.: The choice of toys by early childhood children. Amazonia Investiga **12**(67), 173–184 (2023)

Effects of Landscape Types on Children's Stress Recovery and Emotion

Chong Liu(✉) ⓘ, Hideaki Kanai ⓘ, Tzu-Yang Wang ⓘ, and Takaya Yuizono ⓘ

Japan Advanced Institute of Science and Technology, 1-1 Asahidai, Nomi,
Ishikawa 923-1292, Japan
{s2120423,hideaki,tywang,yuizono}@jaist.ac.jp

Abstract. This study provides insight into the effects of different landscape types on children's stress recovery and emotion regulation. Sixteen participants, aged 6–15, completed the Trier Social Stress Test (TSST). By assessing children's stress recovery in different landscape types (comprehensive parks, children's parks, urban squares), facial images were obtained to measure their emotions. The MEGVII Facial Emotion Recognition API was used to identify facial expressions, generating a dataset of facial emotion feature variables. Psychological reactions were recorded using the State-Trait Anxiety Inventory for Children (STAI-S) and the Children's Perceived Restorativeness Scale (PRCS-C II). The results indicate that Zhongshan Square, as an urban square landscape space, exhibited the highest recovery potential. The differences in landscape spatial features can lead to significant changes in children's emotions, particularly in terms of "happiness," "calmness," and "disgust." The appropriate proportion of green-leaf trees and shrubs, and increased proportion of sky may further enhance children's stress recovery experience, promoting a sense of "calmness" and reducing feelings of "disgust." "Conversely, landscape spatial features by more trees and shrubs, a smaller proportion of sky is associated with higher levels of children's happiness." This study reveals the different impacts of different landscape types on stress recovery and emotions in children. The findings offer insights for urban planning that consider the health needs of children, providing guidance for landscape designers in urban landscape planning.

Keywords: Landscape Types · Children's stress Recovery · Facial Emotion Recognition

1 Introduction

Urban green spaces are the most important and positive component of urban infrastructure in terms of environmental and sustainability impacts. They provide significant benefits to people's health and well-being, especially mental health, and have a positive impact on the physical and mental health of individuals [1–5]. The research has confirmed that green spaces have a significant impact on improving the physical health and social interactions of individuals [6, 7]. Research evidence has shown that contact with nature and green environments has a multifaceted positive impact on human health and improves well-being [8, 9]. Even brief contact with nature has been shown to yielding beneficial psychological effects within minutes [10], alleviating stress [11], providing individuals with opportunities to recover from the demands of busy urban life, and enhancing feelings of happiness and relaxation [10]. In addition to the psychological benefits, green spaces have also been reported to have a direct impact on physical health, including benefits such as lowering blood pressure [12] and reducing heart rate [13].

In an educational system characterized by escalating pressure and a fiercely competitive societal environment, children are confronted with mounting study stress, social challenges, and family conflicts [14, 15]. These stresses have a serious impact on their mental and physical health [16–19]. Therefore, providing appropriate spaces and settings to promote stress recovery and emotional regulation in children in this fast-paced, high-stress environment has become an important challenge for research and design. Some studies have shown that the natural environment has a positive impact on children's mental health and emotional state [11, 20, 21]. Exposure to nature has been shown to help alleviate stress, improve emotion, and enhance cognitive functions in children. However, current research on the effects of different landscape types on stress recovery and emotional well-being in children is relatively limited. This study uses experiments to assess children's stress recovery and emotions in different landscape types (comprehensive parks, children's parks, urban squares), collecting data on perceived restorative psychological responses and capturing facial images to measure physiological response data. The aim of this research is to understand the impact of different landscape types on stress recovery and emotions in children. The findings of this research contribute to identifying and prioritizing landscape types that offer optimal stress relief for children. These insights can guide urban planning and landscape design, helping parents and educators understand which urban environments are most conducive to children's relaxation and recovery, thereby providing more targeted recreation recommendations.

1.1 Related Studies

The Intimate Connection between Urban Green Landscapes and Children's Physical and Mental Health [22, 23]. Recent studies have illuminated the profound relationship between urban green landscapes and the well-being of children [24, 25]. Natural elements and open spaces within natural environments have been found to aid in the restoration of children's attention and improve cognitive abilities [26]. Interestingly, even mere exposure to images of natural landscapes can provide significant restorative effects. These findings suggest a positive response from children towards green landscapes. Furthermore, individuals exhibit more positive emotions (e.g., friendliness) when viewing urban scenes with trees as opposed to urban scenes devoid of life, expressing fewer negative emotions (e.g., sadness) [27]. For instance, children playing in schoolyards rich in natural elements demonstrate fewer issues related to attention and concentration and exhibit improved cognitive and physical functions compared to those in less natural schoolyards [28]. Thus, children can utilize the beneficial effects of natural landscapes to restore cognitive stress and reduce stress and emotional disturbance. However, there is still limited research on which type of landscape provides better recovery effects for children. Moreover, a majority of studies on children predominantly rely on methodologies like surveys [14, 15, 29], observations, and interviews [30] to explore the impact of natural environments on their health.

To bridge this research gap, our study builds on previous findings, employing both qualitative and quantitative research methods. Psychological data is gathered using the State-Trait Anxiety Inventory (STAI-S) and the Perceived Restorativeness Scale for Children (PRCS-C II). Facial emotion recognition technology is introduced, providing an objective, data-driven method to assess children's emotional states and mitigating biases inherent to subjective evaluations [30]. Through this approach, the primary objective of this study was to examine the potential benefits of different landscape types on children's stress reduction.

The sub-objective was to:

1. To explore whether different landscape types can alleviate stress in children.
2. To explore differences in the effects of different landscape types on children's stress recovery and emotion.
3. To explore the relevance of landscape features to children's stress recovery and emotion.

In an educational system characterized by escalating pressure and a fiercely competitive societal environment, children are confronted with mounting study stress, social challenges, and family conflicts [14, 15].

2 Method

2.1 Data Collection

Stimulus Material. The study was conducted in Dalian, located in the northeastern part of China. Dalian boasts a plethora of parks and urban squares frequented by both residents and tourists. To delve into the restorative potential of different landscape types, we selected Labor Park, Children's Park, and Zhongshan Square as our primary research sites (Fig. 1). These sites each possess unique landscape spatial features, capturing a comprehensive range of public spaces that children might frequently visit in the city, thereby enriching the dataset for our research.

After team deliberations, we established the following filming itinerary and methods:

An experienced photographer was appointed to film using the Gopro Hero11 Black. This camera, equipped with the HyperSmooth 5.0 stabilization feature, can capture stable footage at 25 fps under 4k resolution, with an output quality of 1920 × 1080 HD.

All videos were shot following a standardized length and a predetermined route, with each simulated walking film spanning 5 min. To ensure consistent environmental conditions, filming was scheduled between May 24th and 30th, 2023, during clear and windless mornings. The camera was centrally positioned on the pathway at a height of 1.60 m [31].

The original audio was retained in the footage, minimizing disturbances from other individuals, vehicles, or excessive ambient noise, aiming to replicate a realistic environment.

Fig. 1. Video roadmap and site photos of the landscape space. Base map data © OpenStreetMap contributors.

Participants and Experimental Procedure. Eighteen participants, including 9 males and 9 females, were included in this study. During the TSST, the experiment was terminated early due to 2 children having difficulty with stress. Therefore, we ended up with valid data from 16 (8 male, 8 female) participants. These participants were recruited online and met the following criteria: 1) aged between 7 and 15 years; 2) no physical or mental health problems; and 3) not taking any medication before the experiment.

Children were assisted by their parents during their participation in the experiment. Participants watched three random park movies on a computer, and the order of viewing was randomly adjusted via Excel to eliminate order effects. The overall flow of the experiment lasted approximately 40 min and included the Trier Social Stress Test (TSST), completion of the State Anxiety Scale (STAI-S) before and after viewing the movies, observation of the movies, and completion of the Perceived Restorative Components Scale for Children (PRCS-C II). Each child's participation spanned 3 days, and data collection was completed between July 15 and August 20, 2023. The children's participation in the study was based on the following data collection methods. Parental informed consent was obtained for all children's participation, and the experiment was ethically reviewed by the China National Children's Center. The detailed experimental procedure (Fig. 2), and the entire experiment were video recorded.

Initially, captured frames were taken every 5 s from the videos recorded during the experiment, resulting in a total of 4416 facial photos from both the stress and recovery phases (Fig. 3). These photos were subsequently analyzed using the MEGVII Facial Emotion Recognition API to identify children's facial emotions. Currently, this API can recognize seven emotion types: Happiness, Calmness, Surprise, Sadness, Disgust, Anger, and Fear. Through this process, we successfully obtained a facial emotion dataset.

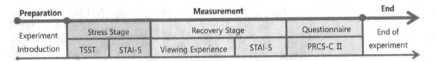

Fig. 2. The procedure of the experiment.

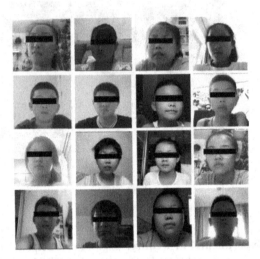

Fig. 3. 16 experimental participants.

2.2 Data Analysis

Data analysis was conducted using IBM SPSS Statistics. For the pre- and post-state anxiety data, a t-test was employed to measure and compare children's stress and anxiety levels. For non-normally distributed facial emotion data, non-parametric tests were employed. The Wilcoxon test was used to compare the extent and significance of emotional changes in children across three different landscape types. Friedman's test was utilized to analyze whether there were significant differences in seven emotional dimensions within the three distinct landscape types. Single-factor analysis of variance (ANOVA) was performed on PRCS-C II data to determine the impact of different landscape types on children's stress recovery. Bivariate correlation analysis was employed to explore the relationship between landscape spatial features and changes in stress recovery and emotions.

3   Results

3.1   Evaluation of Stress Responses and Emotional Changes

Stress Response. Based on the results from the paired sample t-test (Fig. 4), all three landscape types significantly reduced the anxiety levels in children. During the post-stress state and the stress recovery state, there was a significant difference in anxiety scores, and the difference was statistically significant ($p < .01$).

Fig. 4. Changes in STAI-S values from the stress stage to the recovery stage (N = 16, mean ± SEM, *p < .05, **p < .01).

Emotional Change. In this study, we assessed the impact of different landscape types on children's emotional recovery from stress. We compared the emotional changes and significance of three different landscape types in children's transition from a stress state to a recovery state through line graphs and Wilcoxon tests (Fig. 5, Fig. 6, Fig. 7).

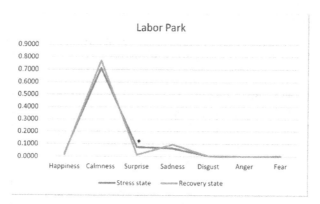

Fig. 5. Comparing changes in children's emotion during labor park stress and recovery states. N = 16, median. * p < .05, ** p < .01, Wilcoxon test.

The results of the Wilcoxon test indicate that, in Zhongshan Square, children exhibited significant recovery effects across four emotional dimensions: "Happiness" (p < .05), "Calmness" (p < .01), "Surprise" (p < .01), and "Disgust" (p < .01). Notably, the significant increase in "Calmness" during the stress recovery state, along with the significant decreases in other emotions, suggests that Zhongshan Square provides an environment conducive to children's emotional regulation and recovery. A slight decrease in "Happiness" during the recovery phase in Zhongshan Square may be attributed to specific environmental factors or the nature of the recovery process. The exact reasons

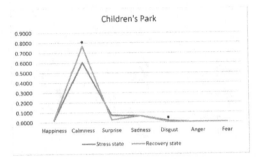

Fig. 6. Comparing changes in children's emotion during children's park stress and recovery states. N = 16, median. * p < .05, ** p < .01, Wilcoxon test.

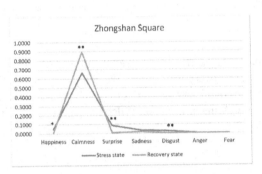

Fig. 7. Comparing changes in children's emotion during Zhongshan square stress and recovery states. N = 16, median. * p < .05, ** p < .01, Wilcoxon test.

for this decrease need to be explored in future research, highlighting the complexity of emotional responses during stress recovery.

In the Children's Park, significant changes were observed in "Calmness" (p < .05) and "Disgust" (p < .05), indicating that the park promotes children's calmness while alleviating feelings of disgust. Changes in "Happiness" (p = .056) and "Surprise" (p = .063) did not reach traditional significance levels, but p-values approaching 0.05 suggest a potential trend, indicating that further research may provide more insights into these two emotional dimensions.

Labor Park showed significant statistical changes in "Surprise" (p < .05). However, the role of "Surprise" as a neutral emotion during the recovery process remains unclear, emphasizing the need for further investigation into this complex emotional response.

Overall, the findings of this study suggest that urban landscape environments have different impacts on children's emotions. Zhongshan Square exhibited the most significant recovery effects across multiple emotional dimensions, while Children's Park and Labor Park also demonstrated positive effects in specific emotional aspects. These insights are crucial for urban planners and public space designers, emphasizing the importance of considering the emotional impact of different environments when creating spaces that contribute to children's psychological well-being.

3.2   Effect of Different Landscape Types on Children's Emotional Recovery

Differences in Perceived Restorativeness Across Landscape Types.   Upon examining the PRCS-C II scores, it was observed that for the landscapes of Labor Park, Children's Park, and Zhongshan Square, all associated PRCS-C II values were positive (Fig. 8). This indicates that children perceived all three landscapes as having a beneficial impact on their psychological recovery. Results from a one-way ANOVA demonstrated significant differences in PRCS-C II values among the three landscapes ($F = 21.894$, $p < .01$). The highest PRCS-C II value was associated with Zhongshan Square, scoring 73.69 ± 1.091, suggesting that Zhongshan Square offered the most optimal recovery effects. This was followed by Children's Park with a score of 68 ± 1.118, while Labor Park showed the least recovery potential, scoring 63.63 ± 1.024.

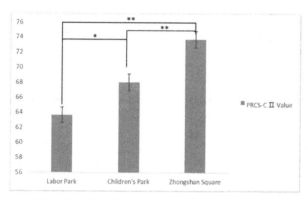

Fig. 8. Comparison of Perceived Restrictiveness of Different Landscape Spaces ($N = 16$, mean $\pm$ SEM, *$p < .05$, **$p < .01$).

Post-hoc tests revealed highly significant differences between Labor Park and Zhongshan Square and between Children's Park and Zhongshan Square ($p < .01$). A significant difference was also noted between Labor Park and Children's Park ($p < .05$). As shown in Table 1, it's clear that children perceive distinct restorative differences across the three landscapes. Specifically, Zhongshan Square stands out with the highest score, showcasing the most favorable perceived restorative attributes for children. This is followed by Children's Park. Labor Park, on the other hand, registered the lowest score, indicating a comparatively diminished restorative effect for children in that setting.

Seven Emotions of Children in Different Landscape Types.   In conjunction with the PRCS-C II assessment, this study combined facial emotion recognition techniques to comprehensively assess the effects of different landscape types on children's emotional responses.

As shown in Table 2, the application of the Friedman test to analyze seven emotional dimensions (Happiness, Calmness, Surprise, Sadness, Disgust, Anger, and Fear) indicates significant differences in the dimensions of "Happiness," "Calmness," and "Disgust" across three distinct landscape spaces.

Table 1. Post-hoc Analysis of Children's Perceived Restorativeness Across Different Locations.

(I) Location	(J) Location	Mean Difference (I-J)	Standard Error	Significance	95% Confidence Interval Lower Limit
Labor Park	Children's Park	−4.375*	1.525	0.006	−7.45
	Zhongshan Square	−10.062*	1.525	<.001	−13.13
Children's Park	Labor Park	4.375*	1.525	0.006	1.3
	Zhongshan Square	−5.687*	1.525	<.001	−8.76
Zhongshan Square	Labor Park	10.063*	1.525	<.001	6.99
	Children's Park	5.688*	1.525	<.001	2.62

Table 2. Emotional Responses Across Different Landscape Spaces: Results from the Friedman Test

Emotion	Labor Park	Children's Park	Zhongshan Square	chi-square	p
Happiness	0.00064(−0.00030, 0.00437)	0.01376(−0.00042, 0.06976) a	0.04352(0.00096,0.07674) a	9.375	.009
Calmness	−0.06059(−0.17958, 0.11550)	−0.06087(−0.20263, 0.02949)	−0.25586(−0.38376, −0.05383) ab	9.500	.009
Surprise	0.00166(0.03295, 0.00296)	0.00852(0.00032, 0.02340)	0.02311(0.00240, 0.07107)	3.375	.185
Sadness	0.00183(−0.07118, 0.06548)	−0.01947(−0.06781, 0.03111)	0.09027(−0.00772, 0.09027)	2.000	.368
Disgust	−0.00166(−0.03295, 0.00296)	0.00852(0.00032, 0.02340)	0.02311(0.00240, 0.07107) ab	9.375	.009
Anger	0.00005(−0.00815, 0.00079)	0.00037(−0.00616, 0.00348)	−0.00033(−0.00506, 0.00320)	1.125	.570

[a] $N = 16$, "a" indicates a significant difference compared to Labor Park, and "b" indicates a significant difference compared to Children's Park, with pairwise comparisons adjusted using Bonferroni correction

Happiness: Significant variations were observed in Happiness levels ($Z = 9.375$, $p < .01$) among Labor Park, Children's Park, and Zhongshan Square. Post hoc analyses indicated that both Children's Park and Zhongshan Square exhibited significantly higher Happiness levels compared to Labor Park ($p < .05$). However, no statistically significant difference in Happiness was found between Labor Park and Children's Park ($p > .05$).

Calmness: Calmness levels demonstrated significant differences ($Z = 9.500$, $p < .01$) across the three landscape spaces. Post hoc analyses revealed that Zhongshan Square displayed significantly higher Calmness levels compared to both Labor Park and Children's Park (p < .05). No significant difference in Calmness was identified between Labor Park and Children's Park (p > .05).

Disgust: The Friedman test indicated significant differences (Z = 9.375, p < .01) in Disgust levels among the three landscape types. Post hoc analyses showed that both Children's Park and Zhongshan Square had significantly lower Disgust levels compared to Labor Park (p < .05). No statistically significant difference in Disgust was observed between Labor Park and Children's Park (p > .05).

In summary, our study findings underscore the impact of different landscape types on children's stress recovery and emotional experiences. Notably, Zhongshan Square consistently emerged as a space that fosters higher levels of happiness and calmness. These results provide valuable insights for urban planning and landscape design, emphasizing the need for environments that positively contribute to children's emotional well-being.

3.3 Landscape Spatial Features and Children's Well-Being

Landscape Spatial Feature Extraction. To analyze the effects of landscape spatial features on children's stress recovery and emotion. In this study, frames from the video were intercepted every 30 s and the proportion of plant and non-plant elements in each photo was calculated, while the background buildings outside the scene were excluded from the statistical analysis due to low relevance to this study. Plant elements were categorized into green-leaf trees, colored-leaf trees, shrubs, grass, and plants. Non-plant elements included water, sky, hardscape, visual dominant elements, and pedestrians. The hardscape included features like a road, gaming facility, parapet, pavilion, and bridge. Visual dominant elements encompassed items such as garbage bins, streetlamps, signboards, seats, pergolas, sculptures, buildings, and stone. Pedestrians included passersby, dog walkers, and other users of the landscape space. Separating animals and pedestrians facilitates the analysis of the impact of these features in the scenes. The obtained images were subjected to image semantic segmentation using the ISAT_with_segment_anything tool[1]. Figure 9 illustrates a schematic diagram of semantic segmentation.

Landscape Spatial Features about Stress Recovery and Emotion. To investigate the relationship between landscape spatial features and stress recovery and emotion. In this study, bivariate correlation analyses were conducted between the quantitative values of landscape spatial features of the three landscape types and the subjects' PRCS-C II scores, happiness difference means, calmness difference means, and disgust difference means. The results are presented in Table 3.

PRCS-C II Analysis: The presence of green-leaf trees (Pearson correlation coefficient = −0.527, p = .002) and shrubs (Pearson correlation coefficient = −0.405, p = .02) were significantly and negatively correlated, suggesting that reductions in the presence of green-leaf trees and shrubs in the landscape were associated with enhanced stress recovery in children. Moreover, sky proportion (Pearson correlation coefficient = 0.434, p = .012) exhibited a positive correlation with PRCS-C II scores. This implies that

---

[1] https://github.com/yatengLG/ISAT_with_segment_anything.

Fig. 9. The overlay of the original image and the image after semantic segmentation.

Table 3. Relationship between landscape spatial features and physiological and psychological recovery effects

		green-leaf trees	colored-leaf trees	shrubs	grass	plant	water	sky	Hardscapes	Visual dominant elements	pedestrians
PRCS-CII	Peason	−.527**	−0.027	−.405*	0.013	−0.246	−0.213	.434*	0.059	−0.003	0.078
	Sig	0.002	0.879	0.02	0.945	0.168	0.233	0.012	0.745	0.987	0.665
Happiness	Peason	−.444**	0.054	−.354*	0.074	−0.254	−0.186	0.337	−0.009	0.012	0.114
	Sig	0.01	0.763	0.044	0.684	0.154	0.300	0.055	0.958	0.949	0.528
Calmness	Peason	.598**	0.142	.442*	0.075	0.212	0.233	−.535**	−0.15	0.023	-0.021
	Sig	<.001	0.432	0.01	0.678	0.236	0.191	0.001	0.403	0.897	0.908
Disgust	Peason	−.431*	0.065	−.345*	0.081	−0.254	−0.182	0.322	−0.019	0.013	0.118
	Sig	0.012	0.718	0.049	0.652	0.154	0.311	0.067	0.918	0.941	0.512

**. Significant correlation at the 0.01 level (two-tailed). *. Significant at the 0.05 level (two-tailed).

increasing the sky proportion may further enhance children's stress recovery experiences. These findings provide valuable insights for designing landscapes tailored to children, emphasizing the importance of specific natural elements in promoting the overall well-being of children.

Analysis of Mean Happiness Differences: Mean happiness differences were calculated by subtracting recovery state data from stress state data. Larger differences indicate relatively lower values during the recovery state, while smaller (or possibly negative) differences indicate relatively higher values during the recovery state. This suggests that the mean differences are negatively correlated with happiness during recovery. Green trees (Pearson correlation coefficient = −0.444, p = .01) and shrubs (Pearson correlation coefficient = −0.354, p = .044) exhibited a significant negative correlation with mean happiness differences. In contrast, an increase in sky proportion (Pearson correlation coefficient $= 0.337$, $p = .055$) showed a significant positive correlation with mean happiness differences. This suggests that a higher level of happiness in children is associated with more trees and shrubs, and a smaller sky proportion.

Analysis of Mean Calmness Differences: Mean calmness differences were calculated by subtracting recovery state data from stress state data. Larger differences indicate relatively lower values during the recovery state, while smaller (or possibly negative) differences indicate relatively higher values during the recovery state. This suggests that the mean differences are negatively correlated with calmness during recovery. Green trees (0.598, $p < .01$) and shrubs (0.442, $p = .01$) showed a significant positive correlation with mean calmness differences, while sky proportion (-0.535, $p = .001$) exhibited a significant negative correlation with mean calmness differences. These findings indicate that reducing the presence of green trees and shrubs and increasing the sky proportion are associated with increased calmness during recovery.

Analysis of Mean Disgust Differences: Mean disgust differences were calculated by subtracting recovery state data from stress state data. Larger differences indicate relatively lower values during the recovery state, while smaller (or possibly negative) differences indicate relatively higher values during the recovery state. This suggests that the mean differences are negatively correlated with disgust during recovery. Green trees (-0.431, $p = .012$) and shrubs (-0.345, $p = .049$) exhibited a negative correlation with mean disgust differences. This suggests that reducing the presence of green trees and shrubs is associated with a decrease in disgust in children during the stress recovery period.

Through an in-depth analysis of the relationship between different landscape spatial features and children's stress recovery and emotional experiences, we draw the following conclusions: in landscape design, a higher proportion of sky, and relatively fewer green-leaf trees and shrubs have a positive impact on promoting children's stress recovery, enhancing calmness emotions, and reducing disgust. The presence of a higher number of green-leaf trees and shrubs, along with a smaller proportion of sky, correlates with children's happiness.

Comparative Spatial Analysis of Landscapes for Children's Well-being. Through the quantitative analysis of spatial characteristics and stress recovery and emotion in Labor Park, Children's Park, and Zhongshan Square, we have gained an understanding of the effects of green leafy trees, shrubs, and sky on children's stress recovery and emotion, while the three landscape spaces have different effects on children's stress recovery and emotion regulation. The results from the one-way ANOVA for each of the 3 landscape spaces Green-leaf Trees, Shrubs, and Sky showed (Fig. 6) (Fig. 10).

For the Green-leaf Trees indicator, there was no significant differences between Labor Park and Children's Park, while the value of Zhongshan Square was significantly lower. ANOVA results showed significant differences between groups ($p < .01$). Shrubs metrics and mean values differed among the three sites. There was no significant difference between Labor Park and Children's Park, while the value for Zhongshan Square was significantly lower. ANOVA results showed a significant difference between groups ($p = .037$). For the Sky metric, the difference between Labor Park and Children's Park was relatively small, while the value for Zhongshan Square was significantly higher. The ANOVA results showed a significant difference between groups ($p = .002$). This

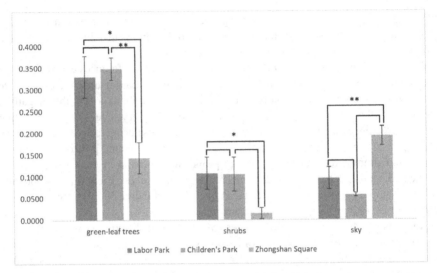

Fig. 10. Comparison of landscape spatial features

comparison reveals that Zhongshan Square has a higher proportion of sky and relatively fewer leafy trees and shrubs compared to Labor Park and Children's Park. These features may be factors contributing to Zhongshan Square's better performance in terms of children's stress recovery and emotional experience.

4 Discussion

4.1 Psychological Reactions

This study highlights the significant impact of different landscape types on children's stress recovery and emotional responses [21, 32]. The selected TSST effectively induced changes in state anxiety and facial emotion recognition. Analysis of PRCS-C II scores yielded that child perceived all three landscapes, Labor Park, Children's Park, and Zhongshan Square, as restorative, which is consistent with the findings of previous studies emphasizing the psychological benefits of green landscapes [33, 34]. However, surprisingly, Zhongshan Square, as an urban square landscape space, exhibited the highest recovery potential, challenging traditional assumptions about the restorative attributes of green spaces. In contrast to traditional green spaces, this comparison suggests that urban landscapes may have inherent restorative properties that were previously overlooked. The study indicates that the proportion of green-leaf trees and shrubs is negatively correlated with PRCS-C II scores, while the sky proportion is positively correlated with PRCS-C II scores. This suggests that an appropriate proportion of green-leaf trees and shrubs, and an increase in sky proportion may further enhance children's stress recovery experiences. These findings provide valuable insights for designing landscapes tailored to children, emphasizing the importance of specific natural elements in promoting the overall well-being of children.

For children, the proportion of green plants is not crucial, but they are more concerned with the openness of space. This aligns with previous research, such as the study by Maryam Allahyar [35], found in a comparative study between children and therapists that children consider coverage to be an unimportant element, while therapists perceive trees as the least important element for enhancing relaxation.

4.2 Emotional Reactions

Happiness. In the current study, the results indicate that different landscape types influence changes in children's happiness. The current findings reveal significant differences in "green-leaf trees," "shrubs," and "sky proportion" about happiness from the perspective of children. Higher levels of happiness in children are associated with more trees and shrubs, and a smaller sky proportion. Similar to our study, Reeve et al. [36] concluded, in a study on the effects of a rehabilitation garden in a children's hospital that patients spending time in the garden reported higher levels of happiness. They also found that the garden provided emotional relief for visitors through appreciating scenic views, being in nature, enjoying time, experiencing therapy, and exposure to outdoor air. Van den Berg et al. [37] compared a park-like forest area with an urban environment and found that parks with a high green view rate generated higher levels of happiness and lower levels of stress, anger, depression, and tension during the recovery period, thereby improving emotion. Some studies suggest that children are particularly fond of water features as they can evoke feelings of joy in children [35]. Although in this study, water features did not show a significant correlation with children's happiness, comparing the features of the three landscape spaces, both Labor Park and Children's Park include water features, while Zhongshan Square does not. This may explain why the happiness changes in Zhongshan Square are lower than in the other two landscape spaces.

Calmness. In the current study, enhancing children's calmness is crucial to stress recovery. From the perspective of children, there are differences in the proportions of spatial features that contribute to increased calmness. Increasing the sky proportion and maintaining an appropriate proportion of green-leaf trees and shrubs are associated with an increase in children's calmness. Ahmad Hami et al.'s research results indicate that open spaces have a positive impact on emotions. They concluded that students prefer areas that are open and spacious based on their preferences for suitable campus landscape patterns [38]. Open green spaces provide opportunities for various activities, and for children, open areas are more important than enclosed ones [39].

Disgust. In the current study, the results indicate that maintaining an appropriate proportion of green-leaf trees and shrubs can effectively reduce children's disgust, positively impacting stress recovery in children. This is consistent with the findings of Simone et al. [40], who investigated the impact of green spaces in the homes of Dutch children on brain structure from birth. They observed a negative correlation between tree coverage density and brain structure in the prefrontal clusters region. In these areas, where trees are more densely concentrated, there may be an adverse impact on the gray matter volume of the prefrontal cortex in children. This suggests that an increase in tree density in these regions may be associated with a negative correlation in the development of brain structures related to cognitive control, emotional regulation, and social behavior in children. In this study, a reduction in green trees and shrubs was positively correlated with a decrease in children's aversion during the stress recovery period. This finding provides design recommendations for creating landscapes that promote positive emotional experiences for children.

4.3 Limitations and Further Study

Due to considerations of fatigue and discomfort that multiple TSST may bring to children, this study focused on the impact of three main urban landscapes on children's stress recovery and emotions. Future research could expand the sample size, including more diverse types of urban landscapes, to comprehensively understand their effects on children. This study initially revealed associations between sky proportion with children's stress recovery and emotional changes. However, future research could further explore the impact of different spatial openness on children's stress recovery and emotional changes.

The limited sample size limits the generalizability of the findings. Expanding the participant group in terms of size and diversity would undoubtedly strengthen the validity of the study. Cacioppo et al. [41] suggested including participants of different age groups to better understand differences in stress recovery. As the current study participants were similar in age, exploring age-related differences was not possible. Future research should extend to populations of different age groups.

This study used video scenes as stimuli, which has advantages in controlling experimental conditions compared to direct on-site experiences. However, participants may not fully engage with scenic scenes solely by watching videos, lacking authenticity and interactivity. Future research could be designed to take participants to actual locations, especially when investigating recovery effects obtained from direct experiences, such as physical activity and social interaction [42, 43].

5   Conclusion

Urban landscapes provide valuable opportunities for improving both the physical and mental health of children. This study, conducted in the Chinese context, reveals the impact of different landscape types on children's stress recovery and emotions. Specifically, increasing the proportion of sky and maintaining appropriate greenery may enhance the stress recovery potential of urban landscapes for children, promoting more "calmness" emotions and reducing the generation of "disgust" emotions, thereby contributing to the enhancement of their emotional well-being. These research findings offer insights for urban planning that consider the health needs of children and provide guidance for landscape designers to create more effective spaces in urban landscape planning. Additionally, this study provides a quantifiable method for researchers and professionals globally to assess how landscape features contribute to changes in children's emotions.

Acknowledgments. This work was supported by the Project of Children's Artificial Intelligence Education Research Institute of China Children's Center (No. CNCCYJY2023010).

References

1. Grahn, P., Stigsdotter, U.A.: Landscape planning and stress. Urban Forest. Urban Green. **2**, 1–18 (2003). https://doi.org/10.1078/1618-8667-00019

2. Kaplan, S.: The restorative benefits of nature: toward an integrative framework. J. Environ. Psychol. **15**, 169–182 (1995). https://doi.org/10.1016/0272-4944(95)90001-2

3. Nordh, H., Østby, K.: Pocket parks for people – a study of park design and use. Urban Forest. Urban Green. **12**, 12–17 (2013). https://doi.org/10.1016/j.ufug.2012.11.003

4. Rodiek S Influence of an Outdoor Garden on Mood and Stress in Older Persons

5. Tsunetsugu, Y., Lee, J., Park, B.-J., Tyrväinen, L., Kagawa, T., Miyazaki, Y.: Physiological and psychological effects of viewing urban forest landscapes assessed by multiple measurements. Landsc. Urban Plan. **113**, 90–93 (2013). https://doi.org/10.1016/j.landurbplan.2013.01.014

6. Allah Yar, M., Kazemi, F.: The role of dish gardens on the physical and neuropsychological improvement of hospitalized children. Urban Forest. Urban Green. **53**, 126713 (2020). https://doi.org/10.1016/j.ufug.2020.126713

7. Maas, J.: Green space, urbanity, and health: how strong is the relation? J. Epidemiol. Commun. Health **60**, 587–592 (2006). https://doi.org/10.1136/jech.2005.043125

8. Campagnaro, T., et al.: General, stress relief and perceived safety preferences for green spaces in the historic city of Padua (Italy). Urban Forest. Urban Green. **52**, 126695 (2020). https://doi.org/10.1016/j.ufug.2020.126695

9. Poortinga, W., Bird, N., Hallingberg, B., Phillips, R., Williams, D.: The role of perceived public and private green space in subjective health and wellbeing during and after the first peak of the COVID-19 outbreak. Landsc. Urban Plan. **211**, 104092 (2021). https://doi.org/10.1016/j.landurbplan.2021.104092

10. Van Dongen, R.P., Timmermans, H.J.P.: Preference for different urban greenscape designs: a choice experiment using virtual environments. Urban Forest. Urban Green. **44**, 126435 (2019). https://doi.org/10.1016/j.ufug.2019.126435

11. Ulrich, R.S., Simons, R.F., Losito, B.D., Fiorito, E., Miles, M.A., Zelson, M.: Stress recovery during exposure to natural and urban environments. J. Environ. Psychol. **11**, 201–230 (1991). https://doi.org/10.1016/S0272-4944(05)80184-7

12. Lee, J., Park, B.-J., Tsunetsugu, Y., Kagawa, T., Miyazaki, Y.: Restorative effects of viewing real forest landscapes, based on a comparison with urban landscapes. Scand. J. For. Res. **24**, 227–234 (2009). https://doi.org/10.1080/02827580902903341

13. Laumann, K., Gärling, T., Stormark, K.M.: Selective attention and heart rate responses to natural and urban environments. J. Environ. Psychol. **23**, 125–134 (2003). https://doi.org/10.1016/S0272-4944(02)00110-X

14. Aggio, D., Smith, L., Fisher, A., Hamer, M.: Mothers' perceived proximity to green space is associated with TV viewing time in children: the Growing Up in Scotland study. Prev. Med. **70**, 46–49 (2015). https://doi.org/10.1016/j.ypmed.2014.11.018

15. Akpinar, A.: How is high school greenness related to students' restoration and health? Urban Forestry Urban Green. **16**, 1–8 (2016). https://doi.org/10.1016/j.ufug.2016.01.007

16. Dimsdale, J.E.: Psychological stress and cardiovascular disease. J. Am. Coll. Cardiol. **51**, 1237–1246 (2008). https://doi.org/10.1016/j.jacc.2007.12.024'

17. Evans, B.E., Buil, J.M., Burk, W.J., Cillessen, A.H.N., Van Lier, P.A.C.: Urbanicity is associated with behavioral and emotional problems in elementary school-aged children. J. Child Fam. Stud. **27**, 2193–2205 (2018). https://doi.org/10.1007/s10826-018-1062-z

18. Hoisington, A.J., et al.: Ten questions concerning the built environment and mental health. Build. Environ. **155**, 58–69 (2019). https://doi.org/10.1016/j.buildenv.2019.03.036

19. Steptoe, A., Brydon, L.: Emotional triggering of cardiac events. Neurosci. Biobehav. Rev. **33**, 63–70 (2009). https://doi.org/10.1016/j.neubiorev.2008.04.010

20. Chang, C.-Y., Chen, P.-K.: Human response to window views and indoor plants in the workplace. HortSci **40**, 1354–1359 (2005). https://doi.org/10.21273/HORTSCI.40.5.1354
21. Wells, N.M., Evans, G.W.: Nearby nature: a buffer of life stress among rural children. Environ. Behav. **35**, 311–330 (2003). https://doi.org/10.1177/0013916503035003001
22. Deng, L., et al.: Empirical study of landscape types, landscape elements and landscape components of the urban park promoting physiological and psychological restoration. Urban Forestry Urban Green. **48**, 126488 (2020). https://doi.org/10.1016/j.ufug.2019.126488
23. Van Den Berg, A.E., Hartig, T., Staats, H.: Preference for Nature in Urbanized Societies: Stress, Restoration, and the Pursuit of Sustainability. J Social Issues **63**, 79–96 (2007). https://doi.org/10.1111/j.1540-4560.2007.00497.x
24. Mårtensson, F., Boldemann, C., Söderström, M., Blennow, M., Englund, J.-E., Grahn, P.: Outdoor environmental assessment of attention promoting settings for preschool children. Health Place **15**, 1149–1157 (2009). https://doi.org/10.1016/j.healthplace.2009.07.002
25. Ward, J.S., Duncan, J.S., Jarden, A., Stewart, T.: The impact of children's exposure to greenspace on physical activity, cognitive development, emotional wellbeing, and ability to appraise risk. Health Place **40**, 44–50 (2016). https://doi.org/10.1016/j.healthplace.2016.04.015
26. Felsten, G.: Where to take a study break on the college campus: an attention restoration theory perspective. J. Environ. Psychol. **29**, 160–167 (2009). https://doi.org/10.1016/j.jenvp.2008.11.006
27. Lohr, V.I., Pearson-Mims, C.H.: Responses to scenes with spreading, rounded, and conical tree forms. Environ. Behav. **38**, 667–688 (2006). https://doi.org/10.1177/0013916506287355
28. Strife, S., Downey, L.: Childhood development and access to nature: a new direction for environmental inequality research. Organ. Environ. **22**, 99–122 (2009). https://doi.org/10.1177/1086026609333340
29. Faber Taylor, A., Kuo, F.E.: Children with attention deficits concentrate better after walk in the park. J. Atten. Disord. **12**, 402–409 (2009). https://doi.org/10.1177/1087054708323000
30. Chawla, L., Keena, K., Pevec, I., Stanley, E.: Green schoolyards as havens from stress and resources for resilience in childhood and adolescence. Health Place **28**, 1–13 (2014). https://doi.org/10.1016/j.healthplace.2014.03.001
31. Wang, X., Rodiek, S., Wu, C., Chen, Y., Li, Y.: Stress recovery and restorative effects of viewing different urban park scenes in Shanghai, China. Urban Forest. Urban Green. **15**, 112–122 (2016). https://doi.org/10.1016/j.ufug.2015.12.003
32. Li, D., Sullivan, W.C.: Impact of views to school landscapes on recovery from stress and mental fatigue. Landsc. Urban Plan. **148**, 149–158 (2016). https://doi.org/10.1016/j.landurbplan.2015.12.015
33. Van Aart, C.J.C., et al.: Residential landscape as a predictor of psychosocial stress in the life course from childhood to adolescence. Environ. Int. **120**, 456–463 (2018). https://doi.org/10.1016/j.envint.2018.08.028
34. Zhu, X., Gao, M., Zhang, R., Zhang, B.: Quantifying emotional differences in urban green spaces extracted from photos on social networking sites: a study of 34 parks in three cities in northern China. Urban Forest. Urban Green. **62**, 127133 (2021). https://doi.org/10.1016/j.ufug.2021.127133
35. Allahyar, M., Kazemi, F.: Effect of landscape design elements on promoting neuropsychological health of children. Urban Forestry Urban Green. **65**, 127333 (2021). https://doi.org/10.1016/j.ufug.2021.127333
36. Reeve, A., Nieberler-Walker, K., Desha, C.: Healing gardens in children's hospitals: reflections on benefits, preferences and design from visitors' books. Urban Forestry Urban Greening **26**, 48–56 (2017). https://doi.org/10.1016/j.ufug.2017.05.013

37. Van Den Berg, A.E., Koole, S.L., Van Der Wulp, N.Y.: Environmental preference and restoration: (How) are they related? J. Environ. Psychol. **23**, 135–146 (2003). https://doi.org/10.1016/S0272-4944(02)00111-1

38. Hami, A., Abdi, B.: Students' landscaping preferences for open spaces for their campus environment. Indoor Built Environ. **30**, 87–98 (2021). https://doi.org/10.1177/1420326X19887207

39. Acar, H.: Landscape design for children and their environments in urban context. In: Ozyavuz, M. (ed.) Advances in Landscape Architecture. InTech (2013)

40. Kühn, S., Schmalen, K., Beijers, R., Tyborowska, A., Roelofs, K., Weerth, C.D.: Green is not the same as green: differentiating between the association of trees and open green spaces with children's brain structure in the Netherlands. Environ. Behav. **55**, 311–334 (2023). https://doi.org/10.1177/00139165231183095

41. Cacioppo, J.T., Tassinary, L.G., Berntson, G.G.: Handbook of psychophysiology. Cambridge Univ Pr (2007)

42. Raney, M.A., Hendry, C.F., Yee, S.A.: Physical activity and social behaviors of urban children in green playgrounds. Am. J. Prev. Med. **56**, 522–529 (2019). https://doi.org/10.1016/j.amepre.2018.11.004

43. Sanders, T., Feng, X., Fahey, P.P., Lonsdale, C., Astell-Burt, T.: The influence of neighbourhood green space on children's physical activity and screen time: findings from the longitudinal study of Australian children. Int. J. Behav. Nutr. Phys. Act. **12**, 126 (2015). https://doi.org/10.1186/s12966-015-0288-z

Author Index

M. Kurosu and A. Hashizume (Eds.): HCII 2024, LNCS 14685, pp. 345–346, 2024.
https://doi.org/10.1007/978-3-031-60412-6

Printed in the United States
by Baker & Taylor Publisher Services